How Americans Can Buy American

The Power Of Consumer Patriotism

Third Edition

Roger Simmermaker

Consumer Patriotism Corporation

How Americans Can Buy American
The Power Of Consumer Patriotism
Third Edition
by Roger Simmermaker

ISBN: 978-0-9801188-0-3

Library of Congress Control Number: 2007908761

Third Edition: January 2008

Published by Consumer Patriotism Corporation

Visit our web site at www.howtobuyamerican.com

Printed in the United States of America

Table of Contents

Acknowledgements

I thank God first for putting the idea for this book on my heart and for the strength to complete it.

A very special thank you goes to my very lovely and loving wife Antonela. For without her help, enduring patience, and trust in me this third edition would not have been possible.

Thanks to Nancy Greystone, Nick Zelinger, Paula Kinnes, Tracie Simmermaker, Kim D'Angelo, Bert Messelink, Tony Maczinski, Steve Kessel, Ryan Julian, Antony Stabile, and Michelle Perkins. Thanks also to the IAM&AW, UAW, and UFCW for their union-made database information.

Thanks also to Neil Cavuto at Fox News, IAM&AW President Tom Buffenbarger, Pat Buchanan, Gus Stelzer, Charley Reese, Pat Choate and Charles W. McMillion.

Criteria

The criteria used in this book for determining if a brand is American owned or foreign owned is the same criteria used by Corporate Affiliations, which was my main source of information. A brand is considered to be American owned only if it is at least 50% owned by an American company. Otherwise, it is considered to be foreign owned.

Disclaimer

The information contained in this book is the result of years of exhaustive research by the author. It is not always possible to be 100% accurate because of erroneous information from references and sources used or human error. However, this book is accurate to the extent that exhaustive research and investigation has been able to create.

Correspondence

How Americans Can Buy American
P. O. Box 780839
Orlando, FL 32878-0839
Email: buyamerican@howtobuyamerican.com
Phone: 1-888-US OWNED (1-888-876-9633)

"Actually, son, whether the glass is half full
or empty isn't important –
it's who *owns* the glass."

Chapter 1

Buying American In Today's Economy

The majority of Americans prefer to buy American. Poll after poll, in recent years, has shown this to be true. A June 2007 *Consumer Reports* magazine poll found that 92 percent of Americans want country-of-origin labels on meat and produce. A nationwide poll conducted by Sacred Heart University in September 2007 found 68.6 percent of Americans now check labels for information like manufacturer, nation of origin, or ingredients, compared to 52.9 percent a year ago. In the same poll, 86.3 percent of Americans would like to block Chinese imports until they raise their product and food safety standards to the level of U.S. standards. An August 7, 2007, Zogby poll showed that one in three Americans would be willing to pay *four times* as much for American-made toys, and 63 percent were willing to join a boycott of Chinese-made goods in general. On August 14, 2007—the same day I was interviewed on Fox News Channel's "Your World with Neil Cavuto"—a FoxNews.com poll asked if it was time to play it safe and buy American in light of the millions of recalled toys coming from China, and 96 percent of those surveyed said "yes." A July 2007 USA Today/Gallup poll showed nearly half of U.S. supermarket shoppers make an extra effort to buy American food items. Sixty-one percent of our senior citizens indicated a preference for American cars, and only 17 percent of Americans overall prefer to buy foreign cars. This is according to a January 8, 2007, *Automotive Digest* poll.

But the desire of Americans to buy American is not merely a recent phenomenon that began in March 2007 when China was found to have been exporting contaminated wheat gluten that was added to pet food and ended up killing our pets. Fifty-four percent of the people surveyed in a June 2004 *Associated Press* poll said that they would pay a higher price for an American-made product rather than pay a cheaper price for a foreign-made product. Over 33 percent regularly look for the "Made in USA" label, and Americans over 60 were reported to be twice as likely to do so, according to the survey. By a margin of over 2-to-1, Americans 60 and above said they would rather purchase American products even when they are more expensive than cheaper foreign goods.

A short time later, a February 2005 *Associated Press* poll, dubbed a "poll on nine nations," showed that 93 percent of Americans would rather buy American products if quality and price were the same as foreign goods. In November 2005, a *Christian Science Monitor* poll asked the question "How often do you look for products that are 'Made in USA?'" Forty-seven percent responded by saying that they do either "most of the time" or "almost always." Only 15 percent said "seldom," and an equal percentage said "never." And an October 2003 *Wall Street Journal*/NBC News poll discovered that 54 percent of Americans think companies that transfer work overseas are giving jobs away.

The *Associated Press'* poll on nine nations also found quite the opposite response when posing the same questions to those in other countries. The public's attitude overseas about American products sold in their countries was not encouraging for Americans who advocate breaking down foreign trade barriers as the best way to promote American products. Of the eight foreign nations polled, Britain, Canada, France, Germany, Italy, and Spain, all said they would prefer not to buy American products if price and quality were equal to their own, with most stating this by a 4-to-1 margin or greater. Only a majority of Mexicans—six in ten—said they would prefer to buy American products. In South Korea, four in ten said they would like to work for an American company. What do these numbers tell us? Simply that America cannot expect or require foreign nations to surrender their market to us just because we have surrendered our market to them. Such a strategy clearly doesn't work. The *Wall Street Journal* reported on September 25, 2006, that foreigners received more money on their investments in the United States than Americans received on their investments in other countries for four quarters in a row.

It is certainly easier to convince Americans to buy American than it is to convince foreigners to do so. In fact, the polls show us that most Americans apparently do not even need convincing. Why do Americans have this desire to buy American, even when it costs them more?

FOREFATHERS KNOW BEST

Americans feel a strong connection to the wisdom of our founding fathers. Travel around our great country, and you will see quotes from these remarkable men gracing the walls and halls of our buildings. One of our greatest statesmen, Thomas Jefferson, offered this about buying American, "I have come to a resolution myself, as I hope every good citizen will, never again to purchase any article of foreign manufacture which can be had of American make, be the difference of price what it may."

And then there's the wisdom of our first president, George Washington—one of the first to advocate a Buy American policy. His personal decisions and actions strengthened America's economy. In the 1760s, Washington's lone cash crop was tobacco, most of which he exported to England, and he relied on an agent to use most of the profits to purchase *imported* finished goods. Later on, Washington formed his own personal Declaration of Independence from England. This came about as a direct result of Washington being unable to audit his agent's activities and being unable to determine whether he was being treated honestly. Washington switched from raising and exporting tobacco to raising corn and wheat, which were sold to local merchants, and he used the profits to buy finished goods from American craftsman. In his historical farewell address, Washington said, "There can be no greater error than to expect or calculate upon real favours from nations."

How many of our presidents, over the last two decades, who have sold globalization and free trade to the American people as the propeller of American prosperity, heeded Washington's words? It is apparent that all of them would have better served our country if they had.

Of course, our economy is different today than it was in the late 1700s, but not in ways that would suggest that we turn away from a Buy

American strategy like the one advocated by George Washington. Today we have a greater volume of imports to choose from, and we also have domestically-produced goods made by foreign companies. These companies have two main objectives. First, to be closer to potential American customers. Secondly, to avoid import restrictions. Back in Washington's day, we really only had two purchasing choices. We would buy American-made goods (buying American) or foreign-made goods (buying imports). It is a pretty safe bet to assume that if a good was imported in the late 1700's, it was produced by a foreign-owned company, and if a good was made here in the United States it was produced by an American-owned company.

PURCHASING CHOICES OF THE PRESENT

Today we have a greater combination of purchasing choices.

1. An American-owned company making their product in the U.S.
2. An American-owned company making their product overseas.
3. A foreign-owned company making their product in the U.S.
4. A foreign-owned company making their product overseas.

I have listed these choices in the order that I believe is the most beneficial to the U.S. economy. Later I will explain them in greater detail. The choices get more complicated when we discover that an American-made product can have a certain percentage of foreign parts (foreign parts content) and a foreign-made product can have a certain percentage of American parts (domestic parts content). So there are actually three parts to the Buy American picture, which I have listed below in the order of importance.

- Ownership: In what country is the company or corporate headquarters based?
- Made: In what country is the product assembled or manufactured?
- Parts content: From what country or countries do the parts come?

How do we sort all this out? It may seem confusing or complicated, but it really isn't. Let me show you why.

BUY AMERICAN: A DEFINITION

When you know the true definition of "buying American," things become clearer. It is not just about buying "Made in USA." While the two terms may sound similar, they do not mean the same thing. Buying American, in the purest sense of the term, means we would buy an American-made product, made by an American-owned company, with as high a domestic parts content within that product as possible. The more we can do this, the more we are truly buying American and the more powerful, positive impact we will have on the U.S. economy. That's good news, isn't it? The better news is that usually this can be done without any extra cost or inconvenience to the consumer. "American-made" is good. "Buying American" is much better!

I have had the honor of speaking to many people across our country. I have watched their interest grow as they comprehend the true definition of buying American. I have seen it grow even more as they learn of the benefits that buying American brings to them as individuals and to us as a nation. It is exciting to be able to express views to people they may have never heard before, and it is gratifying to know that a majority of them are going to respond favorably when they have had the chance to hear these views.

We must prioritize our choices in order to determine which ones are best for the American economy. Ownership is the most important part of the Buy American picture for many, many reasons—the foremost being that American companies pay nearly twice the amount of taxes to the U.S. Treasury as do foreign companies. According to 2003 data from the IRS (the most data recent available), American-owned companies pay 1.29 percent in taxes, while foreign-owned companies only pay 0.72 percent in taxes. But while American-owned companies pay more taxes than comparable foreign-owned companies in the United States, they also pay more taxes than their foreign competition in places like Europe.

In January 2005, the European Commission issued a statement suggesting that member states should stop taxing the dividends of foreign firms (foreign to or based outside of Europe) at a higher rate compared to European companies.

What are some other reasons why ownership is so important? The ownership of a company determines where the profits go, where most of the taxes are paid, and which national economy benefits the most. What exactly does this mean? If we buy a Toyota made in the United States, after the American workers that assembled that car or truck are paid, the remaining profits will go back to Japan. So the taxes on those profits will be paid to the *Japanese Treasury* and *not the U.S. Treasury*. I deal with the pros and cons of buying foreign cars—like Toyotas—assembled in the U.S. in greater detail in Auto Explanations, Chapter 15, but this simple analysis generally applies to all industries. Conversely, all profits made by American-owned companies are taxed in the United States, and those taxes are paid to the U.S. Treasury. All Americans benefit from that.

By definition, American-owned companies are majority-owned by American shareholders and stockholders. These investors are subject to taxes on dividends and capital gains distributed to them from the companies they own, and these taxes are paid to the U.S. Treasury. Dividends and capital gains distributed to foreign persons who have a stake in American-based companies don't pay their taxes to the U.S. Treasury, they pay taxes to foreign treasuries.

REAPING THE REWARDS OF BUYING AMERICAN

What are some of the benefits we get from our tax dollars? Seventy-five percent of all federal spending goes to pay for Social Security, Medicare, defense, education, farm subsidies, highways, parks, and interest on the national debt. Polls show that most Americans are against "government spending" but strongly back these programs.

More taxes collected means more benefits reaped for better public schools, libraries, and hospitals. More taxes collected means a stronger military, a healthier health care system, and a safer NASA space program. If we collect more taxes we will have cleaner public parks, better construction and maintenance of our roads and bridges, and well-equipped fire and police departments.

In some cases, it comes down to respecting your own paycheck. I happen to work for one of America's largest defense contactors, so my wages are funded by tax dollars. For me, it would be blatantly hypocritical to look to the government to fund my livelihood and not do my best to patronize the products that put the most tax dollars into the funds that I draw from. The same thinking should apply to any government employee, contractor, or public service worker. If your salary or wages are derived from tax dollars, you should be concerned about supporting American-owned companies that pay more taxes, which in turn funds your livelihood.

Supporting American companies leads to a more independent America. Ownership equals control, and control equals independence. We cannot claim to be an independent country or control our own destiny if our manufacturing base is under foreign ownership or foreign control. A nation that cannot supply its own needs is not an independent nation. If we are to claim independence from the rest of the world and truly be a sovereign nation, we must begin supplying our own needs once again.

Shared ownership means shared rewards. If General Motors is owned predominantly by Americans (and it is), more Americans will receive a return on their investment than will Americans who own Toyota (since the number of Americans who have invested in that corporation is far fewer.) One thing is for certain, there are fewer rewards to share for Americans, resulting in the prosperity of a foreign corporation.

If foreign ownership did not result in fewer taxes collected by the U.S. Treasury, why would U.S. corporations shift their ownership to Bermuda and the Cayman Islands? To avoid U.S. taxes. *Business Week* reported that American companies are increasingly becoming targets for acquisition by foreign companies, in part because they would pay fewer taxes as a foreign-owned company.

The more profits we can keep circulating within our own economy, the stronger our economy will become. How can we do this? By not sending them across any oceans or over any borders. If we do this, we will see our economy become stronger because our tax revenue will grow, too. Most folks know that our nation is in debt, and as of this writing, that debt is to the tune of $8.87 trillion. The more revenue our U.S. Treasury collects, the closer we will be to chopping our national debt down to size or eliminating it. Eventually our debt will have to be repaid. Why not take as many steps as we can right now while our national debt is more sustainable? One of the steps we *can* take is to support American-owned companies whenever possible so that as many taxes are paid to the U.S. Treasury as possible. Economist Pat Choate once estimated that we lose at least $30 billion a year in tax revenue simply because we patronize foreign-owned companies instead of American-owned companies.

THE NAME GAME:
AMERICAN-OWNED VERSUS FOREIGN-OWNED

The good news is that we can increase the amount of taxes we pay to America through the purchases we are already making with the money that we are already spending and usually with no extra cost or inconvenience to the consumer. This is especially true on products where the consumer is indifferent as to which product to buy. What does that mean? Say you are in the supermarket and bath soap is on your shopping list. You recently discovered that both Irish Spring and Jergens are made in the U.S. So it would be more beneficial to the U.S. economy to buy Irish Spring. (I know, it gets crazy when a foreign sounding brand named Irish Spring is actually American-owned!) Now about Jergens. It is a familiar *sounding* name, isn't it? Sounds like a good old American brand, doesn't it? Wrong. Jergens is owned by the Japanese. How about the price? The difference, if any, is negligible. So there you are at your local market, Irish Spring in one hand and Jergens in the other. What do you do? You perform a simple yet significant act of patriotism. You buy the Irish Spring. And you can do it each and every time you visit the supermarket.

Not only do Americans have trouble identifying American brands, but they also have trouble guessing the right nationality of foreign brands. A June 18, 2007, *Business Week* poll found that only 4.4 percent of Americans knew that Nokia was based in Finland (most guessed Japan), 8.4 percent knew that Lego was based in Denmark (most guessed the United States), 9.8 percent knew that Samsung was based in Korea (most guessed Japan), and only 12.2 percent knew that Adidas was based in Germany (most guessed the U.S.)

Your grocery store is a great place to start buying American. These may be small-ticket items, but that does not really matter. Since we visit the grocery store so frequently, we actually spend more of our money on these items than we do elsewhere on big-ticket items. Fortunately, most grocery store products are usually made, canned, or processed in the U.S. The only difference is the ownership of the company.

Some choices involve a minimal amount of research. In the produce section you'll find lemons from America and limes from Mexico. When I make my morning tea, I like lemon and lime equally, so I just buy more lemons than I do limes. It is simply a choice. It is also a simple way to help America.

I remember shopping at OfficeMax a few months ago. In front of me was a set of ten PaperMate pencils—made in America and priced at ninety-nine cents. Right next to them was a set of ten OfficeMax pencils—made in China and priced at eighty-nine cents. I thought to myself, surely most Americans would think supporting other Americans is worth an extra dime. When we run into examples like these where buying American-made products is more expensive, here is how I think we ought to frame our thinking on the subject. *It is not an extra cost—it is an investment in America.*

Let's take a look at toothpaste. Colgate or Crest toothpaste (American-owned) versus Mentadent toothpaste (foreign-owned). In June 2007, we heard that Colgate toothpaste, *supposedly* imported from South Africa (as indicated on the box) was being counterfeited by an unknown manufacturer and may have contained diethylene glycol. Later the truth came out. Colgate did not even import toothpaste from South Africa. In fact, most Colgate toothpaste (as well as most Crest toothpaste) is made in the United States. The only imported Colgate toothpaste comes from Mexico, and you will be able to identify it by looking at the box. Mentadent sells American-made toothpaste, too, but Mentadent is owned by Unilever (a joint venture between England and The Netherlands). But what else was going on? Several other brands being made in China with names like Dr. Cool, Cooldent, and ShiR Fresh *did* contain diethylene glycol and were pulled from store shelves.

Even before the toothpaste turmoil, our headlines were filled with one tale of China's blatant disregard for one safety issue after another. First there was a massive recall of tainted pet food in March that was killing our pets. Then we discovered some Chinese-made toys were coated with lead paint, while others were filled with kerosene, both posing potential dangers to our children. We then learned that a company named Foreign Tire Sales may have to recall 450,000 Chinese-made tires. Apparently, these tires did not comply with U.S. safety standards designed to prevent the tread from separating, and so American drivers were dying on our highways.

But there is also an often untold story surrounding the issue of product recalls. According to a 2004 study by *Consumer Reports*, over 50 percent of recalled toys and other household goods like appliances are not being brought back to the store for either return or repair. So just because a product is deemed unsafe to the consumer, it does not mean that the risk is automatically going to be eliminated. The subject of whether imports are good or bad for the U.S. economy has been debated since the Boston Tea Party, but I do not think they have ever been perceived to be as threatening to our safety and standard of living as they are today. We import so much apparel from foreign countries these days that even Betsy Ross and her seamstresses would likely be in the unemployment line were they alive today.

The year of 2007 was littered with Chinese recalls and concerns over the safety of all kinds of products imported from that country. China supposedly has stringent safety regulations, but they are rarely enforced. America discovered that nearly all the toys recalled in the United States came from China. We also found that the agency charged with enforcing product safety standards—the Consumer Protection Safety Commission—had only 400 employees, and 80 had been let go over the last ten years. Even though imports have surged in an increasingly global economy, the agency's budget has remained roughly the same.

Concerned consumers can take at least some comfort in the fact that China does not currently export any chicken, beef, pork, or egg products to the United States. But China grows over 50 percent of the earth's vegetables and imports over half of the apple juice and nearly half of the garlic sold in the U.S.

As a result of China's supposedly nonexistent safety issues, 180 food manufacturers closed after 23,000 safety violations were discovered that included putting industrial chemicals in their food products. In 2006, 152,000 food retailers and manufacturers were closed because they were producing fake products of low quality. America loses ground economically, too, when we are forced to accept the consequences of China's lax food-safety standards. As stated by the United States Department of Agriculture, illnesses related to harmful or unsafe foods cost our country almost $7 billion every year.

But the crisis in China goes beyond risking polluting our bodies with lead from paint and chemicals from food. In June 2007, it was discovered that fake blood protein was being sold to pharmacies and hospitals across China. Albumin—the real blood protein—is produced by the liver and is provided to patients who are chronically ill. No one knows for sure if any of the fake blood protein was exported.

All the reports of one safety challenge after another related to Chinese products may have been news to many Americans, but it was not news in China. *Wall Street Journal* columnist David Wessel discovered this in July 2007 when he called a Beijing University professor he had known for years asking him his opinion on the seemingly daily occurrences.

China's own Premier, Wen Jiablo, said in March 2007 that his country's economy is "unstable, unbalanced, uncoordinated, and unsustainable." China's consumer safety watchdog says over 20 percent of the baby clothes and toys made there are substandard. Some Chinese toy makers say removing lead from paint is too expensive, so they are focusing only on the Chinese market instead of exports. Years of pollution has contaminated 10 percent of China's tillable land (over 30 million acres), and experts worry that food grown in the same soil is contaminated as well. No one knows how much tainted food has been exported to the U.S., but Chinese locals have been eating it for years and maybe even decades. In April, China announced that nearly 13 million tons of grain had been contaminated by heavy metals. Thirty-four percent of young Chinese children showed levels of lead in their blood that exceeded the safety limit as defined by the World Health Organization.

Yet China's repeated defense of the quality of their products through all this has been surprising. We clearly cannot expect China to understand and react appropriately to the concerns of the American people. Zong Changbao, president of one of the Chinese toothpaste companies involved in the controversy over diethylene glycol found in toothpaste that was exported to the United States, said that his company has no plans to recall any toothpaste that has already left his factory. According to Mr. Zong, "This problem doesn't exist. It's just a matter of U.S. standards, not a safety problem. The Food and Drug Administration standard is used as a reference in many countries. If China were as powerful as the U.S., we could set the world standard." With quotes like these, is there any more motivation needed to ensure that China does not become more powerful than the United States? Or would we mind if China started setting world standards for us? We might be closer to having to answer these questions than we think. China is now the world's second largest economy (behind the U.S.) when measured by purchasing power parity. A Chinese quality supervision agency official said that China lamented what he claims was an unfair tarnishing of the quality of China's food exports, saying, "We don't really understand why this year suddenly everyone is extremely concerned about this problem." Apparently too many in China do not "get it" as they try to defend the indefensible, so we have to understand that and stand up for American products and American quality.

Chinese companies are also increasing exports of military technology—70 percent in the first half of 2007 compared to all of 2006—to Iran. Chinese officials, who usually accuse us of inadequate evidence, remained silent on the latest figures. Whether you agree or disagree with America's presence in Iraq, it would be an understatement to say that the surge of Chinese military exports to Iran comes at a particularly sensitive time.

Even when we are faced with purchasing options for products we simply need and cannot avoid in an area where the American-made variety is not available, it is still important to support the American-owned company. For instance, if you needed to replace the hard drive on your computer, would you be inclined to buy a foreign-made one from Hitachi, Fujitsu, or Seagate? No disk drive company makes their disk drives in the U.S. If you wanted to support an American company, though, you'd want to buy a Seagate (or a Western Digital—the other major American maker of hard drives) if you were concerned about keeping sensitive information out of the wrong hands. Scott's Valley, California-based Seagate Technology is promoting technology that would cause computer data to be unreadable and lower national security risks later if, say, a Chinese company was to buy Seagate. Bill Watkins, Chief Executive Officer of Seagate, has indicated that he has already been contacted by potential foreign investors and made our government aware of the risks if sensitive information was stored on a computer disk drive that was not *designed* in the United States. Buying American is not only about awareness being the key but also which companies *hold* the key to what's important to America. And who knows? Maybe if enough of us discriminately bought American-owned Seagate hard drives instead of indiscriminately buying Japanese-owned Hitachi or Fujitsu hard drives, Seagate might have enough profits to compel them to produce in America where we demand higher wages than in countries like Singapore where they are being made now.

OUTSOURCING:
A FOUR LETTER WORD (WITH 11 LETTERS)

Let's go back to the toothpaste fiasco. It turns out that Colgate only recently began importing toothpaste from Mexico after closing an older U.S. facility. But because of the mislabeled Colgate toothpaste from China (that Colgate didn't even make), the company now has plans to close their Mexican facility and build a new U.S. plant.

One could argue that a foreign-owned company would have a similar response to an outcry from the American public over a safety issue, but the fact is that the American people hold more influence over American-owned companies than they do over foreign-owned companies. As syndicated columnist Charley Reese said in his review of the first edition of *How Americans Can Buy American* back in 1996, "Toyota, public relations efforts notwithstanding, has its primary loyalty to Japan, as it should. If conditions arise in which Toyota must choose between what is in the best interests of its American subsidiaries and what is in the best interests of Japan, it will choose Japan."

For instance, Japanese-owned Canon has stated that the company wants to "preserve its core competence" by keeping as much manufacturing in Japan as possible. Even though Canon gets 75 percent of its revenue from outside Japan, it has a target of retaining about 60 percent of its production capacity inside Japan. And although American-owned Kodak doesn't make any cameras in the United States (Canon doesn't either), they generate most of their cash from the United States, which is in turn used to help support 40,000 American retirees and their dependents. Canon, as with most Japanese-owned companies, doesn't support nearly as many American workers and retirees as their American-owned competition. This is not an isolated case.

Sometimes, however, it actually makes sense for American companies to cut American jobs, and Kodak is a company that presents one of those situations. In 2004, Kodak stopped making film cameras in the United States but was still making camera film here. The trend was shifting rapidly to digital cameras, and you can bet that if Kodak wasn't making money on film cameras producing them offshore, they certainly weren't making money producing them in the United States. It is clear to me that boycotting Kodak for cutting American jobs would have not been appropriate, and all we would have accomplished is to have re-directed our consumer dollars to fund foreign-owned companies that produced 100 percent of their cameras offshore and de-funded Kodak's 40,000 retirees at the same time.

Even though ownership is the most important part of the Buy American picture, it does not mean that I would automatically be willing to support any company just because it happens to be American-owned. For instance, I don't shop at Wal-Mart for many reasons. Wal-Mart is a company that has taken a lot of heat for their corporate practices—and deservedly so—including being the biggest importer of Chinese goods. But I will not spend too much time here documenting the reasons why Wal-Mart should be avoided, as many concerned consumer groups and labor unions have already done this. I did write an article back in May 2003, which can be viewed at this weblink: http://www.howtobuyamerican.com/simmermaker/ba-030517-wal-mart.shtml

I also would never do business with Bank of America, which in March 2005 paid more than $1 billion in penalties because of various trading and investment banking scandals at the corporate level. Nor would I do business with Citibank, whose CEO, John Reed, recently entertained the option of moving the company headquarters to another country. Why? To escape American banking laws! According to Mr. Reed, the United States is the wrong place for the headquarters of an international bank. But until that occurs—if it ever does—Citibank's deposits are backed by U.S. taxpayers, and Citibank's lobbyists have repeatedly persuaded members of the U.S. Congress to bail out America's troubled commercial banks with multi-million dollar guarantees, saving them from insolvency.

But even with outsourcing becoming as big of an issue as it has, some American companies have actually closed foreign factories and brought jobs back home again. In 2002, Riccar's parent company, Tacony Manufacturing, moved its manufacturing facility from Taiwan to Missouri. According to senior vice-president John Kaido, the company considered moving to China, but they felt that the quality was not quite up to their standards, so they came back to America instead. There have been other changes in the vacuum industry as well. In December 2006, Hong Kong-based Techtronic Corp., agreed to buy Hoover from Whirlpool (who recently bought Maytag). A June 2007 announcement followed detailing how 750 workers would be laid off when they closed their North Canton, Ohio factory in September (the new foreign-owned company transferred production to existing Texas and Mexico plants.) Still, the former owners of Hoover announced that they were committed to economic development in the region to soften the blow to the economy by building an aquarium with a focus on research and education. All Oreck vacuums cleaners (including the one that I own,) are made in Oreck's lone facility in Long Beach, Mississippi. This facility, by the way, was back up and running only two weeks after Hurricane Katrina!

In 2004, after a barrage of customer complaints, Dell, Inc., brought some call center jobs back to America from India. That does not necessarily mean Dell is a bastion of patriotism, nor should you run out and buy one of their computers in the name of "Buy American." Here's why. After pitting North Carolina against Virginia for an American assembly plant in 2005, Dell chose North Carolina after the state agreed to grant $280 million in state and local incentives. The new facility will employ 1,500 people and pay each employee an average of $28,000.00 per year, which is actually lower than the area's average yearly salary of $31,300.00. It seems that we are using the taxpayer's money to fund the creation of new jobs that pay below the wages of the jobs we are losing because we are not protecting them. So much for the promise of jobs in the high-tech industry. In fact, the United States registered a trade deficit in Advanced Technology Products (ATPs) for the first time in 2003—an industry that was supposed to hold promise for America as we lost more traditional manufacturing jobs in sectors like textiles and automobiles. Free trade economists tell us that it is better to support policies that will create new jobs, not protect old ones that can be done more cheaply somewhere else. My question is, *why can't we do both?* If we want to protect the middle class in this country, then we are going to have to do a better job protecting the jobs that pay middle class wages, or that middle class is going to go away.

More disturbing than all of that was the attitude of Dell's vice president of global manufacturing. In quotes to a *Winston-Salem Journal* reporter such as, "Two thousand jobs, shouldn't you be happy with no revenue? Here's what it'll take: 1) free land; 2) free building; 3) no taxes; 4) training at $5 million; 5) participation in creation of future value in the community," and "If a state like North Carolina can't get after this, I'm worried for our country—there's a certain amount of patriotism here."

To be fair, Michael Dell, CEO of Dell, Inc., did take part in an alliance with Bill Gates of Microsoft to donate $130 million to encourage high school graduates in Texas to go to college. But why does his company have to insist on multi-million dollar tax giveaways in other states at the same time?

One good reason to stop multi-million dollar tax giveaways is that the smaller the share of those taxes that a corporation pays to the U.S. Treasury, the larger the share the American taxpayer must pay. In 2003, the share of corporate tax revenue fell to 7.4 percent of total federal receipts—the lowest since 1983 and the second lowest since 1934. A tax analysis in 2004 also revealed that more foreign-owned companies operating in the United States, almost 70 percent of them, claimed they owed no federal taxes in the late 1990s.

It would be far more beneficial to support an American technology company versus a foreign-owned one, like Netherlands-based Philips Electronics. In 2003, Philips closed several chip factories and cut over 1,120 American jobs. While foreign-owned Philips was busy cutting American jobs, American-owned Texas Instruments, also in 2003, was outlining plans for a new $3 billion plant near its headquarters in Richardson, Texas.

But if Dell uses hundreds of millions of dollars in public tax dollars for their own private gain, and you cannot buy a Texas Instruments personal computer (since Texas Instruments does not make personal computers), what would be the best computer company to patronize? In my opinion, it would be best to support a company like Union Built PC, which is featured in Chapter 17.

American companies rarely get the same tax incentives as their foreign-owned competition. This is particularly true in the automotive industry. Why? American companies have been part of the American landscape longer, are based here, and are expected to be more loyal to America. Fair enough, but shouldn't that also mean we should be more loyal to these American companies for the same reasons? Not only do American companies pay more taxes to America, they also employ more workers and support far more retirees and dependents than foreign-owned companies.

Does any American really believe that Venezuelan-owned Citgo would act on behalf of America's best interests over their own interests? American-owned ExxonMobil may be guilty of handing out an extravagant $400 million bonus to its outgoing CEO, but Citgo caused us to change our laws and made us question the sovereign right to defend the enactment of those laws. This happened back when President Bill Clinton was in the White House, and we lost a World Trade Organization dispute, courtesy of Citgo and Venezuela (since Citgo is a state-owned company.) Our president was left with two choices. Weaken our EPA laws or face binding penalties from Venezuela. Rather than hand over your tax dollars to a country that has now vowed to "bring down the United States" and has called President George W. Bush a "madman," Bill Clinton changed our clean air laws. Instead of being outraged, we continue to indiscriminately patronize foreign oil companies like Citgo thinking it just doesn't matter. But it does matter.

According to economist Pat Choate, World Trade Organization (WTO) member countries must "agree to alter their domestic laws, regulations, and administrative practices to conform to WTO agreements and dispute rulings. The only recourse to noncompliance is for the offending government to pay compensation to afflicted parties." *Business Week* reported in April 2003 that the U.S had lost of 13 of the past 15 WTO cases at the time, causing some members of Congress to call for U.S. withdrawal from the organization. A report from the General Accounting Office found that America is not only the biggest loser in WTO decisions but also is slapped with the highest penalties.

CORPORATE RESPONSIBILITY

Every now and then, situations arise that prompt our politicians to stress corporate responsibility. American pressure prodded American-owned Chevron to stop loading oil at Iraqi ports before the Iraq War. The reason? The seemingly imminent attack on Iraq could have disrupted oil imports for U.S. markets. Yet e-mails continue to be circulated across the Internet asking the reader to boycott Exxon or some other American company. If you want to boycott big oil, boycott Citgo. Would Citgo (a Venezuelan government-owned company that openly supports Fidel Castro) have cared about or listened to an America that was about to send their sons and daughters to fight and die in the Middle East? Regardless of how you feel about the necessity of the Iraq War, Venezuela does not care about the lives of American men and women.

Another popular e-mail claims that Target is owned by the French, which is false. Target has been American-owned for at least as long as I have been researching the Buy American issue (since 1994).

In March 2004, IBM announced that it would add 5,000 American jobs to divert criticism of prior plans to move thousands of jobs overseas. Could we have made the same argument against Japanese-owned Sony, for example? Not likely. Sony is not a corporate citizen of the U.S—it is a corporate citizen of Japan. When politicians, or even American citizens, are stressing corporate responsibility, they are talking to American companies since foreign-owned companies owe no loyalty to the United States.

A favorite example of mine in comparing American and foreign products is comparing mustard brands. French's and Grey Poupon are both made in the U.S., but only one of them is American-owned. French's is not owned by the French, it is owned by the British. And even though Grey Poupon sounds like it might be foreign, it is actually an American-owned brand. But perhaps the best example of all is that Swiss Miss is American-owned, but Carnation is owned by the Swiss since it is owned by Nestle, the largest food and beverage company in the world. It would help if we were more diverse in our purchases. Here is what I mean.

DIVERSIFY AND CONQUER

Diversity of consumer purchases means supporting our nationally-owned companies over foreign-owned companies. This keeps profits inside our country as opposed to sending profits out and away, a consequence of supporting foreign-owned companies.

Being diverse in our purchases includes buying as little from China as possible. This is not easy. Chances are you have bought something from China if you own a VCR, DVD, MP3 player, alarm clock radio, or cordless or cellular phone, among many other types of products. Another reason to buy as little as possible from China, even from American-owned companies, is that these American-owned companies producing in China can't repatriate 100 percent of the profits made on the sale of those goods because they aren't 100 percent American-owned. They are often required to enter 50/50 joint ventures with Chinese companies, thereby diluting their ownership.

For American companies that want to set up joint ventures with Indian companies, profits have proven to be elusive. According to a 2005 McKinsey & Co., study, only 3 out of 25 major joint ventures formed by Indian companies and foreign companies between 1993 and 2003 actually survived. To avoid the high failure rate for Indian joint ventures, American companies can try to set up a separate unit that is independent from a current joint venture, but they must first get a "no-objection certificate" from the Indian company if the independent company wants to compete in the same business sector.

WE VOTE EVERY DAY

The good news about buying American is that you do not have to change every single buying habit to be a patriotic shopper. If you have had good luck with a particular foreign brand and you have some brand loyalty to that particular foreign company, do not get too hung up on it. To some degree, everyone has brand loyalties. I realize that. But you might also consider some of the brands I have highlighted in this chapter (as well others throughout this book) where you have no brand loyalty and where one product will do just as well as the other. Are your teeth really going to be better off if you use Mentadent instead of Colgate or Crest? I doubt it. If everyone would change just two, five, or even ten simple buying habits like the ones I have described, the positive impact on our U.S. economy would be nothing short of fantastic.

Why do I say this? Any economist (even the ones who staunchly defend free trade) will tell you that 70 percent of economic activity in America is a result of consumer spending. We may vote every two years in November at the polls, but we vote every single day with our dollars at the stores (or on the Internet). There is a great patriotic duty to vote for the candidate of our choice. But what if, instead of relying on our elected officials to do what they say they will once in office (and hoping it will lead to positive results for our economy), we took matters into our own hands by supporting American workers, shareholders, stockholders, and investors. The beauty of a Buy American strategy is that we can be voting with our dollars while we hold our elected officials accountable at the same time. Our legislators could pass all the laws either for or against buying American that they want, but no legislation can override the free patriotic choices of the American people. If we, as consumers, leave foreign products to rot on the shelves and instead opt for buying the American ones, there is not a political strategy our legislators could devise that would thwart this united effort. This is why buying American is potentially more powerful than legislation. American consumers possess much more power over our economy than we realize. The only missing factor is how to apply that power. Awareness is the key.

In fact, we should put more emphasis on voting with our dollars for positive changes in the U.S. economy than we should count on making those changes at the voting booth. When we as Americans decide to act on our beliefs and put our money where our mouths are, the politics reflecting those beliefs will follow sooner or later. Even a well meaning minority can change the direction of the country.

By October 2003, nine states were considering legislation to require that work done on state contracts must be performed in the U.S. In May 2004, Tennessee's governor signed legislation requiring the state's procurement employees to give special preference to contractors who hire only American workers. And in March 2005, New Jersey voted to ban all work contracted for the state from being done outside the U.S. In July 2007, Minnesota passed a law that made it a misdemeanor to sell American flags in the state that are not made in America.

CHANGING YOUR BUYING HABITS: BYE BYE BIG-BOX

What if it becomes harder and harder for us to buy American in the stores? This could be a result of either bad legislation (or lack of any legislation at all) that fails to help secure the American market for the American producer. We can fight this by simply shifting from buying at big-box retailers to buying through smaller online-only companies. These companies often carry more American products out of sheer patriotic duty. More Americans are already shopping online than ever before. *Business Week* reported back in December 2003 that 54 percent of Americans planned to use the Internet to find Christmas gifts, up from only 46 percent the year before, and subsequent years have seen the rate of online purchases go even higher. In 2006, an annual study from Forrester Research and the National Retail Federation's Shop.org revealed online sales of apparel (including accessories and footwear) jumped 61 percent. At $18.3 billion, apparel catapulted past computer hardware and software web purchases, second only to the travel industry in online sales.

But the very thought of trying to buy American can feel like a daunting task. If an important aspect of your store shopping has been to find the "Made in USA" label, you have no doubt felt the frustration of finding a wide variety of goods made in a wide variety of foreign countries. The temptation is to throw up our hands and say, "What can I do? I can't do anything!" But we really should be saying, "What can I do? I've got to do something!" This was my reaction when I went shopping for American-made apparel in a Florida mall in 1994 and came away with only one t-shirt. Lou Dobbs reported in his 2004 book *Exporting America* that 96 percent of clothing production is done outside our borders.

Sounds depressing, right? Not if you know how and where to find that 4 percent of clothing being produced in the United States. If you do, you can help stabilize the trend of ever-increasing foreign imports and even cause it to reverse direction.

AWARENESS IS KEY

So how can we find that coveted 4 percent? Again, awareness is the key. The good news is that the American-made products are out there, you've probably just been looking in the wrong places. Everything I wear every day is made in the USA, and if I can do it, you can too! And I'm here to tell you I probably don't spend any more money on clothes than you do, and I'm not buying clothes of inferior quality.

Levi's jeans closed their last two American plants on January 6, 2004. I read the announcement and quickly went to the store to snap up several pair of Levi's American-made jeans. I noticed then that the jeans made in Bangladesh and the ones made in America (on the same shelves, in the same store, and right next to each other) were *the exact same price*. I was not paying any extra money to buy American then, and I do not normally pay any extra money to do so today. I guess another option would have been to switch to Wrangler or Lee jeans—at least until 2005. That's when parent company VF Corp., shuttered its last American sewing plant.

One problem with ordering on the web, however, is that even though there is a requirement for Internet sites to divulge whether their products are made in the United States (but not the ownership of the company), not all of them comply. The Federal Trade Commission requires you to file a formal case against a noncompliant company so that a lawyer can determine if the language in their document actually means what it says.

That's one reason why I buy most of my apparel from ZebulonUSA.com, where everything is made in the U.S. (see Chapter 17). The prices are very competitive with the prices in stores like Wal-Mart, but you don't have to spend $3.00 per gallon in gas driving around town looking for American-made goods, which you may not find anyway. You could argue that the outsourcing of apparel production has resulted in lower prices to the American consumer, but you might be surprised at the insignificance of the price difference. In the apparel industry, the lower prices resulting from the transfer of jobs from America to foreign countries have been almost negligible. The *Wall Street Journal* reported that the change in apparel prices from 2005 to 2006 was 1.2 percent. That means that all those lost American textile jobs we shipped overseas in the name of free trade and supposedly increased competition lowered the price of a typical $15.00 garment a total of a meager *eighteen cents*. In fact, the Labor department shows that prices rose for virtually every industry (except apparel) in 2006, despite the supposed guarantee of lower prices due to ever-increasing imports.

But the fact that retail prices do not go down even when we import more goods from cheap-labor countries should not be surprising when you listen to some apparel industry experts and retail company spokespersons. Before the complete phasing out of apparel and textile quotas on January 1, 2005, Peter McGrath, chairman of both the International Trade Advisory Committee for the National Retail Federation and J.C. Penney's purchasing department, said he expected wholesale prices (the prices retailers pay for various goods that they sell) would fall between 8 percent and 18 percent after the quotas ended. But Standard & Poor's apparel analyst, Marie Driscoll, said she figures only about one-third of wholesalers' costs savings would be passed down to consumers. A spokesman for Wal-Mart commented that consumers would not notice much of a price difference at all, and J.C. Penney spokesman Tim Lyons said that his company was not necessarily looking to give the consumers the lowest price possible.

Nike does not want their prices to drop either—regardless of how much money they save by producing exclusively in cheap-labor countries—because they feel it would be dangerous to their image as the king of fashion-forward and cutting-edge designs. In May 2003, when shoe retailer Foot Locker decided to aggressively discount their prices in an effort to increase sales, Nike felt alienated because they didn't like having their footwear marked down.

THE REAL PRICE OF WHAT WE SAVE

Is the fact that we can now spend eighteen cents less on a typical garment worth all the lost jobs? We need to focus on the "cost" of these lost jobs versus the price savings we might see at the cash register. Sometimes we fail to calculate or consider the lost tax revenue (both locally and nationally), among other things. When cabinet maker Merillat closed its Loudonville, Ohio factory in 2003, the city's tax revenue declined about $350,000.00. But most free traders did not care about those American workers. After all, 30 cabinetmakers in China can be hired for what it costs to hire one cabinetmaker in Ohio or North Carolina. But, cabinetmakers in China do not pay taxes to America. Only American cabinetmakers pay taxes to America.

In 2003, I saw a textile factory layoff in the making thanks to the good people at WBTV in Charlotte, North Carolina. They were doing a story on a plant closing in Bowling Green, South Carolina that was to claim 160 jobs. That textile plant paid $100,000.00 in taxes in 2002. The invisible hand of the "free market" was wreaking havoc left and right. It came on the heels of the largest permanent layoff in North Carolina's history—when Pillowtex Corp., went bankrupt. But to many hardworking Americans in the region, the free market was not invisible, not when they had been permanently freed from their jobs.

The Carolina textile workers were not alone in receiving layoff notices in 2003. A Rutgers University study conducted that year found that one in five American workers had been laid off in the last three years, and only one in three received a severance package.

Daniel Lafar, the owner of the plant, told me that Bowling Green Spinning Company spent $2 million to make the plant more efficient, buying the latest and most productive spinning machines available. It did not matter. Due to circumstances beyond its control (including a spike in the price of cotton), the plant was forced to close. Mr. Lafar told me that the plant probably would have closed long ago, but it didn't because it had so much history behind it. It had also been in his family for generations. The Bowling Green, South Carolina plant survived the Great Depression, but it could not survive an economy that was supposed to be on the rebound at the time.

The story behind the closing of the Bowling Green plant, where 160 people lost their jobs, is not what free traders often try to make America's manufacturing plants all about. Free market advocates would have you believe that manufacturing plant closings in America are usually about factories not becoming more efficient and deserving to close because there are more efficient plants overseas. Forget that the machinery at the Bowling Green plant will be shipped overseas to be used by China or Pakistan to make goods once made here in America. Is it really about efficiency? No, it is about cheap labor.

I came away from my WBTV interview and my Charlotte, North Carolina visit with a better idea of what is really happening to American manufacturing. It also reinforced my belief that Americans really *do* care about buying American. Anchorman Paul Cameron of WBTV had this to say about the reaction his station received as a result of the interview, "The response...has been nothing short of overwhelming. The comments were mostly that we didn't do enough. Our 11 p.m. news last night was far and away the ratings winner—with numbers higher than we've seen in a year."

The interview on WBTV was more than just about the plant closing in Bowling Green, South Carolina. It was also about showing people the power they have with their pocketbooks in steering the global economy in a direction that best benefits the United States of America. We visited stores in the area and compared American-owned and foreign-owned products and explained the difference. Similar stories have also run on KSDK-TV in St. Louis as well as Lou Dobbs' program on CNN.

The story of Bowling Green isn't the only example of its kind. Consider the $1.4 billion printing company that is Banta Corp., of Menasha, Wisconsin. In 2003 they switched to all digital input material that used to be produced by hand, resulting in an 80 percent productivity gain per worker. Banta also boosted productivity by installing newer, wider, and faster printing presses. But Chinese printing companies bought the identical $12 million machines, which eliminated any competitive advantage the

American printing company was hoping to achieve.

Even when American companies can invest in the latest, greatest equipment, it becomes difficult to justify the investment to start with since Chinese workers can be hired for a fraction of the wages of an American worker, and American producers know they can't beat the Chinese price, anyway. The reality is that American factories become a less attractive prospect for future investment since investors will perceive lower returns on that investment. And if you cannot justify adequate investment in your facilities, you end up with under-utilized industrial capacity, which makes you even less competitive. It is a vicious cycle.

U.S. producers of high fructose corn syrup estimated in 2003 that a 20 percent Mexican import tax resulted in investment losses of hundreds of millions of dollars because of idle plant capacity as well as $620 million in lost export sales annually.

When William Bachman, president of St. Louis-based Bachman Machine Co., submitted a bid of $595,000.00 to fabricate and produce tools to stamp metal parts for car jacks, he found a Chinese competitor also made a bid on the job. That's all right, you are probably thinking, taking several bids is the way the process works. There is just one problem. The Chinese company was *offering to make the tools for free!*

"It really doesn't matter how much I automate. I can't compete with zero," Mr. Bachman says. And the Chinese company can make the car jack parts from the newly fabricated tools for 50 percent less than Bachman Machine Tool Company, unless Bachman would like to transfer production overseas.

The reason companies and corporations like to shift production to low-wage countries is to pay lower wages, but it is also to pay lower taxes. A lower production cost overseas does not always mean lower prices back home, but it can mean lower wages and a lower investment at domestic factories. If that translates into the threat of an American factory possibly closing, then you've got a worried workforce on your hands, which can further sap productivity. Employees who are constantly worried about layoffs hardly make for an inspired workforce. To be productive, companies *need* inspired employees. Want high productivity? (And what business doesn't?) Then having workers toil for low wages is not the way to go about getting it.

Do you want more proof that foreign companies pay lower taxes than their American-owned competitors? On December 12, 2003, the Treasury Department updated their rules to require American companies that are acquired by foreign-owned companies or move their headquarters overseas to inform the IRS. Why? Because the shift of corporate headquarters overseas means paying lower taxes.

MYTHOLOGY 101

You thought you saw the last of mythology when high school was over, didn't you? But there's a new myth out there regarding China versus the U.S., and it needs de-bunking. It goes like this. The Chinese focus is on cheap, labor-intensive products resulting in low-wage jobs, and the Unites States focus is on high-tech, high-wage jobs. The sound bite *"we think, they sweat"* doesn't apply anymore. In fact, we are in danger of losing both manufacturing and high-tech jobs in today's global economy. According to a June 20, 2005, issue of *Business Week*, Bangalore has 150,000 info tech engineers—more than the Silicon Valley—which has only 130,000.

According to Intel's chief executive officer, Craig Barrett, people in China "are capable of doing any engineering job, any software job, any managerial job that people in the United States are capable of doing." Apparently, we don't have the comparative advantage in any particular industry anymore. The only comparative advantage we might have these days in many cases is in lower wages, if we want to accept them.

Microsoft CEO, Steven Ballmer, says that the shortage of U.S. tech students is the issue that worries him the most. "The U.S. is No. 3 now in the world and falling behind quickly No. 1 [India] and No. 2 [China] in terms of computer-science graduates," he said at a forum in New York in late 2003. But Ballmer also claims, "Low supply is keeping U.S. engineers' wages too high and causing job losses. Lower the pay of U.S. professionals to $50,000.00 and it won't make sense for employers to put up with the hassle of doing business in developing countries."

MYTHOLOGY 102

What about the "jobs that Americans won't do?" Often it is not the job that is unattractive but the wages that come with the job. There is probably a shortage of tomato harvesters willing to work for $6.00 an hour, but there probably isn't a shortage of tomato harvesters willing to work at $14.00 an hour.

Ah, yes, Roger, but you would be paying less for your tomatoes if the workers were paid $6.00 an hour instead of $14.00. Oh really? In the first five years after the North American Free Trade Agreement (NAFTA) was passed, more than 100 Florida tomato farmers lost their farms, 24 packing houses closed, and more than 100 processors and suppliers went belly up. And even though Mexican imports of tomatoes went up 70 percent, in the United States, the American tomato buyer/eater found that tomato prices increased 16 percent. So much for that theory! But then again, that's all free trade is—a theory—and one that often does not hold up well when it is applied in the real world.

THAT'S *COOL*

Luckily, my home state of Florida requires produce to be labeled with the country of origin, so I can easily tell the difference between American tomatoes and Mexican tomatoes. Florida has had this requirement in place since 1980, which takes about two man-hours per week to execute in each Florida store.

But what about other food products like beef, pork, lamb, seafood, and peanuts? For five years now, legislation called COOL, which stands for Country-of-Origin Labeling, has been delayed and would have made such information mandatory. The volume of imported food has almost doubled in the past ten years, and with all this new competition the American farmer is facing, COOL would provide a great way to support those farmers here at home.

Opponents of COOL legislation contend that the labeling process would be too costly. Really? I have never seen one report that says Florida's produce is more expensive than in neighboring states like Georgia,

Alabama, or Louisiana. And to refute accusations of protectionism, American farmers remind us that safety, labor, and environmental laws, which are often more strict than most other nations, are precisely why we have a higher standard of living. Since 92 percent of consumers favor country-of-origin labeling, farmers also remind us that the ability to promote farm products as American would limit the need to resort to tariffs or other import restrictions. Eighty percent of American consumers in a Fresh Trends survey think that food grown in the U.S. is safer and fresher than food grown outside the U.S., and 92 percent said they would eat U.S. meat if they knew it originated here. If we can have labeling guidelines for T-shirts, we can certainly have them for T-bones.

HOPE FOR OUR FARMERS

Another industry that holds promise for the American farmer is corn-based ethanol. If you want to purchase more of our energy from the Midwest instead of the Middle East, corn-based ethanol might be the way. It is not the only new source of income on the horizon for rural America. Kathy White started Rural Sourcing, Inc., after she got fed up with the loss of American technology jobs to India. She found that there were plenty of college towns in more rural areas that had an ample supply of trained workers that would represent 30 percent to 50 percent lower costs to domestic firms in the areas of basic programming and information technology.

HOMESHORING

There is a growing trend in America called *homeshoring*. It promises to keep more jobs in America by making it possible for existing companies to move their workers out of high-overhead call centers back into their own low-overhead homes. Homeshoring jobs grew 20 percent in the course of 2005 alone to 112,000. That figure is expected to nearly triple by 2010. Most *home agents* are stay-at-home moms who dropped out of the workforce. They reside in rural areas, do not want long commutes to call centers, and cannot afford child care. Homeshoring also holds promise for disabled Americans, too, like legally blind Katey Glass, whose $35,000.00 annual salary allowed her to get off of Social Security as she cared for her husband, who is a double amputee and dialysis patient.

What else is great about *home agents* is that they are not just more productive, they are also more loyal. Because of them the company's turnover rate is reduced, and so are call-center company costs. Homeshoring may be a trend whose time has truly come. Sixty-two percent of U.S. consumers complain if they suspect a customer or tech support agent is overseas, and nearly 70 percent say they are less likely to continue doing business with the same company after a bad experience with a call center, according to Opinion Research Corp.

But sadly, the unbridled growth of Chinese imports over the years means that the clock might *literally* be ticking for disabled Americans like Katey Glass, mentioned above. For 30 years now, most of the wall clocks found in government buildings have been made by the nonprofit enterprise Chicago Lighthouse, which was "established to give persons who were blind the chance to become self-sufficient and earn wages." The organization, now over 100 years old, which used to feature Helen Keller at their annual dinners in the 1940s and 1950s, offers employment to blind and visually impaired employees who can assemble a clock in fifty seconds. Sometimes there are instances where we should turn our focus away from our needless drive for cheap products and excessive productivity. But why stop with the disabled? I believe that all Americans share the right to live by the Chicago Lighthouse creed giving Americans the opportunity to become self-sufficient and earn wages.

LABELS: BUY AMERICAN'S BEST FRIEND

Labeling laws make it easy for us to tell whether the apparel we buy is made in the U.S. or imported. Federal law requires that the front of all packages for socks must display the country of origin. Today, you don't have to turn the product over and scour the fine print. I have found through my own research that oftentimes American-made socks are even lower priced than imported socks of similar styles. So much for the widespread belief that imports always save the consumer money. It doesn't necessarily matter that in 2003 alone, China exported 276 million pairs of socks to the United States, or 2,200 percent more than they exported to us in 2001. What *does* matter is that we leave the foreign-made socks on the shelf and buy the American-made ones. Americans will remain employed, and we will save the American sock industry, which out of all the types of apparel sold in the U.S., has the highest domestic market share.

What about other products where the country of origin cannot be found? Remember our home team example of Colgate toothpaste with its label indicating it was from South Africa? Colgate toothpaste made in the U.S. does not need to be labeled "Made in USA" according to the Federal Trade Commission guidelines for complying with the "Made in USA" standard. Are you thinking, *"So what?"* Here's why it is a big deal. If a product is not labeled with a country of origin, what do you think? If you think that no label means it was made overseas, you are not alone. In fact, you are thinking like the vast majority of Americans who are highly suspicious of goods that are not labeled with a country of origin, believing that the product was probably made overseas and its parent company just does not want us to know. But because of our country's labeling laws, no label means the U.S. Customs Department did not require the product to be labeled with a foreign country of origin. That means it was either made in the U.S., or the product was significantly transformed in the U.S., meaning the company *could* apply a label like "Made in the U.S. from Imported Parts," "Made in USA of U.S. and Imported Parts," or "Assembled in USA." But the manufacturer does not have to apply any of these labels to their product. If they do, however, they need to be prepared to back it up with proof. The only label that *needs* to be affixed on tags or labels is the foreign country of origin if it is imported.

To be labeled "Made in USA," a product has to be "all or virtually all" made in the U.S. with negligible foreign content. You can visit the Federal Trade Commission's website at www.ftc.gov for more information. We need labels to indicate that the product is made in the United States (unless labeling laws are being broken). We need to help the consumer make informed choices, and labels can do this, with a little help from our friends at the Federal Trade Commission. It may be a little confusing, but isn't it better to find those labels than one that reads "Made in Honduras?"

AMERICAN COMPANIES DOING RIGHT BY AMERICA

In 2005, Forrester research estimated that by 2015 we would lose $136 billion in wages and 3.3 million jobs (2 percent of the U.S. workforce) from sending jobs offshore. This could result in a $34 billion decline in federal, state, and local tax revenue. Free trade and outsourcing proponents counter that 2 percent of the workforce is a negligible percentage, and so we should not worry. After all, think of all the positives, like saving eighteen cents on that $15.00 shirt compared to last year's prices.

Even though the average annual pay for a CEO is now 369 times the annual pay of an average worker (the ratio was 28:1 in 1970), not all American CEOs are bad. Some have made statements (and even backed them up with actions) that prove they care about the plight of the American worker. Intel CEO Craig Barrett said, "My allegiance is to the shareholders of Intel and to the success of the company. We go after the most cost-effective resources around the world, no matter where they are." But he also said, "As an American citizen, I would have to be worried about whether jobs that are created are created outside the U.S...As a citizen, I see all these resources and I think this puts my country in danger."

In 2005, Intel announced it was building a $3 billion facility in Arizona and investing $345 million in two existing U.S. plants. Admittedly, this was after the American Jobs Creation Act of 2004 was passed, allowing repatriated earnings to be temporarily taxed at 5.25 percent instead of the usual 35 percent, but the fact that Intel already had two factories in the U.S. shows that CEO Craig Barrett backs up his comments with corresponding actions.

Even though it was estimated that American companies repatriated about $350 billion because of the special tax break, the legislation was a bad idea since it does nothing to solve America's competitiveness problem. Instead of lowering taxes of American companies, which is revenue-negative, to make them more competitive with foreign companies (which pay fewer taxes to the U.S. Treasury), we should be raising taxes on foreign companies, which is revenue-positive. In other words, do not lower our standards to theirs—raise their standards to ours!

Soon after the legislation passed, evidence surfaced that indicated that the intended boost for U.S. jobs was not happening. National Semiconductor disclosed in January 2005 that it intended to repatriate $500 million, but on the same day it announced 550 layoffs representing 6 percent of its company work force. National Semiconductor executive, Mr. Weir, who formerly worked on Capitol Hill, questioned the meaning of the "American Jobs Creation Act" title and said that the law should simply be viewed as a tax break.

Also, it has been argued that the idea of blindly handing out tax breaks hoping that it is going to result in more jobs may not be a good policy. Prior to the American Jobs Creation Act of 2004, Congress added a stipulation to an energy bill that restricted a certain tax credit to appliances made in the U.S. Despite the tax credit, Whirlpool announced that it would go ahead with plans to transfer an ice maker production line from Arkansas to Mexico. Whirlpool also said it would likely result in zero layoffs since affected workers in the plant would move to other positions vacated by retirees. In a statement regarding the tax break, Whirlpool's vice president of government relations, Tom Catania, said that although the tax credit was certainly beneficial to their business, it would not eliminate the possibility that the ice maker jobs would move to Mexico.

But free traders might be surprised to hear what Adam Smith, author of the 1776 book *Wealth of Nations* and architect of the modern-day free trade movement, had to say about taxing foreign goods that compete with our own, "When the necessaries of life have been taxed in any country, it becomes proper to tax not only the necessaries of life imported from other countries, but all sorts of foreign goods which can come into competition with anything that is the produce of domestic industry."

BETTING ON THE WRONG HORSE, OR WAS IT ACTUALLY THE RIGHT HORSE?

Sometimes, we fail to recognize which companies are doing right by the American economy, and we even attempt to boycott them. Even though as of March 2005, only 12 percent of Maytag's products were made outside the U.S. when Maytag was feeling the competitive pinch from other companies that had a greater share of their production offshore, many Americans pledged to boycott Maytag for closing a refrigerator plant in Galesburg, Illinois and relocating it to Mexico.

In June of 2004, before Maytag was acquired by Whirlpool, Maytag's CEO, Ralph Hake, proclaimed that even though 96 percent of his employees were in the United States, it "is not an advantage for Maytag." He also told a group of union members and workers concerned about their jobs that consumers were more interested in price than they were in whether a product was made in the United States.

Back in February 14, 2005, I wrote a "Buy American Mention of the Week" article—posted on my website www.howtobuyamerican.com and sent to thousands of e-mail subscribers—explaining how a boycott of Maytag was a mistake. This was true since American consumers who switched their purchases from Maytag to any other appliance company would be supporting a company that had a higher percentage of their workforce employed outside the U.S. as well as a higher percentage of their products made outside the U.S. One e-mail list subscriber who worked for Maytag told me that although Maytag did move their refrigerator jobs to Mexico, they have also recently moved some jobs from Mexico back to America.

At first, it seemed that Maytag was starting down the same path with their washers and dryers as they were with their refrigerators when they transferred production of the electrical wiring harnesses from Newton, Iowa to Mexico. These harnesses were fabricated south of the border and shipped back to Iowa where American union workers installed them in Maytag washers and dryers. But over a period of several months, Maytag discovered quality problems with the harnesses, and the work was moved back to Iowa where workers who once fabricated the electrical harnesses were put back to work.

Had we boycotted Maytag washers and dryers, would the electrical harness work have been transferred to another foreign location instead of to America? Maybe. Would Maytag have suffered losses in profits that might have forced them to explore relocating more work from America, where we demand higher wages, to a different low-wage location like China? Possibly. Would we have instead diverted our American consumer dollars to Swedish-owned Electrolux, makers of Frigidaire, Westinghouse, and Gibson, among others? If so, we would have been rewarding a foreign company that closed a Michigan refrigerator plant in March 2006. Not only were 3,000 jobs destroyed, but Electrolux was the biggest source of local tax revenue. Michigan offered $74 million in tax breaks, and the union offered $32 million in concessions of its own. Still, it wasn't enough to keep Electrolux's doors open. Interestingly, the company never indicated that they were losing money on the Michigan plant or that the company wasn't profitable. *They just weren't making enough.*

And then you've got to wonder why we would have trouble coming up with enough money to buy an American-made Maytag, anyway. According to Maytag CEO Ralph Hake, a Maytag washing machine made in 1974 sold for $499. Today, the same model with more features sells for $439.

Maytag's CEO may not think that "Made in USA" matters to American consumers, but if it doesn't, then why does Tito's Handmade Vodka stress in their radio commercials that theirs is the only vodka brand made in the U.S.? Why did retail chain Rug Décor explain on the front of their July 2007 promotional flyer that Shaw rugs are made in America and encourage potential shoppers to "Buy American and SAVE?" Why did Don Reid Ford, a local auto dealer in the Orlando, Florida area, urge potential car and truck buyers to Buy American in his television ads? Why are toy companies that predominately produce in the U.S. beefing up their American credentials before the Christmas shopping season with bigger and brighter "Made in USA" labels and stickers? And why are toy stores training their employees and placing floor signs to direct patriotic patrons looking for American-made toys to the proper part of the store? The answer is that it is because "Made in USA" *does* matter.

What can happen when we are not aware enough, and we fail to support the right companies while boycotting the wrong ones? In June 2005, Chinese-owned Haier sent Maytag an "indication of interest." This set off a bidding war, which, thankfully, ended with American-owned

Whirlpool outbidding Chinese-owned Haier. Whirlpool is a company that has some of its production overseas. However, on May 18, 2004, it announced that close to $100 million would go toward investment in the company's U.S. facilities. Clearly it is better that Maytag was acquired by American-based Whirlpool than Chinese-based Haier.

Whirlpool's American investment included a new generation of Ohio-made washers and dryers; a new line of Ohio-made dishwashers; new production lines for refrigerators at plants in Arkansas, Indiana, and Tennessee; and cooking products at a Tulsa, Oklahoma plant.

Even though some Haier refrigerators are made in the U.S., it would still be better in the long run to buy a Whirlpool refrigerator made in Taiwan. Why? To keep American companies profitable so that any of our home companies that come under financial stress may be acquired by another American company rather than a foreign-owned company, or better yet, they don't become vulnerable at all. Supporting American companies means funneling financial resources into a company that is much more likely to reinvest in existing American factories or is at least more likely to invest in America. This is better than supporting foreign-owned companies that will oftentimes strive to acquire existing American-owned factories. The end result of that scenario? A greater share of the American pie being transferred overseas.

THE SAD IRONY

If Chinese-owned Haier had prevailed in the bidding war, irony would be stamped all over that transaction. A Chinese company buys an American company with money Americans spent on cheap Chinese products because they thought that buying them raised our standard of living and was a net positive for the U.S. economy.

But those dollars used by Haier to purchase Maytag would not necessarily have been a result of American consumers sending their dollars to China for Chinese-made goods. Since Haier has a factory in South Carolina, I'm sure some consumers figured they were doing the right thing buying an American-made product. Yet few probably realized that they were funding a Chinese company that would someday use that money to try to buy an existing U.S. company, which would only have resulted in transferring more of America's wealth to Beijing. This only reinforces my belief that we should always support the products of American companies even when their factories are located overseas.

After Whirlpool received approval to purchase Maytag on March 26, 2007, they planned to consolidate their washer and dryer production jobs in Newton, Iowa to other locations, but Whirlpool didn't take those jobs overseas. The work was moved to locations in Clyde, Ohio and Marion, Ohio.

STEP INTO AMERICAN-OWNED

The footwear industry represents another area where it is difficult to buy American, but it is by no means impossible. New Balance makes about 30 percent of its shoes in the U.S., and SAS (San Antonio Shoes) makes 100 percent of its shoes in the U.S. And then there are the biggies Nike, Reebok, and Adidas. How many of their shoes are made here? None. What was that figure again? None. Zero. Nike is an American-owned company that often gives multi-million dollar endorsement contracts to NBA athletes, like their $90 million, seven-year endorsement deal with LeBron James and $40 million, four-year deal with Kobe Bryant. Now back to the local hero, New Balance, which had only a 3 percent share of the market in 1992 when it began its *"Endorsed by No One"* promotion. By 2004, it had garnered 13 percent of the market—without any celebrities pitching its products.

Many Americans view the transfer of jobs overseas as a clear indication of corporate greed, but we must be careful to analyze each situation on a case-by-case basis. Since New Balance pays its American employees $13.00 per hour plus benefits, and Nike pays its Chinese employees a small fraction of that amount and few, if any, benefits, could we honestly call it corporate greed if one day New Balance abandoned its U.S. factories like its competitors? I don't believe so, because every company that moves offshore adds to the pressure of the companies that remain in the United States to do the same thing. Smaller companies in particular find that if they don't follow their competitors to China, they won't be able to stay in business.

PROUD TO BE AN AMERICAN...MANUFACTURER... OVERSEAS

There are other companies that are not only proud of their manufacturing capacity in America but also of their American ownership. Just prior to July 4, 2007, A&W Restaurants started their "Moove to American" campaign touting their use of 100 percent U.S. beef, taking shots at competitors like McDonald's for importing beef from places like New Zealand.

Anheuser-Busch, the last remaining major American brewer (Miller is owned by South African Breweries, which in turn is based in England, and Coors was acquired by Canadian-based Molson), has repeatedly emphasized their American roots and ownership. Acknowledging that marketing their beer in Europe as "American" might not be seen as a plus, Stephen Burrows, head of Anheuser-Busch's international arm, still proclaimed, "We are America. We recognize that everybody doesn't want that, but a lot of people do—and those are the people we are after."

Germany, for instance, poses a king-sized problem for the King of Beers since Anheuser-Busch is not allowed to use the "Budweiser" name inside the country. The term "Bud" isn't allowed either because it sounds much like "Bit," which is short for a popular German beer called Bitburger. That presents more than an itty-bitty problem for America's largest brewer marketing to German beer drinkers. Why? Well, what do you think of the name "Anheuser Busch Bud." Not too catchy, is it? That may partly explain why Anheuser-Busch generates only 6.4 percent of its revenue outside the United States.

Most 3M products are made in the United States, despite the fact that they generate most of their revenue overseas. In addition to employing thousands of manufacturing workers, this American company employs 6,000 technical employees at its American-based research centers.

Harley-Davidson has solid American roots, even though its domestic parts content has declined in recent years, and the company has all but ruled out producing in China. CEO Jeffrey Bluestein told a meeting of the National Governors Association, "We cannot sell a motorcycle in China today unless we are willing to manufacture it there and, frankly, I don't think Harley-Davidson with its Americana image and the kinds of quality and features we put into the motorcycle would have the same caché even in China if it were built in China."

Harley-Davidson used to face huge obstacles in penetrating the Japanese market before many years of lobbying got rid of the barriers. Anyone in Japan wishing to own a motorcycle 400cc or larger, like a Harley Davidson, had to pass an exam. Well, that doesn't sound so crazy, you're probably thinking. However, it does if you factor in that one of the parts of the test included *riding the motorcycle across a balance beam.* Two percent of the test-takers passed that part of the test. By the way, these laws were written with strong input from Japan's four large motorcycle competitors. Wouldn't Harley love to have that kind of input if it meant keeping out Honda and Suzuki motorcycles?

Then there's the Japanese law that bans highway access to motorcycles with more than one person riding. Motorcycles with two people, like the ones Harley-Davidson fans like so they can take their spouses along, are relegated to city streets and back roads. That leaves the highways open for single riders of high-performance Japanese bikes.

Other American companies, like Motorola, have faced their own obstacles in penetrating overseas markets. To avoid an emphasis on elimination of customs fraud and smuggling in Russia, Motorola flew a batch of 167,500 cellular phones on a company jet to Russia with the company logo on it. Still, Russian police seized the shipment, and despite the Motorola corporate logo, they designated it as "smuggled goods." And so, 50,000 of the phones were said to be "harmful" and were destroyed. The fate of the other 117,500 phones is still unknown.

It is important to know and support American brand names, not just those made in the U.S., or we could run the risk of ending up like Britain. They have sold off significant symbols of their national identity to foreign investors. Jaguar to American-owned Ford, Rolls Royce to German-owned BMW, and spirits and wine company Allied Domecq to

French-owned Pernod Ricard. Britain's practice of allowing national symbols to become the property of foreigners is now called the "Wimbledon Effect": World-class players competing in a world-class tournament that no Brits are able to win.

My website www.howtobuyamerican.com is filled with American-owned companies, large and small, that are proud of their American ownership and proud to make their products in the United States.

Ownership matters to Americans. And not just "Made in USA." That is why an overwhelming majority of Americans, 73 percent according to a Wall Street Journal/NBC News poll, opposed United Arab Emirates-based Dubai Ports World from taking control of several of America's ports. It is why Marathon Oil Co., uses the slogan "An American Company Serving America." And it is why Venezuelan-owned Smartmatic, a company that manufactured voting machines for American elections, was pressured into selling its Sequoia Voting Systems Company, Inc., to an American company. Ownership matters, which is why there was such a public outcry about the 70 percent Chinese government-owned CNOOC bid to acquire American-owned petroleum company Unocal. It is incredibly rewarding to see, time after time, Americans rushing to defend our companies when we stand a chance of losing them. The next step is for Americans to defend them by buying American every day.

Many companies have also shown that the privilege of using the "Made in USA" logo matters to them as well. Lock manufacturing company Kwikset was sued in California, one of 28 states with country-of-origin laws, for labeling their locks "All American Made" or "Made in USA" even though some of the components in the locks were produced overseas.

In 2004, Sears was handed a class action lawsuit accusing the company of false advertising by stating that the Craftsman tool line was "Made in USA." Over 1,600 tools bearing the Craftsman name are made in the U.S., but Sears gave the perception that the entire line fit the criteria, motivating consumers to buy the tools out of a feeling of patriotism. Months later, Sears blacked out "Made in USA" claims on portions of its website that displayed Craftsman tools.

And at least the perception of "Made in USA" is important to President George W. Bush. In 2003, Bush held a press conference on strengthening the American economy using cargo boxes with their "Made in China" labels covered up and theoretical "Made in USA" labels imposed over them.

I PLEDGE ALLEGIANCE TO THE FLAG
OF MY FOREIGN COUNTRY

When we support foreign companies operating in the United States, we still send our dollars to foreign lands through profits paid to foreign companies, and this money may, and many times has, been used to "invest" back into the United States. When foreigners assume ownership of U.S. land and factories, they become our landlords. We are essentially letting them be the holders of the mortgage on our national treasury. Every time they return their profits to their foreign lands, and pay their taxes to their foreign governments, they dissipate our country's wealth instead of creating it. What can we do about it? For starters, how about trying more American investment in America and less foreign investment in America?

A careful look at foreign investment in the proper light is necessary. This look does not automatically regard foreign investment as a positive for the United States and realizes that foreign companies aren't investing in America for the good of America. More often than not, they are using America to invest in themselves. Our look at foreign investment in the U.S. also must acknowledge that an overwhelming majority of it does not go to upstart production. Rather, it goes to acquiring our existing American-owned operations.

According to 2004 Department of Commerce data, 91 percent of all Foreign Direct Investment in the United States by foreign companies between 1992 and 2002 was used to "acquire and export control of the global assets of American-based corporations." And from 2000 to 2002, a whopping 95 percent of Foreign Direct Investment was used for the *"purpose of merely acquiring and exporting control."* When you consider this and take into account the layoffs that almost always accompany foreign acquisitions of existing U.S. companies, the number of jobs created by foreign investment may actually be a negative. Seen in this light, foreign investment doesn't create jobs in the U.S., *it destroys them.*

Yet, given all of this bad-for-America data, on Friday, July 14, 2004, President Bush told a Chicago audience, "I have no problem with foreign capital buying U.S. companies."

Paul Craig Roberts, former Assistant Secretary of the Treasury in the Reagan administration, said on Lou Dobbs' program that when foreigners acquire our assets, they "acquire ownership of our real estate, of our companies, of the corporate and government bonds so we lose all the future income streams that are associated with the assets when we lose the ownership. So it is a bad thing."

According to the Department of Commerce, foreign investment in the United States increased $161.5 Billion from 2005 to 2006, equaling a jump of 76.7 percent, and investors from the Middle East doubled their American asset acquisitions in the same period. The manufacturing sector was the target of the majority of foreign investment, with computers, chemicals, and electronics leading the way.

Although there are stories of American and foreign companies alike outsourcing jobs to lower-wage countries, American-owned multinational corporations still create more jobs in America than they do overseas. A study focusing on the time period between 1991 and 2001 found that American-based multinationals added five new jobs in the U.S. for every three new jobs added overseas. This shows that American-owned companies are unquestionably more pro-American than foreign-owned companies. And contrary to popular belief, U.S. multinationals operate from foreign countries mostly to serve those foreign markets rather than using them as platforms to export back to America. In 2001, only 11 percent of foreign affiliate sales from American-owned companies went to American consumers.

For example, Heinz came under attack before the 2004 election for having a number of plants overseas. However, Heinz's overseas factories only worked to serve overseas markets, and none of those overseas locations export back into the United States. Heinz does import some of their ketchup from Canada, but this is easily avoided by merely selecting a different size ketchup bottle. For instance, 36 oz., 32 oz., 24 oz., and 20 oz., size bottles are made in U.S., but 50.5 oz., and 44 oz., size bottles are made in Canada. Also, Heinz exports from Ohio and California factories to various places around the world.

American-owned companies also give more money to charity for the benefit of Americans than do foreign-owned companies. A 2003 ranking of the top ten corporate charity donors revealed that no foreign-owned companies were on the list. Foreign companies were also absent from a list of the top five companies committed to employee and supplier diversity as ranked by *DiversityInc* magazine.

It is bad enough when Americans boycott the wrong companies. It is just as bad when the president and other public servants endorse outsourcing. Former Florida Governor, Jeb Bush, did just that when he endorsed outsourcing as a means to save taxpayer money. But the worst is when American retailers attack American manufacturers for defending their American factories against the outsourcing trend. For example, since 2000, Chinese-made wooden furniture has flooded the U.S market. This has destroyed at least 35,000 U.S. jobs at woodworking factories. This represents roughly 27 percent of the workforce. Yet when American furniture companies like Bassett supported proposed tariffs to restrict the flood of Chinese-made furniture, the company became a target of American furniture retailers. This happened even though the *Wall Street Journal* reported that duties as low as 10 percent might *not even be noticed by U.S. consumers*, and that furniture retailers along with their Chinese factories could easily absorb the extra charge. Still, over a dozen retailers nationwide removed Bassett furniture from their showrooms or halted new Bassett orders, eliminating orders totaling $8 million. If all retailers care about is their bottom line and can so easily disregard absorbable tariffs that would help protect other American workers, it is time to make their bottom line bottom out.

MAKING YOUR DOLLARS SPENT MATTER EVEN MORE

So many jobs have been lost in the furniture manufacturing industry that the American Furniture Manufacturers Association dropped the word "Manufacturers" from its name, eliminating a policy that formerly required members to have a minimum of one factory in the U.S.

This brings up yet another angle of the Buy American issue. It is one that consumers rarely think about, but if they did, they'd be helping our country even more. If it is best to buy an American-made product from an American-owned company, and it is, then it is even better to buy those goods from an American-owned *retailer* like Best Buy, which is American-owned, while CompUSA is Mexican-owned. Best Buy's Chief Executive, Bradbury H. Anderson, is a great example of an American boss who cares about his American employees. Anderson rose through the company ranks after starting as a stereo salesman. He declined 934,000 stock options for himself between 2002 and 2004, and instead he distributed them to lower-level employees.

What is another example of a good American retailer that we should be patronizing? Costco. Not only are they a viable alternative to Wal-Mart, they also have a reputation for offering the *best benefits in the retail sector*. At Costco, cashiers can make $40,000 a year, in less than four years of working full time.

As you might guess, Costco has taken some heat from the Wall Street elite for being too generous to their employees and not focusing on shareholder returns instead. That should be a clue to ordinary Americans that Costco is doing something right. Could it be that 82 percent of Costco's employees are covered by (able to afford) company-provided health insurance? Could it be that Costco covers 92 percent of health care premiums for their workers? The answer is "yes" to both questions.

The more health care premiums are covered by successful American companies employing Americans, the less the federal government will be obligated to cover through higher taxes on all of us. Pressure is mounting to find a solution to America's health care crisis. The best solution is obviously not one that shifts more of the health care burden to working Americans. Owning the responsibility of your own business is great, but owning the responsibility of your own health care is a much less attractive proposition.

BOYCOTTS MAKE A DIFFERENCE

One place we may have an impact and serve notice to foreign-owned companies that we mean business is through boycotts. Yet there are times we fail to boycott the right companies. In 2003, claiming France gave "aid and comfort to Saddam Hussein," the South Carolina State Legislature declared, "It makes no sense to buy French products, goods, and services." But the State Senate never acted on the legislation, claiming that since French-owned Michelin has factories in South Carolina, a boycott would be counter-productive. Not true. Here's why.

Continuing to buy French-owned Michelin tires (Michelin also owns B.F. Goodrich) in order to support their American workers means that we're boycotting American-owned Cooper and Goodyear tires, and their American workers, by default. This is too bad because Cooper and Goodyear *both* employ more Americans than French-owned Michelin. Again, we have to look beyond the "Made in USA" *label* and support American *companies*—the ones that pay more taxes to the U.S. Treasury. I just put a new set of Cooper tires on my Michigan-made Lincoln Town Car, and I noticed that every Cooper tire offered at the tire shop was made in the U.S.

Approximately 11 percent of the American workforce today is employed in manufacturing. That means the remaining 89 percent of Americans are employed in other areas like engineering, research and development, design, testing, administration, and advertising. And since the company headquarters for American companies are based in America, it is more likely that these types of jobs are located here as well when we support an American company. So if we buy a Michelin tire made in the U.S., we are "voting" 11 percent American and 89 percent French with our dollars. By buying Cooper tires, we're "voting" nearly 100 percent American since nearly all the tires Cooper sells to America are made here, and Cooper is an American-owned company. So jobs like the ones mentioned above will likely be filled by Americans. By truly buying American in the purest sense of the term, buying American-made products from American-owned companies, we could have boycotted a

French company and supported a net increase of jobs in the U.S. If Michelin had had to trim their workforce, Cooper and Goodyear would likely have added to theirs.

According to a February 25, 2004, article, Michelin cut 10 percent of its workers in North America between 2001 and 2003 because of cost reductions, outsourcing, and plant sales. In South Carolina alone, Michelin cut about 1,200 jobs, which translates into a 13 percent reduction and leaves 8,000 Michelin employees in the state. I know what you're saying, *"Roger, my Uncle Bob works for Michelin, so I'm still going to buy their tires."* Okay, but know that in the process that while you're helping Uncle Bob, you're hurting Uncle Sam.

Do American companies think American jobs matter to the American people? And I mean jobs other than just manufacturing jobs? Absolutely! If not, why does Apple write on the back of their iPods "Designed by Apple in California"? Many American companies also hesitate to outsource the design of their cherished brands since ownership of design comprises a major portion of a company's fundamental value. If a company outsources design, investors might question the amount of intellectual property actually owned by the company. And even more importantly to investors, what percentage of the profit actually returns to the company instead of going to pay foreigners for licensing fees?

The French boycott of 2003 was in response to the disagreement they were having with the U.S. over the Iraq War. But to me, the boycott of French companies provided an opportunity for us to take advantage of a patriotic response and become more economically independent. Americans everywhere were clamoring for knowledge on how to avoid buying French products, and I was happy to provide them with all-American alternatives.

Goodyear and Cooper are also guilty of layoffs in America, but they lay off workers in downturns in other countries as well as in the U.S. In April 2006, Goodyear detailed plans to cut 1,500 jobs as it tried to cope with rising costs of raw materials. What is interesting to note is that these cuts were *mostly outside the U.S.,* including plants in Britain and

Poland. It boils down to this. Support an American company making things in the U.S., like Cooper and Goodyear, or support a foreign company making things in the U.S., like Michelin.

Other foreign companies aren't exempt from criticism in laying off American workers, either. German-owned Continental Tire announced it was laying off 513 North Carolina workers in January 2006 because "manufacturing costs are higher" and "we cannot continue in our current situation." The company also made it clear that it was considering closing the plant if the remaining 573 employees did not agree *to voluntarily lower their wages.*

Japanese-owned Bridgestone/Firestone announced in 2006 that it would close its Oklahoma City plant by year's end, affecting 1,400 American workers. According to a statement from the vice-president of manufacturing operations, it has the same problem Goodyear and Cooper have. Heightened competition from lower-cost countries.

Kyocera, a Japanese maker of telecommunications and electronics equipment, cut 600 jobs in San Diego in 2005.

One in twelve manufacturing workers in the United States now works for a foreign-owned company. Sure, they provide the job if we agree to transfer the ownership of our industries, but in my opinion, you can't trade ownership for prosperity and expect that prosperity to continue in the long run.

FOREIGN DIRECT INVESTMENT

Before going too far into this hot button issue, let's start with a definition to put us all on the same page. To me, Foreign Direct Investment means foreign companies taking ownership of companies that were previously American-owned. In 2005, over $128 million was in the form of foreign investment—more than double the 1995 level. Still, between 2001 and 2004, data show that foreign companies lowered their capital spending in the U.S. and reduced their American workforce by 10 percent. This was happening even though foreign company sales in the U.S. were on the rise. By December 15, 2006,

Japanese firms had acquired 294 foreign companies (foreign as in based outside of Japan) worth $18.1 billion, more than the total for 2005 and twice the total for 2004. To the degree that we've been buying Hondas, Nissans, and Toyotas, even if they were made in the United States, they've been buying our land, factories, and companies with money that used to be ours.

Sometimes foreign companies steal secrets right out from under us. This was the case in 2005 when a California court found Japanese-owned Toshiba guilty of trade secret theft involving flash memory chips from California-based Lexar Media, Inc. The court went on to award damages worth $381 million.

WHAT'S GOOD FOR OUR FAMILIES SHOULD BE GOOD FOR OUR NATION

As parents, many of us teach our kids the American qualities of being independent and self-reliant. We tell them not to depend on anyone for what they can do for themselves. As it goes for the American family, so it should also go for the American nation. Critics call this principal isolationism. The problem with that criticism lies in the simple fact that even if we wanted our world to be that way, it just can't be, and it isn't. Isolationism is not possible today. The word the accusers are looking for starts with an "I" but it is not isolationism—it is independence. It is why we celebrate July Fourth every year. But if we don't support independence, we might as well stay home on July Fourth, because our celebrations will be largely ceremonial.

ALICE WAS RIGHT: "CURIOUSER AND CURIOUSER"

Maybe you're asking yourself, *"Can't we tell if we are supporting an American-owned company by looking at the label?"* The answer is we can't. The label will tell you where the product is *made*, but it will not tell you where the company is *based*. And that is what we need to know when it comes down to supporting our own companies. Even though Lysol lists Parsippany, New Jersey as its home, it is merely the U.S. subsidiary of the larger parent company in Britain.

This example is one reason why the book you are holding is so important to American prosperity and independence. We cannot tell who owns the company for any given product, so many times we end up sending profits overseas to the coffers of foreign companies who in turn pay taxes to foreign governments.

Looking at the tag, label, or product itself will never tell you that a Goodyear tire or a Cooper tire is American-owned and a B.F. Goodrich tire is French-owned or that French's mustard is owned by the British, and Grey Poupon is owned by an American company.

The situation gets even more complex when we try to determine who owns our restaurants, hotels, grocery stores, and other services. In these cases there's not even a tag, label, or product to examine. But services like these are unique because here ownership is the *only* factor to consider. There is no manufacturing location to consider, and there is no parts content to calculate. How would you know that Kroger is American-owned and A&P is German-owned? Did you know that Motel 6 and Red Roof Inns are owned by the French and that Days Inn and Comfort Inn are American-owned? Did you know that 7-Eleven is Japanese-owned and Circle K is Canadian-owned but that Racetrac and Hess are both American-owned? It is a lot to **not** know, and that lack of knowledge isn't good for America.

Let's look at where you do your banking. Domestic banks are more sensitive to pressure from the central bank to expand credit in America. This is especially true in areas that require stimulus. Domestic banks are much more likely to respond to that pressure on behalf of the U.S. economy. Foreign ownership of U.S. assets is a kind of absentee ownership—often being nothing more than a piece of paper indicating shares held by a distant owner. Not only are they "distant owners," they're also *disconnected* owners who feel little social responsibility (or need) to make the land in which they hold a stake any better. It is easier to be less responsible to your employees when you, the owner, are far, far away. Foreign owners are absentee owners, not just because they live elsewhere, but also because they are often absent from our society, our values, and our needs. If they don't live here, why would they care about our infrastructure for roads and bridges? They don't live here and don't use them, so why should they pay for them?

As Dick Gephardt put it in his book *An Even Better Place*, we can only "get back on the right track...reclaiming ownership of the land we love." But how can we do that if Pat Buchanan is right in saying, "By 2002, foreigners owned U.S. assets equal to 78 percent of our Gross Domestic Product (GDP), 13 percent of our equity market, 22 percent of our corporations, 24 percent of our corporate bonds, and 48 percent of the U.S. Treasury market?"

THE POWER OF WEALTH

Friedrich List, a German economist who also lived in America for several years and wrote *The National System of Political Economy* in 1841 before he died in 1846, once said, "The power of producing wealth is...infinitely more important than wealth itself." I would add that by keeping the ownership of our companies, we retain the power to create wealth. Transferring ownership of our wealth (or transferring industries to foreigners) means we're also transferring our streams of future income to foreigners as well. In our future, we'll find it much easier to face difficult decisions if our nation's debt is held by us. Obviously, we are the ones who have the greatest stake and the greatest interest in maintaining our own prosperity.

We cannot trade ownership of our American industries for prosperity. Between 1990 and 2005, America transferred $3.6 trillion of its wealth to foreign countries by selling ownership of its assets. You can only sell the family silver once. And what about all those imports? They are supposed to mean lower prices, which enable shoppers to have money left over to spend elsewhere. But an October 25, 2004, *Business Week* article showed that even though retail sales increased $62 billion during the prior twelve months, imports of motor vehicles, foods and beverages, and consumer goods increased by the exact same amount. All the extra manufacturing jobs that were created to meet the increased production were not created in America but in other countries instead.

I remember reading a story in 2005 about an American who used to live next door to a Russian émigré. One day the émigré asked about something that confused him regarding his new home country. "This place seems very rich but I never see anyone making anything. How does the country earn its money?" The answer was that we seemed to make our living selling houses to each other. Which brings me to my next point—we need to create wealth not just push it around in re-distributive fashion. If we only do that we are creating a system whereby some benefit at the expense of others. We certainly cannot teach prosperity to the rest of the world until we restore our own.

Buying American is rooted and grounded in historical American qualities such as independence, self-reliance, and self-sufficiency. But sovereignty and independence cannot be obtained if we do not even own the engines that result in the production we all celebrate. Only if we own the means of our own production can we rule under capitalism. As William Greider asks in his book *The Soul of Capitalism,* "Can Americans be said to own their own lives? Do they own their work, their voice and self expression? Does the ownership of financial assets have any meaning beyond the portfolio's monthly balance statement? Does it involve any influence or responsibility? Can sovereign citizens claim responsibility for the governing decisions made in their name? Who owns the common assets that are ostensibly shared by all?"

DO UNTO OTHERS DOESN'T APPLY

Free traders seem to be of the mindset that if we continue to buy goods from China and other nations, they will ultimately return the favor and buy more from us. They also adhere to the belief that consumers in foreign countries will buy more American goods if we demonstrate that we will buy more from them first. Anything less invites retaliation, which free traders believe is a struggle we will lose. So the thinking goes if we surrender our market to foreign countries, they will surrender their market to ours—and we will be ahead. It is also believed that as we export our products we are exporting our values and capitalism. But if that's true, it must also be true that when China exports its products to us, we're importing communism.

The fallacy in this thinking is that the people who are most likely to buy American are not foreigners. Who are they? Remember back to the "poll on nine nations?" It is the American people. That's right, it is us. We are the ones most likely to buy American, which tells us that most Americans are concerned with building a better American economy, not a better global economy. In fact, our U.S. Constitution charges us with the responsibility to form a "more perfect Union." It says nothing about striving to form a more perfect global economy.

A May 15, 2007, article in the *Wall Street Journal* revealed that American brands are losing their influence on the Chinese imagination. The former excitement over American products is being replaced by increasing nationalist sentiment in China, and Chinese consumers are now more likely to seek out their own domestic brands.

An April 12, 2004, *Business Week* article reported how even though several (free trade leaning) economists tend to downplay or outright disregard the economic significance of outsourcing, the political significance in the 2004 elections couldn't be so easily overlooked. Forty-seven percent of American voters feared that a friend, relative, or even they themselves might lose their job to a foreign country. And a whopping 83 percent said it was an important election issue.

With poll numbers like the ones mentioned throughout this chapter, you'd think that companies would strive to put as many American-made products in front of consumers as possible. Certainly any politician would respond knowing that 83 percent of their constituents believed a certain way on an issue, so wouldn't a company or corporation respond similarly? Then why don't they? There are two reasons. First, even if Americans wanted to back up their responses to these polls with corresponding American-made purchases in the stores, 76 percent of American consumers say it is increasingly difficult to find American-made products on the shelves of Wal-Mart, Target, Kmart, or Sears. Second, stocking retail store shelves with cheaper imported goods results in higher profits for retailers.

Peggy Smedly, Author of *Mending Manufacturing* and editorial director of *Start* magazine, got the idea for a China-free Christmas list in 2004 and found both American-made and Chinese-made leotards at Target for $14.99. In Wal-Mart (I was doing research there, not shopping there) I found six pair of Hanes socks, made in the U.S., for $4.48. Fruit of the Loom had the same style and the same size, made in Mexico, for the same price.

HISTORICAL FIGURES SAW THE CONNECTION

Many Americans continue to buy cheap foreign-made clothing in malls across America, and probably few would make a connection between that and the importance of supplying our own needs. However, one of our forefathers, Alexander Hamilton, made that connection when he said, "Every nation ought to endeavor to possess within itself all the essentials of a national supply. These comprise the means of subsistence, habitation, *clothing* (my emphasis added) and defense."

President William McKinley had a few things to say about the word "cheap." He said, "I do not prize the word 'cheap.' It is not a badge of honor...it is a symbol of despair. Cheap prices make for cheap goods; cheap goods make for cheap men; and cheap men make for a cheap country!" But unfortunately the wisdom of some of our great former presidents is at odds with our current one. President George W. Bush believes exporting jobs is good for America. According to the 2004 Economic Report of the President, "When a good or service is produced more cheaply abroad, it makes more sense to import it than to provide it domestically." As Connecticut Senator Joe Lieberman asserted in one speech, "Bush's laissez-faire means 'I don't care.'" Free trade and outsourcing is nothing more than an ill-advised attempt to generate prosperity on the cheap. It won't work in terms of generating prosperity, but it will certainly work to cheapen the country.

In 1841, Friedrich List wrote in his seminal work *The National System of Political Economy*, "The forces of production are the tree on which wealth grows...the tree which bears the fruit is of itself of greater value than the fruit itself." List also said national interest was of a higher priority than cheap consumer products purchased from foreign producers.

LACK OF CHOICE MEANS A LACK OF CONSUMER PATRIOTS

Americans often purchase foreign goods not because they have a huge desire or craving for imports but because they are often forced to buy from the options that are placed in front of them. If 85 percent of the goods on the shelves at Wal-Mart are imported, it is no startling revelation that most of the people shopping there will come away with their shopping bags stuffed full of imports. Shoppers don't walk out of Wal-Mart with foreign-made goods because they crave imports. They come away with foreign-made goods because it is what Wal-Mart stocks. I've heard plenty of stories about people looking through several products in stores to find the "Made in USA" logo on them, but I've never heard of anyone searching persistently until they can find one that says "Made in China."

In 2003, the state of New Jersey forced one of the companies operating on a state contract for computer services to move from Bombay back to New Jersey. Just prior to the 2004 elections, Arizona's governor banned outsourcing altogether, ruling that all state work must be performed in the U.S. New Jersey went a step further in 2005 and passed a law preventing any state work from being done outside the U.S. New Jersey's governor, Richard Codey, made no apologies for the bill being "protectionist." He said that sending American tax dollars to foreign countries to pay for domestic services was "bad public policy." Codey also said that the legislation was "an important step to protect our workers and keep jobs from going overseas. If a company wants to take jobs from our hardworking families and send them overseas, then it will not do business with this state."

I'm sure we could end outsourcing tomorrow if we could simply convince the American worker to accept the wage rates of the Chinese worker and convince American citizens and consumers to accept the same lax safety standards found in China as well. Of course, to do that we would also have to accept China's standard of living. We should realize that when businesses in America fire their American workers and send those jobs overseas, they are firing the best customers they could ever have.

But some officials in the Bush administration disagree. The president's chief economic adviser, Gregory Mankiw, put it like this, "Outsourcing is just a new way of doing international trade...more things are tradeable than were tradeable in the past and that's a good thing." Really? Tell that to all the Americans who didn't agree with Mankiw, but make sure you have a lot of time because a 2004 poll revealed that 84 percent did not agree. According to a 2004 CNN/USA Today/Gallup poll, 61 percent of Americans voiced concern that they will lose their current job to a foreign country. (Mankiw later became the chief economic adviser to the Mitt Romney presidential campaign.)

Other legislators flatly deny that outsourcing destroys jobs. Some go as far as to claim that outsourcing *creates* jobs. South Carolina Senator Jim DeMint went as far as to claim that "offshoring...creates three jobs in the United States for every one overseas." What *kinds* of jobs would be created that DeMint is referring to is hard to imagine, and not only because he didn't say.

THE JOBS WE LOSE TO OUTSOURCING

There's a belief that the only jobs we are losing to outsourcing are those low-wage, dead-end jobs. That belief is a mistaken one. In fact, information compiled by Forrester Research and the Bureau of Labor Statistics paints a very different picture. The jobs we are currently losing to outsourcing will probably surprise you, possibly scare you. They include processors of mortgage applications, tax returns, credit card accounts, and payroll and benefits; software development, chip design, and information technology consulting; financial analysis and research for banks, brokerages, and accounting firms; analytics (risk analysis for industrial process and consumer behavior); medical transcription and low-level X-ray analysis; and legal research, biotech research, and news reporting. Here's something to think about. Maybe we wouldn't have to worry about creating so many jobs if we didn't intentionally destroy so many.

Still, people like U.S. Chamber of Commerce President and CEO, Thomas Donohue, continue to recommend outsourcing as a way to make America more competitive and even increase employment. (Donohue must have Senator DeMint's number on his speed-dial.) Donohue says he understands the pain experienced by those who have seen their jobs go overseas because of offshoring, estimated at 250,000 a year by one government estimate. But Donohue also believes that Americans affected by offshoring trends should just "stop whining." I wonder how loudly he would be "whining" if he lost his CEO job and salary to offshoring.

Other proponents of outsourcing point to a practice they call "insourcing" as evidence that Americans should not be as concerned about the negative effects of trade as they have become. The big problem with this thinking is the fact that foreign companies that are insourcing jobs to America aren't the least bit motivated to do so by their knowledge that American companies are outsourcing. Foreign companies operate inside the U.S. because it is often advantageous to be closer to their customers in the United States or to avoid existing tariffs or any future import restrictions, not because of any loyalty to the United States or American workers.

On the campaign trail in 2004, George W. Bush claimed that Honda's investment in Ohio resulted in 16,000 direct jobs and 128,000 total jobs, considering what's called the "multiplier effect" or the jobs that are created as a result of supporting the initially created jobs. Guess what Bush failed to mention? The 2003 announcement by Honda that it was going to outsource production of its Inspire sedan from Ohio to Japan. Bush also failed to mention that most insourcing numbers are a result of foreign companies acquiring American companies. For example, when Germany's Daimler-Benz bought Chrysler in 1998, 97,000 Americans were simply reclassified as being employed by a foreign company. This type of reclassification resulted in 2.78 million jobs being *insourced* between 1991 and 2001.

In his book *An Even Better Place*, Dick Gephardt said, "If you don't vote, you may eventually lose the right to vote." Many Americans today would say that we have a right to buy American, and if we don't exercise that right now, we may lose it as well. It was partly out of the concern for losing that ability that I made a decision to do something from my experience in the mall in 1994. I thought to myself, "I'm an American. I live here, work here, and pay taxes here. Why is it so difficult to support other Americans who live here, work here, and pay taxes here?"

FOLLOWING IN DAD'S FOOTSTEPS

Occasionally in the media you'll hear about the benefit of greater availability of imports as giving Americans more freedom of choice in their buying decisions. But we have to guide consumer ambitions in a way that does not ultimately undercut what is best for the country. It is true that part of freedom is having the right to make choices, but with that right comes the responsibility of accepting the results of those choices.

Let's look at "freedom" from another vantage point. What about our freedom to choose the industry in which we want to be employed? What if you want to follow in the footsteps of your father or grandfather or you have a sense of family tradition? Maybe you feel a great sense of family pride and loyalty, and you want to work in the footwear industry, or the television industry, or the textile industry?

Since our government has decided to allow once-thriving industries to die in the face of cutthroat foreign competition, Uncle Sam is essentially saying, *"I'm sorry son or daughter, I'm afraid we've caused that industry or career choice to be unavailable for you. But don't worry, you still have the freedom to buy whatever goods from whatever country you choose, you just don't have the freedom to choose any industry for your career. Sorry. Can't have everything, right?"* So much for American freedom. And since most Americans change jobs much more often than in the past because of the instability of the job market, exactly how does one define the term "career" in a work environment that seems to actually discourage continuity?

According to Joseph Stiglitz, from his book *The Roaring Nineties*, "...even with Western individualism, today, we recognize our interdependence; it is hard to imagine life as a hermit, without goods that we receive, somehow, from others." Even though I respect Mr. Stiglitz, who received the Nobel Prize in 2001, he tends to exaggerate on this point. Buy American advocates don't wish to cease receiving any and all goods from others, we just want to emphasize our independence as opposed to the interdependence of which Mr. Stiglitz speaks. And few, if any, Buy American advocates believe that advancing a Buy American policy would cause us to live our lives as "hermits."

If we can't commercially grow bananas in the United States, I think few would perceive our independence as a nation was at risk for importing bananas. Many Americans also believe, for instance, that we can't grow coffee in America either, but the USA Coffee Company offers us 100 percent American coffee from tree to cup (see Chapter 17).

As Pat Buchanan states in his book *Death of the West*, "Independence is more precious than power." I would add that it is also more precious than efficiency, profits, or productivity figures. Our great country is known for its Declaration of Independence. Today it feels like we're heading toward a Declaration of *Inter*dependence, Declaration of Efficiency, or Declaration of Productivity. We shouldn't be heading that way. Again, as Pat Buchanan puts it, what is at stake now is far more important than whether our economy grows at 3 percent or 4 percent.

BUY AMERICAN: THE WORKPLACE EDITION

There's another unique way that Americans can influence patriotic purchases and benefit our country. This one comes from an avid supporter of *How Americans Can Buy American*, a man who works for a major American corporation. He influenced the decision of this company to use an American-owned vendor for the purchase of about $750,000.00 worth of hand-held computers over a foreign-owned computer vendor.

This is a new, yet interesting way to influence patriotic purchases at our workplaces every day. But you do not have to focus on big-ticket items to make a difference. It could be something as simple and insignificant as office supplies. An American-owned Sanford highlighter over a French-owned Bic highlighter, for instance, or American-owned

PaperMate pens instead of French-owned Bic pens. Of course the possibilities go well beyond PaperMate and office products. And many of these office product choices reflect *no price difference* whatsoever. It is a great way for you to help America prosper and not even have your company spend any extra money.

OUR TAX DOLLARS HARD AT WORK

In addition to the services and benefits we get as Americans from our tax dollars that I've already listed in this chapter, here are some others we might not be thinking about:

- Industry, states, and municipalities spent $25 billion on clean air initiatives.
- FDA inspections on food imports.
- $200 million on security improvements for airports and shipping ports in Los Angeles alone.
- $8 billion for nationwide airport security.
- $24.6 million to upgrade LA County's bioterrorism lab.
- $10.4 million under-graduates attending publicly funded institutions in 2003 alone.
- $100 million on technology to make American passports smarter, adding a chip that will store information like biometric data and facial measurements.
- Government-funded basic biomedical research.
- The Securities and Exchange Commission to protect investors.
- The Family and Medical Leave Act.
- $320 million the U.S. Army spent on recruitment in 2006.
- $200 billion (federal only) in rebuilding costs after hurricane Katrina.
- $1.5 billion a year for the U.S. Coast Guard.
- $6 million per year to aid small-and medium-sized companies in reducing energy use (which generates $40 million in savings and trains more efficiency experts).

- $5 million for the National Renewal Energy Laboratory in Golden, Colorado.
- $115 billion for federal research and development, which includes $26 billion for the National Institutes of Health.
- Funding for the Department of Health and Human Services, partly to educate the public on comparing the quality of nursing homes.
- $15.5 billion annually for the NASA space program.
- $616 million to double the family-separation allowance pay for military households and increase combat pay 50 percent.
- $29.4 billion in Homeland Security spending.
- $40 billion annually in prison incarceration costs.
- $12 billion annually on employment and training initiatives.
- Funding to take illegal Mexican immigrants back home instead of just dropping them off at the border.
- $13.3 billion annually to improve education for disadvantaged students.
- Caring for the 17 percent of U.S. soldiers who return from Iraq and the 6.2 percent returning from Afghanistan who have at least one major mental health problem.
- $14.5 billion disaster-aid bill to re-seed the Gulf Coast's oyster beds and tap natural gas reserves in Alaska.
- $447 billion to raise military pay 3.5 percent and better health care for reservists.
- $100 million to increase military pensions, health insurance, and benefits for retirees' widows.
- $286 billion for a six-year highway construction and mass transit bill.
- Funding to ensure 911 cellular phone calls provide the originating location.
- $200 billion to create a national network of electronic health records.
- $1.8 billion federal energy-assistance program, prohibiting utility companies from turning off power in extreme cold weather.

Extreme heat, which caused 650 deaths in Chicago alone in 2005, is not covered.

- $52.7 billion in unemployment benefits.
- $500 million for the Pentagon to develop the next latest, greatest supercomputer.
- $7.1 billion to prepare for a pandemic influenza threat.
- Food and Drug Administration funding to add trans-fat content on food labels and labeling for allergen groups: wheat, soybeans, peanuts, fish, milk, and eggs.
- $8.9 billion in federal school breakfast and lunch reimbursements (annually).
- Federal gas taxes to finance 45 percent of all public road improvements annually.
- $70 billion (annually) for United States Department of Agriculture testing of cows for mad cow disease.
- Federal spending on research for each lung cancer death: $1,830; breast cancer death: $23,475; prostrate-cancer death: $14,370.
- $175 million for traffic congestion initiatives.
- Funding for the Federal Air Marshal Service.
- $5 billion for a satellite-based air traffic control system.
- Fifty-one cents per gallon of gasoline federal subsidy.
- Funding for our $1.6 trillion deficit, according to the American Society of Civil Engineers, in our nation's transit infrastructure needs, power grids, dams, drinking water, and wastewater treatments, through 2010 for maintenance and repairs.

Cheap foreign labor does not contribute to any of the programs above that Americans favor and depend upon. Perhaps we will eventually realize that we cannot have our cheap Chinese goods and have a strong infrastructure, too. If we only stopped and thought before we bought some of these cheap products, we might find we have enough money to buy the right products—the ones made in the U.S. by American-owned companies!

The plain truth is that buying American provides more tax dollars to help fund these important benefits. It also helps prevent potential cuts for several others, such as the war on cancer, which has for the first time in history caused the number of Americans who die from it to decline. More tax dollars could help fund improvements for on-base housing for our military, 60 percent of which is considered substandard. The Department of Transportation says the cost of traffic congestion is 2 percent of the Gross Domestic Product, or $200 million annually, not to mention all the extra pollution and wasted fuel, the contamination of our environment, and either advancing our dependence on foreign oil or creating more pressure for yet more government subsidies for ethanol. Americans already waste 38 hours in traffic delays every year.

In 2005, victims' rights advocates organized to counter a Bush administration bid to cut over $1 billion from a fund for violent crime victims. What was the reason for the funding cut proposal? To cut the federal budget deficit.

In 2003, when over 40 states and several local governments were facing a severe budget crisis due to a sharp decline in tax revenue from a plunging stock market, many states cut vital services as a result. Staff cuts in the Oregon State Police force left only one ballistics expert. One of the experts who got laid off from her modest $27,000-a-year job had just linked two homicides to ballistic markings on shell casings and bullets.

Directing our dollars to foreign companies and foreign workers just won't cut the American mustard anymore. It also won't pay for the things that "We, the People," have demanded from our tax dollars. The key is to buy American while there is still American left to buy. We may not be able to stop foreigners from buying our American land, factories, and companies, but we can definitely stop giving them the money with which to do it.

Guide To Abbreviations

Andorra	AND	Luxembourg	LUX
Argentina	ARG	Malaysia	MAL
Australia	AUS	Mexico	MEX
Austria	AST	Netherlands	NETH
Belgium	BGM	New Zealand	NZ
Bermuda	BMD	Norway	NOR
Brazil	BZL	Pakistan	PAK
Canada	CAN	Peru	PER
Chile	CHL	Philippines	PHIL
China	CHN	Portugal	POR
Colombia	COL	Russia	RUS
Denmark	DEN	Samoa	SAM
Finland	FIN	Saudi Arabia	SAUD
France	FRA	Singapore	SNG
Germany	GER	Slovenia	SLO
Greece	GRE	South Africa	SAF
Hong Kong	HK	Spain	SP
Iceland	ICE	Sweden	SWE
India	IND	Switzerland	SWI
Indonesia	INDO	Taiwan	TWN
Ireland	IRE	Thailand	THAI
Israel	ISR	Turkey	TUR
Italy	ITL	United Kingdom	UK
Japan	JAP	Unilever*	UKN
Jordan	JOR	Venezuela	VEN
Korea	KOR		

*Unilever is a joint venture between England and The Netherlands

Chapter 2

Transportation/Automotive

(**American owned in bold** / *Foreign owned in italic*)

ANTI-FREEZE

Fleet	USA
Green Mountian	USA
Havoline	USA
Heet	USA
Pah-Nol	USA
Peak	USA
Prestone	USA
Security	USA
Sierra	USA
STP	USA
Streettguard	USA
Zerex	USA

AUTOMOBILES

Acura	JAP
Alfa Romeo	ITL
Aston Martin	USA
Audi	GER
Bentley	GER
BMW	GER
Buick	USA
Cadillac	USA
Chevrolet	USA
Chrysler	USA
Datsun	JAP
Dodge	USA
Ferrari	ITL
Fiat	ITL
Ford	USA
GMC	USA
Honda	JAP
Hyundai	KOR
International Trucks	USA
Isuzu	JAP
Jaguar	USA
Jeep	USA
Kia	KOR
Lamborghini	GER
Lexus	JAP
Lincoln	USA
Lotus	UK
Maserati	ITL
Mazda	JAP
Mercedes	GER
Mercury	USA
Mitsubishi	JAP
Nissan	JAP
Oldsmobile	USA
Opel	USA
Peugot	FRA
Pontiac	USA
Porsche	GER
Renault	FRA
Rolls Royce	GER
Saab	USA
Sachs	GER
Saturn	USA
Subaru	JAP
Suzuki	JAP
Toyota	JAP
Volkswagen	GER
Volvo	USA

CAR POLISH

American Show Car	USA
Armor All	USA
Blue Coral	NETH
Body Magic	USA
Festival	USA
Finish 2001	USA
Minute Wax	USA
Raindance	USA
Rally	USA

Turtle Wax	USA	Martin	USA
Vehiclean	USA	Mobil	USA
Wash And Wax	USA	Murphy USA	USA
Wash N' Wax	USA	Phillips 66	USA
Wax As-U-Dry	USA	Prist Fuel Additive	USA
Zecol	USA	*Shell*	*NETH*
Zip Wax	USA	Sinclair	USA
		Sinopec	*CHN*
CAR RENTAL		*Sohio*	*UK*
Alamo	USA	Sonoco	USA
Avis	USA	Soy Plus Biodiesel	USA
Budget	USA	Sunoco	USA
Enterprise	USA	Tenneco	USA
Hertz	USA	Texaco	USA
Imperial	*SAF*	Ultramar	USA
National	USA	Union 76	USA
Sears	USA	Zephyr	USA
Thrifty	USA		
		MOTOR OIL	
GASOLINE		*Amoco*	*UK*
76 Stations	USA	Ams Oil	USA
Amoco	*UK*	*Assuron*	*UK*
Arco	*UK*	Cardinal	USA
BP	*UK*	*Castrol*	*UK*
BP Amoco	*UK*	Chevron	USA
Chevron	USA	*Citgo*	*VEN*
Citgo	*VEN*	Coastal	USA
Coastal	USA	Convoy	USA
Conoco	USA	*Fire & Ice 2000*	*NETH*
Exxon	USA	Fleetgard	USA
Fina	*FRA*	Havoline	USA
Gas Express	USA	Huskie	USA
Getty	*RUS*	Mobil/Mobil 1	USA
Gulf	USA	Motorcraft	USA
Hess	USA	Nano-Chem	USA
Kerr-McGee	USA	Penn-Grade	USA
Marathon	USA	*Pennzoil*	*NETH*

Motor Oil (cont.)

Brand	Country
Phillips 66	USA
Proforce	USA
Proline	USA
Quaker State	NETH
Red Tack	USA
RPM	USA
Shell	NETH
Slick 50	NETH
Sonoco	USA
STP	USA
Streetts Superior	USA
Sunoco	USA
Supergard	VEN
Valvoline	USA

MOTORCYCLES

Brand	Country
BMW	GER
Buell	USA
Gold Wing	JAP
Harley-Davidson	USA
Honda	JAP
Husky/Husqvarna	SWE
Katana	JAP
Kawasaki	JAP
Suzuki	JAP
Yamaha	JAP

TIRES

Brand	Country
Avon Tyres	USA
BF Goodrich	FRA
Bridgestone	JAP
Continental	GER
Cooper	USA
Dayton	JAP
Dean	USA
Dunlop	AUS
Duraking	USA
Firestone	JAP
Fortera	USA
Futura	USA
General	GER
Giant	USA
Goodyear	USA
Hankook	USA
Hercules	USA
Kelly Springfield	USA
Lumber Jack	USA
Manx	USA
Mastercraft	USA
Merit	USA
Merit Metric	USA
Michelin	FRA
Mickey Thompson	USA
Mohawk	JAP
Momku	USA
Nitto Tire	JAP
Pirelli	ITL
Power Trax	USA
Private Label	JAP
Razr	USA
Roadmaster	USA
Sava	USA
Scorpion AT	ITL
Secura	USA
Semperit	GER
Sertaservis	USA
Servetica	USA
Short Track	USA
Sigma	JAP
Signet	USA
Snow Hog	USA
Snow Traks	USA
Snowprox	JAP

Snowsport	*ITL*	*Transforce*	*JAP*
Snowtrac	*NETH*	**Transmaster**	**USA**
Soft Turf	**USA**	*Traxion*	*NETH*
Solo Llantas	**USA**	*T-Trac*	*NETH*
Sottozero	*ITL*	*Turbo-Tech*	*JAP*
Space Master	*NETH*	**Turf Tec II**	**USA**
Sport Veloce	*ITL*	**Tyre Pro**	**USA**
Sportrac	*NETH*	*Ultrac*	*NETH*
Sprint	*NETH*	*Uniroyal*	*GER*
Sprint-Dirt	**USA**	**Unisteel**	**USA**
Star	**USA**	*Vanco*	*GER*
Starfire	**USA**	*Vanderbilt*	*JAP*
Stunner	*ITL*	*Vario V1*	*JAP*
Sumitomo	*JAP*	**Ventura**	**USA**
Super Miler	*KOR*	*Ventus*	*KOR*
Sure Trax	**USA**	*Widetrax*	*FRA*
Terra Trooper	**USA**	**Winqfoot**	**USA**
Tireco	**USA**	**Wrangler**	**USA**
Touring	*ITL*	*Xtreme*	*NETH*
Towmaster	**USA**	*Yokohama*	*JAP*
Toyo	*JAP*	*Zero*	*ITL*
Tractor Transport	*NETH*	*Zovac*	*KOR*

Chapter 3

Retail Stores

(**American owned in bold** / *Foreign owned in italic*)

AUTO PARTS STORES

AutoZone	USA
Bennet Auto Parts	USA
Big O Tires	USA
CarQuest	USA
O'Reilly	USA
R & S Strauss	USA
Strauss Discount Auto	USA

AUTO REPAIR CENTERS

Aamco	USA
Big O Tires	USA
Discount Tire	USA
Earl Scheib	USA
Firestone	*JAP*
Goodyear	USA
Meineke	USA
Merchant's Tire	
& Auto Centers	*JAP*
Monro Muffler/Brake	USA
Mr. Transmission	USA
National Tire & Battery	*JAP*
Precision Lube	USA
Precision Tune	USA
Quick 10	USA
Sears Auto Centers	USA
Speedy Auto Service	
by Monro	USA
Sullivan Tire and Auto	USA
Tire Kingdom	*JAP*
Tread Quarters	
Discount Tire	USA
Tuffy	USA
VIP	USA

BOOKSTORES

B. Dalton	USA
Barnes & Noble	USA
Bookland	USA
Books & Co.	USA
Books-A-Million	USA
Bookstar	USA
Bookstop	USA
Borders	USA
Doubleday	USA
The Bookend	USA
Times The Bookshop	*SNG*
Waldenbooks	USA
WH Smith	*UK*

CONVENIENCE STORES

7-Eleven	*JAP*
Beacon	USA
Becker's	*CAN*
Big K	USA
B-Kwik Food Stores	*NETH*
Break Time	USA
Brunswick Dead River	USA
Capitol Street	
Food Trend	USA
Caribou Food Trend	USA
Cash Mart	USA
Circle K	*CAN*
Coastal Mart	USA
Convenient Food Mart	USA
Country Cupboard	USA
Cumberland Farms	USA
Dairy Mart	USA
Depot	USA
Diamond Shamrock	USA
Economy Food Stores	USA
Enmark	USA
Etna	USA
Express 1 Stop	USA

Convenience Stores (cont.)

Extramile Market	USA	Mr. Mike Market	USA
Farm Mart	USA	Mr. Mike Mini Mart	USA
Farm Stores	USA	Olympian	USA
Farmingdale Food Trend	USA	On The Way	USA
Fast Fare	USA	Pilot Travel Centers	USA
Fast Lane	USA	Presque Isle Food Trend	USA
Fast Max	USA	Quick Stop	USA
Fiesta Mart	USA	Quiktrip	USA
Flyers	USA	Racetrac	USA
Flying J Travel Plazas	USA	Raceway	USA
Food Chief	USA	*Red Rooster*	*CAN*
Getty Mart	*RUS*	Rumford Food Trend	USA
Golden Gallon	USA	Scot Markets	USA
Gray Food Trend	USA	*Servus*	*SWE*
Harper's	USA	Shamrock	USA
Hess Express	USA	Smokers Express	USA
Hess Mart	USA	Speedway	USA
Holiday	USA	SpresStop	USA
Houlton Food Trend	USA	Sprint	USA
Huck's	USA	Stop N Go	USA
Hungry Murphy's	USA	SuperAmerica	USA
Kangaroo	USA	The Pantry	USA
Krauszer's	USA	Topsham Dead River	USA
Kwik Pantry	USA	Uni Marts	USA
Kwik Star	USA	United Dairy Farmers	USA
Kwik Trip	USA	Wareco	USA
Lil' Champ	USA	White Hen Pantry	USA
Little John's	USA	Wicker Mart	USA
Mac's	*CAN*	*Winks*	*CAN*
Mapco	*ISR*	Xtra Mart	USA
Marathon	USA	Zip Mart	USA
Marche Plus	*FRA*	Zippy Mart	USA
Market Express	USA		
Mexico Food Trend	USA	**DEPARTMENT STORES**	
MiniMart	USA	Ann Taylor	USA
Minitman	USA	*Au Printemps*	*JAP*
Mr. Cut-Rate	USA	Beall's	USA
		Big Lots	USA

Bloomingdale's	USA	Ross Stores	USA
Bon-Macy's	USA	Saks Fifth Avenue	USA
Boston Store	USA	Schottenstein Stores	USA
Burdines	USA	Sears	USA
Carson Pirie Scott	USA	Service Merchandise	USA
Catherines	USA	Shopko	USA
Dillard's	USA	Stage	USA
Elder-Beerman	USA	Stein Mart	USA
Famous-Barr	USA	Strawbridge's	USA
Filene's	USA	Target	USA
Foley's Department Store	USA	The Bon	USA
Fortunoff	USA	The Bon Marche	USA
Fred Meyer	USA	The Jones Store	USA
Goldsmith-Macy's	USA	*V&D*	*NETH*
Hecht's	USA	Von Maur	USA
Herberger's	USA	Younkers	USA
J.C. Penney	USA		
Jacobson	USA		
Kaufmann's	USA	**DRUG STORES**	
Kmart	USA	Brooks	USA
Kohl's	USA	CVS	USA
Lazarus	USA	Longs	USA
Lord & Taylor	USA	Osco	USA
Lotte	*JAP*	Pathmark	USA
Macy's	USA	Pay Less	USA
Masters	USA	Pharmaprix	USA
McRae's	USA	Rite Aid	USA
Meier & Frank	USA	Savon Drugs	USA
Meijer	USA	*Shoppers Drug Mart*	*CAN*
Mervyn's	USA	Smith's	USA
Neiman Marcus	USA	Supervalu Food & Drug	USA
Nordstrom	USA	*The Medicine Shoppe*	*CAN*
Palais Royal	USA	*Uniclinique*	*CAN*
Parisian	USA	*Unipharm*	*CAN*
Proffitt's Inc.	USA	*Uniprix*	*CAN*
Rich's-Macy's	USA	Walgreen	USA
Robinsons-May	USA		

EYE CARE CENTERS

Binyons Optical	USA
BJ's Optical	*ITL*
Cambridge Eye Doctors	USA
Costco Wholesale	USA
D.O.C. Eyeworld	USA
Doctor's Valuevision	USA
Eyemasters	USA
Horner Rausch	USA
J.C. Penney	USA
Kent Optical	USA
LensCrafters	*ITL*
Pearle Vision	*ITL*
Royal Optical	USA
Sam's Club	USA
Sears Optical	*ITL*
ShopKo	USA
Specttica Fashion Opticians	*ITL*
Target Optical Stores	*ITL*
TLC Laser Eye Centers	*CAN*
Vision World	USA
Visionworks	USA
Wesley-Jessen	*SWI*

FURNITURE STORES

Arbek Furniture	USA
Ashley	USA
Crossroads	USA
Ethan Allen	USA
Framers Home Furniture	USA
Gallery Furniture	USA
Globe Furniture Rentals	USA
Ikea	*NETH*
Jennifer Convertibles	USA
Kane	USA
La-Z-Boy Galleries	USA

Levitz	USA
Rhodes	USA
Rooms To Go	USA
Roomstore	USA
Savon	USA
Seaman	USA
Storehouse	USA
Sure Fit	USA
The Bombay Company	USA
Thomasville	USA

GENERAL RETAIL

Aaron Brothers	USA
Aaron Rents, Inc	USA
Abercrombie & Fitch	USA
Adray	USA
Aeropostale	USA
Afaze	USA
After Hours Formalwear	USA
Afterthoughts	USA
Alfred Dunhill	*SWI*
Al's Formalwear	USA
American Eagle Outfitters	USA
Ann Taylor	USA
Annie Sez	USA
Appleseed's	USA
Arden B.	USA
Ashley Avery Collectibles	USA
Ashley Stewart	USA
Atlanta Apparel Mart	USA
August Max	USA
Babbage's	USA
Babies "R" Us	USA
Baby Gap	USA
Bachrach	USA
Baldwin	USA

Banana Republic	USA	CookieTree Cookies	USA
Barneys New York	USA	Cork & Cap Liquor	
Bath & Body Works	USA	Shops	USA
Bavarian Village	USA	Country General Stores	USA
Bebe Stores	USA	Crate & Barrel	USA
Bed, Bath & Beyond	USA	CVS	USA
Bentley's Luggage	USA	Dairy Barn	USA
Berean Christian	USA	Dara Michelle	USA
Best Buy	USA	David's Bridal	USA
Big Daddy's Liquor	USA	Deb Shops	USA
Big Lots	USA	Deck The Walls	USA
Big O Tires	USA	Dollar General	USA
Blockbuster	USA	Dollar Tree	USA
Blooming Basket		Dress Barn	USA
Floral Shop	USA	Duckwall-Alco	USA
Body Shop	USA	Duron Paint Stores	USA
Bon Appetit	USA	Eddie Bauer	USA
Braum's Dairy	USA	Electronics Boutique	USA
Braum's Ice Cream	USA	Encore Recycled	
Camelot Music	USA	Appliances	USA
Cara Shop	CAN	Factory Card &	
CardSmart	USA	Party Outlet	USA
Casual Corner	USA	Family Christian Stores	USA
Casual Male XL	USA	Family Dollar	USA
Caswell/Massey	USA	Fannie May Candy Shops	USA
Catherines	USA	Fanny Farmer Candy	
Cato Plus	USA	Shops	USA
Champs Sports	USA	FAO Schwarz	USA
Christopher & Banks	USA	Fashion Bug	USA
Circuit City	USA	Fiesta Mart	USA
Claire's Boutiques	USA	Flanigan's	USA
Clark Camera Shops	USA	Foot Locker	USA
Clothestime	USA	Frank's Nursery & Crafts	USA
Club Libby Lu	USA	Frederick's	
Coconuts Music		of Hollywood	USA
& Movies	USA	Frisco	USA
CompUSA	MEX	Funcoland	USA
Contempo Casuals	USA	Gadzooks	USA

General Retail (cont.)

GameStop	USA
Gap	USA
GapKids	USA
Garden Master	USA
Garden Ridge	USA
Gateway Country	*TWN*
Geoffrey	USA
Gingiss Formal Wear	USA
Golden Rule Lumber Centers	USA
Good Guys	*MEX*
Goody's Family Clothing	USA
Great American Cookie Co.	USA
Great Earth	USA
Guitar Center	USA
Gump's	USA
Hallmark	USA
Hallmart	USA
Hammacher Schlemmer	USA
Hammons Pantry	USA
Hancock Fabrics	USA
Harold Powell	USA
Harvey	USA
Hollywood Video	USA
Hot Topic	USA
Ikea	*NETH*
J&R Music World	USA
J.J. Newberry	USA
J. Jill	*JAP*
Jacobson	USA
Jo-Ann Fabric & Crafts	USA
K&G Men's Center	USA
K-B Toys	USA
Kids "R" Us	USA
King Koil Bedquarters	USA
Kinko's	USA
Kirkland's	USA
Ladies Sportswear Discounters	USA
Land's End	USA
Lane Bryant	USA
Levi's Outlets	USA
Liberty House	USA
Limited Too	USA
Linda Karen	USA
Linens 'N Things	USA
Longs Drug Stores	USA
Love's Country Stores	USA
Magnolia Audio Video	USA
Mandee	USA
Men's Wearhouse	USA
Merchant's Tire & Auto	USA
Mothers Work	USA
Movies & More	USA
Musicland	USA
National Farm & Shop	USA
National Tire & Battery	USA
NordicTrack	USA
Nordstrom	USA
NPD	USA
Off 5th	USA
Office Depot	USA
OfficeMax	USA
Old Navy	USA
Old School	USA
Once Upon A Child	USA
OSCC Bespoke	USA
Pacific Sunwear of California	USA
Paul Stuart	USA
PC World	*UK*
Perfumania	USA
Petite Sophisticate	USA
Petsmart	USA

Pier 1 Imports	USA	**Structure**	USA
Piercing Pagoda	USA	*Sumesa*	*MEX*
Planet Music	USA	*Sunglass Hut*	*ITL*
Pottery Barn	USA	**Swiss Colony**	USA
Price Costco	USA	**T.J. Maxx**	USA
Priscilla of Boston	USA	*Talbots*	*JAP*
Radio Shack	USA	*Tesco*	*UK*
Rag Shops	USA	*The Bargain Shop*	*CAN*
Rainbow Apparel		*The Bay*	*CAN*
Distribution	USA	*The Body Shop*	*FRA*
Rand McNally	USA	**The Dress Barn**	USA
Ray's Dugout Stores	USA	**The Gap**	USA
Rose's	USA	*The Good Guys*	*MEX*
Ross Stores	USA	**The Great Frame Up**	USA
RV Depot	USA	**The Limited**	USA
S&K Menswear	USA	*The Link*	*UK*
Saks Fifth Avenue	USA	**The Original Mattress**	
Sam Goody	USA	**Factory**	USA
San Francisco Music Box	USA	**The Popcorn Factory**	USA
Saturday Matinee	USA	**The Rag Shop**	USA
See's Candy Shops	USA	**The Sharper Image**	USA
Seiyu	*JAP*	*Things Remembered*	*ITL*
Sephora	*FRA*	**Thrifty Acres**	USA
Service Merchandise	USA	*Tie Rack*	*ITL*
Sharon Young	USA	**Tobacco Outlet Plus**	USA
Smith & Hawken	USA	*Tommy*	*CHN*
Software Etc.	USA	**Torrid**	USA
Sound Advice	USA	**Toys "R" Us**	USA
Sound Warehouse	USA	**Tuesday Morning**	USA
Spec's	USA	**Tweeter Etc.**	USA
Spencer Gifts	USA	**Ulla Popken**	USA
Spirit Halloween		*Uniqlo*	*JAP*
Superstore	USA	**UPS Store**	USA
Staples	USA	**Urban Outfitters**	USA
Star Lumber & Supply	USA	**Victoria's Secret**	USA
Strawberries	USA	**Village Crafts**	
Stride Rite	USA	**by Michaels**	USA
Strouds	USA	*Vintage Cellars*	*AUS*

General Retail (cont.)

Vitamin World	USA
Wal-Mart	USA
Wamsutta	USA
Watch Station	*ITL*
Watch World	*ITL*
Wet Seal	USA
Wherehouse Music	USA
Wicks 'N' Sticks	USA
Wilsons-The Leather Experts	USA
Woodie's DIY	*IRE*
Zellers	*CAN*
Zutopia	USA

GROCERY STORES

A & P	*GER*
Acme	USA
Albertson's	USA
Aldi	*GER*
Big Bear	USA
Bi-Lo	*NETH*
Bi-Lo Foods	USA
BJ's Wholesale	USA
Bozzuto's	USA
Bruno's	USA
Buehler's	USA
Butera	USA
Carrs	USA
Cash Mart	USA
Charles & Co.	USA
Coles	*AUS*
Copps	USA
Costco	USA
Country Cupboard Food Stores	USA
County Market	USA
Cub Foods	USA
DelChamps	USA
Dick's	USA
Dominick's	USA
Dominion	*GER*
Easy Way	USA
Econofoods	USA
Economart	USA
Family Thrift Center	USA
Farm Fresh	USA
Farmer Jack	*GER*
Finast	*NETH*
Food 4 Less	USA
Food City	USA
Food Emporium	*GER*
Food Fair	USA
Food Giant	USA
Food Lion	*BGM*
Food Tiger	USA
Food World	*NETH*
FoodMax	USA
Foodtown	USA
Fresh Fruits	USA
Fresh Pride	USA
Furr's Family Dining	USA
Gelsons	USA
Giant Eagle	USA
Giant Food Stores	*NETH*
Gristede's	USA
H. Foods	USA
Hannaford	*BGM*
Harp's Food Stores	USA
Harris Teeter	USA
Harvest Foods	USA
Homeland	USA
IGA	USA
Ingles	USA
Jack & Jill	USA
Jay C. Food Stores	USA

Jewel/Osco	USA	Sam's Club	USA
Jungle Jim's	USA	*Sav-A-Centers*	*GER*
Kaiser's Grocery Store	*GER*	*Save 'N Pack*	*BGM*
Kash N' Karry	*BGM*	Save-A-Lot	USA
Kessel Food Markets	USA	Sav-U Foods	USA
King Soopers	USA	Schnucks	USA
Kohl's	*GER*	Sedano's	USA
Kroger	USA	Shaw's	USA
Mayfair	USA	Shop 'N Save	USA
Metro Market	USA	Shopper's Food	
Minitman	USA	Warehouse	USA
National	USA	Shoprite	USA
O'Malia	USA	Smith's	USA
Our Family Foods	USA	Spencer	USA
P&C Foods	USA	Star Markets	USA
Pak 'N Save	USA	*Stop & Shop*	*NETH*
Pathmark	USA	*Super G*	*NETH*
Pay Less	USA	*Super GB*	*FRA*
Pick 'N Save	USA	Supersaver Foods	USA
Piggly Wiggly	USA	*Supersol*	*ISR*
Price Chopper	USA	*Supervalu*	*IRE*
Priceless Foods	USA	*Sweetbay*	*BGM*
Publix	USA	Thriftway	USA
Pueblo	USA	Tom Thumb	USA
QFC	USA	*Tops*	*NETH*
Quality Markets	USA	True Value	USA
Quix Food Stores	USA	*Valufoods*	*CAN*
Rainbow Foods	USA	Valumarket	USA
Ralphs	USA	*Victory*	*BGM*
Randalls	USA	Vons	USA
Ray's Food Place	USA	Wal-Mart Supercenter	USA
Ray's Shop Smart Food		Wegmans	USA
Warehouse	USA	Weis	USA
Red Apple	USA	Western Family Foods	USA
Rego's Fresh Market	USA	Whole Foods Market	USA
Rini-Rego	USA	Wholesale Food Market	USA
Riverside Markets	USA	Wild Oats	USA
Rosauer's	USA	Winco Foods	USA

<u>Grocery Stores (cont.)</u>

Winn-Dixie	USA
Woodman Food Market	USA

HARDWARE STORES

Ace Hardware	USA
B&Q	*UK*
Coast To Coast	USA
Do It Center	USA
Fastenal	USA
Hardware Hank	USA
Home Depot	USA
Lowe's	USA
Orchard	USA
Pro Hardware	USA
Restoration Hardware	USA
Servistar	USA
Sterling	USA
Strongarm	USA
Super Susan	USA
True Valu	USA
Trustworthy	USA
Trustworthy Howe	USA

JEWELRY STORES

Bailey Banks & Biddle	USA
Caldwell's	USA
Carlyle	USA
Fred Meyer	USA
Friedman's Jewelers	USA
Gordon's	USA
H. Samuel	*UK*
Helzberg	USA
J.B. Robinson	*UK*
Jared - The Gallery Of Jewelry	*UK*
Kay	*UK*

Littman	USA
Lundstom	USA
Marks & Morgan	*UK*
Marks Bros.	USA
Mayor's	*CAN*
Merksamer	USA
Michael Anthony	USA
Park Prominade	USA
Regency	USA
Samuels	USA
Schaap & Citroen	*NETH*
Siebel	*NETH*
Whitehall	USA
Zales	USA

RENTAL STORES

Colortyme	USA
Grantree	USA
Rent-A-Center	USA
Ryder	USA
Selix Formal Wear	USA
Taylor Rental	USA
TRS Rental Co.	USA
U-Haul	USA
United Rentals	USA

SHOE STORES

Athlete's Foot	USA
Athletic Attic	USA
Bostonian	*UK*
Butler	USA
F.X. Lasalle	USA
Famous Footwear	USA
Finish Line	USA
Florsheim	USA
Foot Locker	USA
FootAction USA	USA

		SPORTING GOODS STORES	
Hanover	*UK*		
Jarman	**USA**	Big 5	USA
Johnston & Murphy	**USA**	Champs	USA
Journeys	**USA**	Dick's	USA
Just For Feet	**USA**	Galyan's Trading Co.	USA
Keds	**USA**	Gart Sports	USA
Naturalizer	**USA**	Hibbett	USA
Nike Town	**USA**	Modell's	USA
Nine West	**USA**	Oshman's	USA
Payless Shoe Source	**USA**	Sport Chalet	USA
Shoe Carnival	**USA**	*Sport Check*	*CAN*
Shoe Pavilion	**USA**	*Sport Mart*	*CAN*
Sportshoe Center	**USA**	Sports Authority	USA
		Sportsman's	USA

Chapter 4

Food Products

(**American owned in bold** / *Foreign owned in italic*)

ARTIFICIAL SWEETENER

Canderel	USA
Equal	USA
Nutra Taste	USA
Nutrasweet	USA
Semble	USA
Slim Up	*JAP*
Splenda	USA
Sucaryl	USA
Sugar In The Raw	USA
Sugartwin	USA
Suketter	USA
Sunett	USA
Sweet 'N Low	USA
Sweet Rite	USA
Sweet Thing	USA
Sweetex	USA
Sweetmate	USA
Tagatose	USA

BABY FOOD/FORMULA

Alete	*SWI*
Alimentum	USA
Alprem	*SWI*
Baby's First	USA
Bean Stalk Pocari	*JAP*
Beech-Nut	USA
Bledina	*FRA*
Carnation	*SWI*
Earth's Best (organic)	USA
Eledon	*SWI*
Enfalac	USA
Enfamil	USA
Enfapro	USA
Farley's	USA
Gain	USA
Gerber	*SWI*
Good Start Supreme	*SWI*

Heinz	USA
Isomil	USA
Lait Guigoz	*SWI*
Lofenalac	USA
Mellin	*FRA*
Nan	*SWI*
Nativa	*SWI*
Nature's Goodness	USA
Neosure	USA
Nestum	*SWI*
Pregestimil	USA
SGM	*NETH*
Similac	USA
SNM	*NETH*
Stages	USA
Sun	*INDO*
Tabletime	USA
Vita Plus	*NETH*
Vitalac	*NETH*
Xylisorb	*FRA*

BAKING/COOKING AIDS

4C	USA
Accugel	USA
Alsa	*UKN*
American Ingredients Co.	*NETH*
Argo	*UKN*
Arm & Hammer	USA
Arrozina Corn Starch	*UKN*
Aunt Jemima	USA
Aunt Sweeties	USA
Bakemark	*NETH*
Baker Cake & Pastry Fillings	USA
Bakers Ease	USA
Baker's Joy	USA
Bakin' Miracle	USA
Benchmate	*AUS*

Baking/Cooking Aids (cont.)

Benson's Corn Starch	*UKN*
Bertolli Olive Oil	*UKN*
Betty Crocker	**USA**
Biskin Vegetable Oil	**USA**
Brown & Polson	*UKN*
Cake Mate	**USA**
Calumet Baking Powder	**USA**
Chipits	**USA**
Clabber Girl	**USA**
Colorado Corn Starch	**USA**
Cream Corn Starch	*GER*
Cremogema	*UKN*
Crisco Shortening	**USA**
Dakota Maid	**USA**
Defiance	*AUS*
Del Destino Olive Oil	**USA**
Dover Flour	*CAN*
Duncan Hines	**USA**
Duryeas	*UKN*
Early Harvest	**USA**
Econa	*JAP*
Econobake	**USA**
Fearn	**USA**
Fleischmann's Yeast	*AUS*
Ideal	**USA**
Indian Head Corn Meal	**USA**
Karp's	*NETH*
KC	**USA**
Kre-Mel	*UKN*
Lady's Choice	*UKN*
Maizena	*UKN*
Majala	*UKN*
Malile	*UKN*
Martha White	**USA**
Master Chef Cooking Oil	**USA**
Mateus	*UKN*
Mazola Cooking Oil	*UKN*

Mini Chips Chocolate	**USA**
Montemps Cake & Pancake Mix	*JAP*
Mrs. Crutchfield's	**USA**
Olean Cooking Oil	**USA**
Palmia Cooking Oil	**USA**
Pam Cooking Spray	**USA**
Poti	*UKN*
Puritan Oil	**USA**
QA Products	*NETH*
Satin Donut Fry	**USA**
Smucker's Baking Healthy	**USA**
Toll House Morsels	*SWI*
Triumph	*JAP*
Waha	**USA**
Wesson	**USA**
White Cap	*JAP*

BREAD & BAKED GOODS

Arnold	*CAN*
Aunt Sweeties	**USA**
Bakers' Select	**USA**
Barowsky's	**USA**
Bay City	**USA**
Beefsteak	**USA**
Betsy Ross	**USA**
Bimbo	*MEX*
Blue Ribbon	**USA**
Bohemian Hearth	*CAN*
Bouyea	*UKN*
Bread Du Jour	**USA**
Brick Oven	*UKN*
Bridgford	**USA**
Brownberry	*UKN*
Bunny	**USA**
Butter Krust	**USA**
Buttercup	*UK*

Buttermaid	USA	*Hearth Farms*	*CAN*
Butternut	USA	Heritage Ovens	USA
Cable Car	USA	Holsum	USA
California Goldminer	*CAN*	Home Pride	USA
Calise	USA	Hometown	USA
Castle	USA	Honey Berry Bran	USA
Chee-Zee	USA	Honeybran	USA
Chef David	USA	Hostess	USA
Cobblestone Mill	USA	*Hovis*	*UK*
Cottage Hearth	USA	*Jacquet*	*FRA*
Country Bake	*UK*	Kings Hawaiian	USA
Country Harvest	*CAN*	Kreamo	USA
Country Hearth	USA	*Levy's*	*UKN*
Country Kitchen	USA	Lumberjack	USA
Country Split	*UK*	Mackinaw Milling Co.	USA
Dare	USA	Maestro	USA
Douville	USA	Maryann	USA
Earth Harvest	*CAN*	Meijer	USA
Eddy's	USA	Merita	USA
Elgin D-Lux	USA	Millbrook Farms	USA
Entenmann's	*CAN*	*Molenberg*	*UK*
European Bakers	USA	*Montmartre*	*JAP*
Evangeline Maid	USA	*Mother's Pride*	*UK*
Farmhouse	USA	Mrs. Cubbison's	USA
Fibre Goodness	*CAN*	Mrs. Karl's	USA
Flavor-Kist	USA	Mrs. Wrights	USA
Fleur De Lait	*FRA*	National	USA
Flowers	USA	Nature's Own	USA
Franz	USA	New York	USA
Freihofer's	*CAN*	Nickles	USA
Golden Crème	USA	*Nimble*	*UK*
Golden Hearth	USA	Nutri-Bran	USA
Gonnella	USA	*Old Country*	*UKN*
Granary	*UK*	*Old London*	*UKN*
Grande	USA	Old Tyme	USA
Grant's Farm	USA	*Orowheat*	*CAN*
Grin N Carrot	USA	Ovenfresh	USA
Harvest Recipe	USA	Palagonia	USA

Bread & Baked Goods (cont.)

Parisian	USA
Pasco	*JAP*
Patak's	*UK*
Pepperidge Farm	USA
Power Kids	USA
Rich Grain	USA
Roman Light	USA
Roman Meal	USA
S. Rosen	USA
Sahara Pita Bread	*UKN*
Sara Lee	USA
Seattle International	USA
Sensables	USA
Simple Pleasure	*CAN*
Smart Nutrition	USA
Snak N' Fresh	USA
Snyder	USA
Snyder's	USA
Sojola	*BGM*
St. Allery	*BGM*
St. Auvent	*BGM*
Stone-Buhr	*UKN*
Stroehmann	*CAN*
Suandy	*MEX*
Sun Grain	USA
Sunbeam	USA
Sunicrust	*UK*
Sunnuntai	*FIN*
Sunny Doodles	USA
Sunset Harvest	*MEX*
Sweetheart	USA
Swirl	USA
Tasty	USA
Tasty Grahams	USA
Tasty-Klair	USA
Tentazione	*PER*
The Bake Shop	USA

Thomas'	*CAN*
Tia Rosa	*MEX*
Toscana	USA
Toscano	USA
Tres Leches	USA
Via Panera	USA
Vleminckx	*BGM*
Weston	*CAN*
Whitewheat	USA
Williams'	USA
Wolfermans	USA
Wonder	USA

BUTTER/MARGARINE

Banquet	USA
Becal	*UKN*
Blue Bonnet	USA
Brummel & Brown	*UKN*
Compakt Reddies	USA
Country Crock	*UKN*
Dawn Butter	*IRE*
Dawn Light Butter	*IRE*
ETA	*UK*
Fiesta	USA
Flavor-It	USA
Fleischmann's	*UKN*
Flora	*UKN*
Golden Nugget	USA
Heart Beat	USA
I Can't Believe It's Not Butter	*UKN*
Imperial	*UKN*
Lactantia	*ITL*
Lady's Choice	*UKN*
Land O' Lakes	USA
Linea	*UKN*
Luna	*TUR*
Mazola	*UKN*

Meadow Lee	*UK*
Mom's	*UKN*
Monarch	*UKN*
Mrs. McGregors	*UK*
Nucoa	**USA**
Parkay	**USA**
Praise	*UK*
Promise	*UKN*
Rama	*UKN*
Roaster Fresh	**USA**
Royal	*UKN*
Savory	*JAP*
Savourin	*CAN*
Sello De Oro	*PER*
Shedd's Country Crock	*UKN*
Spectrum Organic	**USA**
Sunglow	*JAP*
Veggie Butter	**USA**
Veggie Honey Butter	**USA**
Vitelma	*BGM*

CANDY

100 Grand Bar	*SWI*
3 Musketeers	**USA**
5th Avenue	**USA**
Abadallah	**USA**
Abba-Zaba	**USA**
Abra Cabubble	*CAN*
After Eight	*SWI*
Aha!	*NETH*
Allan	*UK*
Almond Coconut Delight	**USA**
Almond Joy	**USA**
Almond Roca Toffee	**USA**
Alpenliebe	*NETH*
Alpine White	*SWI*
Altoids	**USA**
Amazing Fruit	**USA**

America's Premium Chocolate	*SWI*
Andes	**USA**
Anise Buttons	**USA**
Annabelle	**USA**
Aplets	**USA**
Assorted Fruit Buttons	**USA**
Assorted Fruit Candy Roll	**USA**
Astro Pops	**USA**
Atomic Fireballs	**USA**
Baby Ruth	*SWI*
Baci	*SWI*
Balisto	**USA**
Bar None	**USA**
Bassett's	*UK*
Bazooka	**USA**
Bear Brand	*SWI*
Beech-Nut	**USA**
Beich	*SWI*
Beldent	*UK*
Belgian Cremes	**USA**
Bicentennial	**USA**
Big Balloon	**USA**
Big Hunk	**USA**
Big League Chew	**USA**
Big Red	**USA**
Big Tex Jelly Beans	**USA**
Bio Fruits	**USA**
Bisc & Bounty	**USA**
Bit-O-Honey	*SWI*
Black Forest Gummi	**USA**
Black Licorice Dollars	**USA**
Black Magic	*SWI*
Blasters Bubble	**USA**
Blue Peppermint	**USA**
Blue Razz	**USA**
Bold Beans Jelly Beans	**USA**

Candy (cont.)

Boston Baked Beans	**USA**
Bouquet D'Or	*UK*
Bournville	*UK*
Brach	*CAN*
Brach's	*CAN*
Breakaway	*UK*
Breath Savers	**USA**
Brown & Haley	
Selections	**USA**
Bubbaloo	*UK*
Bubbas	*UK*
Bubbaxtreme	*UK*
Bubble Jug	**USA**
Bubble Tape	**USA**
Bubble Yum	**USA**
Bubblicious	*UK*
Buckeyes Chocolates	**USA**
Buddy Bears Gummi	
Bears	**USA**
Bug City	**USA**
Burst Gum	*UK*
Butterfinger BB's	*SWI*
Butterfinger	*SWI*
Butterfinger Crisp	*SWI*
Butterkist	*UK*
Buttermint	*UK*
Butterscotch Buttons	**USA**
Buttons	*UK*
Cadbury	*UK*
Cadbury's	*UK*
Caffarel	*SWI*
Cailler	*SWI*
Callard & Bowser	**USA**
Canada Mints	**USA**
Candy Cupboard	**USA**
Caramac	*SWI*
Carambar	**USA**

Caramel Apple Pops	**USA**
Caramello	*UK*
Caramilk	*UK*
Carefree	**USA**
Cashmere Milk	
Chocolate	**USA**
Cella's	**USA**
Certs	*UK*
Chappies	*UK*
Charleston Chew	**USA**
Charms	**USA**
Charms Blow Pops	**USA**
Checkerbar	**USA**
Cheese Crax	**USA**
Chelsea	*JAP*
Cherry Blossom	**USA**
Cherry Lump	**USA**
Chew Beez	**USA**
Chew-ets	**USA**
Chiclets	*UK*
Childhood Sticks	**USA**
Child's Play	**USA**
Chips And Chews	**USA**
Choco Loco	**USA**
Choco Pie	**USA**
Chocolat Suisse	**USA**
Chocolate Koka	*JAP*
Chocos	*UK*
Chomp	*UK*
Chuckles	**USA**
Chunky	*SWI*
Cinn-A-Burst	*UK*
Cinnamon Imperials	**USA**
Cinnamon Teddy Bears	**USA**
Circus Peanuts	**USA**
Clara Stover	**USA**
Clorets	*UK*
Club Chocolate Bars	*FRA*

Coconut Slice Candy Bar	USA	**Elana Chocolates**	USA
Coconut Wave	USA	**Ethel M Chocolates**	USA
Coffee Buttons	USA	**Excel**	USA
Coffee Shop	USA	**Extra**	USA
Color Boom	USA	**F&F Peppermint**	USA
Connaisseurs	SWI	**Famous Sqwish**	
Cool Blast	USA	**Candy Fish**	USA
Cote D'Or	USA	**Farley's**	USA
Cows Toffees	USA	**Fast Break**	USA
Crazy Dips Lollipop	USA	**Fingers**	USA
Creamsicle	USA	*Five Star Chocolate*	UK
Cremesavers	USA	*Flake Chocolate*	UK
Cremosa Lollipop	USA	**Flavor Rolls**	USA
Crispy Crunch	UK	**Fluffy Stuff**	
Crunchie	UK	**Cotton Candy**	USA
Curley Wurley	UK	**Foxes**	USA
Cyberspeak	USA	*Fox's Glacier Mints*	SWI
D&P Rock Candy	USA	*Freddo Frog*	UK
Daily-C	USA	**Freedent**	USA
Daim Chocolate	USA	*Freshen Up*	UK
Dairy Box Chocolates	SWI	*Frigor*	SWI
Dandy	UK	*From A to Z*	UK
Deemints	USA	**Frooties**	USA
Demet's	SWI	**Fruit Allsorts**	USA
Dentyne	UK	**Fruit Jammers**	USA
Designer Choco Bons	USA	**Fruit Stripe**	USA
Dots	USA	*Fry's Chocolate*	UK
Double Decker	UK	*Fun Dip*	SWI
Double Dippers	CAN	*Galak Chocolate Bras*	SWI
Doublemint	USA	**Gelrite**	USA
Dove Chocolate	USA	**Genugel**	USA
Dovebar	USA	**Ghirardelli**	USA
Drifter	SWI	**Giant Kiss**	USA
Dum Dum Gum Pops	USA	**Glosette Peanuts**	
Dum-Dum Suckers	USA	**& Raisins**	USA
Eagle Brand	USA	**Godiva**	USA
Eat-More	USA	**Gold Leaf Chocolate**	USA
Eclipse	USA	**Golden Almond**	USA

Candy (cont.)

Golden Bomber	USA	JB	USA
Goobers	*SWI*	Jelly Basler Belly	USA
Good & Plenty	USA	Jelly Belly	USA
Good News	*SWI*	Jet-Puffed	USA
Goose Eggs	USA	Jolly Rancher	USA
Got Milk?	USA	Joseph Schmidt	USA
Green Apple Buttons	USA	Judson-Atkinson	USA
Guernsey Milk		*Juicefuls*	*GER*
Chocolate	USA	Juicy Fruit	USA
Halls	*UK*	Jujyfruits	USA
Harmony Snacks	USA	Jungle Jollies	USA
Haviland	USA	Junior Mints	USA
Hearty	*UK*	*Kandos*	*SWI*
Heath Bar	USA	Kelcogel	USA
Herbert Candies	USA	Kenny's	USA
Heritage Milk Chocolate	USA	Key Lime Buttons	USA
Hershey	USA	*Kinder*	*ITL*
Hershey Hugs	USA	Kisses	USA
Hershey Kisses	USA	*Kit Kat*	*SWI*
Hershey Miniatures	USA	*Kohler*	*SWI*
Hershey's Classic		Koolerz	USA
Caramels	USA	*Krema*	*UK*
Hershey's Cookies		Kudos	USA
'N' Crème	USA	*La Pie Qui Chante*	*UK*
High Sierra Chocolate	USA	La Vie	USA
Hofbauer	*SWI*	*Laffy Taffy*	*SWI*
Hollywood	*UK*	*Le Confiseur French*	
Honey Queen Bees	USA	*Truffles*	*SWI*
Hospitality Chocolate	USA	Leman	USA
Hot Tamales	USA	Lemon Buttons	USA
Hubba Bubba	USA	Lemonhead Lollipops	USA
Hueso	*UK*	Lemonheads	USA
Hugs	USA	LifeSavers	USA
Ice Blue Mint Coolers	*CAN*	*Lingots*	*SWI*
Ice Breakers	USA	Linguanotto	USA
Ice White	USA	*Lion Bar*	*SWI*
Intense Mints	USA	*Lion Jellied Sweets*	*UK*
		Lockets	USA

Look	USA	**Monster Malts**	USA
Lunch Bar	*UK*	*Moro Chocolate*	*UK*
M&M's	USA	**Mounds**	USA
Malabar	*UK*	**Mountain Bar**	USA
Mallo Cup	USA	*Mr. Big*	*UK*
Malta Sweet	*UK*	**Mr. Goodbar**	USA
Maltesers Chocolate	USA	**Mrs. Stover's Candies**	USA
Mamba	*GER*	**Murray Mints**	USA
Manner Wafers	USA	**Musica**	USA
Mantecol	*UK*	**My Buddy**	USA
Maple Nut Goodies	*CAN*	**My Gummy**	USA
Mars	USA	**Nabisco**	USA
Mars Bar	USA	**Narbles**	USA
Marshmallow Peeps	USA	**Natural Mint Snow**	USA
Mary Jane Taffy	USA	**Necco**	USA
Mason	USA	**Neon Bubble Strips**	USA
Mason Crows	USA	*Nerds*	*SWI*
Mason Dots	USA	*Nestle*	*SWI*
Masterpieces Chocolate	USA	*Nestle Crunch*	*SWI*
Matchmakers	*SWI*	*Nestle Quik Bar*	*SWI*
Mega Smarties	USA	**Nibs**	USA
Meller	*NETH*	**Now and Later**	USA
Meltykiss Chocolate	*JAP*	**Nut Chocolate**	USA
Mentos	*UK*	**Oban Wafers**	USA
Merci Chocolates	USA	*Oh Henry!*	*SWI*
Mexican Hats	USA	**Old Dutch Chocolate**	USA
Mi-Cho-Ko	*UK*	**Orbit**	USA
Mike & Ike	USA	**Orora**	USA
Milk Duds	USA	**P.K.**	USA
Milka	USA	**Panda Licorice**	USA
Milky Way	USA	**Park Avenue**	USA
MilkyBar	*SWI*	*Pascall*	*UK*
Mini-Dickman's		*Pascall Licorice*	*UK*
Chocolate	USA	*Pascall Toffee*	*UK*
Mint Balls	USA	**Payday**	USA
Mint Lumps	USA	**Peanut Butter Cup**	USA
Mint-A-Burst	*UK*	**Peanut Butter Log**	USA
Mon Amor Mints	*ITL*	**Peanut Roll**	USA

Candy (cont.)

Pearson	*SWI*
Pearson's Nips	*SWI*
Peeps	**USA**
Pe-Kons	**USA**
Pepperidge Farm	**USA**
Perk	*UK*
Pernigotti Chocolate	**USA**
Perugina	*SWI*
Perugina Baci	*SWI*
Peter Paul Almond Joy	**USA**
Peter Paul Mounds	**USA**
Petit Assort Chocolate	**USA**
Pez	**USA**
Piasten	*UK*
Picnic	*UK*
Picture Pops Lollipops	**USA**
Pirates Gold	
Chocolate Coins	**USA**
Pixy Stix	*SWI*
PM Mix	**USA**
Polo	*SWI*
Pot Of Gold	**USA**
Poulain Chocolates	*UK*
Premier Chocolate	**USA**
Prince Noir	*SWI*
Providence Milk	
Chocolate	**USA**
Punch Buttons	**USA**
Quality Street	**USA**
Queen Anne	**USA**
Quench Gum	**USA**
Quik Flip	**USA**
Radiant Morsels	**USA**
Rain-Blo	**USA**
Rainbow Cherry	**USA**
Raisinets	*SWI*
Rang	**USA**

Recaldent	*UK*
Red Hot Dollars	**USA**
Red Tulip	*UK*
Red Vines	**USA**
Redhots	**USA**
Reese's	**USA**
Reese's Nutrageous	**USA**
Reese's Peanut	
Butter Cups	**USA**
Reese's Pieces	**USA**
Reesesticks	**USA**
Refreshmints	**USA**
Riesen	*GER*
Ring Pop Lollipops	**USA**
Roca	**USA**
Roca Bits	**USA**
Rocky Mountain	
Chocolate Factory	**USA**
Rocky Mountain Mints	**USA**
Rocky Road	**USA**
Rocky Road Mint	**USA**
Rolo	*SWI*
Root Beer Buttons	**USA**
Rowntree	*SWI*
Runts	*SWI*
Russell Stover Candies	**USA**
Sabel Milk Chocolate	**USA**
Sae-Al Chocoball	**USA**
Saf-T-Pop Lollipop	**USA**
Saf-T-Pops	**USA**
Sanagola	*UK*
Santa Claus	*SWI*
Sasha	*JAP*
Sathers	**USA**
Scenic	**USA**
Scharfeen Berger	**USA**
Schokomac	*SNG*
Scotch Candy	*JAP*

Seafoam	USA	*Special Toffee*	*UK*
See's	USA	*Special Treasures*	*CAN*
Sense Mint	*FIN*	*Sperlari*	*ITL*
Sen-Sen	USA	*Sprengel*	*CAN*
Sevigny	USA	**Sprig-O-Mints**	USA
Sherbets	*UK*	**Squires Choice**	USA
Sherwood	USA	**Sqwish**	USA
Sherwood Cows	USA	**Star**	USA
Sherwood Hard Candy	USA	*Star Brites Mints*	*CAN*
Signature	USA	**Starburst**	USA
Signature Line	USA	**Stark**	USA
Simplesse	USA	*Stimorol*	*UK*
Skai	*SWI*	*Stophoest*	*NETH*
Skittles	USA	*Storck*	*GER*
Skor	USA	**Strip-O-Pops**	USA
Slo Poke	USA	*Sudzucker*	*GER*
Smartzone	USA	**Sugar Babies**	USA
Smint	USA	**Sugar Daddy**	USA
Smooth 'N Melty	USA	**Sugar Sanded**	USA
Smucker's Puckers	USA	**Sugar-Free Delights**	USA
Snak-Stop	USA	**Suisse**	USA
Snaps	USA	**Summer Fruit Mix**	USA
Snickers	USA	*Sundrop*	*UK*
Sno-Caps	*SWI*	*Sunfud*	*JAP*
Soft Cinnamon	USA	*Sunfuns*	*JAP*
Soft Mint	USA	**Sunnybrook**	USA
Softfruits	*UK*	**Sunray**	USA
Softmints	*UK*	*Super Dickmann's*	*GER*
Solitaire	USA	**Super Ropes**	USA
Sophie Mae	USA	*SuperBomba*	*UK*
Sour Bloops	USA	**Sutter**	USA
Sour Fruit Burst	USA	*Swedish Fish*	*UK*
Sour Jacks	USA	**Sweet Dreams**	USA
Sour Patch Kids	*UK*	**Sweet Stripe Mint Twists**	USA
Sour Punch	USA	*Sweetarts*	*SWI*
Spangler	USA	**Sweet's Cinnamon Bears**	USA
Sparkies	*UK*	**Sweet's Orange Sticks**	USA
Spearmintlets	USA	**Sweet's Saltwater Taffy**	USA

Candy (cont.)			
Swiss Confisa	SWI	Triple Blasts	USA
Swiss Thins	SWI	Trolli	USA
Swiss Tradition	SWI	Tudor Gold	SNG
Swoops	USA	Turkish Delight	UK
Symphony	USA	Tuxedos	USA
Tabu	NETH	Twin	USA
Tango	SNG	Twinkles	SNG
Tastetations	USA	Twisty Punch	USA
Taz	UK	Twizzlers	USA
Teenee Beenee		Two Two Candy	KOR
Jelly Beans	USA	U-NO	USA
Tempo	UK	V6	UK
Tendermint	USA	Van Houten	SNG
Terry's	USA	Van Leer	CAN
The London Mint	USA	Velamints	USA
Tic Tacs	ITL	Vida	UK
Tiki	USA	Vigorsol	NETH
Toblerone	USA	Visconti	USA
Todds	USA	Vitafreze	USA
Toffifee	GER	Vivident	NETH
Tofita	UK	Voldrop	NETH
Tofy	UK	Wacle	FIN
Toll House	SWI	Wagon Wheels	USA
Tomtom	UK	Waleeco	USA
Tongue Tattoo	USA	Washburn	USA
Tootsie Pops	USA	Watermelon Buttons	USA
Tootsie Roll	USA	Wedel	UK
Topdrop	NETH	Weather's Original	GER
Topi	UK	Whatchamacallit	USA
Topmix	SNG	Whistle Pops	USA
Topsi	COL	Whitman's	USA
Torino	SWI	Whoppers	USA
Tornado Bar	USA	Wiggle Worms	USA
To-You	FIN	Wilbur	USA
Treasures	SWI	Wilbur Buds	USA
Trebor	UK	Wild Cherry	USA
Trident	UK	Wild 'N Fruity	CAN
		Willy Wonka's	SWI

Winterfresh	USA	*Sport*	*COL*
Wonka	*SWI*	**Sugar Puffs**	USA
World's Finest	USA	**Sunbelt**	USA
Wow	*FIN*	*Telma*	*UKN*
Wow Bubble	*FIN*	*Tender O's*	*CAN*
Wrapped	USA	**Toasty O's**	USA
Wrigley's	USA	**Weetabix**	USA
Xantural	USA	**Weetos**	USA
X-Treme Sour Smarties	USA	*Yo Baby*	*FRA*
Xylish	*JAP*		
Yardstick Bubble Gum	USA	**CHEESE**	
York Peppermint Patty	USA	*Alouette*	*FRA*
Yorkie	*SWI*	**Alpine Lace**	USA
Zagnut	USA	**American Heritage**	USA
Zed	USA	**American Slice**	USA
Zero	USA	*Apericube*	*FRA*
Zingos	USA	*Apetitto Zelatva*	*FRA*
Zinties	*SNG*	*Appenzeller*	*SWI*
Zours	USA	*Armstrong*	*CAN*
		Arpin	*FRA*
CEREAL		**Asadero**	USA
Alpen	USA	**Athenos**	USA
Breadshop	USA	**Auribella**	USA
Ciscorn	*JAP*	**Baby Jack**	USA
Cream Of Wheat	USA	*Babybel*	*FRA*
Dunkin' Donuts	USA	*Balderson*	*ITL*
Familia	*SWI*	**Barrel Cheddar**	USA
General Mills	USA	**Bar-Scheeze**	USA
Kashi	USA	*Bayernland*	*GER*
Kellogg's	USA	**Beddar With Cheddar**	USA
Nabisco Shredded Wheat	USA	*Bel Paese*	*FRA*
Nestle	*SWI*	*Belle Des Champs*	*FRA*
Oats 'N Fiber	USA	*Black Diamond*	*ITL*
Old Mill Oatmeal	USA	*Boisange*	*FRA*
Post	USA	*Bonbel*	*FRA*
Quaker	USA	**Bongards**	USA
Shredded Heritage Bites	*CAN*	**Borden**	USA
Soy Plus	*CAN*	**Cache Valley**	USA

Cheese (cont.)			
Calvita	USA	*Kaukauna*	*FRA*
Caprice Des Dieux	*FRA*	Korsholm	USA
Chamois D'or	*FRA*	Kraft	USA
Cheesestrings	*ITL*	*Laughing Cow*	*FRA*
Cheez Whiz	USA	Light N' Lively	USA
Churny	USA	*Malthe*	*DEN*
Clearfield	USA	McCadam	USA
Cotiga	USA	Mexican Medley	USA
Country Crock	*UKN*	*Mini Bonbel*	*FRA*
County Line	USA	Mitchelstown	USA
Cracker Barell	USA	*Montagnard*	*FRA*
Creamy Harvati	USA	Monte Carlo	USA
Delico	USA	*Mountain Farms*	*FRA*
Di Giorno	USA	Muenster and Brick	USA
Edam Loaf	USA	*New Holland*	*FRA*
Enchilado	USA	Noon Hour	USA
Entremont	*FRA*	Norrgreeve Swiss	USA
Etorki	*FRA*	Northland Star	USA
Farmer's	USA	Oaxaca	USA
Fine Bouche	*FRA*	Old English	USA
Fontina	USA	Old Wisconsin	USA
Friendship	USA	Pizazz	USA
Galbani	*FRA*	Polly-O	USA
Geramont	*FRA*	Prastost	USA
Gerard	*FRA*	*Precious*	*FRA*
Gervais	*FRA*	*President*	*FRA*
Graddost	USA	Presidents Pride	USA
Great Lakes	USA	*Puck*	*DEN*
Gulost	USA	Queso Blanco Fresco	USA
Harvest Moon	USA	Queso Fresco	USA
Healthy Choice	USA	Queso Quesadilla	USA
Heluva Good	*NETH*	Ranchero	USA
Herrgard	USA	Real California	USA
Hoffman's	USA	Rex	USA
Il Primo	USA	Ribbon	USA
Intensacheddar	USA	Romano	USA
Jockey	*FRA*	Roselli	USA
		Rosenborg	*DEN*

Rowntree's	SWI	**Vasterbotten**	USA
Sandhurst Farms	ITL	*Vaudreuil*	CAN
Saputo	CAN	**Velveeta**	USA
Sargento	USA	**Verdaccio**	USA
Sartori Foods	USA	**Vibrante**	USA
Scandic	USA	*Wildberg*	SWI
School Choice	USA	**Wisconsin**	USA
Schreiber	USA	*Wispride*	FRA
Senda	CAN	**Woody's**	USA
Shapesters	FRA	**Wrapped Robbin**	USA
Skim Swiss	USA		
Sorrento	FRA	**COFFEE CREAMER**	
Soy A Melt	USA	*Brite*	SWI
Star Valley	USA	*Carnation*	SWI
Stella	CAN	**Coffee Rich**	USA
Sticksters	FRA	*Coffee-Mate*	SWI
Stringsters	FRA	**Cremora**	USA
Super Swiss	USA	**Farm Rich**	USA
Swiss Garden	USA	**International Delight**	USA
Swiss-American, Inc.	USA	*Krem-Top*	SWI
Sylphide	FRA	**Mocha Mix**	USA
Syrokrem	FRA	**N-Joy**	USA
Taluhet	CAN	**Silk Soy Creamer**	USA
Tartare	FRA	*Yorker*	SNG
Tasty-Lite	USA		
Terra Nostra	FRA	**CONDIMENTS**	
Tete De Moine	SWI	*Alacena*	PER
The Good Slice	USA	*Amora*	FRA
The Laughing Cow	FRA	**Atkins**	USA
Tillamook	USA	**B&G**	USA
Tilsiter	SWI	*Best Foods*	UKN
Toastinette	FRA	**Bick's**	USA
Tofutti Soy-Cheese Slices	USA	**Blue Plate**	USA
Treasure Cave	CAN	**Brooks**	USA
Trikalino	GRE	**Cains**	USA
Twin Falls	USA	**Cates**	USA
Vacherin	SWI	**Chef's Choice**	USA
Vachon	CAN	**Chili Dog**	USA

<u>Condiments (cont.)</u>

Chipico	USA
Chirat	*UKN*
Claussen	USA
Clements	USA
Daddies Ketchup	*FRA*
Del Monte	USA
Delinaise	USA
Dijonnaise	*UKN*
ETA	*UK*
Farman's	USA
French's	*UK*
Fruco	*UKN*
Garden Club	USA
Gattuso	USA
Goodall's	*UKN*
Grey Poupon	USA
Gulden's	USA
Habitant	USA
Heifetz	USA
Heinz	USA
Heinz Lite	USA
Hellmann's	*UKN*
Hunt's	USA
Jack Daniels	USA
JB	*UKN*
Kosciusko	USA
Kraft	USA
Lesieur	USA
Livio	*UKN*
Lizano	*UKN*
London Pub	USA
McLarens	USA
Mrs. Fanning's	USA
Nalley's	USA
Nance's	USA
Nathan's	USA
Natural Stone Ground	USA

Oxford	USA
Pan Yan	*SWI*
Peter Piper	USA
Plochman's	USA
Pomodorissimo	*UKN*
Praise	*UK*
Purity Gourmet	USA
Rose	USA
Sandwich Sensations	USA
Schwartz	USA
Sport Pepper	USA
State Fair	USA
Steinfield	USA
Telma	*UKN*
Terrapin Ridges Gourmet Line	USA
Vlasic	USA
Zatarain's	USA

<u>FLOUR</u>

Allinson	*UK*
Baker's Joy	USA
Cardinal	USA
Crutchfield's	USA
Dakota	USA
Duryeas	*UKN*
Gibralter	USA
Gold Medal	USA
Heritage Blend	USA
Highloaf	*CAN*
Hudson Cream Flour	USA
King Arthur	USA
La Pina	USA
Masathentic	USA
Miller's Choice	USA
Pathfinder	USA
Peerless	USA
Pillsbury	USA

Pizza Superiore	USA
Polly	UKN
Progressive Baker	USA
Qualitate	USA
Red Band	USA
Robin Hood	USA
Segitiga Biru	INDO
Sensation	CAN
Serenade/Vesta Cake	USA
Softasilk	USA
Spring Hearth	USA
Spring King	USA
Sunflour	USA
Textratein	USA
Tia Rosa	MEX
Vita-Grain	USA
Vitamilho	UKN
White Lily	USA
White Wings	USA

GENERAL FOOD PRODUCTS

4C	USA
A-1 Steak Sauce	USA
Act II	USA
Adolph's Seasoning	UKN
Akebono	JAP
Al Fresco	USA
Algood	USA
Allen	USA
Allens	USA
Allen's	USA
Alliance Nutrition	USA
Alpro	NETH
Always Tender Pork	USA
Ambrosia Desserts	UKN
American Foods Group	USA
American's Best	USA
America's Choice	GER

Amicelli	USA
Amigo Bananas	USA
Amish	USA
Amish Kitchen	USA
Amoy Chinese Sauces	FRA
Anchor Foods	USA
Andy Boy Vegetable	USA
An-Joy	USA
Apple Time	USA
April Hill	USA
Aquarian	USA
Arctic Gold	THAI
Arden International Kitchens	USA
Ardenelli's Italian	USA
Armanino	USA
Armor Soy	USA
Armour Canned Meats	GER
Arnott's Biscuits	USA
Aromat Food Seasoning	UKN
Arrezio	USA
Arrow Head	USA
Arrowhead Mills	USA
Ashley Farms	USA
Asian Gold	THAI
Atalanta	USA
Aunt Jemima	USA
Aunt Nellies	USA
Austex	USA
Austin Blues	USA
Authentico	USA
Award	USA
Awrey Pastries	USA
Azteca Tortillas	USA
B&G	USA
B&M	USA
Babe & Kris	USA
Bachman	USA

General Food Products (cont.)

Bacos	USA	Bettercreme Icing	
Bagel Bites	USA	& Filling	USA
Bagel Dogs	USA	Better'N Eggs	USA
Bag'N Season	USA	Betty Crocker	USA
Bahia Gold	*THAI*	Big AZ	USA
Bak-A-Fry	USA	Big Johns	USA
Baker's Chocolate	USA	Big Valley	USA
Bakers Hard Wheat	USA	Bigger Better Bagles	USA
Bakey Pies	*KOR*	Bird's Desserts	USA
Balance Bar	USA	Birds Eye	USA
Bama	USA	Bishop	USA
Bambino Cheese Spread	USA	Bisque Cocktail Sauce	USA
Bandito Salsa	USA	Blast O Butter	USA
Banquet	USA	*Blue Bay*	*CAN*
Batchelors	*UK*	Blue Bird Pastries	
Batter Gold	USA	& Cakes	USA
Battersweet	USA	Blue Boy Vegetables	USA
Bay City	USA	Blue Ribbon French Fries	USA
Bay Winds Seafood	USA	Blue Star	USA
Bayside Bistro	USA	Blueberry Squares	USA
Bean Cuisine	USA	Bob Evans Sausage	USA
Beanee Weenee	USA	*Boboli Pizza Crusts*	*UKN*
Bearitos	USA	Boca Meat Alternative	USA
Bel Maestro	USA	Bonehead's Seafood	USA
Belin	*FRA*	Bonner Raisins	USA
Bell & Evans Chicken	USA	Bookbinder Cocktail	
Bell Carter Olives	USA	Sauce	USA
Bellissimo	USA	*Booth*	*CAN*
Bell's	USA	Bordeau	USA
Bender Bagels	USA	Borelli	USA
Benson's Old Home	USA	Bowl Appetit	USA
Bernard	USA	Bradshaw's Honey	USA
Berri Basket Vegetables	USA	Bravo	USA
Berries Galore Vegetables	USA	Brer Rabbit	USA
Bertolli	*UKN*	Briar Hill	USA
Best Foods	*UKN*	Brilliance Shortening	USA
Best's Kosher	USA	Brooks	USA
		Brossard	USA

Brown & Polson	UKN	Casa Solana	USA
Brown 'N Serve	USA	*Cascade Select*	JAP
Bruce Foods	USA	Cassano Pizza Dough	USA
Buckwheat Honey	USA	Castellari	USA
Buena Vida Tortillas	USA	Castleberry's	USA
Bugs Bunny's Carrots	USA	Catalina	USA
Buitoni	USA	Catalina Tomato Sauce	USA
Bunker Hill Brand	USA	*Caterpac French Fries*	CAN
Bunny Love Carrots	USA	*Cattleman's Barbecue*	
Bureleson's Honey	USA	*Sauce*	UK
Bush's Best	USA	Celebrations	USA
Butter Boom	USA	Certified Red Label	USA
Butter Buds	USA	Champion Raisins	USA
Butter Kernel	USA	Charlene's Fruit Filling	USA
Butter Licious	USA	Charlies	USA
Butterball	USA	Cheez Whiz	USA
Butterfield	USA	Chef Allen's Sauce	USA
Butter-Licious	USA	Chef BoyArDee	USA
Buy 'N Save	USA	*Chef Francisco*	BGM
Byerlys	USA	Chef Magic Hot Sauce	USA
C&W	USA	Chef Sandridge	USA
Cajun King	USA	*Chef-Mate*	SWI
Calavo	USA	Chef's Choice	USA
Calorie Check	USA	*Chef's Classic Seasonings*	IRE
Calorie Control	USA	*Chef's Pride*	JAP
Calypso	USA	Cherry Central	
Cambarrel	USA	Applesauce	USA
Campbell's	USA	Chester's	USA
Canoe Creek	USA	Chi Chi's	USA
Cap'N Pride Seafood	USA	Chicago Town Pizza	USA
Captain Cook	JAP	*Chicken Tonight*	UKN
Captain's Catch	CAN	Chico Bananas	USA
Carapelli	USA	Chihuahua	USA
Carnation	SWI	Chilli Man	USA
Carolina Rice	SP	Chiquita Bananas	USA
Carroll Shelby	USA	*Chirat*	UKN
Casa Fiesta	USA	Chitosan Noodles	USA

General Food Products (cont.)

Chun King	USA	Crinkle Cut Coins	
Cinta Azul Rice	*SP*	Carrots	USA
Classic American Foods	USA	Crispura French Fries	USA
Clearsoy	USA	Crispy 'N White	USA
Clements	USA	Crisscut Fries	USA
Clover Honey	USA	*Crosse & Blackwell*	*SWI*
Clover Leaf	*CAN*	Crown Prince Seafood	USA
Clover Maid Honey	USA	Crunch 'n Munch	USA
Cloverdale Foods	USA	Crystal Hot Sauce	USA
Colavita	USA	Crystal Lake Egg	
Colonna	USA	Products	USA
Coltina	*JAP*	C-Town	USA
Comstock	USA	Cub Foods	USA
ConAgra	USA	Culinary Select	USA
Coney Bites	USA	*Cup Noodles*	*JAP*
Conimex	*UKN*	Curley QQQ Fries	USA
Conquest French Fries	USA	Custom Gold Label	USA
Contadina	*SWI*	Dai Day	USA
Continental Chef Sauces	USA	Dairy Sweet	USA
Cookies & Crazy Hair	USA	Dall'cuore	USA
Cool Whip	USA	Dan's Prize	USA
Coqueiro Fish	USA	De Ruijter	USA
Coral Seafood	*CAN*	Dead Heat Hot Sauce	USA
Cornados	USA	Decadence Biscotti	USA
Cotees	*UK*	Dei Fratelli	USA
Country Gold Mix	USA	Del Carbie	USA
Country Kitchen	USA	Del Monte	USA
Country Manor	USA	*Delacre Biscuits*	*UK*
Country Skillet Poultry	USA	Deli Break	USA
Countrys Delight	USA	Delight Bites	USA
Crab Delights	USA	Delimex	USA
Cracker Jack	USA	Delsey's	USA
Craisins	USA	*Delta Rice*	*UKN*
Cranfruit Sauces	USA	Dennisons	USA
Creative Components	USA	Devil's Spit BBQ Sauce	USA
Crema Rancherito	USA	Di Giorno	USA
Crema Supremo	USA	Diamond Crystal	USA
		Diana Sauce	USA

Diet Lean	USA	El Lago Mexican	USA
Dillon's	USA	El Monterey	USA
Dilly Veggie Dip	USA	El Torito	USA
Diners' Choice	USA	Elan Foods	USA
Dining Treat	USA	Elgin Whip Topping	USA
Dinner Supreme	*SWI*	Eli's Cheesecake	USA
Dinty Moore	USA	Elita Cheese Spread	USA
Dolce Sauce	USA	Elite Kosher Foods	USA
Dole	USA	*Ellio's*	*CAN*
Dolly Madison	USA	el-Rio	USA
Dolmio	USA	Elsie	USA
Don Miguel Mexican	USA	Embasa Mexican	USA
Dona Maria	USA	Empires Treasure	
Doxsee	USA	Seafood	USA
Drake's	USA	*Empress*	*JAP*
Dream Whip	USA	Enrico's Salsa	USA
Dri-Flo Honey	USA	*Entenmann's*	*CAN*
Du Chef Syl	*UKN*	Equal	USA
Dude	USA	Eucalyptus Honey	USA
Dulce De Leche Pudding	USA	European Pudding	USA
Duncan Hines	USA	Excel	USA
Durkee	*UK*	Express Bowl	USA
Dutch Delight Vegetables	USA	EZ Marinader	USA
Dutch Farms Ice	USA	Fairbury Brand	USA
Dutch Gold Honey	USA	Fajita Marinade	USA
Dutch Harbor	*JAP*	*Family Buffet*	*IRE*
Dutch Mill	USA	Family Entrée	USA
Duyvis	USA	Fanfare	USA
E.M. Todd	USA	Fantasia Bakery Products	USA
East Texas Fair Peas	USA	Farm Rich Vegetables	USA
Eat Smart	USA	Farmer's Harvest	
Ebly	USA	Vegetables	USA
Eckrich	USA	Farmhouse Eggs	USA
Eden Blend	USA	Farmhouse Foods	USA
Edwards Frozen Desserts	USA	Fast Choice	USA
Egg Beaters	USA	Fastbites	USA
Eggo Waffles	USA	Fastshake Pancake Mix	USA
El Charrito	USA	Faust Seafood	USA

General Food Products (cont.)

Fazer Biscuits	*FRA*
Felix	**USA**
Fiesta Seasonings	**USA**
Fine Cuisine	*SWI*
Finest	**USA**
Fisher Boy	*CAN*
Fisher Nuts	**USA**
Fisherings	*CAN*
Flavacol Seasoning Salt	**USA**
Flav'R Top	**USA**
Florentine Lasagna	**USA**
Floresta	*CAN*
Florigold Citrus Fruits	*BGM*
Food Club	**USA**
Fortuna	**USA**
Fowl Play	**USA**
Fram Fresh	**USA**
Franco American	**USA**
Franklin Farms	**USA**
Frank's Canned Foods	**USA**
Frank's RedHot Sauces	*UK*
Freezer Queen	*IRE*
Freihofer's	*CAN*
French's	*UK*
Fresh Gourmet	**USA**
Fresh 'N Ready Desserts	**USA**
Freshlike	**USA**
Friendship	**USA**
Frigodan	*DEN*
Frionor	**USA**
Frisco	*SWI*
Frosty Seas	**USA**
Frosty Whip	**USA**
Frozfruit	**USA**
Fruit Naturals	**USA**
Fruitrients	**USA**
Fry's	**USA**

Frz	**USA**
Full Circle Organic	**USA**
Funa Sauces	*UKN*
Fun-C	**USA**
Funyuns Onion Rings	**USA**
Furman's Processed Vegetables	**USA**
Gala Honey	**USA**
Galaxy Nutritional Foods	**USA**
Galvanina	**USA**
Garden Club	**USA**
Garden Delight	**USA**
Garden Soup Company	**USA**
Gardenfare	**USA**
Garlic Plus	**USA**
Garlic Zing	**USA**
Gattuso	**USA**
Gayelord Hauser	**USA**
General Mills	**USA**
Generation 7 Fries	**USA**
Georgia Mustard BBQ Sauce	**USA**
Ghigi	**USA**
Gibbs	**USA**
Gilardi Foods	**USA**
Gilroy	**USA**
Gina Italian Village	*CAN*
Glazers Doughnuts	**USA**
Global Grill	**USA**
Glosette	**USA**
Gold Kist Farms	**USA**
Gold Label	**USA**
Gold Star	**USA**
Golden Cob	**USA**
Golden Crisp	**USA**
Golden Days	**USA**
Golden Meadow Honey	**USA**
Golden Shore Seafood	**USA**

Golden State Almonds	USA	Health Smart	
Gold's Condiments	USA	Condiments	USA
Gonnella	USA	Health Valley	USA
Good Heart Organics	USA	Healthy Choice	USA
Good News Eggs	USA	Healthy Pop Microwave	USA
Good-O	USA	Hearthside Select	USA
Gooey Buns	USA	Hebrew National	USA
Gorton's	*UKN*	Heinz	USA
Gourmet Table		*Heluva Good*	*NETH*
Condiments	USA	Hemingway Marinades	USA
Goya	USA	Herbal Bouquet	USA
Grand River Ranch	USA	*Heritage Salmon*	*CAN*
Grand Valley		Hershey Syrup	USA
French Fries	USA	Hickory Farms	USA
Grandma's Seasonings	USA	Hickory Hill Sausage	USA
Great Ocean		Hickory Liquid Smoke	USA
Canned Hams	USA	*High Liner*	*CAN*
Great Value	USA	Hilltop	USA
Green Giant	USA	Hilton Seafood	USA
Green Peacock Rice	*SP*	Hilton's	USA
Greenleaf	USA	Hoffman	USA
Gregg	USA	Holiday Harvest	
Griffin Food Co.	USA	Cranbury Sauce	USA
Grillwich Mexican	USA	Holiday Island	
Groko	*DEN*	Fruit Cake	USA
Grossmann Chilled		Holiday Pantry	USA
Salads	*UKN*	Homestyle Bakes	USA
Gulf Kist Shrimp	USA	Homestyle Bowls	USA
Gulfstream Seafood	USA	*Homestyle Entrée*	*IRE*
Habitant	USA	Honey in the Rough	
Hain Pure Foods	USA	Honey	USA
Hak Vegetables	USA	Honey Stung Poultry	USA
Hamnik	USA	Honeysoy	USA
Hand Fulls Sandwiches	USA	Hormel	USA
Hanover	USA	Hostess	USA
Happy Time	USA	Hot Digity Subs	USA
Harvest Moon	USA	*Hot Pockets*	*SWI*
		House of Tsang	USA

General Food Products (cont.)

Hungry Jack Pancake		Juliennes French Fries	USA
Mix	USA	Jus-Rol	USA
Hungry-Man	USA	Just Pikt	USA
Huntley & Palmers		K.C. Masterpiece	USA
Biscuits	*FRA*	Kan Tong	USA
Hunt's	USA	*Kaukauna Cheese Spread*	*FRA*
Hunt-Wesson	USA	Kellogg's	USA
Iberia	*UKN*	Kern	USA
Icelandic Seafood	*ICE*	Kerr	USA
Icicle Seafood	USA	Kettle Corn	USA
Icy Point	USA	Kettle Mania	USA
Idaho Supreme	USA	Kettle Pops	USA
IGA	USA	Kid Cuisine	USA
Igloo	*UKN*	Kineret	USA
Imo Food Dressings	USA	King Kold	USA
Indian Summer Vinegar	*JAP*	*King Oscar*	*CAN*
Indo	USA	King Soopers	USA
Inn Maid Noodles	USA	Kitchen Crisps	
International Entrée	USA	French Fies	USA
Italian Holiday	USA	Kitchen Treat	USA
Italian Village	*CAN*	*Knorr*	*UKN*
J & M	USA	Knott's Berry Farm	USA
Jack Rabbit	USA	Kosher King	USA
Jack's	USA	Kraft	USA
Jacky	*SWI*	Krasdale	USA
Jacob's Biscuits	*FRA*	*Kre-mel Desserts*	*UKN*
James River	USA	Krusteaz	USA
Jardine's	USA	Kuner	USA
JB Olives	*UKN*	L.K. Bowman	USA
Jell-O	USA	La Abuelita	USA
Jiffy	USA	La Casa Salsa	USA
Jiffy Pop	USA	La Choy	USA
Jimmi	*UKN*	*La Lechera*	*SWI*
Jimmy Dean Sausage	USA	La Primera Sausages	USA
Joan of Arc	USA	La Restaurante Salsa	USA
John West	USA	*La Rosa Biscuits*	*SWI*
Jolly Time	USA	*La Victoria Salsa*	
		& Sauces	*MEX*

Lady Aster	USA	Louis Kemp Seafood	USA
Lakeside	USA	Louisiana Hot Sauce	USA
Lamb Weston	USA	Lucca Italian	USA
Lamb's Supreme	USA	Lucky Leaf	USA
Lamisoy	USA	*Lucky Whip*	*UKN*
Lance	USA	Lunch Makers	USA
Land O' Lakes	USA	Lunchables	USA
Larrowe's Pancake Mix	USA	Luster Fruits	USA
Lascco Seafood	USA	Lustersoy	USA
Lassie	USA	Luzianne	USA
Lawry's Seasonings	*UKN*	Lynn Wilson's Mexican	USA
Le Gourmet Rice	USA	Mama Rosa'a	USA
Lea & Perrins	*FRA*	Mama Tisch's	USA
Lean Cuisine	*SWI*	Mandalay Rice	USA
Lean Gourmet	USA	Manwich	USA
Lean Ole Mexican	USA	*Maple Leaf*	*CAN*
Lean Pockets	SWI	*Maplehurst*	*CAN*
Lender's	USA	Mariner French Fries	USA
Leone Bianco	USA	Mario Olives	USA
Leon's	USA	Marrakesh Express	
Libby	USA	Couscous	USA
Libby's	*SWI*	Marshall's Canned	
Lidano	*UKN*	Seafood	USA
Light Tonight Fish		Martel Canned Seafood	USA
Fillets	USA	Marval	USA
Lil-Salt	USA	Mary Kitchen	USA
Lily Seafood	USA	Marzetti	USA
Link-N-Dog	USA	*Master Choice*	*GER*
Little Pig Barbeque		Masterfoods	USA
Sauce	USA	Maurice (imported)	USA
Lloyd's Entrees	USA	Mayfair Cake	USA
Log Cabin	USA	*Mazola Corn Oil*	*UKN*
Loma Linda Meat		*McCain*	*CAN*
Alternatives	USA	McCann's Oatmeal	USA
London Pub	USA	*McDougall's*	*UK*
Lone Star	USA	McKenzie's	USA
Longhorn Grill	USA	Meridian	USA
Longmont Turkey	USA	*Mette Munk*	*DEN*

General Food Products (cont.)

Mexene	USA	MTC Japanese Food	USA
Michelina's	USA	Murry's	USA
Midway's Finest Caramel	USA	Musco Olives	USA
Minh Egg Rolls	USA	Musselman's	USA
Minute Rice	USA	Myers	USA
Mirabel Seafood	USA	Nabisco	USA
Miracle Maize Corn		Naks-Pak	USA
Bread Mix	USA	Nalley's	USA
Mitia Mexican	USA	*Napolina*	*UKN*
Miyako	USA	Nathan's Seafood	USA
Moe's Southwest	USA	Natreen	USA
Mondo	USA	Natural Resource	
Mooreland Honey	USA	Produce	USA
Morningstar Farms	USA	Natural Touch	USA
Morrison & Schiff	USA	NaturalCrisp French	
Morton House		Fries	USA
Canned Meat	USA	Naturally Fresh	USA
Mosey's Corned Beef	USA	Nature's Choice	USA
Mother's Kosher Foods	USA	Nature's Own Instant	
Mott's	*UK*	Potatoes	USA
Mountain House	USA	Nature's Path Organic	USA
Mountain Top Pies	USA	Naturfresh	USA
Mr. Freeze	USA	Near East Side Dishes	USA
Mrs. Butterworth's	USA	Nelson's Oysters	USA
Mrs. Cubbison's	USA	*Nestival*	*SWI*
Mrs. Dash	USA	*Nestle*	*SWI*
Mrs. Difillippo's		New York	USA
Meatballs	USA	New York Bagel Boys	USA
Mrs. Freshley's	USA	Newman's Own	USA
Mrs. Friday's	USA	Nile Spice	USA
Mrs. Grass Soups		Ninos	USA
& Dry Mixes	USA	*Nissin Foods*	*JAP*
Mrs. Grimes	USA	Noon Hour	USA
Mrs. Paul's	USA	North American Honey	USA
Mrs. Smith's Desserts	USA	North Side Foods	USA
Mrs. T's Pierogies	USA	Oaxaca	USA
Mrs. Weiss Noodles	USA	Ocean Beauty Salmon	USA
		Ocean Spray	USA

Ocean's Harvest	USA	Paco Rico Mexican	USA
Oceanway Seafood	USA	Pagoda Egg Rolls	USA
Oh Boy	USA	*Pampas Pastry*	*UK*
Ohse	USA	Panetini	USA
O-Ke-Doke	USA	Papa Lynn Mexican	USA
Okray's	USA	Papetti's	USA
Old American	USA	Par Excellence Rice	USA
Old Dutch	USA	*Pasco Cakes*	*JAP*
Old El Paso	USA	Pasta Perfect	USA
Old Fashioned Pudding	USA	Pasta Roni	USA
Old Mill	USA	*Patak's*	*UK*
Old Salt Seafood	USA	Patak's Ethnic Foods	USA
Old Time	USA	Patio	USA
Old VA Apple Butter	USA	Pavone	USA
Old Wisconsin	USA	*Paxo*	*UK*
Olde Cape Cod	USA	Payette Farms French	
On Top Non-Dairy		Fries	USA
Topping	USA	Peloponnese	USA
On-Cor	USA	Pemmican Meat Snacks	USA
O'New Pies	USA	Peppadew Picnate Fruit	USA
Onion Magic	USA	Pepperidge Farm	USA
Open Pit Barbeque Sauce	USA	*Perfect Bar*	*JAP*
Orange Honey	USA	Perfection	USA
Orchard Boy	USA	Peri-Peri	USA
Ore-Ida	USA	*Peter Pan Seafoods*	*JAP*
Orien Bites	USA	Pet-Ritz Frozen Pies	USA
Original Deluxe		*Pfanni Potato Products*	*UKN*
Fruit Cakes	USA	Phillips (processed)	USA
Orleans Seafood	*CAN*	Picnic Cold Cuts	USA
Ortega	USA	Pictsweet Vegetables	USA
Orville & Wilbur's	USA	Pie Piper Dessert	USA
Orville Redenbacher	USA	Pierre	USA
Oscar Mayer	USA	Pillar Rock Canned	
Our Family	USA	Seafood	USA
Oven Fry Coating Mix	USA	Pillow Pack	USA
Owen's Spring Creek	USA	Pillsbury	USA
Oxford Biscuits	*FRA*	Pinata	USA
Pace Picante Sauce	USA	*Pizza Quick*	*UKN*

General Food Products (cont.)

Plymouth Colony	
Desserts	USA
Polonaise	USA
Pop Secret	USA
Pop-Ice	USA
Pop-Tarts	USA
PopWeaver	USA
Poss	USA
Potato Pearls Mashed	
Potatoes	USA
Poti Desserts	*UKN*
Poundo Yam	*UK*
Prairie Farms	USA
Preformers Potato	
Products	USA
Prego	USA
Prelate Seafood	USA
Presidents Pride	USA
Pride Canned Vegetables	USA
Pride French Fries	USA
Pride of Alaska Seafood	*JAP*
Pride of Antartica	
Seafood	USA
Pride Of The Fram	USA
Prima Porta Sausages	USA
Prima Rosa Mexican	USA
Princella	USA
Private Label Angel	
Food Cake	USA
Progresso	USA
Proof-Perfect Pizza	
Dough	USA
Provena	USA
Prudence	USA
Pubhouse Seafood	USA
Puck & Bowercow	USA
Puritan Canned Meats	*UKN*
Puritan Pancake Mix	USA
Purity	*CAN*
Quaker Rice Cakes	USA
Quality Fare	*CAN*
Que Bueno Mexican	*SWI*
Queso Anejo Enchilado	USA
Queso Rancherito	USA
Queso Sierra	USA
Quick Whip Topping	*UKN*
Quick-Start Chili Mix	USA
Raga Muffins	USA
Ragu	*UKN*
Raised Donut Mix	USA
Ranch Style	USA
Rapibarritas Seafood	*CAN*
Rapicocinados Seafood	*CAN*
Raris	USA
Ready Crust Pie Crust	USA
Real Cream Whipped	
Topping	USA
Realean	USA
Reames	USA
Recess Lunch Kit	USA
Red & White	USA
Red Cloud Fruits	USA
Reddi Whip	USA
Redicel Processed Celery	USA
Redi-Shred	USA
Reese	USA
Reputation	USA
Reser's	USA
Revels	USA
Rib Nibblers	USA
Rib-B-Q	USA
Rice Dream Desserts	USA
Rice-A-Roni	USA
Riceland Rice	USA
Richard's Cajun Food	USA

Right Course	*SWI*	*Saudia*	*SAUD*
Rio Grande Eggs	USA	**Saus-A-Rage**	USA
Rita Miller's Honey	USA	**Sau-Sea**	USA
Rite Foods Seafoods	USA	**Saverite**	USA
Robin Hood	USA	**Savon**	USA
Rocky Pop	USA	**Savor Notes**	USA
Rokeach Kosher Foods	USA	**Savory Wheat Beer**	
Roman Meal Waffles	USA	**Bread Mix**	USA
Romanoff Cavier	USA	**Savorysoy**	USA
Ron Son	USA	**SBS**	USA
Rosarita	USA	*Scanpro*	*DEN*
Rosarita Mexican Food	USA	**Schwan's**	USA
Rowntree's	*SWI*	**Scott's Foods**	USA
Royal Danube	USA	**Scott's Oats**	USA
Royal Kerry Wafers		**Scrub Club**	USA
& Biscuits	USA	**Sea Alaska**	USA
Royal Mahout	USA	*Sea Fresh*	*CAN*
Royal Prince	USA	*Sea Pasta*	*JAP*
Royalty Pineapple	USA	**Sea Spray**	USA
Ruiz	USA	*Sea Stix*	*JAP*
Ruiz Mexican	USA	*Sea Tails*	*JAP*
S&W	USA	**Sea-Best**	USA
Sage Honey	USA	**Seabrook Farms**	USA
Salad Shoppe Toppings	USA	**Seafarer**	USA
Salmon Chef	USA	**Sealegs**	USA
Salsa Express	USA	**Sealicious**	USA
Salsalito	USA	**Seashells**	USA
Sam's American Choice	USA	**Seaside**	USA
San Biscuits	*FRA*	**Season**	USA
Sanderson Farms	USA	*Seastar*	*ICE*
Sandwich Maker	USA	**Seawatch**	USA
Sans Sucre	USA	**Seaway**	USA
Santa Fe Salad Kit	USA	**Second Nature**	USA
Santiago Refried Beans	USA	**Seeds Of Change**	USA
Santoka Noodles	*JAP*	**Select Recipe French**	
Sara Lee	USA	**Fries**	USA
Sarimi Noodles	*INDO*	*Selecta*	*UK*
Sartori Foods	USA	**Seltzer**	USA

General Food Products (cont.)			
Seneca	USA	*Simmerin*	*JAP*
Senna	*AUS*	**Simple Traditions**	USA
Senseo	USA	**Simplot**	USA
Sensient	USA	**Simply Organic**	USA
Serano Pickled Peppers	USA	**Simply Potatoes**	USA
Serve 'N Store	USA	**Simply Serve**	USA
Seto Fumi	*JAP*	**Singleton**	USA
Shaheen	USA	**Sinu-Health**	USA
Shake 'N Pour Pancake Mix	USA	*Sisig*	*PHIL*
		Sister Schubert's	USA
Shake'N Bake	USA	**Skansen Herring**	USA
Shaman	USA	*Ski*	*UK*
Shang Teng Egg Rolls	USA	**Skinny**	USA
Shape Ups	USA	*Skips*	*UK*
Shasta	USA	**Skyfries**	USA
Shaws	*IRE*	**Skyland**	USA
Shenandoah	USA	**Skyline Chili**	USA
Shiitake	*JAP*	**Slidinglid**	USA
Shimeji	*JAP*	**Small Planet Foods**	USA
Shoestrings	USA	**Smart Bites**	USA
Shogun	USA	**Smart Menu**	USA
Shopfast	*AUS*	**Smart Start**	USA
Shur Fine	USA	**Smartfood**	USA
Shurfine	USA	*Smedley's*	*UK*
Shurfresh	USA	**Smiths**	USA
Side-by-Side	USA	**Smokie Grill**	USA
Sierra	USA	**Smucker's**	USA
Sig	USA	*Snack Man*	*AUS*
Siggi's	*AUS*	**Snackees**	USA
Signature	USA	**Snackin' Cake**	USA
Signature Of Iowa	USA	*Snap Packs*	*IRE*
Silk Road	*JAP*	**Snoboy**	USA
Silver Fleece	USA	*Snowberry Cakes*	*JAP*
Silver Floss Sauerkraut	USA	**Snowfloss Sauerkraut**	USA
Silver Lining	USA	**Snow's**	USA
Silver Skillet	USA	*So Crispy (organic)*	*NETH*
Simba	USA	*Sofia Express*	*COL*
		Softstix	USA

Solo Cakes	USA	Stuffed Tater	USA
Sorbee	USA	Sue Bee Honey	USA
Soup Starter	USA	Sugary Sam	USA
Souplantation	USA	*Sultana*	*UK*
Sourdough	USA	*Sumire Noodles*	*JAP*
Southern Pride	USA	Summer Fruit	USA
Southern Winds	USA	Summite	USA
Soy Dream	USA	Sun Crop French Fires	USA
Soya Kaas	*NETH*	Sun Lee	USA
Soyco Foods	USA	Sun Meadow	USA
Soytreat	USA	Sun Ripe	USA
Spaghettios	USA	Sunfresh	USA
Spark Plugs	USA	Sun-Maid Raisins	USA
Spectrum Naturals	USA	Sunny Fresh	USA
Spice Advice	*UK*	Sunny Square	USA
Spices Of The Orient	*SNG*	Sunnyland	USA
Sports Blast	USA	Sunripe Tomatoes	USA
Spreadin' Honey	USA	Sunshine	USA
Spudsters	USA	Sunspire	USA
Squeez 'N Go	USA	*Suntory*	*JAP*
St Ivel	*UK*	Sun-Vista	USA
Stadler Country Hams	USA	Super Chipper Desserts	USA
Stafano's	USA	*Super Cup Noodles*	*INDO*
Stagg	USA	*Super Mi Noodles*	*INDO*
Stagg Corned Beef Hash	USA	Super1Foods	USA
Star Cross	USA	Supercel	USA
Star Signature	USA	*Supercrisps French Fries*	*CAN*
State Fair	USA	Superior	USA
Static Guard	USA	Supermelts	USA
Steak House Fries	USA	*Superquinn*	*IRE*
Steakhouse	USA	*Superstars French Fries*	*CAN*
Stealth French Fries	USA	Supervalu	USA
Stefano Foods	USA	Supreme Valu	USA
Stingers	USA	Supremo	USA
Stocki Pancake Mix	*UKN*	Sure Fine	USA
Stokely's	USA	Suzi-Wan	USA
Stouffer's	*SWI*	Svenhard's Pastries	USA
Stove Top	USA	Swan	USA

General Food Products (cont.)		The Big Cheez	USA
Swanson	USA	The Bomb	USA
Swedish Glace	USA	The Fresh 1	USA
Sweet Kiss	USA	The Funnel Cake Factory	USA
Sweet Sue	USA	The Golden Pig	USA
Swift Meat Products	USA	The Max	USA
Sysco	USA	The Nature's Basket	USA
T. Marzetti's	USA	The Royal Cherry	USA
T.J. Cinnamons	USA	The Royal Olive	USA
Taco Bell	USA	Thermalink	USA
Taj Mahal Noodles	*INDO*	Thiel Cheese Spread	USA
Takenoko	*JAP*	*Thomas'*	*UK*
Tangle Wood Farms	USA	*Thomas' English Muffins*	*UKN*
Tarte Julie	*UK*	Three Bears Honey	USA
Tartex	*NETH*	*Tia Berta*	*MEX*
Tastee Choice	USA	Tia Pei	USA
Tasteespud French Fries	USA	*Tia Rosa*	*MEX*
Tasty	USA	Tiger Bay	USA
Taterboy	USA	Tiger Power	USA
Tawisa	*MEX*	Time Savor Line	USA
TBK	*SAF*	*Tina's Burritos*	*JAP*
Teasdale	USA	*Tinkies*	*SAF*
Telma	*UKN*	Tinytums	USA
Tem-Cote	USA	Tio Pepe's	USA
Tem-Plus	USA	Tita Biscuits	USA
Tempting Biscuits	USA	Titan	USA
Tender Basket	USA	Tivoli	USA
Tender N' Easy	USA	Toastchee	USA
Tenderflake Pastry	*CAN*	Toast'Em	USA
Tenshin Meisai	*JAP*	*Toaster Melts*	*JAP*
Terra Chips	USA	*Toaster Pizza*	*JAP*
Tesco	*ITL*	Toaster Scrambles	USA
Tesori Dell'Arca	*ITL*	Toaster Strudel	USA
Texas Pride	USA	Tobin's Mother	USA
Texas Signature Foods	USA	Toddy Chocolate Powder	USA
Textured Soy Protein	USA	Toffee Crunch Pies	USA
TGI Friday's	USA	Tofutti	USA
The Big Blitz Pies	USA	Tongue Torch	USA

Tonk Biscuits	*FIN*	**Udon Noodles**	USA
Top	USA	**Ultra-Soy**	USA
Top Cat French Fries	USA	**Uncle Ben's**	USA
Top Crest	USA	**Uncle Ray's**	USA
Top Ramen	*JAP*	**Underwood**	USA
Tornio	*FIN*	*Unicord*	*THAI*
Torry Harris	USA	*Unisea*	*JAP*
Torta Tiramisu Pies	USA	**Up-Country Organics**	USA
Tortiricas	*MEX*	*Uppercrust*	*UK*
Totino's	USA	**Upstate Farms**	USA
Tracker	USA	**V. Pearl**	USA
Trader's Choice	*UK*	**V.W. Joyner**	USA
Traditional Recipe	USA	**Val U Pak**	USA
Trappey's	USA	**Valerian-Poppy**	
Tree Of Life	*NETH*	**Supercomplex**	USA
Tree Top Apple Sauce	USA	*Valley Fresh*	*IRE*
Tres Estrellas	*MEX*	**Valley Grille**	USA
Tri-Co	USA	**Valu Time**	USA
Trident Seafoods	USA	*Value America*	*CAN*
Trifoglio	USA	**Value Choice**	USA
Trio Supreme	*SWI*	**Valutime**	USA
Triunfo Biscuits	*FRA*	**Van Camp's**	USA
Trix	USA	**Van de Kamp's**	USA
Tropical	USA	*Vandemoortele*	*BGM*
Tropical Paradise	USA	**Vanilla Blend**	USA
Tropical Source	USA	*Vea*	*NETH*
Tropicana	USA	**Veg-All**	USA
Truly Indian	*IND*	**Vegamina**	USA
Tucchetti	USA	**Vege-Sal**	USA
Tulelake	USA	*Velemint*	*GER*
Tulip	USA	**Venise**	USA
Tuna Spirals	USA	*Ventura Foods*	*JAP*
Tung-I	*TWN*	**Verdelli**	USA
Twin Cup Noodles	*JAP*	**Verdi**	USA
Twister Fries	USA	**Vic's**	USA
Twisty Grahams	USA	**Victor**	USA
Tycoon	USA	**Victory Wings**	USA
U.F.O. Fried Noodles	*JAP*	*Vienetta*	*UKN*

<u>General Food Products (cont.)</u>

Vienna	PHIL	White & Buttery	USA
Vigan Longanisa	PHIL	White Cheddar	USA
Village Farms	USA	White Chief	USA
VIP	USA	White Crown	USA
Virginia Brand Honey	USA	White House	USA
Virginia's Choice	USA	White Rose Foods	USA
Vita Burst	CAN	White Swan	USA
Vitashure	USA	Whitney's	USA
Vitex Supercomplex	USA	*Whole Earth (organic)*	NETH
Vito	USA	*Wiener/Viennese*	AUS
Voimix	FIN	Wild Berry Splash	USA
Vruit	JAP	Wild Honey	USA
Wacky Mac &		*William Saurin*	FRA
Cheese Dinners	USA	Win Schuler's	USA
Wacky Pack	USA	Windsor Frozen Food	USA
Wagon Master	USA	Wing Demons	USA
Walden Farms	USA	Winter Gardens	USA
Walkers	USA	Winter Glow Fruit	USA
Wall's	IRE	*Wishbone*	UKN
Walnut Acres (organic)	USA	Wolf Brand	USA
Wanchai Ferry	USA	Wolferman's	USA
Wasabi Fu	JAP	Wolff's	USA
Washington	USA	Wolfgang Puck's	USA
Wattie's	USA	Women's One	USA
Weaver	USA	*Wonderbar*	SAF
Webber Farms	USA	Wonderbites	USA
Weight Watchers	LUX	W-R	USA
Wel Pac	JAP	Wright's	USA
Welch's Juicemakers	USA	Wyler's	USA
Wesson	USA	Xangos Desserts	USA
Westbrae Natural	USA	*X-Treme Fries*	CAN
Western Bagel	USA	X-Trude	USA
Western Family	USA	Yano	USA
Westfarm Foods	USA	Yoder's	USA
Westpac	USA	Yoshida	USA
Westsoy	USA	Yu Sing	USA
Wheatex	USA	*Yukari*	JAP
		Yummy Cheese	USA

YumYum	*JAP*	*Fruit-Line*	*UKN*
Yves Veggie Cuisine	**USA**	*Fudgsicle*	*UKN*
Zalads	**USA**	*Godiva*	*CAN*
Zap'Ems	**USA**	**Golden Gopher**	**USA**
Zappetizers	**USA**	*Good Humor*	*UKN*
Zax Suace	**USA**	**Greens**	**USA**
Zerto	**USA**	*Haagen-Dazs*	*SWI*
Zesto Pesto	**USA**	**Healthy Choice**	**USA**
		Homemade Brand	**USA**
ICE CREAM		**Hygeia**	**USA**
3 Musketeers	**USA**	*Kidwich*	*UKN*
Absolutely Nuts	**USA**	*Klondike Bar*	*UKN*
Arctic Blast	**USA**	**Knudson**	**USA**
Baldwin	**USA**	**Mayfield**	**USA**
Baskin-Robbins	*UK*	**Meadow Gold**	**USA**
Beatrice	*ITL*	**Mello Frozen Yogurt**	**USA**
Ben & Jerry's	*UKN*	**Mellobuttercup**	**USA**
Bison Crunch	**USA**	**Melona**	**USA**
Blue Bell	**USA**	**Muddy Sneakers**	**USA**
Blue Bunny	**USA**	**Natuur**	**USA**
Bomb Pop	**USA**	**North Star**	**USA**
Borden	**USA**	*Oh Henry*	*UKN*
Bresler	*CAN*	**Penn Farms**	**USA**
Breyer's	*UKN*	**Perry's**	**USA**
Brigam's	**USA**	**Pet**	**USA**
Calypso	**USA**	**Pierre's French**	
Candy Counter	**USA**	**Ice Cream Co.**	**USA**
Cascade	*SWI*	*Popsicle Brand*	*UKN*
Dove Ice Cream Bars	**USA**	**Private Label**	**USA**
Dreamery	*CAN*	*Push-Ups*	*SWI*
Dreyer's	*SWI*	*Quebon*	*UKN*
Drumstick	*SWI*	**Reiter**	**USA**
Dusty Roads	**USA**	*Revello*	*UKN*
Eagle	**USA**	*Saudia Premium*	*SAUD*
Edy's	*SWI*	**Schoep's**	**USA**
Eskimo	*CAN*	**Schwan's**	**USA**
Eskimo Pie	*CAN*	**Sealtest**	**USA**
Frisco	*SWI*	**Shamrock Farms**	**USA**

Ice Cream (cont.)

Skinny Cow	*SWI*
Snow Moji	*SWI*
Softscoop	**USA**
Spirit Of America	**USA**
Starbucks	**USA**
Stouffer's	*SWI*
Thronton's	*UK*
Tuscan	**USA**
UFO	*SAUD*
Viennetta	*UKN*
Whole Fruit Sorbet	*CAN*
Yoplait	*IRE*

JAMS, JELLIES & PRESERVES

Algood	**USA**
Bama	**USA**
Berry Patch	**USA**
Branston Pickle	**USA**
Cap Design	**USA**
Casa De Mateus	*UKN*
Clements	**USA**
Country Inn Classics	**USA**
Country Sides	**USA**
Coventrygarden	**USA**
Crosse & Blackwell	*SWI*
Delicious	**USA**
Dickinson's	**USA**
Dutch Girl	**USA**
Evergreen Collection	**USA**
Frank Cooper	*UKN*
Garden Club	**USA**
Hartleys	**USA**
House Design	**USA**
Ideal	**USA**
J.M. Smuckers	**USA**
Just For Kids	**USA**
Kist	*UKN*

Knott's Berry Farm	**USA**
Kraft	**USA**
Kukui	**USA**
Lost Acres	**USA**
Mary Ellen	**USA**
Mateus	*UKN*
Olde Cape Cod	**USA**
Pacific Mountain	**USA**
Polaner	**USA**
Pomodorissimo	*UKN*
Purely Fruit	**USA**
Purely The Finest	**USA**
R-Line	**USA**
Rowntree's	*SWI*
Savory	**USA**
Smucker's	**USA**
Sorrell Ridge	**USA**
The Dickinson Family	**USA**
Welch's	**USA**

MEATS

Allen's	**USA**
Alpine	**USA**
Alpine	**USA**
Ambassador Sausage	**USA**
Aoste	**USA**
Argal	**USA**
Bake Eze	**USA**
Ball Park	**USA**
Banner Brand Sausage	*GER*
Bassett's Sausage	**USA**
Beaver Falls	**USA**
Beer Brat Bratwurst	**USA**
Beyond Nutrition	**USA**
Big Mama Sausage	**USA**
Bird Alert Poultry	**USA**
Black Angus Reserve	**USA**
Black Label Bacon	**USA**

Block & Barrel	USA	Country Skillet	USA
Blue Ribbon	USA	Country-Carved Hams	USA
Blue Ribbon Sausage	USA	Cure 81 Ham	USA
Boars Head	USA	Curemaster Ham	USA
Bolita Sausage	USA	Daisysealed Pork	USA
Braselton Poultry	USA	Dakota Pork	USA
Breakaway	USA	Dakota Supreme Beef	USA
Breast Zestees Chicken	USA	Dakota Valley Pork	USA
Briar Street	USA	*Danepak Bacon*	*DEN*
Bryan Foods	USA	Danish Crown	
Buckhead Beef	USA	Canned Ham	USA
Buddig	USA	Dean Kosher Poultry	USA
Budget Wise Turkey	USA	Decker	USA
Bunker Hill Brand	USA	*Denny*	*IRE*
Butcher Wagon Sausage	USA	Dinner Bell	USA
Butterball	USA	Double Diamond	USA
Cab	USA	Dubuque	USA
Captain's Chicken	*CAN*	Eckrich	USA
Carlton	USA	Empire Kosher Poultry	USA
Carlton's	USA	Esskay	USA
Celebrity	USA	Falls Poultry	USA
Chef Italia	USA	Family Tradition Turkeys	USA
Chef Pleaser Bacon	USA	Farmer Boy	USA
Chefs-In-A-Bag Chicken	USA	Farmers Hickory Brand	USA
Chesapeak Valley Farms	USA	Farmer's Pride Natural	
Chic-O-Steak	USA	Chicken	USA
Chorizo Sausage	USA	Farmland Foods	USA
Circle U Dry Sausage	USA	Farmland Pork	USA
ConAgra	USA	Fast Favorites Chicken	USA
Cook'D Right	USA	Fast 'N Easy	USA
Cookin' Good Poultry	USA	Firecracker Turkey	USA
Corky's	USA	Firedog Beef Sausage	USA
Cornby	USA	*Foodane*	*DEN*
Country Boy Sausage	USA	Freezer Queen	USA
Country Creek Farm	USA	Galil Kosher Poultry	USA
Country Cupboard	USA	Galileo	USA
Country Mill Sausage	USA	Gold Label	USA
Country Pride Poultry	USA	Gold' N Honey Poultry	USA

Meats (cont.)

Gold Ribbon Hams	USA
Golden Prairie Pork	USA
Golden Superb Pork	USA
Gold'N Plump	USA
Gourmet Selection Pountry	USA
Green Bay Dressed Beef	USA
Grillmaster	USA
Grogans	USA
Gwaltney	USA
Hamilton's	USA
Harker's Steaks	USA
Harot Kosher Poultry	USA
Harrington's Ham	USA
Hatfield	USA
Healthy Choice	USA
Hebrew National	USA
Herta	*SWI*
Hickory Farms	USA
Hillshire Farms	USA
Homeland Hard Salami	USA
Honey Baked Ham	USA
Honeysuckle White	USA
Hormel	USA
Hostess Hams	USA
Hunter	USA
Hygrade	USA
Il Primo	USA
Iowa Quality	USA
J.C. Potter	USA
James River	USA
Jamon Pietran	USA
Jennie-O	USA
John Morrell	USA
Julia's Poultry	USA
Jumbo Griller	USA
Kahn's	USA
Kayem	USA
Kentuckian Gold	USA
Kentucky Legend Ham	USA
Kings Delight Poultry	USA
Kitchen Sensations	USA
Krakus	USA
Kretschmar	USA
Lake Lanier Farms Poultry	USA
Lamb's Natural	USA
Larkwood Farms Poultry	USA
Lazy Maple Bacon	USA
Lean Generation Pork	USA
Light & Lean	USA
Liguria	USA
Li'l Butterball Turkey	USA
Little Sizzlers Pork	USA
Little Smokies Sausage	USA
Longmont Turkey	USA
Louis Rich	USA
Luter's	USA
Lykes	USA
Marval Turkey	USA
Master Choice	*GER*
Mayrose	USA
McKenzie Of Vermont	USA
Medford's	USA
Meester	*NETH*
MeisterChef	USA
Mickelberry's Ham	USA
Millers and Robirch Pork	USA
Minit Chef	USA
Minute Menu	USA
Morton House Canned	USA
Mr. Host Ham	USA
Mr. Turkey	USA
Muncheze	USA
Murry's	USA

National Deli	USA	Range Brand	USA
Nature's Farm	USA	Rapelli	USA
New Orleans Sausage	USA	Rath Black Hawk	USA
Newport Meat	USA	Ready Crisp Bacon	USA
Nistria	*NETH*	Redi-Steak	USA
Nutristrips	USA	Regal Poultry	USA
Odom's Tennessee Pride	USA	Rex	USA
Ohse	USA	Riojana Cold Cuts	USA
Old Town	USA	Roast Rite Turkeys	USA
Old Tyme	USA	Rockingham	USA
Old Wisconsin	USA	Rodeo	USA
Old World Premium	USA	Rose	USA
Old World Sausage	USA	Roselli	USA
Olde Smithfield	USA	Rosina Meatballs	USA
Ole South	USA	Rudy's Farm	USA
Omaha Steaks	USA	Russer	USA
Oscar Mayer	USA	Sanderson Farms	USA
Oscherwitz Glatt Kosher	USA	*Schneider Foods*	*CAN*
Oven Stuffer	USA	Schoneland's	USA
Owens Country Sausage	USA	Schwan's	USA
Palm River Grill King	USA	Scott Petersen Sausage	USA
Partins	USA	Seitz	USA
Patrick Cudahy	USA	Sever's Choice Pork	USA
Perdue	USA	Sheboygan Deli	USA
Peyton's	USA	Shofar Kosher	USA
Pick of the Stick	USA	*Shopsy's*	*CAN*
Picnic Cold Cuts	USA	Shorty's	USA
Pilgrim's Pride	USA	Showcase Supreme Beef	USA
Pit Barbecue	USA	Sibio Pork	USA
Plantation Turkey	USA	Simmons	USA
Plymouth Pride Turkey	USA	Sinai	USA
Presidents Pride	USA	Sir Steak	USA
Prime Part Chicken	USA	Six Gun Meat Loaf	
Pristine Cuisine Chicken	USA	Mixin's	USA
Pruden Ham	USA	Slick Chick	USA
Purdue Chicken	USA	Smartserve	USA
Puritan	*UKN*	Smithfield	USA
Ranchers Reserve	USA	*Smokey Joes*	*IRE*

Meats (cont.)

Smokrest Pork	USA
Special Seasonings Pork	USA
Speedy Bird Chicken	USA
Spring Creek Farm	
Brand	USA
Stadium Brats Bratwurst	USA
Steak-Eze	USA
Steak-It-Easy	USA
Stegeman	USA
Sterling Silver	USA
Sugar Lake Farms	USA
Sugardale	USA
Sun Land	USA
Sunnyland	USA
Superior	USA
Swiss American Sausage	USA
Tegel	USA
Tenderbird	USA
Tenderbites Chicken	
Nuggets	USA
Tendriade	*FRA*
Texan Weiners	USA
Texas Beef	USA
Texas Smokehouse	
Sausage	USA
The Fat Boy Sausage	*CAN*
The Original Texas	
Smokehouse	USA
TicinellaSWI	
Tobin's First Prize	USA
Top Dogs	*CAN*
Tornado	USA
Townsends	USA
Trinca	*SWI*
Triple M Spiral Hams	USA
Trunz	USA
Tyson	USA

Tyson's Pride	USA
Vincello Veal	USA
Virginia Reel	USA
Wampler Foods	USA
Wayne Farms	USA
Western Beef	USA
William Fischer	USA
Williams Country	
Sausage	USA
Wilson Deli	USA
Wings Of Fire Poultry	USA
Worthington	USA
Wranglers Franks	USA
Wright	USA
Wunderbar	USA

MILK & DAIRY PRODUCTS

Actimel	*FRA*
Albertson's	USA
Alta Dena	USA
Alto	USA
Ambrosia	*UKN*
Anlene	*NZ*
Avonmore	*IRE*
Axelrod	USA
Barber	USA
Beatrice	*ITL*
Berkeley Farms	USA
Better Than Cream	
Cheese	USA
Bison Dip Sour Cream	USA
Blue Bunny	USA
Blue Star	USA
Bonus Milk Powder	USA
Borden	USA
Bovine Colostrum	USA
Breaka	*ITL*
Breakstone's	USA

Brelactis	USA	**Darigold**	USA
Bridel	FRA	**Dean**	USA
Bridelice	FRA	**Eggland's Best**	USA
Broughton	USA	**El Mexicano**	USA
Cabot	USA	**Englewood Farms**	USA
Calci Skim	USA	*Every Day (Powdered)*	SWI
Carnation	SWI	**Farm Rich Non Dairy**	
Cenprem	USA	**Creamer**	USA
Centurion	USA	*Farmland*	ITL
Clinton	USA	**Foremost**	USA
Club Yogurt Drink	SWI	**Fram Fresh**	USA
Coburg	USA	**Friendship**	USA
Coleman	USA	*Froth Top*	ITL
Columbo	FRA	*Frusion*	FRA
Cool Cow	USA	**Fundo**	USA
Country Delight	USA	**Galaxy**	USA
Creamland	USA	**Gandy's**	USA
Crema Centroamericana		*Go-Gurt*	FRA
Sour Crème	USA	**Gold Star**	USA
Crema Mexicana		**Golden Crème**	USA
Sour Crème	USA	**Greens**	USA
Crema Poblana		*Grinner Becher*	SWI
Sour Crème	USA	**Hershey's Chocolate**	USA
Crema Salvadorena		**Horizon**	USA
Sour Crème	USA	**Hunter**	USA
Crosse & Blackwell	USA	**Hygeia**	USA
Crowley	NETH	*Ice Break*	ITL
Curtis Farm	ITL	*Ideal*	SWI
Dairy Ease	USA	**Intense**	USA
Dairy Fresh	USA	**Isolac**	USA
Dairy Smart	USA	**Kemps Dairy Products**	USA
Dairy Wise	ITL	**Knudsen**	USA
Dairylane	USA	**Kohler**	USA
Danette	FRA	**Kraft**	USA
Danimals	FRA	*Lactaid*	ITL
Dannon	FRA	*Lactel*	FRA
Danone	FRA	**Lakeview Farms**	USA
Dany	FRA	**Lampak**	USA

Milk & Dairy Products (cont.)

Light 'N Fit	FRA	**Philadelphia Cream Cheese**	USA
Light N' Lively	USA	*Physical*	ITL
Lite Time	USA	*Physical Skim*	ITL
Lucerne	USA	*Pilkil*	JAP
Lunebest	SWI	**Plas And Magic**	USA
Maplehurst	USA	**Polly-O**	USA
Mayfield	USA	**Prairie Farms**	USA
McArthur	USA	*Praise*	UK
Meadow Brook	USA	*President*	FRA
Meadow Fresh	NZ	**Price's**	USA
Meadow Gold	USA	**Primeros Anos**	USA
Melody Farms	USA	**Purity**	USA
Mid-America Farms	USA	**Ray's**	USA
Milk Mate	USA	**Reiter**	USA
Milkmaid	SWI	*Riviera*	ITL
Millennium	USA	**Robinson Dairy**	USA
Milnot	USA	**Rod's**	USA
Model Dairy	USA	**Ruggles**	USA
Moovers	USA	*Rush*	ITL
Morning Glory	USA	*San Regim*	ARG
National Champion	USA	*Sancor*	ARG
Naturally Yours	USA	*Sandhurst Farms*	ITL
Nature's Touch	USA	**Sauder Quality Eggs**	USA
Neilson	CAN	*Saudia*	SAUD
Nespray	SWI	**Schenkel's**	USA
Nido	SWI	**Schepps**	USA
Nutrish AB	USA	**Sealtest**	USA
Oberweis	USA	*Semper*	DEN
Organic Cow	USA	**Shamrock Farms**	USA
Parmalat	ITL	**Silcreme**	USA
Pauls	ITL	**Silk Is Soy**	USA
Peak	USA	**Silver Star**	USA
Penn Maid	USA	*Ski*	AUS
Penn Supreme	USA	*Skinny*	ITL
Pensupreme	NETH	*Slavyanochka*	RUS
Pet	USA	*Slim*	ITL
Peters & Brownes	USA	*Slimline*	SWI

Sno	IRE	*Ultra'Milk*	CAN
Snow Brand	JAP	**United**	USA
Snowcream	IRE	**United Dairy Farmers**	USA
Sofuhl	JAP	*Vaalia*	ITL
Sokreem Sour Cream	USA	*Vaudreuil*	CAN
Soprole	NZ	**Veggie Cream Cheese**	USA
Sport Shake	USA	**Veggie Milk**	USA
Sprinkl'ins	FRA	**Veggie Sour Cream**	USA
Starter Kit	USA	**Verifine Dairy**	USA
Stassano	NETH	*Vida*	ARG
State Brand	USA	*Vifit*	NETH
Stonyfield Farm	FRA	*Vigortone Lacto Edge*	FRA
Stroh's	USA	*Vita*	CHN
Sun Break	USA	*Vitasnella*	FRA
Sun Soy	USA	*Wave*	UK
Sunspray	NZ	**Weeks**	USA
Super Calf-Kit	USA	**Winter Star**	USA
Super Guard	USA	*Yazoo*	NETH
Superior	USA	*Yo-Flex*	DEN
Surefine	USA	*Yogho Yogho*	NETH
Sweet Acidophilus	USA	*Yogo*	AUS
Sysco	USA	*Yogs*	ARG
T G Lee	USA	*Yo-Most*	NETH
Tapporosso	ITL	*Yoplait*	IRE
Tararua	NZ	**Zoologic Doc**	USA
Tetra Brik	ARG		
Tillamook	USA	**PASTA**	
Tip Top	NZ	*Alianza*	PER
Top Hat	NZ	**American Beauty**	USA
Total	GRE	**Anthony's**	USA
Transition Plus	NETH	**Antiones**	USA
Trauth Dairy	USA	**Arthurs**	USA
Tres Ninas	ARG	*Barilla*	ITL
Trix	USA	**Bean Cuisine**	USA
Trutaste	CAN	**Bernardi**	USA
Tuffi	NETH	*Birkel*	FRA
Tuscan	USA	**Bistro**	USA
Tzatziki	GRE	*Buitoni*	SWI

Pasta (cont.)		San Giorgio	USA
Classico	USA	*Santa Rosa*	*PER*
Colavita	USA	Skinner	USA
Colonna	USA	*Stella*	*JAP*
Columbia	USA	*Top Ramen Noodles*	*JAP*
Creamette	USA	*Torino*	*FIN*
Cushpack Noodles	USA	*Trinca Pasta*	*SWI*
Dal Raccolto	USA	*Victoria*	*PER*
Deboles	USA	Healthy Harvest	USA
Di Giorno	USA	Piccolino	USA
Dreamfield Foods	USA		
Globe A-1	USA	**PASTA SAUCE**	
Honig	USA	Aunt Millie's	USA
Lady's Choice	*UKN*	*Barilla*	*ITL*
Light 'N Fluffy Noodles	USA	Campbell's	USA
Luxury	USA	Classico	USA
Mona	USA	Colonna	USA
Monterey	USA	*Contadina*	*SWI*
Mrs. Grass	USA	Del Monte	USA
Mrs. Weiss	USA	Di Giorno	USA
Mueller's	USA	Enrico's	USA
Napolina	*UKN*	*Five Brothers*	*UKN*
Nates	USA	Gattuso	USA
Olivieri	*CAN*	Gianni	USA
P&R	USA	Healthy Choice	USA
Pasta Montana	*JAP*	Hunts	USA
Pasta Perfect	USA	McCormick	USA
Pasta Select	USA	Medei Cuisine	USA
Pennsylvania Dutch	USA	*Napolina*	*UKN*
Ponte	*FRA*	Newman's Own	USA
Prince	USA	Pastorelli Four Cheese	USA
R & F	USA	*Pizza Quick*	*UKN*
Reames	USA	Prego	USA
Reimassas	*SWI*	Progresso	USA
Ronzoni	USA	*Ragu*	*UKN*
Roselli	USA	*Trinca Sauce*	*SWI*
Rosetto	USA	Walden Farms	USA
Royal	*UKN*		

PEANUT BUTTER

Adams	USA
Algood	USA
American	USA
Austin	USA
Best Foods	*UKN*
Blue Plate	USA
Cap Design	USA
Cap'N Kid	USA
Garden Club	USA
Houstyons	USA
Jif	USA
Kitchen King	USA
Lady's Choice	*UKN*
Laura Scudder's	USA
Peter Pan	USA
Reese's	USA
Savory	USA
Skippy	USA
Smucker's	USA

PET FOOD

3-D	USA
9-Lives	USA
Alpo	*SWI*
American Beefhide	USA
Amore	USA
Atta Boy	USA
Atta Cat	USA
Basic Plus	USA
Beef Jerky	USA
Beggin' Strips	*SWI*
Bestfriend	USA
Betta	USA
Bil-Jak's	USA
Bird's Favorite	USA
Blue Seal Dog Biscuits	USA
Buffet	*SWI*
Butcher's Blend	*SWI*
Cadillac	*CAN*
Calo	USA
Canigou	USA
Canine Carry Outs	USA
Canine Health Nutrition Maxi	USA
Canine Plus	*CAN*
Cat Chow	*SWI*
Catsan	USA
Cesar	USA
Chappie	USA
Classic Lite Cat	USA
Classic Nutritionals	USA
Come 'N Get It	*SWI*
ConAgra	USA
Country Cat	USA
Country Cousin	USA
Cycle	USA
Dad's	USA
Deli Cat	*SWI*
Delight	USA
Dog Chow	*SWI*
Dr. Ballard's	*SWI*
Eukanuba	USA
Evolve	USA
Fancy Feast	*SWI*
Felin Mignon	USA
Fit 'N Trim	*SWI*
Friskies	*SWI*
Frolic	USA
Fromm	USA
Gold'N Glow	USA
Gourmet	*SWI*
Gravy Train	USA
Hearty Brand	USA
Hill's	USA
Hi-Pro	*SWI*

Pet Food (cont.)		Prescription Diet	USA
Hi-Tor	USA	Pro Energy	USA
Husky	USA	*Pro Plan*	*SWI*
Iams	USA	Pro-Form	USA
Jerky Treats	USA	Pup-Peroni	USA
Jim Dandy	*SWI*	*Puppy Chow*	*SWI*
Kal Kan	USA	Puppy Gold	USA
Kam	USA	Puppy Prime	USA
Ken-L Ration	USA	*Purina*	*SWI*
Kent Feeds Adult Prime	USA	Reward	USA
Kibbles & Chunks	*SWI*	*Ringoos*	*SWI*
Kibbles 'N Bits	USA	*Rollitos*	*SWI*
Kit E Kat	USA	Ronron	USA
Kit 'N Kaboodle	*SWI*	Royal Canine Feline	
Kitekat	USA	Nutrition	USA
Kitten Chow	*SWI*	Science Diet	USA
Kitty	USA	*Sensible Choice*	*FRA*
Kozy Kitten	USA	*Shur-Gain*	*CAN*
Matzinger	*SWI*	*Size Nutrition*	*FRA*
Meaty Bone	USA	Snausages	USA
Mighty Dog	*SWI*	Song And Beauty	USA
Milk Bone Dog Biscuits	USA	Songbird Seeds	USA
Mini Chunks	USA	Sprout	USA
Moist And Meaty	*SWI*	Star Pro	USA
Moments	*SWI*	Strongheart	USA
My Dog	USA	Sun Pro	USA
Natural Blend	USA	Sunshine	USA
Natural Harmony	USA	Tasty Nuggets	USA
Nature's Choice		Tony	USA
Bird Feed	USA	Triumph	USA
Nature's Recipe	USA	Tuffys	USA
Nylabone Dog Chews	USA	Twin Pet	USA
Ol' Roy	USA	Vita Bone	USA
Pedigree	USA	Wild Finch Food	USA
Pet Treats	*SWI*	Wild Wing	USA
Pets All Agree	USA	Winterlife	USA
Pointer	USA		
Pounce	USA		

PIZZA

Appian Way	*GER*
Belafino	**USA**
Boboli	*UKN*
Celeste	**USA**
Chicago Town	**USA**
Dessert Delight	**USA**
Di Giorno	**USA**
Ellios	*CAN*
Gattuso	**USA**
Greek Masterpizza	**USA**
Grotto	**USA**
Healthy Choice	**USA**
Heavens' Bistro	**USA**
Jack's	**USA**
Jeno's	*UK*
Kraft	**USA**
Kroger	**USA**
Meat-E-Or	**USA**
Pillsbury	**USA**
Pizza Quick	*UKN*
Proof Perfect	**USA**
Red Baron	**USA**
Rising Crust (organic)	**USA**
Salubre	**USA**
Schwan's	**USA**
Spinoccoli	**USA**
Stouffer's	*SWI*
Tombstone	**USA**
Tony's	**USA**
Totino's	**USA**
Trinca Pizza	*SWI*
Veggie Patch	**USA**

RICE

Adolphus	*SP*
Arroz Sos	*SP*
Blue Ribbon	*SP*
Canilla	**USA**
Carolina	*SP*
Chef-Way	**USA**
Cinta Azul	*SP*
Colusa	*SP*
Comet	*SP*
Curry-O	*JAP*
Delta	*UKN*
Golden Canilla	**USA**
Gourmet House	*SP*
Green Peacock	*SP*
Mahatma	*SP*
Pearl Blossom	*SP*
S&W	*SP*
Saludaes	*SP*
Success	*SP*
Sunwest Organics	**USA**
Tastic	*SAF*
Texmati	**USA**
Uncle Ben's	**USA**
Watermaid	*SP*
Zatarain's	**USA**

SALAD DRESSING

Bernstein's	**USA**
Best Foods	*UKN*
Black Olive	**USA**
Blanchard & Blanchard	**USA**
Cains	**USA**
Calve	*UKN*
Cardini's	**USA**
Chef's Choice	**USA**
Clements	**USA**
Conway	**USA**
Conzelo	**USA**
Dorothy Lynch	**USA**
Elite	*UKN*
Girard's	**USA**

Salad Dressing (cont.)

Good Seasons	USA
Goodall's	UKN
Health Smart	USA
Heidelberg	UKN
Hellmann's	UKN
Henri's	UKN
Hidden Valley	USA
Ken's	USA
Knott's Berry Farm	USA
Kraft	USA
La-Flora	USA
Lesieur	UKN
Lighten Up!	USA
Maple Grove Farms	USA
Marie's	USA
Marzetti	USA
Miracle Whip	USA
Nalley's	USA
Newman's Own	USA
Olde Cape Cod	USA
Pasta Mates	USA
Pfeiffer	USA
Praise	UK
Purity Gourmet	USA
Riviera	USA
Roux	USA
Salad Lite	USA
San-J	JAP
Seven Seas	USA
Soja And Ginger	SP
Spin Blend	USA
Star	SP
Tirreno	UKN
Village Garden	USA
Walden Farms	USA
Western	UKN
Wish Bone	UK

SAUCES

Ah-So Barbecue	USA
Amoy	FRA
Atlantic Cocktail Sauce	USA
Buitoni	SWI
Bull Hot Sauce	USA
Bull's-Eye Barbecue Sauce	USA
Chirat	UKN
Crosse & Blackwell	SWI
Di Giorno	USA
Heinz	USA
Heinz 57 Steak Sauce	USA
Homepride Sauces	USA
Hot Stuff BBQ	USA
House Of Tsang	USA
Hunt's Spagetti Sauce	USA
Indi-Pep Hot Sauce	USA
Jackaroo	USA
JB	UKN
K.C. Masterpiece	USA
Kikkoman	JAP
Knorr	UKN
La Victoria Salsa	MEX
Las Palmas	USA
Lawry's	UKN
Lea & Perrins	FRA
Little Pig BBQ Sauce	USA
Lizano	UKN
London Pub	USA
Louisiana Hot Sauce	USA
Lousiana Hot Sauce	USA
Maille	USA
Makin Cajun	USA
Medei Cuisine Pasta Cuisine	USA
Mesquite Liquid Smoke	USA
Mexi-Pep Hot Sauce	USA

Mrs. Dash	USA
Mustard Cocktail	USA
Napolina	*UKN*
Nathan's	USA
Old Smokehouse Steak Sauce	USA
Old World	USA
Open Pit Barbeque	USA
Pace	USA
Patak's	*UK*
Real Fresh Cheese Sauces	USA
Richa & Sassy BBQ Sauce	USA
Roselli	USA
Sagawa's	USA
San-J Soy Sauce	*JAP*
Santa Fe Chili Co. Salsa	USA
Sauceworks	USA
Saucy Susan	USA
Shane's Sauce BBQ Sauce	USA
Sue Bee Barbecue Sauce	USA
Sysco	USA
Tabasco	USA
Taxco Hot Sauce	USA
Taxquena Hot Sauce	USA
Telma	*UKN*
Terrapin Ridges Gourmet Line	USA
Texas Best BBQ Sauce	USA
Texas Pit BBQ Sauce	USA
Tiger	USA
Tokusen Marudaizu Shoyu	*JAP*
Tony Roma's Red Hots	USA
Tree Top	USA
Uncle Dave's	USA
Zatarain's	USA

SNACKS

3D's	USA
Air Crisps	USA
Airsweep Potato Chips	USA
Almond Accents	USA
Almond Facts	USA
Anderson Pretzels	USA
Andy Capp's	USA
Archway	*ITL*
Austin	USA
Bachman	USA
Bagel Bites	USA
Baked Flake	USA
Baked Lays	USA
Baked Tostitos	USA
Baken-ets	USA
Bakers Best Pretzels	USA
Bakery Wagon	*ITL*
Bakey Pies	*KOR*
Ballerina	USA
Barnum's Animal Crackers	USA
Barrel O' Fun	USA
Bar-Schips	USA
Bearitos	USA
Beef Jerky	USA
Beef Snack Stix	USA
Beer Nuts	USA
Belin	*FRA*
Bertolli	*UKN*
Better Cheddars	USA
Better Made	USA
Bickel's	USA
Biscos	USA
Blue Luna Chips & Dips	USA
Bluebird (flowers)	USA
Bluebird (Goodman Fielder)	*UK*

Snacks (cont.)

Bocabits	USA	*Colonial*	*ITL*
Bon-Bons	USA	Combos	USA
Bonne Maman	USA	Confetti Almonds	USA
Bonton	USA	Cookie Jar Classic	USA
Borden's Peanuts	USA	Cookie Tree	USA
Boston Better Snacks	USA	Cool Cuts	USA
Bridgford	USA	Corn-tillas	USA
Britos	USA	Cracker Jack	USA
Bugles	USA	Creamy Caramel Rounds	USA
Cabana	USA	Crispin	USA
Cabaret	USA	Crisp-Ums	USA
Café Crème	USA	Crispy O	USA
Cal Almond Peanuts	USA	Crispy Snacks	USA
Cape Cod	USA	Crown Pilot	USA
Captain's Wafers	USA	Crujitos	USA
Carazza	USA	Crunch 'n Munch	USA
Carson's Meat Snacks	USA	Cumberland Ridge	USA
Celebration Almonds	USA	Dad's	USA
Cheddairs	USA	Dan Dee	USA
Cheese Doodles	USA	Deluxe Grahams	USA
Cheese Nips	USA	Demitasse	USA
Cheesestrings	*ITL*	Devil Dogs	USA
Cheetos	USA	*Devonsheer*	*UKN*
Cheez Explosion	USA	Diamond of California	USA
Cheez Whiz	USA	Diamond Walnuts	USA
Cheez-it	USA	Ding Dongs	USA
Chex Mix	USA	Dolly Madison	USA
Chip Thunder	USA	Doo Dads	USA
Chipitos	USA	Doritos	USA
Chips Ahoy!	USA	Drake's	USA
Chips Deluxe	USA	*Drumsticks*	*SWI*
Chip-Stirr Potato Chips	USA	Ducales	USA
Choclait Chips	USA	Dunkaroos	USA
Choco Jet	USA	Durangos	USA
Churrumais	USA	Easy Cheese Spread	USA
Club & Cheddar	USA	Eat-A-Snax	USA
Coffee Break	USA	El Nacho Grande	USA
		Emerald Nuts	USA

Eta	FRA	Golden Wavy	
Evon's Nuts	USA	Potato Chips	USA
Family Favorites	USA	Goldfish	USA
Famous Amos	USA	Gourmet Twists Pretzels	USA
Fandangos	USA	Grandaddy's	USA
Fat Freddie	USA	Grandma Shearers	
Fiddle Faddle	USA	Potato Chips	USA
Firecracker	USA	Grandma Utz's	USA
Fireside	USA	Grandma's Cookies	USA
Fisher Nuts	USA	*Grany Granola Snack*	FRA
Flavor Crisps	USA	Greens+ Energy Bar	USA
Flavor Tree Nuts	USA	Hammons Nuts	USA
Flavor-Kist	USA	Hampton Peanuts	USA
Fleetwood Snacks	JAP	Handi Snacks	USA
Flipz	SWI	Happy Trails Beef Snack	USA
Frito-Lay	USA	Harmony Snacks	USA
Fritos	USA	Harvest Chewy Bars	USA
Fruit by the Foot	USA	Harvest Road Pretzels	USA
Fruit Rippers	CAN	*Heluva Good*	NETH
Fruit Roll-Ups	USA	Hickory Sticks	USA
Fruit Snacks	USA	Ho Hos	USA
Funny Bones	USA	Homestyle Pretzels	USA
Gamesa	USA	Honey Maid	USA
Gary's Peanuts	USA	Hoody's Peanuts	USA
Gentle-Flo Potato Chips	USA	Hostess Snack Cakes	USA
Ginger Snaps	USA	Hot Sticks	USA
Glosette Peanuts		Hot Stuff	USA
& Raisins	USA	Hunter Sausage	USA
Go Snacks	USA	Hunt's Snack Pack	USA
Gold N Chees	USA	Husman Potato Chips	USA
Golden Crisp Potato		Invitation Almonds	USA
Chips	USA	Jack Links Beef Jerky	USA
Golden Flake	USA	*Jacob's*	FRA
Golden Grahams Treats	USA	*Jane Parker*	GER
Golden Ridges		Jax Cheese Twists	USA
Potato Chips	USA	Jays Potato Chips	USA
Golden Wave		Jell-O	USA
Potato Chips	USA	Keebler	USA

Snacks (cont.)

Kettle Chips	*AUS*
Kidzels Pretzels	USA
King Nut	USA
Kings Delicious Nuts	USA
King's Dried Beans	USA
Klein	USA
Klondike Ice Cream Bar	*UKN*
Knott's Berry Farm	USA
Koala Yummies	*JAP*
Konitos	USA
Krinkle Potato Chips	USA
Krunchers! Potato Chips	USA
Kudos Granola Bars	USA
La Restaurante Chips & Salsa	USA
Lance	USA
La-Nut Peanuts	USA
Laura Scudder's	USA
Lay's Fries	USA
Lay's Potato Chips	USA
Leksand	USA
Little Bear Organic	USA
Little Debbie	USA
Lorna Doone	USA
Lozza Mozza	USA
Lunchables	USA
Mac Farms of Hawaii	USA
Maizetos Tortilla Chips	USA
Mallomars	USA
Mani La Especial	USA
Marlene's	USA
Marry Me Bars	USA
Marshmallow Circus Peanuts	USA
Marshmallow Twirls	USA
Martins Potato Chips	USA
Marzetti	USA
Mauna Loa Nuts	USA
Mexicali	USA
Mickey	USA
Milano	USA
Mini Chessmen	USA
Mint'ees Almonds	USA
Miss Vickie's Potato Chips	USA
Mother's Cookies	*ITL*
Mr. Kipling	*UK*
Mr. Twister Soft Pretzels	USA
Mrs. Field's	USA
Mrs. Goodcookie	USA
Munchmates	USA
Munchos Potato Crisps	USA
Munchrights	USA
Murray	USA
Nabisco	USA
Nabs	USA
Nachitos	USA
Nalley's	USA
Nantucket	USA
Napoli Wafers	USA
National Arrowroot	USA
National Pretzels	USA
Natural Lays	USA
Nature Snacks	USA
Nature Valley Granola Bars	USA
Newtons	USA
Nilla Wafers	USA
Nips	*SWI*
Nut Thins	USA
Nutter Butter	USA
Nutzels	USA
Oasis Energy Bars	USA
Oat Bran Sticks	USA
Oberto	USA

Old Fashioned	USA	Rice Krispies Bars	
Olde Tyme Pretzels	USA	& Treats	USA
Oreo	USA	Ridgetts	USA
Otis Spunkmeyer	USA	Ring Dings	USA
Oupost Brand Beef Jerky	USA	Ritz	USA
Party Club	USA	Rold Gold Petzels	USA
Peak Freans	USA	Roman Meal	USA
Peanut Crunch	USA	Roos Pretzels	USA
Pecan Passion	USA	Royal Lunch	USA
Pemmican	USA	Rudolph Pork Rinds	USA
Penrose	USA	Ruffles Potato Chips	USA
Pepperidge Farms	USA	Ruger Wafers	USA
Peterson's Nuts	USA	Rustler's Meat Snacks	USA
Phileas Fogg	*UK*	Salt & Vinegar Rumble	USA
Pinnacle Orchards	USA	*Saltin Noel*	*COL*
Pinwheels	USA	San Saba Pecans	USA
Pirouettes	USA	*San-J*	*JAP*
Pizzarias	USA	Santitas	USA
Planters	USA	Sara Lee	USA
Pop-Ice	USA	Sausalito	USA
Poporon	*JAP*	Screaming Yellow	
Poppycock	USA	Zonkers	USA
Pop-Tarts Mini	USA	*Sesame*	*FIN*
Pop-Up Pastries	USA	SGD Cookie Express	USA
Popweaver	USA	Shapes Of The Cape	USA
Pow Wow	USA	Slim Jim	USA
Powerbar	*SWI*	Smiths Potato Chips	USA
Premium	USA	Smiths Sensations	USA
Pretzel Fillers	USA	Smucker's	USA
Pretzelfils Pretzels	USA	Snack A Jacks	USA
Pringle's	USA	Snackadamias	USA
Puresnax	USA	Snackbarz	USA
Puticrape	*JAP*	Snackin' Fruits	USA
Quaker	USA	Snack-In-A-Box	USA
Quavers Potato Snacks	USA	Snackwell's	USA
Quinlan Pretzels	USA	Snaps	USA
Realtree	USA	Snickers	USA

Snacks (cont.)		Tom's	USA
Snyder of Berlin	USA	Torengos	USA
Snyder's of Hanover	USA	*Tosh*	*COL*
Social Tea	USA	Tostados	USA
Soda Victoria	*PER*	Tostitos	USA
Sonrick's	USA	Town House	USA
Sonric's	USA	*To-You*	*FIN*
Special K Bar	USA	*Tradia*	*INDO*
Spring Glen	USA	Trails Best	USA
Spud Jumpers	USA	Triple Cheese Twisters	USA
Spudz	USA	Triscuit	USA
Stacy's Pita Chips	USA	Trix-Kino	USA
Stella D'Oro	USA	Troyer Farm Potato	
Stormy	USA	Chips	USA
Summer Harvest	USA	Twin Dragon	USA
Sun Chips	USA	Twinkies	USA
Sunbelt	USA	Twist Pretzels	USA
Sun-Maid	USA	Twix	USA
SunNuts (organic)	USA	Uneeda	USA
Sunshine	USA	Urge	USA
Sweetie Pie	USA	UTZ	USA
Tato Skins	USA	*Vachon*	*CAN*
Tayto	*UK*	Value Zone	USA
Teddy Grahams	USA	Van-O-Lunch	USA
Tenny	*INDO*	Veggie Crisps	USA
Terti-Kino	USA	Versalpeel	USA
Texas Style	USA	*Victoria*	*PER*
The Good Dog	USA	Village Fair Cakes	USA
The Good Slice	USA	Vine-Maid	USA
The Kidz	USA	*Vinta*	*CAN*
Thin 'N Right Pretzels	USA	Vitners	USA
Thunder	USA	*Voortman Cookies*	*CAN*
Ticinella Tre Stelle Nuts	*SWI*	Wakefield Peanuts	USA
Tiny Butter Sticks	USA	Walker's	USA
TLC Crackers	USA	*Warfe*	*KOR*
Toasty	USA	Waverly	USA
Toggi	USA	Wavy-Lay's	USA
Tom Scott Nuts	USA	Welch's Fruit Snacks	USA

Wetzels Pretezls	USA	*Funa*	*UKN*
Wheat Thins	USA	Habitant	USA
Wheatsworth	USA	Health Smart	USA
Whims	USA	Healthy Choice	USA
White Smile	*FIN*	Honig	USA
Wild Bill's	USA	*Knorr*	*UKN*
Wotsits	USA	*Lawry's*	*UKN*
Yankee Doodles	USA	Liebig	USA
Yodels	USA	*Lipton Cup-A-Soup*	*UKN*
Young's Sweet Gold	USA	*Maggi*	*SWI*
Yoyo	*INDO*	Mrs. Grass	USA
Yummy Bears	USA	Myers	USA
Zapp's	USA	*Napolina*	*UKN*
Zec	*JAP*	Nile Spice	USA
Zesta	USA	Olde Cape Cod	USA
Zingers	USA	Progresso	USA
Zoneperfect Nutrition		Purity Gourmet	USA
Bars	USA	*Pursoup*	*FRA*
Zoo Zoo	*KOR*	Reames	USA
Zwleback	USA	*San-J*	*JAP*
		Soup At Hand	USA
SOUP		Soup Starter	USA
Anderson's	*FRA*	Supper Bakes	USA
Aunt Patsey's	USA	Swanson	USA
Bean Cuisine	USA	*Telma*	*UKN*
Bistro	USA	Wyler's	USA
Bovril	*UKN*	*Younong*	*JAP*
Campbell's	USA		
CasBah	USA	**SPICES/SEASONINGS**	
Chunky Southwestern	USA	2-Alarm Chili	USA
Colonna	USA	Ac'cent	USA
Country Cup	*UK*	*Aji-Ngon*	*JAP*
Crosse & Blackwell	*SWI*	Alaga Hot Sauce	USA
Cup-A-Soup	*UKN*	Beef Mate Flavoring	USA
Dominique's	USA	Bell's Pie Spicer	USA
Donald Duck	*SWI*	Champions Choice	USA
Donbei	*JAP*	Colonna	USA
Erasco	USA	*Condimix*	*UKN*

Spices/Seasonings (cont.)

Ducros	USA
Fiesta	USA
Flavor-Cap Flavorings & Spices	USA
Fruco	UKN
Funa	UKN
Goodall's	UKN
Jimmi	UKN
Kitano	UKN
Knoor	UK
Knorr	UKN
Lawry's	UKN
Lowerys	USA
Maggi	SWI
Makin Cajun	USA
Masako Seasoning Mixes	JAP
McCormick	USA
Mexicana Joes	USA
Molly McButter	USA
Morton Table Salt	USA
Mrs. Dash	USA
Napolina	UKN
Naturally Cajun	USA
Newmenu	HK
Old Plantation	USA
Peloponnese	USA
Peppermill Grind Pepper	USA
Primerba	UKN
Produce Products	SWI
Rajah Indian	FRA
Red Devil	USA
Ros Dee Seasonings	JAP
Salt Sense	USA
Saute Sensations	USA
Sazon	JAP
Schwartz	USA

Sensient	USA
Six Gun Taco Mixin's	USA
Spice Hunter	USA
Spice Islands	UK
Stange	USA
Stock-Aid	USA
Sugar Cure	USA
Swedish Kitchen	USA
Vegit	USA
Wagners	USA
Weidudu	JAP
Yumyum	JAP

SUGAR

Arometti	GER
Big Chief	USA
C & H	USA
Country Cane	USA
Crystal	USA
Daddy	FRA
Diamond Crystal	USA
Dixie Crystals	USA
Domino	USA
Flosweet	USA
HC&S	USA
Holly	USA
Imperial	USA
Jack Frost	USA
Maui Brand Raw Sugar	USA
Pillsbury	USA
Pioneer	USA
Plantation White	USA
Premium Turbinado	USA
Savannah Gold	USA
Spreckels	USA
Western Sugar	UK

SYRUP

Alaga	USA
Aunt Jemima	USA
Bee Hive	*UKN*
Brer Rabbit Molasses	USA
Cheryl Lyn	USA
Clements	USA
Country Kitchen	USA
Crown Brand	*UKN*
Cusenier	*FRA*
Dolce	USA
Garden Club	USA
Gingham Band	USA
Golden Griddle	*UKN*
Hungry Jack	USA
Karo	*UKN*
Knott's Berry Farm	USA
Log Cabin	USA
Luau	USA
Maple Grove Farms	USA
Mrs. Butterworth's	USA
Nalley's	USA
Old Tyme	*UKN*

Passion	USA
Plow Boy	USA
Spontin	*BGM*
Sweetmeadow Farms	USA
Tastee	USA
Vermont Maid	USA
Wotsits	USA
Yellow Label	USA
Walden Farms	USA

TUNA

America's Choice	*GER*
Blue Bay	*CAN*
Bumble Bee	*CAN*
Celebrity	USA
Chicken of the Sea	*THAI*
Clover Leaf	*CAN*
Deep Blue	USA
Greenseas	USA
Prime Catch	USA
Progresso	USA
Star-Kist	USA

Chapter 5

Home & Office Products

(American owned in bold / *Foreign owned in italic*)

AIR FRESHENERS

Airwick	*UK*
Ambi-Pur	USA
Avon	USA
Banish	USA
Baskets	USA
Bayberry	USA
Berry Burst	USA
Bissell	USA
Cherry-O	USA
Cor-Aire	USA
Cormatic Aire	USA
Elite	USA
Fresh Scents	USA
Full Bloom	USA
Glade	USA
Happy Malodor	USA
Hide-A-Disc	USA
Hillyard	USA
Magic Lantern	USA
Parry's	USA
Renuzit	*GER*
Round-The-Clock	USA

BABY PRODUCTS/ EQUIPMENT

Baby Orajel	USA
Baby's First Year	*UK*
Baby's Own	*UK*
Century Baby Strollers	USA
Century Car Seat	USA
Cosco Carseat	*CAN*
Enesco	USA
Evenflo	USA
Famar	USA
Fisher-Price Carseat	USA
Graco Snugride	USA
Johnson's Baby Products	USA

Musical Toilette Plus	*CAN*
Next Step Carseat	USA
Nexus Carseat	USA
OshKosh B'Gosh	USA
Ovation Car Seat	USA
Petit Cheri	USA
Portabout Car Seat	USA
TLC Car Seat	*CAN*

BAKEWARE/COOKWARE

All-Clad	*UK*
Amberware	USA
Bakers Secret	USA
Calphalon	USA
Canon	*JAP*
Chefco	USA
Chef's Ware	USA
Corning	USA
Cuisinart	USA
Dansk	USA
Ekco	USA
Farberware	USA
KitchenAid	USA
Magnalite	USA
Mirro	USA
NordicWare	USA
Oven Essentials	USA
Pampered Chef	USA
Pyrex	USA
Regal Ware	USA
Revere	USA
Saladmaster	USA
Smartvent	USA
Tefal	*FRA*
T-Fal	*FRA*
Tornado	USA
Xylan	USA
Zipseal	USA

CHAIN SAWS

Craftsman	**USA**
Husqvarna	*SWE*
Poulan	*SWE*
Stihl	*GER*

CUTLERY/SILVERWARE

Air Ranger Hunting	
Knives	*FIN*
Anastasia	**USA**
Apollo	**USA**
Bantum	**USA**
Beau Manor	**USA**
Becker Necker	**USA**
Bowie Knife	**USA**
Brute Knife	**USA**
Buck Knives	**USA**
Bucklite	**USA**
Chefco	**USA**
Chicago	**USA**
Classicware	**USA**
Combat Bowie	**USA**
Combat Knife	**USA**
Combat Utility	**USA**
Cometware	**USA**
Connoisseur	**USA**
Corporal Knife	**USA**
Cougar Kinfe	**USA**
Crewman Knife	**USA**
Cutco	**USA**
Defender Damascus	
Knife	**USA**
Dexter	**USA**
Dexter/Russell	**USA**
Ducks Unlimited	**USA**
Duke	**USA**
Dura Edge	**USA**
Edge2X	**USA**

Extremeops	**USA**
Farberware	**USA**
Folding Hunter	**USA**
Gerber	*FIN*
Ginsu	**USA**
Gorham	**USA**
Grosvenor	*AUS*
Heirloom	**USA**
Hermes	*FRA*
Hoffritz	**USA**
Hunter's Pal	**USA**
Imperial Cutlery	**USA**
Integral Knife	**USA**
Laser	*AUS*
Lev-R-Lok	**USA**
Lightning HTA	**USA**
Masterpiece	**USA**
Maxx Stiletto	**USA**
Metropolitan	**USA**
Mini Buck	**USA**
Moderna	**USA**
Montana	*FIN*
Mundial	*BZL*
Odyssey	**USA**
Old Timer	**USA**
Oneida	**USA**
Pilot Knife	**USA**
Poppy	**USA**
Professional's	**USA**
Ranger	**USA**
Reflection	**USA**
Regent Sheffield	*AUS*
Rodd	*AUS*
Rogers	**USA**
Rosenthal	*IRE*
Russell	**USA**
Russell Green River	**USA**
Russell International	**USA**

Sabatier	*AUS*	**Whitehunter**	**USA**
Saint Andrea	**USA**	**Wildtoter**	**USA**
Sani Safe	**USA**	*Wiltshire*	*AUS*
Scout	**USA**	**Yello-Jacket**	**USA**
Sergeant	**USA**	**Zipper**	**USA**
Silver Knights	*FIN*		
Silver Sword	**USA**		
Silver Trident	*FIN*		

DISHWASHING LIQUIDS & DETERGENTS

Silverlion Micarta	**USA**	*All*	*UKN*
Six Star	**USA**	**American Fare**	**USA**
Skinmaster	**USA**	*America's Choice*	*GER*
Skinner	**USA**	**Amway**	**USA**
Sofgrip	**USA**	**Ayudin**	**USA**
Solstice	*FIN*	**Cascade**	**USA**
Sportec	**USA**	**Dawn**	**USA**
Squire	**USA**	**Dermassage**	**USA**
Stanley Roberts	**USA**	**Det-O-Jet**	**USA**
Staysharp	*AUS*	*Dial*	*GER*
Stockman	**USA**	*Dove*	*UKN*
Strachan	*AUS*	*Electrasol*	*UK*
Strider	**USA**	**Ivory Liquid**	**USA**
Sushi	**USA**	*Jet Dry*	*UK*
Tactool	**USA**	**Joy**	**USA**
Tail-Gater	**USA**	*Lux*	*UKN*
Thunder	**USA**	**Palmolive**	**USA**
Thuya	**USA**	*Sunlight*	*UKN*
Towle Silversmiths	**USA**	**Yes**	**USA**
Town Craft Stainless	**USA**		
Trail Guide	**USA**		

FURNITURE

Trendy	*FIN*	*Ability*	*CAN*
Tristar	**USA**	**Academy**	**USA**
Ulti-Mate	**USA**	**Acanthus**	**USA**
Velcro	**USA**	**Acapulco**	**USA**
Victorinox	*SWI*	**Accent Oak**	**USA**
Viking & Nordsman	**USA**	**Accolade**	**USA**
Waidbesteck	**USA**	*Adshel*	*AUS*
Waidblatt	**USA**	**Aliesa Designer Chairs**	**USA**
Western Cutlery	**USA**	**Alloya (office)**	**USA**

Furniture (cont.)

American Drew	USA	Congress	USA
American Legacy	USA	Contempra	USA
American of Martinsville	USA	Drexel	USA
American Seating	USA	Drexel Heritage	USA
Ameriwood	*CAN*	Drexel Studio	USA
Anguilla	USA	Falcon	USA
Antigo	USA	Founders	USA
Anywhere Chair (office)	USA	Gardenella	USA
Arabesque	USA	Good Bedroom	USA
Aria	USA	Harden	USA
Arise	USA	Hearthside (outdoor)	USA
Artec (office)	USA	Henredon	USA
Aura	USA	Heritage	USA
Avenir	USA	Herman Miller (office)	USA
Avenue	*GER*	Hickory Chair	USA
Avery	USA	International	USA
Avon	USA	Jennifer Convertibles	USA
Azteca	USA	Karges by Hand	USA
Baker	USA	Karpen	USA
Bassett	USA	Kindel	USA
Bedbase	USA	Kinetics	USA
Berkshire	USA	Kroehler	USA
Bigham	USA	Lane	USA
Bombay	USA	La-Z-Boy	USA
Botany Bay	USA	Lee Jofa	USA
Brayton (office)	USA	Lexington	USA
Brentwood	USA	Marlo	USA
Bristol	USA	Mastercraft	USA
Broyhill	USA	Matilda Bay	USA
Bush (office)	USA	Metropolitan	USA
Calliope	USA	Mity-Lite	USA
ChaiseLounger	USA	Montego Bay	USA
Chesterfield	USA	Mulberry	USA
Cocktail Height	USA	*Natuzzi*	*ITL*
Collage	USA	Nautical	USA
Collegian	USA	NCI	USA
Colony Lounge	USA	O'Sullivan (office)	USA
		Pennsylvania House	USA

Peters-Revington	USA	*Seatwise (office)*	*GER*
Relay	USA	**Secant (office)**	USA
Rhodes	USA	**Sedan**	USA
Salone	USA	**Sedona**	USA
Salterini (outdoor)	USA	**Segment (office)**	USA
Salzburg	USA	**Segments**	USA
Sammy	USA	**Segno**	USA
Samuel	*ITL*	**Sem**	USA
San Antonio	USA	**Sena**	USA
San Fran	*CAN*	**Senator**	USA
San Franciscan	USA	**Sensor (office)**	USA
San Francisco	*CAN*	**Separates**	USA
San Martino	USA	**Sequence**	USA
Sand	*UK*	**Serenade**	USA
Sand Hill	USA	**Serene (office)**	USA
Sandpiper	USA	**Serenissima**	USA
Sandra	USA	**Serenissimo**	USA
Sannibel	USA	**Serenity**	USA
Santa Ana	USA	*Seriana*	*UK*
Sante Fe	USA	**Series K**	USA
Sanzeno	USA	**Serpentine**	USA
Sapporo	USA	**Session (office)**	USA
Sara	USA	**Seville**	USA
Sarah	USA	**Shadowline**	USA
Sarasota	USA	**Shaker**	USA
Sardinia	USA	**Shana**	USA
Sauder (office)	USA	**Shannon**	USA
Savanna	USA	*Shape (office)*	*GER*
Savannah Settee	USA	**Shawe**	USA
Savera	*CAN*	**Sheffield**	USA
Savoy	USA	**Shelby**	USA
Scamps	USA	**Shelby Williams**	USA
Scarborough	USA	**Sheraton**	USA
Scarlette	USA	**Sherbrooke**	USA
Sciangai	USA	*Shermag*	*CAN*
Scottsdale	USA	*Sherwood*	*UK*
Scroll	USA	**Shoreline**	USA
Seating in Motion	USA	**Sidewalk (office)**	USA

Furniture (cont.)			
Sierra	USA	*Soda*	*CAN*
Sierra Towers	USA	*Sofia*	*CAN*
Sieste (office)	USA	Soho	USA
Sigma	USA	Solana	USA
Sigmund	USA	Solano	USA
Signature	USA	Solarbronze	USA
Silhouette	USA	Soldier	USA
Silk Road	USA	*Solitar*	*CAN*
Silva	USA	Solon	USA
Silver (office)	USA	Solstice	USA
Simple Pleasures	USA	Solutions	USA
Simplicity	USA	Somerset	USA
Simplicity II (office)	USA	Somnar	USA
Simply Yours	USA	Sonata (office)	USA
Sinclair Lounge Chairs	USA	Sonic	USA
Singolo	USA	Sonnet	USA
Sipario	USA	Sonoma	USA
Sistema	USA	Sonora	USA
Skinny	USA	Sonrisa	USA
Skye	USA	Sophia	USA
Slate	USA	Sophisticate	USA
Slater	USA	*Sophy*	*CAN*
Sleep Haven	USA	Soroya	USA
Sleeper Chair	USA	Sotheby	USA
Sleepover	USA	Sourcebook	USA
Sleepy	USA	South Beach	USA
Sleigh	USA	South Hampton	USA
Slim	USA	South Seas	USA
Slipper Chairs	USA	Southhampton	USA
Sloane Square	USA	Sovereign	USA
Smart Seating (office)	USA	Space	USA
Smart Tables (office)	USA	Spacesaver	USA
Smartworks	USA	Sparrow	USA
Smoke (office)	USA	Spec	USA
Snap Clip	USA	*Speciality Line (office)*	*GER*
Snodgrass (office)	USA	Spectra	USA
Society Row	USA	Speedy (office)	USA
		Spica	USA

Spinnaker	USA	Stiletto (office)	USA
Spinz (office)	USA	Stockholm	USA
Spirit Millennium	USA	Stockton	USA
Splash	USA	Stonington	USA
Spokane	USA	*Stora*	*UK*
Springboard (office)	USA	Storefront	USA
Springfield	USA	Storm	USA
St. Andrews	USA	Stow Davis	USA
St. Charles	USA	Stowe	USA
St. Clair (office)	USA	Stradella	USA
St. Etienne	USA	Stratford	USA
St. Germain	USA	Stratos	USA
St. James	USA	*Stressless*	*NOR*
St. Martin	USA	Structure	USA
St. Pierre	USA	Stuart	USA
Stackaways (office)	USA	Stuart Clark	USA
Stadium Lounge Chairs	USA	Studimo	USA
Stafford	USA	Studio	USA
Standard	USA	Styline	USA
Stanton Hall	USA	*Suad*	*ITL*
Stanton-Cooper	USA	Suffolk	USA
Stanwood	USA	Sumara	USA
Star	USA	Summerhaven	USA
Starlight	USA	Summerton	USA
Sta-Soft	USA	Summit	USA
Station Master (office)	USA	Sun Valley	USA
Stature	USA	Sundance	USA
Status	USA	Super Erecta	USA
Steamer	USA	Surfside	USA
Steelcase (office)	USA	Surprise (office)	USA
Stefano	USA	Sussex	USA
Stefano Lounge	USA	Sutton	USA
Stephanie Odegard		Suzanne	USA
Collection	USA	*Svane*	*NETH*
Stepmaster	USA	*Swarthmore*	*CAN*
Sterling	USA	Swathmore (office)	USA
Stevenson	USA	Sway	USA
Stickley	USA	Swedish Home	USA

Furniture (cont.)		Taupe	USA
Sweetheart	USA	Taurus	USA
Switch (office)	USA	Tea Cup	USA
Swivel	USA	Teamwork (office)	USA
Sydney	USA	Teardrop	USA
Syllabus (office)	USA	Technique (office)	USA
Symphony	USA	Techno	USA
Syncro (office)	*GER*	Tecrete (office)	USA
Synopsis	*CAN*	Tecta	USA
Syntop (office)	USA	Teen Bungalow	USA
Syroco	*FIN*	*Teknion*	*CAN*
Systembuild	*CAN*	Tekno	USA
Systemseating	USA	*Telly*	*CAN*
Systemwall	USA	Temba	USA
Tactics	USA	Temecula	USA
Taftville (office)	USA	Tempe	USA
Tag	USA	Template (office)	USA
Tahira	*ITL*	Tempo	USA
Tahoe	USA	Tempus	USA
Taiqa	*CAN*	Tennis Queen	USA
Take Five	USA	*Teo (office)*	*GER*
Taliesin	USA	Terazzo (office)	USA
Talisman	USA	Tercero (office)	USA
Talk	USA	Teres	USA
Tally	USA	Terrace Place	USA
Talon	USA	Terrain	USA
Tammy	*CAN*	Terre	USA
Tango	USA	Teso (office)	USA
Tanis	USA	*Tessa*	*CAN*
Tankini	USA	*Tex*	*ITL*
Tanner	USA	Texacraft	USA
Tasha	USA	Texwood Furniture	USA
Task	USA	The Casa Collection	USA
Tassel	USA	The Shores (outdoor)	USA
Tate Access Floors	USA	The Stash	USA
Tateflex	USA	Thebes	USA
Tato And Tatino	USA	Theo	USA
Tatone	USA	Theorem (office)	USA

Think (office)	USA	*Tos (office)*	*CAN*
Thistle	USA	Toscana	USA
Thomas	USA	Toscana Bureau	USA
Thomas Day	USA	Touchdown (office)	USA
Thomasville	USA	Touchmotion	USA
Thonet	USA	Town & Country	USA
Thoreau	USA	*Towne Square*	
Thornton	USA	*Rocking Chair*	*CAN*
Thurston	USA	Townhouse	USA
Tidewater	USA	Townsend	USA
Tiempo (office)	USA	Trade Street	USA
Tiffany	USA	Tradewinds	USA
Tiger Maple	USA	Traditional	USA
Tilt Swivel	USA	Traditions Made Modern	USA
Timberform	USA	Traffix	USA
Timberlake	USA	Train (office)	USA
Timberlane	USA	Tranquility	USA
Timeless	USA	*Transit (office)*	*CAN*
Timeless Retreat	USA	Transitions	USA
Timothy	*CAN*	Translation	USA
Tiper (office)	USA	Traveler's Retreat	USA
Tivoli	USA	Traverse	USA
Tocotta	USA	Travertine	USA
Todo (office)	USA	Travo	USA
Toga	USA	Trax	USA
Tokyo Pop	USA	Trebbiano	USA
Tomato	USA	Trek	USA
Tomlinson/Erwin-		Trellis	USA
Lambeth	USA	Tremont	USA
Tommy	*CAN*	Trendmaster	USA
Tonga (office)	USA	Trendwall	USA
Topaz (office)	USA	Trestle	USA
Topo (office)	USA	Trevor	USA
Tori	USA	Triad	USA
Torina	USA	Tribeca	USA
Toronto	*CAN*	Tricia	USA
Torre	USA	Trigger	USA
Torsion	USA	Trinidad	USA

Furniture (cont.)

Trio Plus (office)	USA	Uni-Koat	USA
Tripoli	USA	Union Square	USA
Triton	USA	Unison (office)	USA
Trophy (office)	USA	Unity (office)	USA
Tropic Craft	USA	Universal	USA
Tropi-Kai	USA	Uno	USA
Truman	USA	Upholstery	USA
Truro	*UK*	Upstart (office)	USA
Trutype Americana	USA	Uptown	USA
TR-View	USA	UR GR8	USA
Tube-It	USA	Urban Comfort	USA
Tucker	USA	Urban Jazz	USA
Tucson	USA	Urbano	USA
Tuff	USA	Usoa	USA
Tuffy	USA	Utica	USA
Tuffyland Products	USA	Utility	USA
Tulip	USA	Vail Conversation	USA
Turkey Trot (office)	*GER*	*Valencia*	*UK*
Turnbury	USA	Valet (office)	USA
Turnstone	USA	Valhalla	USA
Tusk	USA	Valido (office)	USA
Tux	*CAN*	Value Stacker	USA
Tuxedo	USA	Vancouver	USA
Twain	USA	Vanese	USA
Twiggy	USA	Vanessa	USA
Twilight	USA	Vanguard (office)	USA
Twin	USA	Vanity	USA
Twist	USA	Vantage	USA
Twofour Series	USA	Varitask	USA
Tympani	USA	*Vasari*	*CAN*
Tyndall	USA	Vaughn Bassett	USA
Ultimate	*UK*	Vecta	USA
Ultimo	USA	Vecta (office)	USA
Ultrastack	USA	Vegas	USA
Umbria	*CAN*	Vendome Lounge Chairs	USA
Unanimous	USA	Veneto	USA
Uniframe	USA	Venice	USA
		Venicia	USA

Ventaglio	USA	Walden Inn	USA
Ventana	USA	Walk-And-Talk (office)	USA
Veracruz	USA	Wallaby (office)	USA
Verandah	USA	Wallaway	USA
Vercelli	USA	Walls In Motion	USA
Verona	USA	Wallsaver	USA
Veronique	USA	Wallstreet (office)	USA
Versa	USA	*Wally*	*CAN*
Versailles	USA	Walpole	USA
Verso	USA	Waltham	USA
Vertebra	USA	Waltham (office)	USA
Vesa	USA	Warren	USA
Vesuna	*CAN*	Washington	USA
Vesuvius	USA	Washington Valley	USA
Vicenza	USA	Watch Hill	USA
Victor	USA	Waterfall	USA
Victorian	USA	Water's Edge	USA
Videne (office)	USA	Watersaver	USA
Viewpoints	USA	Wave	USA
Vigo	*UK*	Waverly	USA
Villa	USA	Waverly Hall	USA
Villa Antica	USA	Waveworks	USA
Villa Gallia	USA	Weathermaster	
Villager	USA	(outdoor)	USA
Vineyard	USA	Web Shelving (office)	USA
Vintage	USA	Wellsley	USA
Vintage Elway	USA	Wenger Eibelino	USA
Virginia	USA	Wenlock	USA
Virtuoso	USA	Wentworth	USA
Visions	USA	Werndl (office)	USA
Vivi	USA	*Wessex*	*UK*
Volterra	*CAN*	West	USA
Vostra	USA	West Elm	USA
Vulcano	USA	West Indies	USA
Wabash Valley	USA	Westbrook	USA
Wainwright	USA	Westlake (office)	USA
Wakeby	USA	Weston	USA
Walden (office)	USA	Westport Armless	USA

Furniture (cont.)

Westwood	UK	*Wordsworth*	UK
Whartin	USA	*Work*	CAN
Wheaton	USA	**Work Manager (office)**	USA
Whitehall	USA	**Workmaster (office)**	USA
Whitfield	USA	**Works**	USA
Whitley	USA	**Works Desk**	USA
Whitman	USA	**Workzone**	USA
Whitmore	USA	**Woven**	USA
Whitney	USA	**Wow**	USA
Widdicomb	USA	*Wyndmoor*	CAN
Wiley	USA	**Wynwood**	USA
Wilkhahn (office)	USA	**Yale**	USA
William Alan	USA	**Yardley**	USA
Williamsburg	USA	**Yield House**	USA
Williamsport	USA	**York**	USA
Williams-Sonoma Home	USA	**Young American**	
Willow	USA	**by Stanley**	USA
Willow Creek (office)	CAN	**Youth Airplane**	USA
Wilmington	USA	**Youth Petite**	USA
Wilshire	USA	**Zane**	USA
Windermere	USA	**Zanzibar**	USA
Windham	USA	**Zaragoza**	USA
Windsor	USA	**Zen**	USA
Windy	USA	**Zena**	USA
Wing	USA	**Zenith Lounge Chairs**	USA
Winston	USA	*Zennah*	UK
Winterhaven	USA	**Zeno**	USA
Winthrop	USA	**Zero**	USA
Wireworks	USA	**Zeta**	USA
Wish	USA	**Zetro**	USA
Woodard	USA	**Zig Zag**	USA
Woodbury	USA	*Zione*	UK
Woodford	USA	**Zodiac**	USA
Woodley	USA	**Zoe**	USA
Woodmark	USA	*Zone*	CAN
Woodsmiths	USA	**Zoom Derby (office)**	USA
Woodstock	USA	**Zoom Victory (office)**	USA
		Zuma	USA

Zumafrd	USA	*Bayclin*	*GER*
Zuniga	USA	Betco Express	USA
Zylo	USA	Betcobest	USA
		Bio-Bowl	USA

FURNITURE POLISH

Admire	USA	Bissell One Step	USA
Behold	USA	Borax	USA
Endust	USA	Bowl Cleanse	USA
Favor	USA	Bowl Fresh	USA
Gleem	USA	Bowl Patrol	USA
Highlight	USA	Breath-O-Pine	USA
Jubilee	USA	*Bref*	*GER*
Lustre-Mist	USA	Brillo Pads	USA
Mansion	*UK*	Brimax	USA
Pledge	USA	Brite Floor Polish	USA
		Brown Out Carpet Care	USA
		Capture	USA

GARAGE DOOR OPENERS

Chamberlain	USA	Carpet Science	USA
Craftsman	USA	CBC Plus Bowl Cleaner	USA
Genie	*JAP*	Cidex Opa Solution	USA
Liftmaster	USA	Clean Release	USA
		Clear Mint Disinfectant	USA
		Clear Pine Disinfectant	USA

HOUSEHOLD CLEANERS

A World of Difference	USA	Clear Window Cleaner	USA
Accelerate	USA	Clorox	USA
American Fare		CLR	USA
Disinfectant	USA	Comet	USA
Amway	USA	Crystal Glass Cleaner	USA
Anachlor Disinfectant	USA	C-Thru	USA
Aqua Bowl	USA	*Decap Four*	*GER*
Arela	USA	*Destop*	*UK*
Arm & Hammer	USA	*Domestos*	*UKN*
Armstrong Floor		Drano	USA
Cleaner	USA	Dustall	USA
Assurance	USA	*Easy-Off*	*UK*
Atlas	USA	Ever Fresh	USA
Austin	USA	Fantastik	USA
Ayudin	USA	First Mate	USA
		Fluss	USA

Household Cleaners (cont.)		New Bowl	USA
Formula 409	USA	Nilosol	USA
Germ Warfare		Nilotex Stain Remover	USA
Disinfectant	USA	Noil Floor Care	USA
Germ-X Disinfectant		*O-Cedar*	*GER*
Spray	USA	O-Cel-O	USA
Glade	USA	Olde Master	USA
Glare	USA	Once Over	USA
Glass Express	USA	One Plus Floor Polish	USA
Glass Pro	USA	One Step	USA
Glassex	*UK*	Orange All	USA
Glo-Coat Floor Polish	USA	Orange Clean	USA
Glory Rug Cleaner	USA	Para-Gone	USA
Goddard's Polish	USA	Perfi-Clean	USA
Gold Label Hand Cleaner	USA	Perma Brite	USA
Gold N Shine	USA	Pine-Sol	USA
Goop	USA	Pinex	USA
Gum-Go	USA	Pinexo	USA
Handi-Wipes	USA	Pinoluz	USA
Hi-Phene Disinfectant	USA	Pledge	USA
Keeps Bowl Cleaner	USA	Point After Floor Care	USA
Kimberly-Clark	USA	Polaris Ultra Floor Care	USA
Klean 'N Shine	USA	Power Bowl Cleaner	USA
Klear Floor Polish	USA	Power Green	USA
Kleen Guard	USA	Pre-Pare Carpet Care	USA
Like New	USA	Pretty Polly	USA
Lime-A-Way	USA	PT-4 Drain Cleaner	USA
Liquid S	USA	Raise Rug Shampoo	USA
Liquid Swabby	USA	Rapidyne	USA
Liquinox	USA	Renuzit	USA
Lysol	*UK*	Room Sense	USA
Magic Bath	USA	Roto-Mop	USA
Mistolin	USA	Rug Aroma Carpet	
Mox	USA	Freshener	USA
Mr. Clean	USA	Rug Doctor	USA
Mr. Muscle Oven Cleaner	USA	S. C. Johnson	USA
Murphy's Oil Soap	USA	*S.O.S.*	*GER*
Neat Sweep	USA	Sani-Dex	USA

Sani-Flush	UK	**White Sun**	USA
Sani-Hands	USA	**Winda Shine**	USA
Scrub Free	USA	**Windex**	USA
Scrub 'N' Toss	USA	**Windo-Clean**	USA
Scrubbing Bubbles	USA	**Window Wash**	USA
Sharpshooter	USA	**Wipe Away**	USA
Sheer Magic	USA	**X-14**	USA
Shout	USA	*Zout*	GER
Shower Patrol	USA		
Shower Shine	USA	**INSECT REPELLENT/**	
Sidol	GER	**INSECTICIDES**	
Snobol	USA	**Aloe Up**	USA
Soft Scrub	GER	**Ambush**	USA
Sparkle	USA	**Amdro**	USA
Spectrum	USA	*Annihilator*	GER
Spinsweep	CHN	**Ant Rid**	USA
Spray 'N Sparkle	USA	**Applaud**	USA
Spray Nine	USA	*Arena*	JAP
Stain Begone	USA	**Asana**	USA
Stain Eraser	USA	*Atabron*	JAP
Strip And Shine	USA	*Autan*	GER
Strip Away	USA	**Avaunt**	USA
Super-Croix	GER	**Aztec**	USA
Swiffer	USA	**Banish**	USA
Tempo	USA	*Baygon*	GER
Tile Action	USA	**Black Flag**	USA
Tile Brite	USA	*Bolstar*	GER
Tilex Fresh Shower	USA	**Buzz Off**	USA
Tip-Off	USA	**Capture**	USA
Toilet Duck	USA	**Catch**	USA
Top Clean	USA	**Combat**	USA
Top Crest	USA	**Curfew**	USA
Top Mop	USA	**Cutter**	USA
Twenty Mule Team Borax	GER	**Deep Woods OFF!**	USA
Twist Assist Mop	USA	**Dibrom**	USA
Vanish	USA	**Duratrol**	USA
Vertiklean Mop	USA	**Dursban**	USA
Wash'N Go	USA	**Empire**	USA

Insect Repellent/Insecticides (cont.)

Enda-Bug	USA
Evergreen	USA
Exponent	USA
Fortress	USA
Goodknight	USA
Homekeeper	USA
Hopperguard	USA
Hot Shot	USA
Insectape	USA
Intruder	USA
Lorsban	USA
Lure-N'-Kill	USA
Monitor	USA
Mosquito Shield	USA
Mustang Max	USA
MVP	USA
Natrapel	USA
OFF!	USA
Oil-N-Wick	USA
Ortho	USA
Padan	USA
Phosdrin	USA
Point-Guard	USA
Polo	USA
Predator	USA
Raid	USA
Raid Max	USA
Raid Roach Controller	USA
Rescue	USA
Ridsect	USA
Roach	USA
SBP	USA
Sea-Green	USA
Selton	USA
Shotgun	USA
Skintastic	USA
Sta-Home	USA
Steward	USA
Supracide	SWI
Suprathion	ISR
Surround	USA
Suscon Blue	AUS
Talstar	USA
Terminex	USA
Termite Kill III Concentrate	USA
Thiodan	USA
Thionex	ISR
Tiny Whacker	USA
Tracer	USA
Ultrathon	USA
Vendex	USA
Voltage	JAP
Vydate	USA
Wasp & Hornet Killer Plus	USA
Weed Beater	USA
Xmate	USA

LAUNDRY PRODUCTS

Ace Bleach	USA
Ajax	USA
All	UKN
Amway	USA
Aqua Soft	USA
Ariel	USA
Arm & Hammer	USA
Attack	JAP
Ayudin Bleach	USA
Big Value	USA
Biotex	USA
Biz	USA
Blanquita Bleach	USA

Bold	USA	*Spray 'N Wash*	*UK*
Bounce	USA	**Suavitel**	USA
Brillo	USA	**Sunny Sol Bleach**	USA
Cheer	USA	**Super Globo Bleach**	USA
Cling Free	*UK*	*Surf*	*UKN*
Clorisol Bleach	USA	**Tide**	USA
Clorox	USA	*Twenty Mule Team Borax*	*GER*
Colour More Bleach	USA	*Vanish*	*UK*
Dash	USA	**Laundry Products**	USA
Dosia	*UK*	*Wisk*	*UKN*
Downy	USA	*Woolite*	*UK*
Dreft	USA	**Xtra**	USA
Dryel	USA	**Yuhanrox Bleach**	USA
Dynamo	USA	*Zout Stain Remover*	*GER*
Easy-On Spray Starch	*UK*		
Enzimax	USA	**LAWN & GARDEN**	
Era	USA	**Amend**	USA
Final Touch	*UKN*	**American Made**	USA
Flor	*UK*	**Asef**	USA
Gain	USA	**Assault Weed Killer**	USA
Gemini	USA	**Barefoot**	USA
Ivory	USA	*Bargain Garden*	*NOR*
Ivory Snow	USA	**Black Beauty**	USA
Limpido Bleach	USA	**Bob-Cat**	USA
Miracle White	USA	**Bonus S Weed & Feed**	USA
Niagara	*UKN*	**Brigss & Stratton**	USA
Old Blue	USA	**Brush-B-Gone**	USA
Orange Miracle	USA	**Celaflor**	USA
Oxydol	USA	**ChemLawn**	USA
Parozone Bleach	*UK*	**Deep Green**	USA
Pure Power	USA	**Eagle Garden Tools**	USA
Purex	*GER*	**Earthgro**	USA
Radion	*UKN*	**Emerald Edge**	USA
Rinso	*UKN*	*Enviroworks*	*FIN*
Sello Rojo Bleach	USA	**Evergreen**	USA
Shout	USA	*Fiskars*	*FIN*
Snuggle	*UKN*	**Flowtron**	USA
Solid Stainaway Bleach	USA	*Flymo*	*SWE*

Lawn & Garden (cont.)

Garden Claw	USA	Rubbermaid	USA
Garden Devils	*FIN*	Scottkote	USA
Garden Pride	USA	Scotts	USA
Garden Weasel	USA	Sea Island	USA
Hedge Hog	USA	Serrano	USA
Hefty	USA	Shake 'N Feed	USA
Husqvarna	*SWE*	Shamrock	USA
Ingersoll	*GER*	Sheridan	USA
Insley Backhoes	USA	Sierra	USA
Jiffy-7	*NOR*	Sierrablen	USA
Jiffy-Mix	*NOR*	Smith & Hawken	USA
Jiffy-Pots	*NOR*	Sof 'N-Soil	USA
Jiffy-Strips	*NOR*	*So-Green*	*CAN*
Jobe's	USA	*Solartex*	*FIN*
KB	USA	Spectracide	USA
Killex	USA	Sport-Zooms	USA
Lawn Doctor	USA	Spring Lawns Alive!	USA
Lebanonturf	USA	St. Croix	USA
Levington	USA	Sta-Green	USA
Miracle-Gro	USA	Stow N Go	USA
Moisture Master	*FIN*	Substral	USA
NK	USA	Swan Garden Hose	USA
Ortho	USA	Terrace	USA
Parker 1/2 Runner	USA	Thatchmaster	USA
Pathclear	USA	*Thrive*	*AUS*
Pax Fertilizer	USA	Tree Gard	USA
Peters	USA	Trinidad	USA
Plant Hart's Seeds	USA	True Temper	USA
Poly-S	USA	Trugreen	USA
Preen 'N Green	USA	Tuff-Sak	USA
Rally	*SWE*	Turf Alive!	USA
Razor-Back Garden		Unionpro	USA
Tools	USA	Uniontools	USA
Regency	USA	Vanderbilt	USA
Ross	USA	Verandah	USA
Roundup	USA	*Victa*	*AUS*
Rout	USA	*Victorian Garden*	*CAN*
		Villano	USA

Wallace Garden Tools	FIN	**John Deere**	USA
Watercolors Garden		*Kubota*	JAP
Hose	USA	**Lawn-Boy**	USA
Waterwise	AUS	**MTD**	USA
Waterworks Garden		*Murray*	CAN
Hose	USA	**Mustang Tractor**	USA
Weed Popper	USA	*Poulan*	SWE
Weed-B-Gon	USA	*Rally*	SWE
Weedol	USA	**Sears Craftsman**	USA
Werga	FIN	**Simplicity**	USA
West Indies	USA	**Snapper**	USA
White Outdoor	USA	**Tiger**	USA
Wilson	CAN	**Toro**	USA
Xenoy	JAP	**Troy-Bilt**	USA
Yard 'N Garden	USA	**Vulcan**	USA
Yardmate	CAN	*Weed Eater*	SWE
Yardworks	CAN	**Wheel Horse**	USA
Yates	AUS	**Yard Machines**	USA
Yazoo/Kees	SWE		
Zero	AUS		
Zooms	USA	**MAGAZINES**	
		4-Wheel & Off Road	USA
		4X4	USA
LAWN MOWERS		**5.0 Mustangs &**	
Aircap	USA	**Super Fords**	USA
American Lawn	USA	**Allure**	USA
Ariens	USA	**Altitude**	USA
ATZ	USA	**Amateur Gardening**	USA
Black & Decker	USA	**Amateur Photographer**	USA
Bolens	USA	**Amazing Stories**	USA
Briggs & Stratton	USA	*American Artist*	NETH
Command	USA	**American Baby**	USA
Craftsman	USA	**American City**	
Cub Cadet	USA	**& Country**	USA
Dixon	USA	**American Heritage**	USA
Garden Pride	USA	**American Iron**	USA
Honda	JAP	*American Journal*	
Husqvarna	SWE	*of Nursing*	NETH
Ingersoll	GER	**American Observer**	USA

Magazines (cont.)

American Rodder	USA	*Billboard*	NETH
American School	USA	**Birders World**	USA
American Snowmobiler	USA	**Black Enterprise**	USA
American Theater	USA	**Boat Trader**	USA
American Woodworker	USA	**Bon Appetit**	USA
Anna	GER	**Bowhunter**	USA
Apple Paperbacks	USA	**Boy's Life**	USA
Architects Journal	UK	**Bride's**	USA
Architectural Digest	USA	**BusinessWeek**	USA
Architectural Lighting	UK	*Car And Driver*	FRA
Architectural Review	UK	**Car Craft**	USA
Architecture	NETH	*Catholic Digest*	FRA
Army Times	USA	**Child**	USA
Astronomy	USA	**Christian History**	USA
Auto Bild	GER	**Christian Parenting Today**	USA
Auto Mart	USA	**Christianity Today**	USA
Auto Motor	GER	**Circle Track**	USA
Auto Plus	UK	**Classic Toy Trains**	USA
Auto Racing Digest	USA	**Classic Trains**	USA
Auto Trader	USA	**Coins**	USA
Auto World Magazine	USA	**Conde Nast Traveler**	USA
Automotive Digest	UK	*Construction News*	UK
Autoweek	USA	**Consumer Reports**	USA
Aviation Week	USA	*Corporate Traveler*	UK
B.A.S.S. Fishing Techniques	USA	**Corvette Fever**	USA
Backpaker	USA	**Cosmopolitan**	USA
Barron's	USA	**Country Gardens**	USA
Baseball Digest	USA	**Country Home**	USA
Bass Player	UK	**Country Life**	USA
Bassmaster	USA	**Country Living**	USA
Beads & Bulton	USA	**Country Weekly**	USA
Better Homes and Gardens	USA	**Crafts Showcase**	USA
Bicycling	USA	**Crayola Kids**	USA
Bike	USA	**Crochet World**	USA
Biker	USA	**Custom Classic Trucks**	USA
		Cycle Sport	USA
		Cycling Weekly	USA

Dance	USA	Glamour	USA
Decorative Woodcrafts	USA	God's Word Today	USA
Deer & Deer Hunting	USA	Golf	USA
Dirt Rider	USA	*Golf Digest*	*GER*
Diversion	USA	Good Housekeeping	USA
Do It Yourself	USA	Good Old Days	USA
Dollhouse Miniatures	USA	Gourmet	USA
Easyriders	USA	Grit	USA
Ebony	USA	*Guitar Player*	*UK*
Elle	*FRA*	Guns & Ammo	USA
Entertainment Weekly	USA	Hair	USA
Entrepreneur	USA	Handguns	USA
Episodes	USA	Harpers & Queen	USA
ESPN	USA	Harper's Bazaar	USA
Esquire	USA	Highlights For Children	USA
Family Circle	USA	Home Theater	USA
Family Handyman	USA	Hot Bike	USA
Family Money	USA	Hot Rod	USA
Farm Forum	USA	House & Garden	USA
Fate	USA	House Beautiful	USA
FHM	*UK*	How	USA
Field & Stream	USA	*Impressions*	*UK*
Finescale Modeler	USA	*Interiors*	*NETH*
Fishing	USA	IronWorks	USA
Fit Pregnancy	USA	Jack and Jill	USA
Fitness	USA	Jet	USA
Flash	USA	Joypad	USA
Flex	USA	*Keyboard*	*UK*
Fly & Glide	USA	Ladies' Home Journal	USA
Fly Fish America	USA	Living Fit	USA
Food & Wine	USA	*Looks*	*UK*
Football Digest	USA	Mad Magazine	USA
Forbes	USA	Mademoiselle	USA
Fortune	USA	Marie Claire	USA
Four Wheeler	USA	Marriage Partnership	USA
Fox	USA	Men's Fitness	USA
Freeze	USA	Men's Health	USA
Gentlemen's Quarterly	USA	Men's Journal	USA

Magazines (cont.)

Midwest Living	USA	Parents	USA
Minx	*UK*	PC World	USA
Model Railroader	USA	People	USA
Model Retailer	USA	*Performance Computing*	*UK*
Money	USA	*Playstation 2*	*JAP*
Money Management	*UK*	Popular Mechanics	USA
Mopar Muscle	USA	Popular Science	USA
More	USA	Popular Woodworking	USA
Motor Boating	USA	Powder	USA
Motor Magazine	USA	Practical Parenting	USA
Motor Trend	USA	Prevention	USA
Motorcycle Cruiser	USA	Printing Impressions	USA
Motorcyclist	USA	Progressive Farmer	USA
Mountain Bike	USA	Psychology Today	USA
Mountain Bike Rider	USA	Publishers Weekly	USA
MPH	USA	Railway	USA
Muscelcar Review	USA	Readers Digest	USA
Muscle & Fitness	USA	*Red*	*UK*
Mustang & Fords	USA	Redbook	USA
Mustang Monthly	USA	*Refrigeration &*	
National Fisherman	USA	*Air Conditioning*	*UK*
National Geographic	USA	Renovation Style	USA
National Hog Farmer	USA	Reptiles	USA
National Lampoon	USA	Rifle Shooter	USA
National Review	USA	Rod & Custom	USA
Nation's Restaurant News	USA	Rodale's Scuba Diving	USA
New Civil Engineer	*UK*	Rolling Stone	USA
New York	USA	Rugby World	USA
Newsweek	USA	Runner's World	USA
Nursing Times	USA	Sail	USA
NYSE Magazine	USA	Sailing World	USA
O, Oprah Magazine	USA	Salon Today	USA
Official Xbox Magazine	USA	Sarasota	USA
Outdoor Life	USA	Saturday Evening Post	USA
Paper Crafts	USA	Savage	USA
Paperworks	USA	Saveur	USA
Parent & Child	USA	Scale Auto	USA
		Scholastic	USA

Scouting	USA	Sport Driver	USA
Screen International	*UK*	Sport Fishing	USA
Scrye	USA	Sport Rider	USA
Scuba Diving	USA	Sport Truck	USA
Seagate	USA	*Sports Car Classics*	*UK*
Self	USA	Sports Collectors Digest	USA
Seventeen	USA	Sports Illustrated	USA
Shallow Water Angler	USA	*Stamp & Coin Mart*	*UK*
Shape	USA	Stamp Magazine	USA
Sharper Image	USA	*Star Inc.*	*CAN*
Shifter	USA	Starlog	USA
Ships Monthly	USA	Stereophile	USA
Shoot Monthly	USA	Stock Car Racing	USA
Shooting Times	USA	*Stocks*	*GER*
Shuttle Sheet	USA	Storage Magazine	USA
Silver Papers	*FIN*	Street Customs	USA
Skateboarder	USA	Student Loan Funding	USA
Skyguide	USA	*Studio Magazine*	*UK*
Slam	USA	Stuff	USA
Smart Source	USA	Style Weekly	USA
Smartmoney	USA	Sunset	USA
Snowboarder	USA	*Super Review*	*NETH*
Soap Opera Digest	USA	Super Street	USA
Soap Opera Weekly	USA	Superbike	USA
Software Development	*UK*	Surfer	USA
Software News	USA	Swine Practitioner	USA
Software Release	*NETH*	T&L Golf	USA
Sojourns	USA	Tailgate	USA
Soundings	USA	Taste of Home	USA
Southeast Farm Press	USA	Tattoo	USA
Southern Living	USA	Teaching	USA
Southwest Farm Press	USA	Tech	USA
SPA	USA	*Technology & Learning*	*UK*
Space News	USA	Teen Vogue	USA
Spectra News	*SWI*	Texas Monthly	USA
SpiritLed Woman	USA	The American Enterprise	USA
Sport Auto	*UK*	The Atlantic Monthly	USA
Sport Bild	*GER*	The Auburn Trader	USA

Magazines (cont.)

The Bassmaster Tour	USA	Trading Post	USA
The Broadcaster	USA	Trains	USA
The Corn And Soybean		Transworld	USA
Digest	USA	Trapper & Predator	
The Digest	USA	Caller	USA
The Entertainer	UK	Travel & Leisure	USA
The Field	USA	Travel + Romance	USA
The Fun Zone	USA	Travel Week	NETH
The Golf	USA	Trends	UK
The Grower	USA	Truck Trend	USA
The Guitar Magazine	USA	Trucking	USA
The Hacks Series	USA	Trucking Times &	
The Lookout	USA	Sport Utility	USA
The National Enquirer	USA	TrueCareers	USA
The National Historical		Tuff Stuff	USA
Society	USA	Turkey & Turkey	
The New American	USA	Hunting	USA
The New Yorker	USA	Turnberry	USA
The Packer	USA	Turtle	USA
The Pet Product News	USA	TV Guide	USA
The Saturday Evening		U.S. News & World	
Post	USA	Report	USA
The Spectator	UK	Unica	SWI
The Sporting Life	USA	US Weekly	USA
The Sporting News	USA	Valhalla	USA
The Washingtonian	USA	Vanity Fair	USA
The Writer	USA	Variety	NETH
This Old House	USA	Veranda	USA
Tiger Beat	USA	Verena	GER
Time	USA	Vibe	USA
Top Gear	UK	Vida Cristiana	USA
Top Of The Pops	UK	Vitals	USA
Town & Country Travel	USA	Vogue	USA
Toy Cars & Models	USA	VQ	USA
Toy Shop	USA	V-Twin	USA
Toybox	UK	W	USA
Tradin' Times	USA	Wakeboarding	USA
		Wallpaper	USA

Washington Technology	USA	Bassett	USA
Water Garden News	USA	Beautyrest	USA
Watercolor	*NETH*	Beautysleep	USA
Watercolor Magic	USA	Body Perfect	USA
Waterski	USA	Body System	USA
Waves	*UK*	Craftmatic	USA
Weight Watchers	USA	Dr Gjust for Teens	USA
Western Farm Press	USA	Dr. Fuller	USA
Wild Animal Baby	USA	Ecstasy	USA
Wildbird	USA	Englander	USA
Wildfowl	USA	Euro Rest	USA
Windows News	*UK*	Gold Bond	USA
Windsurfing	USA	Health Comfort	USA
Wired	USA	Highland House	USA
Wiredscholar	USA	Imperial Comfort	USA
Womens Day	*AUS*	J.G. Hook	USA
Women's Health	USA	King-O-Pedic	USA
Womens Weekly	*AUS*	Kingsdown	USA
Wood & Wood Products	USA	Laura Ashley	USA
Woodall	USA	Legget & Platt	USA
Woodshop News	USA	Luxury Comfort	USA
Woodworking	USA	Marrakech	USA
World Coin News	USA	Martha Stewart	USA
Xbox Magazine	*UK*	Medi-Coil	USA
Yacht Trader	USA	MemoryTouch	USA
Yankee Magazine	USA	New Experience IV	USA
Yankees Magazine	USA	Original Mattress	
Young Money	USA	Factory	USA
Young Rider	USA	Perfect Night	USA
Your Back Yard	USA	Perfect Sleeper	USA
Zanders	*FIN*	Perma Grip	USA
Zero Breakdowns	USA	Posture Center	USA
		Posture Cushion	USA
MATTRESSES & BEDDING		Posturepedic	USA
Arabella	USA	Queensdown	USA
Atelier Martex	USA	*Regal*	*UK*
Austin	USA	Rip Van Winkle	USA
Baby Beautyrest	USA	Rockleigh	USA

Mattresses & Bedding (cont.)			
Royal Kingsdown	USA	Supreme Dimensions	USA
Schlaraffia	BGM	Surrey	USA
Sealy	USA	Swedish Mattress	USA
Sealy Posturepedic	USA	*Swissflex*	BGM
Secret	USA	Sycamore	USA
Sedona	USA	Symbol Mattress	USA
Select Comfort	USA	Symphony	USA
Sembella	BGM	*Tamanrassat*	PAK
Sentry	USA	Tanchoi	USA
Serta	USA	Teen Central	USA
Sheridan	USA	Tempered	USA
Shiloh	USA	Tempur	USA
Sigma-Flex	USA	Tempur Pedic	USA
Simmons	USA	The Learning Line	USA
Sleep Number	USA	The Sleep Express	USA
Sleepeezee	UK	Ther-A-Pedic	USA
Sleeping Beauty	USA	*Tiara*	UK
Slumber	USA	Tiffany	USA
Somerset	UK	*Toile*	UK
Spine Support Collection	USA	True Balance Sleep	
Spiralok	USA	System	USA
Spire	USA	True U	USA
Spirit Duo	USA	True-Flex	USA
Spring Sleep	USA	Tuscan Rose	USA
Springhill	USA	*Ubica*	BGM
St. Germain	USA	*Union*	UK
Stapleton	USA	Utica	USA
Sta-Tite	USA	Venetain	USA
Stearns & Foster	USA	Verlo	USA
Sterling	USA	Versalok	USA
Sublime	UK	*Victoria*	UK
Summer	UK	*Vintage*	UK
Summit	USA	Visco	USA
Super Edge	USA	*Vi-Spring*	UK
Super Snuggy	USA	Vitagenic	USA
Superba	BGM	Vivaldi	USA
Superframe	USA	Waldorf	USA
		Wamsutta	USA

Waterford	USA
Wave	USA
Web Lok	USA
Westbury	*UK*
Westland	USA
Whistler Pine	USA
Wildlife	USA
Wilmington	USA
Windermere	USA
Yarmouth	USA
York	*PAK*

OFFICE SUPPLIES

Acco	USA
Acco Staplers	USA
Accodata	USA
Amberg	USA
American Eagle	USA
Arrow Staplers	USA
Avery	USA
Book Tray	USA
Boone Bulletin Boards	USA
Boorum & Pease	USA
Boston Staplers	USA
Boxelope	USA
Cambridge	USA
Campbellrhia	USA
Columbian Envelopes	USA
Docu-Lok Envelopes	USA
Docu-Lope Envelopes	USA
Duralite Envelopes	USA
Eastlight	USA
Elements	USA
Elmer's Glue	USA
Esselte	USA
Fashion Write Envelopes	USA
Fiskars	*FIN*
Fuller's Glue	USA

Grip Seal Envelopes	USA
Hon	USA
Jiffy Mailer	USA
Mead	USA
Nature Saver	USA
Panel-Lok Envelopes	USA
Post-It Notes	USA
Prime	USA
Rexel Staplers	USA
Shredman Shredder	*JAP*
Shredmaster Shredder	USA
Smead	USA
Superstax	USA
Swingline Staplers	USA
Tuff Pocket	USA
Tuffgard	USA
Tyvek	USA
Viking	USA
Westvaco	USA

PAINT

Accu-Tone	USA
Acry-Bond	USA
AcryPlex	USA
Aluminall	*GER*
Ambassador	USA
Ameritone	*UK*
Anchor	USA
Aqua Borne	USA
Aqua Gloss	USA
Aqua Lac	USA
Arctic Kote	USA
Artex	*UK*
Aspects	*AUS*
Asphaltum	USA
Behr	USA
Benjamin Moore	USA
Blatz	USA

Paint (cont.)			
Blockaid	UK	*Imperial Touch*	UK
Bond Ad	USA	**Iowa Paint**	USA
BPS	USA	**Krylon**	USA
California	USA	**Kurfees**	USA
Color Key	UK	*Lifemaster*	UK
Cover Perfect	UK	**Lyt-All**	USA
Coverall	USA	**Mab**	USA
Crayola	USA	**Maestro Colors**	USA
Davis	USA	**Magicolor**	USA
Decorator	USA	**Martha Stewart**	USA
Dezignrite	USA	**Masterpiece**	USA
Dulux	UK	**Mastertone**	USA
Dunn-Edwards	USA	**Masury**	USA
DuPont	USA	**Mautz**	USA
Duracolor	USA	**Maximum**	USA
Duratone	USA	**McCloskey**	USA
Duron	USA	**Metalhide**	USA
Dutch Boy	USA	**Microflo Process**	USA
Dutch Brand	USA	**Model Master**	USA
Easy Care	USA	**Moorgard**	USA
Effecto	USA	**Moorglo**	USA
Elegante	USA	**Muresco**	USA
Elite	USA	**Olympic Weatherscreen**	USA
Endurance	UK	*Opal*	HK
Enterprise	USA	**Overcoat**	USA
Envirobase	USA	**Pactra**	USA
Ezy-Cote	USA	**Perma-Kote**	USA
Fabulon	USA	**Permalize**	USA
Fixall	USA	**Perry & Derrick**	USA
Formby's	USA	**Pitt-Cryl**	USA
Glamor	USA	**Pittsburgh**	USA
Glidden	UK	**Plastic Kote**	USA
Graham	USA	**Polycron**	USA
Harris	UK	**Polyflex**	USA
ICI	UK	**Pop-Free**	USA
Illinois Bronze	USA	**Porter Paints**	USA
Imperial Gold	UK	**Pratt & Lambert**	USA
		Pro Line	USA

Pro Tech	USA	**Stays Clear**	USA
Progress Industrial	USA	**Sterling**	USA
Pro's Choice	USA	**Stop Stain**	USA
Red Devil	USA	**Stormpruf**	USA
Regency	UK	*Stripaway*	AUS
Reward	USA	**Studio Finishes**	USA
Royal Gard	USA	**Style Perfect**	USA
Royale	UK	**Suprema**	USA
Rustmaster	UK	**Symphony**	USA
Rust-Not	USA	**Tempgard**	USA
Rustop	USA	**Terminator**	USA
Sara Technology	CAN	**Testor**	USA
Screamers	USA	**The Color Authority**	USA
Seal Kote	USA	*The Color Key Program*	UK
Sears	USA	**The Crown Jewel**	USA
Sheboygan	USA	*The One Day Deck*	CAN
Sherwin Williams	USA	**Thompson's**	USA
Sicoceram	CAN	*Tikkurila*	FIN
Sicopoxy	CAN	**Titancoat**	USA
Siding In A Can	USA	**Trim Chips**	USA
Sinclair	FRA	*Triple Cover*	UK
Skylight	USA	**Trutest**	USA
Smartpaint	USA	**Tuscan Villa**	USA
Smooth Cote	USA	**Ultimatte**	USA
Solagard	AUS	*Ultrasolid*	CAN
Solotex	USA	**Unicoat**	USA
Solver	AUS	**Uniprep**	USA
Sontara	USA	**Uniprime**	USA
Spartaglo	USA	**Utilac**	USA
Spartagloss	USA	**Valueshade**	USA
Spartasheen	USA	**Varsity**	USA
Spartashell	USA	**Versaflat**	USA
Speedcote	UK	**Versa-Glo**	USA
Speedeck	USA	**Versa-Gloss**	USA
Speed-Wall	UK	**Versasatin**	USA
Spray-Day-Lite	UK	**Vexcon Chemicals**	USA
Spred	UK	**Wall Cover**	USA
Standox	USA	**Walltone**	USA

Paint (cont.)

Waste Paint Hardener	*CAN*	Snap-Pac	USA	
Weather Master	USA	So-Dri	USA	
Weatherall	USA	Sofpull	USA	
Weatherperfect	USA	Soft'N Gentle	USA	
Weather-Tite	USA	Sparkle	USA	
Wonder Guard	*UK*	Tenderly	USA	
Wonder Shield	*UK*	*Tessy*	*MEX*	
Wood Gel	*AUS*	Tidynap	USA	
Yenkin-Majestic	USA	Viva	USA	
Zin-Tox	USA	White Cloud	USA	
		Zee	USA	

PAPER GOODS

Angel Soft	USA	ATX	USA
Aqua Soft	USA	Avante	USA
Bella	USA	Berol	USA
Bess	USA	*Bravo*	*JAP*
Bounty	USA	**Calligraphic**	USA
Brawny	USA	**Crayola**	USA
Charmin	USA	*Crest*	*FRA*
Conserv	USA	**Cross**	USA
Coronet	USA	**Dixon Ticonderoga**	USA
Cottonelle	USA	**Gillette**	USA
Ecosoft	USA	*Hybrid-2*	*JAP*
Elegance	USA	**Kodak**	USA
Essence	USA	*Lancelot*	*JAP*
Fluff-Out	USA	**Mead**	USA
Georgia-Pacific	USA	**Monte Marco**	USA
Hi Line	USA	**Paper Mate**	USA
Kleenex	USA	**Parker**	USA
Kowtowls	USA	**Penatia**	USA
Northern	USA	*Pentel*	*JAP*
Puffs	USA	*Pilot*	*JAP*
Sani Hanks	USA	*Pro Am*	*JAP*
Scott	USA	*Quicker Clicker*	*JAP*
Serviette	*SAF*	**Radiance**	USA
Sherbets	USA	*Razor Point*	*JAP*
Shoppro	USA	**Readi-Pencils**	USA

PENS, PENCILS & MARKERS

Rolling Writer	JAP	**Townsend**	USA
Rub-A-Dub	USA	**Trades Marker**	USA
Sanford	USA	*Trigon*	GER
Scripto-Tokai	USA	**Tri-Grip**	USA
Sensa	USA	**Ultima**	USA
Sense-A-Mark	ITL	**Uni-Ball**	USA
Sensematic	ITL	**Uni-Blazer**	USA
Sentinel	FRA	*V Razor Point*	JAP
Sharp	JAP	*Vanishing Point*	JAP
Sharpie	USA	*Varsity*	JAP
Sheaffer	FRA	*VBall*	JAP
Shimmers	FRA	*Vinci*	ITL
Sign Pens	JAP	**Vista Gripper**	USA
Signia	USA	**Waterman**	USA
Silver Marker	JAP	*Wearever*	ITL
Skillcraft	USA	*White Dot*	FRA
Skrip	FRA	**Y&C**	USA
Solo Classic	USA		
Spectrace	USA	**PLASTIC & PAPER**	
Spoiller	JAP	**SERVERWARE**	
Stardust	USA	**Banana Boat**	USA
Stylist	USA	**Diamond**	USA
Summitt	USA	**Forster**	USA
SuperSharpie	USA	**Frost Flex**	USA
Swiss Army	SWI	**Guildware**	USA
Targa by Sheaffer	FRA	**Hot 'N Kold Handle**	
Technica-X	JAP	**Cups**	USA
Techniclick	JAP	**Jazz**	USA
Texpen	USA	**Jubilee**	USA
Text Accent	USA	**Kingsmen**	USA
Textliner Inkjet	GER	**Krazy Kritters**	USA
Textliter	USA	**Petal Mist**	USA
Textsurfer	GER	**Premierware**	USA
The Intrigue	FRA	**Refresher**	USA
The Shaker	JAP	**Serv-Ease**	USA
Ticonderoga	ITL	**Solo**	USA
Titanium	USA	**Solo Cups**	USA
TK-Fine	GER		

TABLEWARE

Allendale	JAP
Allure	IRE
Alpena	USA
Ambience	JAP
American Atelier	USA
American Rose	USA
American Royalty	USA
American Whitehall	USA
Ameriwhite	USA
Amethyst	USA
Amore	USA
Amy	USA
Anabel	IRE
Anchor Hocking	USA
Andrea	USA
Anthea	IRE
Apple Orchard	USA
Aqua Mate	USA
Arcadia	USA
Arcoroc	FRA
Ardmore	JAP
Aria	JAP
Ashland	JAP
Atlanta	IRE
Atlantis	USA
Aynsley	UK
Best China	USA
Buffalo	USA
Camelot	USA
Casamoda	USA
Classicware	USA
Coloniale	ITL
Colony	USA
Cometware	USA
Complements	USA
Confections	USA
Corelle	USA
Correleations	USA
Darkland	USA
Desert Winds	USA
Durus	USA
Elegance	USA
Elements	USA
Envoy	USA
Fieldware	USA
Fiesta	USA
Fostoria	USA
Franciscan	UK
Frost Flex	USA
Fruit Bounty	USA
Garden of India	USA
Gothic	USA
Gwynever	USA
Herbes De Provence	USA
High Sierra	USA
Homer-Laughlin	USA
International Silver	USA
Jenaer Glas	GER
Just Life	USA
Kingline	USA
Lenox	USA
Libby	USA
Luminarc	USA
Lutece	USA
Lyrica	USA
Madeira	USA
Majesticware	USA
Marc Aurel	USA
Masterpiece	USA
Meadow	USA
Milford	USA
Monica Ivory	USA
Monticello	USA
Mount Vernon	USA
Petit Rose	USA

Pfaltzgraff	USA	Simon Pearce	USA
Presentations	USA	Simplicity Rose	USA
Pristine	USA	Small Bites	USA
Pyrex	USA	Sonnet	USA
Queen Anne	USA	Sonoma Villa	USA
Radius	USA	Sonoran	USA
Reflection	USA	*Sorrento*	*JAP*
Reflex	USA	*Southhaven*	*JAP*
Romance	USA	Sovona	USA
Rosenthal	*IRE*	*Spectrum*	*JAP*
Royale	USA	Spinelle	USA
Sakura	USA	Spiro	USA
Salviati	*FRA*	*Spode*	*IRE*
San Remo	USA	*Spring*	*IRE*
Sand Dune	USA	Spring Time	USA
Sanderville	*JAP*	*Squirewood*	*JAP*
Sanibel	*JAP*	St. Moritz	USA
Sansbury	*JAP*	St. Tropez	USA
Santa Fe	USA	*Stanwyck*	*IRE*
Sara	USA	Stepping Out	USA
Sardinia	USA	Stiletto	USA
Satin	USA	*Stoneleigh*	*JAP*
Satin Lace	*JAP*	*Stratford*	*JAP*
Satinique	USA	Strauss	USA
Saturn	*IRE*	*Studio Nova*	*FRA*
Scarlatti	USA	*Summer Estate*	*JAP*
Schott	USA	*Susan Sargent*	*JAP*
Scribble	USA	*Sweet Leilani*	*JAP*
Sea Shells	USA	Sweet Pea	USA
Serene Meadow	*JAP*	*Symmetry*	*IRE*
Sestina	USA	*Tahoe*	*JAP*
Seville	USA	Taraza	USA
Sevres	USA	*Tempo*	*JAP*
Shells	USA	*Tennyson*	*IRE*
Shenandoah	*JAP*	Thar	USA
Sheraton	USA	The Grande Baroque	USA
Signature	*IRE*	The Newbury Collection	USA
Silhouette	USA	The Sheffield Collection	USA

Tableware (cont.)

Thomas	IRE
Thomas by Rosenthal	UK
Thornhill	USA
Tiffany & Co.	USA
Today's Home	USA
Tones	USA
Torsada	USA
Toulon	USA
Towne Fine	USA
Toyo	PAK
Tracy Porter	USA
Traviata	JAP
Tribeca	USA
Tropic Seas	USA
Troy	JAP
Turning Point	JAP
Unity	USA
Uptown	USA
Vectra	USA
Vendome	JAP
Venetian Scroll	JAP
Verdi	USA
Verlaine	USA
Villeroy & Boch	GER
Vineyard	USA
Vino	USA
Vogue	USA
Volletta	USA
Warsteiner	GER
Waverly	USA
W-C Designs	IRE
Wedgwood	IRE
Wellesley	IRE
Westminster	USA
Westover	JAP
Whitecliff	JAP
Whitehaven	IRE

Williamsburg	USA
Woodstock	USA
Yasmin	JAP
Zoom	JAP
Zrike	USA

TOOLS

Acesa	USA
Aeg	SWE
Allen	USA
Alligator Power Saw	USA
Amco	USA
American Saw & Manufacturing	USA
Ames Taping Tools	USA
AMT	USA
Apex Bits & Sockets	USA
Aro	BMD
Arrow Fastener Staple Guns	USA
Asco	USA
Bear Claw	USA
Black & Decker	USA
Black & Silver	USA
Blue-Point	USA
Capewell Saw Blades	USA
Carpenter's Pride	USA
Climax Portable	USA
Columbian Clamps	USA
Craftsman	USA
Crown Cut	USA
De Walt	USA
Disc Farm Tools	USA
DIY	USA
Doall Saw Blades	USA
Doler	USA
Double Duty	USA
Dremel	USA

Dymorig	*SWE*	**Profrom**	USA
Endurance	*SWE*	**Pro-Grip**	USA
E-Z Swing	USA	**Quattro Power Tools**	USA
Fatmax	USA	**Rear Blades Farm Tools**	USA
Fish & Hook	USA	**Reed**	USA
Goldblatt	USA	**Ridge**	USA
Hammer Head	USA	**Ridgid**	USA
Hanita	USA	**Rotowrench**	USA
Hardware House	USA	**RTW**	USA
Hasting	USA	*Ryobi*	*JAP*
Hitachi	*JAP*	**Sanborn**	USA
Hole Hawg	*SWE*	**Sandflex**	USA
Hole Shooters	*SWE*	**Sata**	USA
Holgun	USA	**Scies Sawblades**	USA
Husky	USA	**Semitec Saw Blades**	USA
Ingersoll-Rand	USA	**Simpson Nails**	USA
Irimo	USA	**Sioux**	USA
J.H. Williams	USA	*S-K*	*FRA*
Jensen	USA	*Skilsaw*	*GER*
Klein	USA	*Sludge Sucker*	USA
Lindstrom	USA	*Smaragdol*	*GER*
Makita	*JAP*	**Smart-Grip Pliers**	USA
Matco	USA	**Snap-Let**	USA
McCrary Saw Blades	*GER*	**Snap-On**	USA
Milwaukee	*SWE*	*Spannfix*	*GER*
Moore	USA	**Spectrum Tools**	USA
NAPA	USA	**Speed-Band Saw Blades**	USA
Palmera	USA	**Spinlock**	USA
Permalock	USA	**Stanley**	USA
Pickup Stick	USA	**Steel Eagle**	USA
Pirhana Saw Blades	USA	**Stormguard Nails**	USA
Plumb	USA	**Studsensor Pro**	USA
Porter Cable	USA	**Super Lute**	USA
Precisioncraft	USA	**Superior Tool**	USA
Primecut Saw Blades	USA	**Super-Pro**	USA
Pro Swing Wrenches	USA	**Supersteel Hammers**	USA
Profile Plus Ratchets		**Telewire-Digicon-S**	USA
& Sockets	USA	**Texoma**	USA

Tools (cont.)

TGE	USA	Vic-Let	USA
Thera-Band	USA	Vic-O-Well	USA
Torx	USA	**Westward**	USA
Tough Tools	USA	**Williams**	USA
Trade Duty Saw Blades	GER	*Wilton Clamps & Vises*	SWI
Trex Nails	USA	**Wiremaster Pliers**	USA
Turboshear	USA	**Wonder Broom**	USA
Uniloy	USA	**Xeri-Man**	USA
Van Keuren	USA	*Xtend Saw Blades*	GER
Vermont American	GER	**Zag**	USA
Viat	SP	**Zipin**	USA

Chapter 6

Health & Beauty Aids

(**American owned in bold** / *Foreign owned in italic*)

BODY SOAPS & SANITIZERS

Amaze	UKN
Attention	USA
Aura of Patchouli	USA
Aveeno	USA
Avon	USA
Big Red	USA
Bliw	USA
Body Fantasies	
Shower Gel	USA
Calgon	UK
Camay	USA
Caress	UKN
Caressa	USA
Carex	USA
Castillian	USA
Challenge	USA
Coast	GER
Coleo	USA
Control	USA
Cra-Z Soap	USA
Curel	JAP
Derma Klear	USA
Derma Klenz	USA
Dial	GER
Dove	UKN
Dr. Hunter's Castile	USA
Elegance	USA
Emerald	USA
FA	USA
Farmaco	USA
Gelatti	USA
Gentle Touch	JAP
Georgia-Pacific	USA
Gran Federal	USA
Grandpa	USA
Hand San	USA
Imperial Leather	UK
Irish Spring	USA
Ivory	USA
Jergens	JAP
Kidz	USA
Lana-Lotion	USA
Lava	USA
Lever 2000	UKN
Lifebuoy	UKN
Lifter Hand Cleaner	USA
Loanda	USA
Lux	UKN
Micrell	USA
Monchel	USA
Moniler	USA
Natural Orange	
Hand Cleaner	USA
Neutrogena	USA
Oil of Olay	USA
Olay Bath Bar	USA
Old Spice	USA
Orange Goop	USA
Palmolive	USA
Parr Hand Cleaner	USA
Pingu	USA
Pink Pearl	USA
Protection Plus	USA
Pure & Natural	GER
Purell Hand Sanitizer	USA
Radience Hand Soap	USA
Rich Pink Hand Soap	USA
Roger & Gallet	USA
Safeguard	USA
San-Ell Hand Cleaners	USA
Sani-Dex Hand Cleaner	USA
Sani-Hands Hand	
Cleaner	USA
SBS Natural Lotion Soap	USA
Shea Butter	USA

Shield	*UKN*	*Aire De Loewe*	*FRA*
Shower Up	USA	**Almay**	USA
Soap Staytion	USA	**Alpine Spice**	USA
Softcide	USA	**American Original**	USA
Softsoap	USA	**Amplifeye**	USA
Solvol Hand Cleaner	USA	*Anais Anais*	*FRA*
Soyaseal	USA	*Angel Innocent*	*FRA*
Soycoat	USA	**Ann**	USA
Soyl Hand Cleaner	USA	**Ann Taylor**	USA
Squeeze Hand Cleaner	USA	*AOK*	*GER*
Suave	*UKN*	**Apricot Honey**	USA
Supro Max Hand Cleaner	USA	**Aqua Velva**	USA
Surgi-Bac Hand Soap	USA	**Aramis**	USA
Surrey Men	USA	**Ardell**	USA
Sweet Pea	USA	**ArdenBeauty**	USA
Tea Room	USA	**Artmatic**	USA
Tone	*GER*	**Aspen**	USA
Trome	*PER*	*Aspril*	*JAP*
Tropical Escape	*GER*	**Aveda**	USA
Tropical Pink Hand Soap	USA	**Aviance Night Musk**	USA
Trounce Hand Cleaner	USA	**Avon**	USA
Valcure	USA	*Ayura*	*JAP*
Vapro	USA	**Aziza**	USA
Verbena	USA	*Azzaro*	*FRA*
Veritas	USA	*Azzura*	*FRA*
Wash Away Your Sins	USA	**B Bognar Woman**	USA
Waterlily	USA	**Babe**	USA
Wright's	*UK*	**Babiegoz**	USA
Zest	USA	**BeautiControl**	USA
		Being Together	USA

COSMETICS & FRAGRANCES

		Benefit	*FRA*
212	*SP*	**Benjamin Ansehl**	USA
5th Avenue	USA	**Betrix**	USA
A Little Sexy	USA	**Bill Blass**	USA
Accenti	USA	*Biotherm*	*FRA*
Acqua Di Gio	USA	**Black Radiance**	USA
Adidas	USA	*Bliss*	*FRA*
Afta After Shave	USA	**Body Fantasies**	USA

Cosmetics & Fragrances (cont.)

Body Flowers	USA	Curlicue Mascara	USA
Bogner	*UK*	Curve	USA
Bora Bora	USA	Cutex Nail Polish	
Brisk	USA	Remover	USA
Brit	USA	*D Program*	*JAP*
British Sterling	USA	Davidoff's	USA
Brut	USA	Decollete	USA
Cacharel	*FRA*	Delice	USA
Cachet	USA	Denivit	USA
Calvin	*UKN*	*Dermablend*	*FRA*
Canoe	USA	Design	USA
Chakra	USA	Designer Imposters	USA
Chantilly	USA	Destination	USA
Charles of the Ritz	USA	Destiny	USA
Charlie	USA	*Diadermine*	*GER*
Cheekers	USA	*Dior Addict*	*FRA*
Chiemsee	USA	*Dioressence*	*FRA*
Christian Dior	*FRA*	*Diorissimo*	*FRA*
Cindy Crawford	USA	Domain	USA
cK One	*UKN*	Donna Karen	USA
Claiborne	USA	*Drakkar Noir*	*FRA*
Claire Burke	USA	Dream	USA
Clarins	*FRA*	Dreamlife	USA
Clarion	USA	*Dune*	*FRA*
Clinique	USA	Dunhill	USA
Colorstay	USA	Earth Gems	USA
Confess	USA	*Eau Sauvage*	*FRA*
Continuous Color		Ebone	USA
Lipstick	USA	Eddie Bauer	USA
Cool Arctic	USA	Elige	USA
Coriandre	USA	Elizabeth Arden	USA
Cotton Candy	USA	Elizabeth Taylor	USA
Countess Isserlyn	USA	Ellen Tracy	USA
Cover Girl	USA	Emeraud	USA
Creamy Flo-Matic	USA	Emporio Armani	USA
Creations	USA	English Leather	USA
Cucumber Melon	USA	Enigma	USA
		Enjoli	USA

Enjoue Musk	USA	Giorgio Beverly Hills	USA
Epoch	USA	Globe	USA
Escada	USA	*Gloria Vanderbilt*	*FRA*
Esencia Femme	USA	Glow by J. Lo	USA
Estee Lauder	USA	Grace Collection	USA
Euro Collections	USA	Gravity	USA
Exclamation	USA	Great Life	USA
Expert-Eyes	*FRA*	Gucci	USA
Extase	USA	*Guerlain*	*FRA*
Eye Express Eyeliner	*FRA*	Gummi Bears	USA
Eyedevotion Eye Shadow	USA	*Guy Laroche*	*FRA*
Eyesicles	USA	Heaven Sent	USA
Eyestyle Eyeshadow	USA	Heirloom	USA
Fahrenheit	*FRA*	*Helene Curtis*	*UKN*
Fairchild	USA	Herbal Logix	USA
Fashion Fair	USA	*Hermes*	*FRA*
Fire & Ice	USA	High Speed	USA
Flowing Velvet	USA	Holly Pine	USA
Fly With Me	USA	*Hugo Boss*	*ITL*
Forever Elizabeth	USA	ICI	USA
Forever Lip Color	*FRA*	Il Bacio	USA
Francesco Smalto	*THAI*	*Illegal Lengths Mascara*	*FRA*
Free Soul Piccadilly	USA	Impact For Men	USA
Freesia	USA	Incognito	USA
Frescolat	*GER*	*Infinitif*	*UK*
Fresh	*FRA*	*Ipsa*	*JAP*
Fresh Musk	USA	Irisch Moos	USA
Gabriel Sabatini	USA	Irma Shorell's	USA
Gale Hayman	USA	*Issey Miyake*	*JAP*
Galileo	*GER*	Jacques Esterel	USA
Gardenia	USA	*J'Adore*	*FRA*
Gelatti	USA	Jean Courterier	USA
Georgette Klinger	USA	Jean Philippe	USA
Germaine Monteil	USA	Jeanne Gatineau	USA
Gerry Weber	USA	Jess by Jessica	
Ghost	USA	McClintock	USA
Giorgio	USA	JMF	USA
Giorgio Armani	*FRA*	Jovan Musk	USA

Cosmetics & Fragrances (cont.)			
Juice Bar	USA	*Maybelline*	*FRA*
Kenzo	*FRA*	Merle Norman	USA
Kiehl's	*FRA*	Mexx	USA
Klein's	USA	Midnight	USA
La Perla	*THAI*	Midsummer	USA
La Roche-Posay	*FRA*	*Miss Dior*	*FRA*
Laforre	*THAI*	*Moisture Whip*	*FRA*
Lancaster	USA	Moisturewear	USA
Lancome	*FRA*	*Molto Smalto*	*THAI*
Legend of Love	USA	Monsieur De Givenchy	USA
L'Heure Bleu	*FRA*	Montblanc	USA
Lip Smacker	USA	Mood Magic Lipstick	USA
Lipdvotion	USA	Mosscara	USA
Liquid Eyes	*FRA*	Musk	USA
Live	USA	My Islands	USA
Liz Claiborne	USA	Mystic	USA
Lone Star	USA	*Nahema*	*FRA*
Long 'N Lush	USA	Naomi Campbell	USA
Longing	USA	Naturade	USA
Lord & Berry	USA	Natural Basics	USA
L'Oreal	*FRA*	Naturistics	USA
Lou Lou	*FRA*	Navy	USA
Love's Baby Soft	USA	*Nerval*	*GER*
Magic	USA	Neutrogena	USA
Magnolia	USA	New Musk	USA
Make Up For Ever	*FRA*	New York Nights	USA
Makeupmate	USA	Nines	USA
Malibu Musk	USA	Ninja	USA
Marathon Mascara	USA	Norel	USA
Marc O'Polo	USA	Norell	USA
Marilyn Miglin	USA	Nouriche	USA
Mary Kay	USA	*Now How*	*THAI*
Mascara Plus Rose	USA	Nu Skin	USA
Maserati	*THAI*	Odalisque	USA
Max Factor	USA	OGM	USA
Max Mara	USA	OPI	USA
Maxx	USA	Opium	USA
		Orlane	*FRA*

Oscar	USA	*Ralph Lauren*	*FRA*
Outdoor Glow Lipstick	USA	**Raspberry Fantasy**	USA
Paco Rabanne	*THAI*	**Really Ripped Abs**	USA
Pajama Party	USA	**Red by Giorgio**	USA
Paloma Picasso	*FRA*	**Regency**	USA
Park Avenue	USA	*Rene Furtherer*	*FRA*
Passion	USA	**Revlon**	USA
Passionate Plumeria	USA	**Rocco Baracco**	USA
Patti LaBelle	USA	**Rochas**	USA
Pearl Fantasy	USA	*Roger & Gallet*	*THAI*
Perfect Blend Eye Pencils	USA	*Roller Color Eyeshadow*	*FRA*
Perry Ellis	USA	**Royal Selections**	USA
Personnelle	USA	**Sally Hansen**	USA
Pheromone	USA	**Salon Formula**	USA
Philip Rockley	USA	**Sandalwood**	USA
Pias	*THAI*	**Santa Fe**	USA
Pierre Balmain	USA	**Satin Finish**	USA
Pierre Cardin	USA	**Scaasi**	USA
Pierre Fabre	*FRA*	*Scarves*	*FRA*
Pleasures	USA	**Scavenol**	USA
Plumeria Fantasy	USA	*Scorpio*	*GER*
Polo Ralph Lauren	USA	**Sensation**	USA
Precious Moments	USA	**Sensi-Tech**	USA
Pre-Electric	USA	**Sensuale**	USA
Preferred Stock	USA	*Sergio Tacchini*	*AND*
Prestige	USA	*Shalimar*	*FRA*
Primo	USA	**Sheer Face Powder**	USA
Prince Matchebelli	USA	**Sheer Halston**	USA
Priscilla Presley	USA	**Shimmerstick Eyeshadow**	USA
Professional	USA	*Shine Free*	*FRA*
PS Fine Cologne	USA	**Shinning Effects**	USA
Pur Blanca	USA	*Shiseido*	*AND*
Pure Care	*THAI*	*Shu Uemura*	*FRA*
Pure Tiffany	USA	**Silox**	USA
Pure-Fume	USA	**Silver Brights**	USA
Qualite	USA	*Sjal*	*AND*
Quorum	*THAI*	**Skin**	USA
Radio Girl	USA	**Skin Beneficial**	USA

Cosmetics & Fragrances (cont.)			
Skin Bracer	**USA**	*Tera XYL*	*GER*
Skin Musk	**USA**	*Testimo Lipstick*	*JAP*
Skot	*FRA*	*The Classics*	*FRA*
Sky High Curves	*FRA*	**Tiffany & Co.**	**USA**
Smacker	**USA**	**Time To Play**	**USA**
Smackers Lip Frosting	**USA**	**Tiosperse**	**USA**
Smooth	**USA**	**Tocade**	**USA**
Smooth N Shine	**USA**	**Tom Tailor**	**USA**
Smooth Result	*FRA*	*Tommy Girl*	*CHN*
Solaroil	**USA**	**Tony & Tina**	**USA**
Spark	**USA**	**Tosca**	**USA**
Stella MaCartney	*AND*	**Total Finish**	**USA**
Stendhal	*NZ*	*Touch*	*UK*
Stetson	**USA**	**Trapp**	**USA**
Stolen Kisses	**USA**	**Tree Hut**	**USA**
Strenesse	**USA**	*Tricia*	*SLO*
Subtle Effects	**USA**	**Tropez**	**USA**
Sugar Vanilla	**USA**	*True Star*	*CHN*
Sui Dreams	**USA**	**Tuberose Musk**	**USA**
Sui Love	**USA**	**TZ Sperse**	**USA**
Sumatra Rain	**USA**	**Ultima**	**USA**
Summer Highlights	**USA**	**Unbound**	**USA**
Sun Mix	*SLO*	**Unforgettable**	**USA**
Suncare	*JAP*	**Unscented**	**USA**
Sunflowers	**USA**	**Uproar**	**USA**
Sunset	**USA**	**Uruku**	**USA**
Super Lustrous Lipstick	**USA**	**U-Two**	**USA**
Superiore	**USA**	**U-You**	**USA**
Sweet Georgia Brown	**USA**	*Vademecum*	*GER*
Swirl Gloss	**USA**	**Vanilla Fantasy**	**USA**
Tabu	**USA**	**Vanilla Fields**	**USA**
Tahoe	**USA**	*Versace Profumi*	*AND*
Take-Off	**USA**	*Very Irresistible*	
Teddy Bear	**USA**	*Givenchy*	*SWI*
Tekno	**USA**	*Vetiver*	*FRA*
Temperamento	**USA**	*Veto*	*GRE*
Tendre Poison	*FRA*	*Vichy*	*FRA*
		Vicky Teil	**USA**

Viedor	JAP	*Zen*	JAP
Vision	USA	**Zero Frizz**	USA
Visions	BGM	**Zonite**	USA
Vitaskin Fitolift	SLO		
Viva Di Tosca	USA	**COTTON SWABS**	
Vivienne Westwood		**Johnson & Johnson**	USA
Boudoir	AND	*Q-Tips*	UKN
Vocalise	JAP	**Senti-Swabs**	USA
Vol De Nuit	FRA	**Transplex**	USA
Volare	BGM		
Vo-Lip-Tuous	USA	**DEODORANT**	
Volume Express	FRA	*8x4*	GER
Volupte	NZ	**Almay**	USA
Wanna Play?	USA	**Arm & Hammer**	USA
Warm Sugar Vanilla	USA	**Arrid**	USA
Waterlove	USA	*Axe*	UKN
Waterproof Mascara	USA	*Ban*	JAP
WB International	USA	*Brut*	UKN
Wear 'N Go	FRA	*Chantal*	UK
Weekend	UK	*Degree*	UKN
Welbox	AND	*Dial*	GER
White Ginger	USA	*Dove*	UKN
White Shoulders	USA	**Dry Idea**	USA
Wild Wind	USA	**English Leather**	USA
Wind Song	USA	**Feel Free**	USA
Wings	USA	**Foot Guard**	USA
Woman	USA	**Grandpa Le Stick**	USA
Women of Earth	USA	**Hex**	USA
Wonder Curl	FRA	**Irish Spring**	USA
X	USA	**Jovan Musk**	USA
X-Centric	USA	*Lady Power Roll-On*	UKN
Xeryus	SWI	*Lady Power Stick*	UKN
Yardley	USA	**Lady Speed Dry**	USA
Yoohoo	USA	**Lady Speed Smooth-On**	USA
Ysatis	SWI	**Lady Speed Stick**	USA
YSL	FRA	**Lady's Choice**	USA
Yves Saint Laurent	FRA	**Mennen**	USA
Z-14	USA	**Mitchum**	USA

Deodorant (cont.)

No Sweat	USA
Norforms	USA
Old Spice	USA
One Drop	USA
Pierre Cardin	USA
Power Stick	*UKN*
Right Guard	USA
Secret	USA
Speed Stick	USA
Suave	*UKN*
Sure	USA
Tag Body Spray	USA
Teen Spirit	USA
Tom's of Maine	USA
Top Care	USA
Ultramax	USA

FEMININE HYGIENE PRODUCTS

Alldays	USA
Always	USA
Always Alldays	USA
Always Plus	USA
Anyday	USA
Bergamon	USA
Bodyform	USA
FDS Feminine Deodorant	USA
Femtex	USA
Gards	USA
Kotex	USA
Massengill	*UK*
Maxithins	USA
Modess	USA
Monistat	USA
New Freedom	USA
O.B.	USA

Poise	USA
Safe & Soft	USA
Soft & Thin	USA
Sprintec	USA
Summer's Eve	USA
Tampax	USA

HAIR CARE PRODUCTS

A Touch of Sun	USA
Ace	USA
Ace Combs	USA
Aderans	USA
Adorn	USA
African Gold	USA
Alberto Balsam	USA
Alberto VO5	USA
Allianz	USA
Aloegen	USA
Aloxxi Chroma Color	USA
Alpha	USA
American Crew	USA
Amplify	*FRA*
Antiall	USA
Apollo	USA
Aqua Net	*UKN*
Arista	USA
Array	USA
Arteffex	USA
Aussie	USA
Avon	USA
Baby Don't Cry	USA
Bain De Terre	*JAP*
Balsam Color	USA
Bare Elegance	USA
Beau Kreme	USA
Beauty Maid	USA
Bed Head	USA
Be-Gone	USA

Behave	USA	Dena-Vie	USA
Better Locks	USA	Denorex	USA
Biolage	*FRA*	*DEP*	*GER*
Black & Beautiful	USA	Design	USA
Blaune	*JAP*	Design Hairspray	USA
Blondo Gel	USA	Designer Touch	USA
Blondor	*GER*	DH-12	USA
Bobbi	USA	Dippity Do Sport	USA
Body Essence	USA	Dusharme	USA
Bolty	*JAP*	Earth Born	USA
Born Blond	USA	Earth Secrets	USA
Braun	USA	Equate	USA
Brylcreem	USA	Escalol	USA
Bumper Curling Iron	USA	European Mystique	USA
Carbonoel	USA	Fabulaxer Hair	
Cerasynt	USA	Straightener	USA
Clairol	USA	Fantastic Silver	USA
Clear Benefit	USA	Final Net	USA
Clear Ice	USA	*Finesse*	*UKN*
Clubman	USA	Finflx	USA
Color Charm	USA	Finisheen	USA
Color Perfect	USA	Fixona	USA
Color Protect	USA	Fold N' Go	USA
Colorific	USA	Folicure	USA
Comb-Thru	USA	Forest Essence	USA
Commander	USA	Formula ZP II	USA
Conair	USA	Framesi	USA
Condition 3-In-1	USA	Free & Lovely	USA
Conditioneze	USA	Free 'N Easy	USA
Cossack	USA	Frizz Ender	USA
Crazy Curl	USA	Frost & Glow	USA
Crème Relaxer	USA	Frost & Tip	USA
Crisan	USA	*Fructis*	*FRA*
Curlax	USA	Gaffix	USA
Curlemaster Curling Iron	USA	Gafquat	USA
Curl-Oil	USA	Gantrez	USA
Daniel Galvin	USA	*Garnier*	*FRA*
Dena	USA	Gentle Treatment	USA

Hair Care Products (cont.)			
Georgette Klinger	USA	Just So	USA
Gillette Super Volume	USA	Kadus	USA
GLH #9	USA	Kelate	USA
Gloss Drops	USA	Kerastase	FRA
Gold Medal	USA	Kiessling	USA
Golden Girl	USA	Koleston	USA
Goldwell	JAP	Kolestral	USA
Goody	USA	Kolor-Bak	USA
Grandpa's Pine Tar		L.A. Looks	GER
Shampoo	USA	La Femme	USA
Grecian Formula	USA	Lady Catherine	
Guys and Dolls	USA	Hairbrush	USA
Hairpainting	USA	Lady Lora	USA
Hairsaver	USA	Lancome	FRA
Hask	USA	Lasting Color	USA
Head & Shoulders	USA	Lectrify	USA
Heart	USA	Lemon Up	USA
Heat Seal	USA	Liquid Hair	USA
Helene Curtis	UKN	Lively Set	USA
Herbal Deep Clean	USA	Living Colors	JAP
Herbal Essence	USA	Logics Hair Color	FRA
High Hair	USA	Londa	USA
Hold & Clean	USA	L'Oreal	FRA
Hold Tight	USA	Love	USA
Hydrience Hair Color	USA	Loving Care	USA
Hypalon	USA	Lucky Kentucky	USA
Infusium	USA	Lustrasilk	USA
Ionil Plus	USA	Luticin	USA
It's Organic Naturally	USA	Lycra	USA
Ivory	USA	Matrix	FRA
Jheri Redding	USA	Medalo	USA
Jhirmack	USA	Men's Choice	USA
Johnson's Baby	USA	Meta 1 Step	USA
Jojoba Farms	USA	Meta Henna Crème	USA
Just 5	USA	Milk N Honey	USA
Just For Me	USA	Milk Plus 6	USA
Just For Men	USA	Mill Creek	USA
		Miss Clairol	USA

Mizani	*FRA*	**Proficare**	**USA**
Moistcure	**USA**	**Progaine**	**USA**
Moisture Max	**USA**	**Prom**	**USA**
Motions	**USA**	**Promotor**	**USA**
Mountain Herbery	**USA**	**Propecia**	**USA**
Natural Instincts	**USA**	**Psoriasin**	**USA**
Natural Mystique	**USA**	**Pure Shine**	**USA**
Neutrogena	**USA**	**Pure-A-Tea**	**USA**
New Life Gel	**USA**	**Quantum**	**USA**
New Man	**USA**	**Rapithix**	**USA**
Nexxus	**USA**	*Rave*	*UKN*
Nice 'N Easy	**USA**	**Ready Set**	**USA**
Nicky Clarke	**USA**	*Redken*	*FRA*
Nioxin Scalp Therapy	**USA**	**Renova**	**USA**
Nizoral	**USA**	**Retin-A**	**USA**
Nuances	**USA**	**Revitalique Hair**	
Nutritonic	**USA**	**Coloring**	**USA**
Olapon	**USA**	**Revlon**	**USA**
Omnirez	**USA**	**Rocket 2000**	**USA**
Optaform	**USA**	**Rogaine**	**USA**
Palmer's Hair Success	**USA**	**Roux Hair Coloring**	**USA**
Pantene	**USA**	**Royal**	**USA**
PBB	**USA**	**Royal Crown**	**USA**
PCJ	**USA**	**Royal Shield**	**USA**
Perfect Control	**USA**	**Salon Control**	**USA**
Perm Life	**USA**	*Salon Formula Dep*	*GER*
Pert	**USA**	*Salon Selectives*	*UKN*
Physique	**USA**	**Salon Set**	**USA**
Phyto-Life	**USA**	*Salon Silhouettes*	*CAN*
Pingu	**USA**	**Satin Gro Styling Tool**	**USA**
Pink	**USA**	**Saxon**	**USA**
Placenta Plus	**USA**	**Sea Buckthorn**	**USA**
Plusbelle	**USA**	**Sea Spa**	**USA**
PM Shines Hair Color	**USA**	**Seaware**	**USA**
Por Equal	**USA**	**Sebastian**	**USA**
Power Gro	**USA**	*Secret Professional*	*FRA*
Prell	**USA**	**Selenium Natural**	**USA**
Pro Hair	**USA**	**Selsun Blue**	**USA**

Hair Care Products (cont.)

Shasta Brushes	USA
Shergrip Brushes	USA
Sherlock Brushes	USA
Shiny Styles	USA
Shockwaves	USA
Shortcut Brushes	USA
Shower Up	USA
SHS	*ITL*
Silk	*JAP*
Silvakrin	USA
Si-Tec	USA
Sleek Look	*FRA*
Smoothly Defined	USA
Soft & Beautiful	USA
Softip Brushes	USA
Softsheen Carson	*FRA*
Spa Bath	USA
Spartan Styling Tool	USA
Spectozole	USA
St. Ives Swiss Formula	USA
Stabileze	USA
Stephan's	USA
Stiff Stuff	USA
Straight FX	USA
Straight Styles	USA
Strait Shades	USA
Stronghold	USA
Structure And Strength	USA
Stuck-Up	USA
Styler Dryer	USA
Styleze	USA
Stylinfoam	USA
Stylingel	USA
Suave	*UKN*
Sulfur-8	USA
Sun Shade	USA

Sun-In	USA
Sunsilk	*UKN*
Super Clips	USA
Super Doo-Z Brushes	USA
Super/Fab Brushes	USA
Super/Pro Brushes	USA
Supersonic	USA
Supreme Beauty	USA
Surfadone	USA
Surgi-Care	USA
Swimmer's	USA
Swimmers & Sports	USA
Systeme Biolage	*FRA*
Taft Styling	*GER*
Tagrol	USA
Tall Grass	USA
Tame	USA
Tessera	*JAP*
Texture Care	*JAP*
The Dry Look	USA
Theorie	*GER*
Thermacell	USA
Thermasilk	*UKN*
Thicker Fuller Hair	USA
Thin To Thick	USA
Tight Curl II	USA
Tight Curls	USA
Titania	USA
Tom's of Maine	USA
Top Care	USA
Total Control	USA
Trendsetter	USA
Tresemme	USA
Trim & Shape	USA
Tritein	USA
Trix	*FRA*
Twisters	USA

Ultraperm	USA	**MEDICATIONS**	
Ultrastat Brushes	USA	2nd Skin	USA
Ultraswim	USA	*Abreva*	*UK*
Uminouruoisou	*JAP*	Ace Bandages	USA
Unwind Detangler	USA	Aci-Jel	USA
Urban Natural Styles	USA	Acne-Aid	USA
Vavoom	*FRA*	Actifed	USA
Vegecell	USA	Acutrim	USA
Vegecol	USA	Advil	USA
Venture	USA	Afrin	USA
Venus Hair	*UK*	*Aleve*	*GER*
Vibrance	*UKN*	*Alka-Mints*	*GER*
Vidal Sassoon	USA	*Alka-Seltzer*	*GER*
Vigoral	USA	Allegra	USA
VIP Pro	USA	Alu-Cap Antacid	USA
Vista	USA	Anacin	USA
Vitalis	USA	Anbesol	USA
Vivality	USA	Anusol	USA
VO 5	USA	*Aquaphor*	*GER*
Volumekind	USA	*Aquasite*	*SWI*
Wash 'N Curl	USA	Arth Aid	USA
Wash'N Straight	USA	Arthricare	USA
Wella Balsam	USA	Arthriten	USA
Whirly Girl	*AUS*	Arthritis Hot	USA
White Camellia	USA	Arthritis Pain Formula	USA
White Rain	USA	Asmanex	USA
Wide Boy Brushes	USA	Aspercreme	USA
Wild Wind	USA	Aspi Cor Aspirin	USA
Wooster Combs		Astelin Nasal Spray	USA
& Brushes	USA	Atwater Carey	USA
Wrap-N-Styl	USA	Auro Ear Drops	USA
Y Serum	USA	Axid Antacid	USA
Yachtsman Brushes	USA	Backaid	USA
Young Styling	USA	Backaid PM	USA
Youthair	USA	*Bactine*	*GER*
Zincon	USA	Band-Aid	USA

Medications (cont.)

Bausch & Lomb		Creo-Terpin	USA
Moisture Drops	USA	*Curad*	*GER*
Bayer Aspirin	*GER*	*Daniprol*	*DEN*
Baytril Antibacterial	*GER*	**Dayquil**	USA
Beecham's Pills	*UK*	**Delsym**	USA
Benadryl	USA	**Dent's Ear Wax Drops**	USA
Ben-Gay	USA	**Dent's Toothache**	
Benylin	USA	Treatment	USA
Benzac AC	*FRA*	**Derma-Gel**	USA
Benzamycin	*FRA*	**Dermoplast**	USA
Benzodent	USA	**Dexatrim**	USA
Big Slixx Lip Balm	USA	**Dimetapp**	USA
Bi-Solution	USA	*Disprin*	*UK*
Blistex	USA	*Disprol*	*UK*
BodyMate	USA	**Diurex**	USA
Bufferin	USA	*Doan's Pills*	*SWI*
Candie's	USA	**Doctor's Choice Eye**	
Cap-Max6	USA	Drops	USA
Capzasin	USA	**Dolobid**	USA
Carter's Little Pills	USA	**Dovonex**	USA
Celluvisc	USA	*Dristan*	*JAP*
Chapstick	USA	**Drixoral**	USA
Chericol Cough Syrup	USA	*Dulcolax*	*GER*
Chloraseptic	USA	**Duragesic**	USA
Circus	USA	**Efferdent**	USA
Clean & Clear	USA	**Emetrol**	USA
Clear Care	*SWI*	**Ensure**	USA
Clear Eyes Eye Drops	USA	*Ex Lax*	*SWI*
Clearasil	USA	**Excedrin**	USA
Coach	USA	**Ezy-Sleep**	USA
Cold Sore Relief	USA	**Fast Dry Lozenge**	USA
Cold-Eeze	USA	**FiberCon**	USA
Compound W	USA	**Fixodent Denture**	
Compoz	USA	Adhesive	USA
Coricidin	USA	**Fleet Phospho-Soda**	
Correctol	USA	Laxative	USA
Cortizone	USA	**Flex-All 454**	USA
		Foille	USA

Formula 44 Cough Syrup	USA	Nasalcrom	USA
Gelusil	USA	Nascobal	USA
Hall's Cough Drops	*UK*	*Nasonex*	*GER*
Head & Chest	USA	Nauzene	USA
Healthy Mouth Breath Drops	USA	Nexcare	USA
Herbie	USA	*Nicoderm*	*FRA*
Ibutab	USA	*Niquitin CQ*	*UK*
Icy Hot	USA	Norwich Aspirin	USA
Imodium A-D	USA	Nose Better	USA
Incyte	USA	*Novalgin*	*FRA*
Indiplon Sleep Aid	USA	NP-27 Athlete's Foot	USA
Inzo	USA	Nu-Gel	USA
Ivarest	USA	Nyquil	USA
Just-In-Case	USA	Ocean Nasal Spray	USA
Kank-a	USA	Ocuflox	USA
Labrosan Lip Care	*ITL*	Off-Ezy Wart Remover	USA
Lanacane	USA	Omnigest EZ	USA
Lanacort	USA	*Opti-Clean Lens Cleaner*	*SWI*
Lemsip	*UK*	Orabase	USA
Lidopain HM	USA	Orajel	USA
Lip-Ex Lip Balm	USA	*Otosrporin Ear Drops*	*UK*
Liposic Dry Eye	USA	*Otrivin*	*SWI*
Lotrimin AF	USA	*Oxy*	*UK*
Luden's Throat Drops	USA	*Oxyclean*	*UK*
Lumigan	USA	Painaid	USA
Maalox	*SWI*	Pamprin	USA
Maltsupex	USA	Pancrease	USA
Metamucil	USA	Pediacare	USA
Micatin Itch Medication	USA	Pedialyte	USA
Midol	*GER*	Pediatric Formula 44	USA
Monistat	USA	Pedicare Leg Crème	USA
Motrin	USA	Pepcid AC	USA
Muellergesic	USA	Pepto-Bismol	USA
Muellerkold	USA	Percogesic	USA
Murine Eye Drops	USA	Peroxyl	USA
Mylanta	USA	Phenergan	USA
Mylicon	USA	Phrenilin	USA
		Pinadol	USA

<u>Medications (cont.)</u>

Podiacin	USA	Simply Sleep	USA
Preparation H	USA	Sinequan	USA
Prontalgine	GER	Sinex Nasal Spray	USA
Propa Ph Acne Care	USA	Singulair	USA
Prozac	USA	*Sintonal*	GER
Refresh Contacts	USA	Sinucheck	USA
Refresh Endura	USA	Sinutab	USA
Relief	USA	*Skinoren Acne Treatment*	GER
Rennie	GER	*Sleepmate*	JAP
Restore	USA	Slice	USA
Rhinospray Nasal Spray	USA	Snore Relief	USA
Ricola	SWI	Sof Foam	USA
Riopan	GER	*Softlips*	JAP
Robitussin	USA	*Solfa*	JAP
Rolaids	USA	Solu	USA
Rondec	USA	Somavert	USA
Rub A535	USA	Sonata	USA
Ryna	USA	Soothe And Shine	USA
Salve Bandage &		*Soothe Eye Drops*	SWI
Adhesive	USA	*Spacehaler*	BGM
Samarin	USA	Spheramine	USA
Santyl Ointment	USA	St. Joseph's Aspirin	USA
Scorba	JAP	Staphvax	USA
Sea-Band	USA	*Stelazine*	UK
Seasorb Soft	DEN	Sterisomes	USA
Selles Medical	UK	*Stimul*	BGM
Seloken	UK	Sting-A-Way	USA
Semprex	UK	*Sucrets*	UK
Senokot Laxative	UK	Sudafed	USA
Sensipar	USA	Sul-Ray	USA
Sensit	BGM	Sunshield	USA
Sensorcaine	UK	*Supertendin*	BGM
Septrin	UK	*Suplasyn*	CAN
Seretide	UK	Surfaxin	USA
Serevent	UK	Surpass	USA
Seroquel	UK	*Symbicort*	UK
Seroxat	UK	Synarel	USA
		Syn-Rx	BGM

Systane Eye Drops	SWI	*Trentadil*	BGM
Tabloid	UK	*Triaminic*	SWI
Tagamet	UK	*Trimovate*	UK
Tamiflu	**USA**	**Tristar**	**USA**
Tantum	BGM	*Trivax*	BGM
Tao	**USA**	*Trizivir*	UK
Telcyta	**USA**	**Trobicin**	**USA**
Telintra	**USA**	**Truvada**	**USA**
Telzir	UK	*Tuberculin Evans*	BGM
Temodar	**USA**	**Tucks**	**USA**
Temovate	UK	*Tums*	UK
Tempo	**USA**	**Tunes**	**USA**
Tenoretic	UK	**Turbovac**	**USA**
Tenormin	UK	**Tussi-12**	**USA**
Tensiomin	BGM	*Tussionex*	BGM
Terramycin	**USA**	*Twinrix*	UK
Tesoprel	BGM	**Tylenol**	**USA**
Theo 24	BGM	*Typherix*	UK
Theraflu	SWI	*UCB*	BGM
Theralene	BGM	*Ultiva*	UK
Thorazine	UK	**Ultracet**	**USA**
Thyromed	**USA**	**Ultraklenz**	**USA**
Ticar	UK	**Ultravac**	**USA**
Tiger Balm	SNG	**Ultrex**	**USA**
Tikosyn	**USA**	**Unasyn**	**USA**
Timentin	UK	**Unicap**	**USA**
Tiseel	**USA**	*Unimax*	UK
Tisercin	BGM	**Unisom**	**USA**
Tissomat	**USA**	**Urobiotic**	**USA**
Titan	**USA**	*Valstar*	BGM
Tobi	**USA**	*Valtrex*	UK
Tolinase	**USA**	*Vanquish*	GER
Tomudex	UK	**Vantin**	**USA**
Toposar	**USA**	*Varilrix*	UK
Toprol	UK	*Vectavir*	SWI
Tracrium	UK	**Velac**	**USA**
Tramake	UK	*Veletri*	SWI
Tranzfect	**USA**	*Ventadur*	BGM

Medications (cont.)			
Ventide	UK	Zarontin	USA
Ventodisks	UK	Zaroxolyn	BGM
Ventolin	UK	Zestril	UK
Versiva	USA	Zetia	USA
Vfend	USA	Ziagen	UK
Viagra	USA	Zigg	USA
Vibramycin	USA	Zinacef	UK
Vibrilase	USA	Zinecard	USA
Vicks	USA	Zineryt	BGM
Vicodin	USA	Zinnat	UK
Vicoprofen	USA	Zithromax	USA
Victors	USA	Zmax	USA
Vioxx	USA	Zocor	USA
Viracept	USA	Zofran	UK
Viractin	USA	Zoladex	UK
Viravan	USA	Zoloft	USA
Viread	USA	Zomig	UK
Visine	USA	Zovirax	UK
Vistaril	USA	Zubrin	USA
Vistide	USA	Zyban	UK
Vivalan	UK	Zyloric	UK
Volmax	UK	Zymar	USA
Vytorin	USA	Zyrtec	USA
Wart-Off	USA		
Wellbutrin	UK	**ORAL CARE**	
Wellness Cough	USA	Aim	USA
Wellvone/Mepron	UK	Aloe Brite	USA
Xalatan	USA	Aquafresh	UK
Xanax	USA	Arm & Hammer	USA
Xcelonase Nasal		Astriginsol	UK
Medicine	USA	Blendax	USA
Xcelovair	USA	Butler	JAP
Xolair	USA	Chloraseptic	USA
Xylocaine	UK	Cleardent	JAP
Xyrem	USA	Close-Up	USA
Xyzal	BGM	Colgate	USA
Zantac	USA	Crest	USA
		Dentist Preferred	USA

Email Diamant	USA	Flex Control	USA
Freshburst	USA	Flicker	USA
Gillette Advantage	USA	Gillette	USA
Gleem	USA	Good News	USA
Gum-Critters	*JAP*	Groomsman	USA
Health Mouth	USA	Jheri Redding	USA
Interplak	USA	Lady Braun	USA
Jordan	USA	Lady Remington	USA
Lavoris	*GER*	Lady Wahl	USA
Listerine	USA	Micro Screen	USA
Listermint	USA	Microtrac	USA
Mentadent	*UKN*	*Norelco*	*NETH*
Nutrismile	USA	Oster	USA
Oral-B	USA	Outliner II	USA
Pearl Drops	USA	Pal	USA
Pepsodent	*UKN*	*Panasonic*	*JAP*
Plax	USA	Personna	USA
Premier	USA	*Prepare*	*JAP*
Prodent	USA	Quattro	USA
Protect	*JAP*	Remington	USA
Quad-Grip	*JAP*	Schick	USA
Reach	USA	Shower Shaver	USA
Rembrandt	USA	Silk Effects	USA
Scope	USA	*Softwin*	*FRA*
Sea Fresh	USA	Stubble Device	USA
Sea Friends	*JAP*	Trac II	USA
Sensodyne	*UK*	*Twin Lady Shaver*	*FRA*
Shape 1	*JAP*	Wilkinson Sword	USA
Tom's of Maine	USA	Xtreme 3	USA
Top Care	USA		

RAZORS/SHAVERS

Atra	USA		
Bic	*FRA*		
Braun	USA		
Daisy	USA		
Daisy Plus	USA		
Face-Guard	USA		

SHAVING CREAM

Aveeno	USA
Barbasol	USA
Bikini Bare	USA
Brut	*UKN*
Burma Shave	USA
Colgate	USA
Edge	USA

Shaving Cream (cont.)

Gillette	USA
Gyro	USA
Lectric Shave	USA
Noxema	USA
Old Spice	USA
Palmolive	USA
Prep	USA
Razoride	USA
Rise	USA
Schick	USA
Tom's of Maine	USA
Williams Mug Shave Soap	USA

SKIN CARE PRODUCTS

AcnePlex	USA
Acqua-Biomin	USA
Actea Heart	*JAP*
Adrien Arpel	USA
Almay	USA
Aloe Sun	USA
Aloe Vesta	USA
Aloecare	USA
Aloederm	USA
Aloegen	USA
Aloette	USA
Alpha	USA
Ambroderm	USA
American Fare	USA
Andrea	USA
Anessa Trans Wear	*JAP*
Anne French	USA
Anthelios SX	*FRA*
Anti-Aging Physician	USA
A-Plex	USA
Aquell	USA
Ardell	USA

Atrac-Tain	*DEN*
Atrix	*GER*
Aupres	*JAP*
Avage	USA
Avalon Organic Botanicals	USA
Aveeno	USA
Aween	*DEN*
Azelex	USA
Badedas	USA
Bain de Soleil	USA
Baktolan	*GER*
Balancing Astringent	USA
Banana Boat	USA
Beauticontrol	USA
Beauty Without Cruelty	USA
Be-Gone	USA
Belleza Latina	USA
Benefiance	*JAP*
Benefique	*JAP*
Bikini Bare	USA
Bio-Performance	*JAP*
Biore	*JAP*
Biotherm	USA
Body Clear	USA
Body Drench	USA
Body Fantasies	USA
Bop	*JAP*
Brasivol	USA
Brevoxyl	USA
Bullfrog	USA
C My Lips	USA
Calming Complex	USA
Carbonoel	USA
Carit	*JAP*
Carmol	USA
Castor Ceresters	USA
Ceramides	USA

Ceraphyl	USA	Foot Print	USA
Charles of the Ritz	USA	Fresh Face	USA
Clarins	FRA	Full Volume	USA
Clearasil	USA	GA Revitalizer	USA
C-Light	USA	Gale Hayman	USA
Clindet's	USA	Ganex	USA
Clobevate	USA	Gelatti	USA
Complex	USA	Gly-Miracle	USA
Confettit	USA	Gold Mine	USA
Coppertone	USA	Ha Sol	USA
Cos-Kelp	USA	Hand Medic	USA
Crema Occhi Intensiva	USA	Handsan	USA
Curash	USA	Hawaiian Tropic	USA
Curederma	USA	Heritage	USA
Curel	JAP	Hydra Dior	FRA
Cush	USA	Hydracare	USA
Daily Essentials	USA	Hyper-Cserum	USA
D-Clog	USA	Intimate Lotion	USA
Deep-C	USA	Kiehl's	FRA
Delicat	USA	Lacticare	USA
Dena-Vie	USA	Lanacane	USA
Derma Klenz	USA	Lancaster	USA
Dermal C	USA	Linked Papain	USA
Derma-Sure	USA	Lubrajel	USA
Dermavite	USA	Lubriderm	USA
Dove	UKN	Lumar	USA
Duac	USA	Luxiva	USA
Dual Fusion	USA	Luzier	USA
Eight Hour Cream	USA	M.D. Forte	USA
Emulsynt	USA	Mariner's Lotion	USA
Epilyt	USA	Melarrest	USA
Escalol	USA	Mill Creek	USA
Eudemin	USA	Miracol	USA
Eudermine	USA	Moistureguard	USA
Fabulous Feet	USA	Moistureshine	USA
Factan	USA	Nadinola	USA
Flowergenics	USA	Nair Dipilitory	USA
Fluoroplex	USA	Nanocel	USA

Skin Care Products (cont.)		Protective Veil	USA
Natural Harmony	USA	Provon	USA
Natural Thigh Rx	USA	Pureness	USA
Nature's Kiss	USA	Reflect	USA
NaturEssence	USA	Rejeuvenigue	USA
Naturgo	USA	Rejuven Q10	USA
Neoteric	USA	Relaxing Fragrance	USA
Neutrogena	USA	Renova	USA
New Cell Therapy	USA	Retin-A	USA
New Hands	USA	Rite Aid	USA
Nivea	GER	Roc Dermatalogic	USA
Noxema	USA	Rosac	USA
Oenotherol	USA	Rose Milk	USA
Oil of Olay	USA	Royal	USA
Oilatum	USA	Salicylic	USA
Ombrelle	USA	Sanicare	USA
Orchid Complex	USA	Saniclenz	USA
Origins	USA	Sanisept	USA
Orlane	FRA	Sanityze	USA
Overnight Success	USA	Sarna	USA
Pacquin	USA	Sastid	USA
Palmer's	USA	Sayman	USA
Panoxyl	USA	SBS	USA
Pavana	USA	SBS-71	USA
Phyotamine	USA	Scarzone	USA
Piz Buin	USA	Scrubmate	USA
Plenitude	FRA	Sea Buckthorn	USA
Plexajel	USA	Sea Results	USA
Polytar	USA	Sea Spa	USA
Pond's	UKN	Seaacids	USA
Poupina	USA	Sealastin	USA
Power Primer	USA	Seamollient	USA
Premium Body	USA	Seaware	USA
Preventage	USA	*Sebum Pack*	JAP
Procare	USA	Selenium Natural	USA
Programme Solaire	ITL	Sensicare	USA
Prolipid	USA	Septisoft	USA
Prom	USA	Septisol	USA

Shea Butter Formula	USA	Sunfrog	USA
Shiseido	*JAP*	Sunright	USA
SK-II	USA	Super-C	USA
Skin Activator	USA	Super-Lube	USA
Skin Medica	USA	Swedish Beauty	USA
Skin Milk	USA	*Swedish Care*	*BGM*
Skin Renewal	USA	*Sween*	*DEN*
Skin Structures	*BGM*	Swimmer's	USA
Skinanswer	USA	Tazorac	USA
Skinceuticals	*FRA*	Therapy	USA
Skinlights	USA	Tinamed	USA
Skin-So-Soft	USA	Tisserand Aromatherapy	USA
Soft N Sure	USA	Titania	USA
Soft Sense	*JAP*	*Towada*	*JAP*
Soft Touch	USA	Trendy	USA
Softguard	USA	Tricalgoxyl	USA
Solar Sense	USA	Trilastene	USA
Solarcaine	USA	Trioxygen C	USA
Solarcat	USA	Tri-Phasic White	USA
Sonoma Soap Co.	USA	Tru Face	USA
Soraya	USA	Two-Night Watch	USA
Soy Max	USA	Udder-Wize	USA
Special Care	USA	Ultra-C	USA
Spectozole	USA	Ultraswim	USA
Sportscreme	USA	Under Cover	USA
Sproam	*DEN*	Ungentine	USA
St. Ives Swiss Formula	USA	Un-Petroleum	USA
Static Free	USA	Vaniqa	USA
Stendhal	*FRA*	*Vaseline*	*UKN*
Stomahesive	USA	Vegecell	USA
Stri-Dex	USA	Vegecol	USA
Suave	*UKN*	Villa De Jerome	USA
Sudden Change	USA	Visibly Even	USA
Sulfoxyl	USA	Vistabel	USA
Sulfur Soap	USA	*Vital-Perfection*	*JAP*
Sun Shade	USA	Vitamin C Absolute	USA
Sunbrellas	USA	Water Babies	USA
Sundance	USA	Weightless Volume	USA

Skin Care Products (cont.)			
Wet Ones	USA	*Eunova*	UK
Whirl-Sol	DEN	**Family Pharmacy**	USA
White Camellia	USA	**Femiron**	USA
White Diamonds	USA	**Fiber Greens+**	USA
Whiteness	JAP	*Flintstones*	GER
Wild Wind	USA	**Funny Chew Chews**	USA
Wild Yam	USA	**Gerahealth Tabs**	USA
Witch	USA	*Geritol*	UK
Woltra	USA	**Good N' Natural**	USA
Women Wise	USA	**Greens+**	USA
X-Tend	USA	**Health Hair**	USA
Xtra-Care	DEN	**Hudson Vitamins**	USA
Z Sperse	USA	**Imutabs**	USA
Za Skin	JAP	**Jungle Greens+**	USA
Zeasorb	USA	**KHG-7**	USA
Zetacet	USA	**Kindermins**	USA
Zia Natural	USA	*Lamberts*	DEN
ZNP	USA	**Li'l Critters**	USA
		Magna II	USA
		Malpotane	USA
VITAMINS		**Mega Stress**	USA
Abtei	UK	**Multiplex**	USA
Active Health Teen	USA	**Nature Blend**	USA
All Women	USA	*Nature Made*	JAP
Alluna	UK	*Nature's Best*	SWI
Avimin	DEN	**Nature's Bounty**	USA
Becoplex	DEN	**Nu Skin**	USA
Berocca	GER	**Nutri Mega**	USA
Bodyonics	USA	**Nutri-Hair**	USA
Bugs Bunny	GER	**Ocuvite**	USA
Camu Plus	USA	**One Source**	USA
Centrum	USA	*One-A-Day*	GER
Cetebe	UK	**Origin**	USA
Chocks	GER	*Oscal*	UK
Coral Calcium+	USA	**Pharbio**	USA
Covitol	GER	**Phytofem**	USA
Doctor's Choice	USA	**Poly-Vi-Sol**	USA
Ester-C	USA	*Protecton*	UK

Protein Greens+	USA	**Take One**	USA
Puritan's Pride	USA	*Takeda*	*JAP*
Radiance	USA	**Thermo Greens+**	USA
Rexall	USA	**Tonalin**	USA
S.F.6	USA	**Triplelean**	USA
Sam-E	*JAP*	**Tummy Care**	USA
Sea Buddies	USA	**Ultimate Health**	USA
Sesame Street	USA	**Ultra-Vite**	USA
Shaklee	USA	**Vistavitamins**	USA
Skin Eternal Plus	USA	*Vitaneurin*	*JAP*
Sleep N Restore	USA	**Vitaplan Rx**	USA
Soy Care	USA	**Vitaplex**	USA
Stresstabs	USA	**Vitasystems**	USA
Stuart Prenatal	USA	**Wellness**	USA
Sundown	USA	**Whole Heart**	USA
Supradin	*GER*	**Zero Flush**	USA
Sweet Essentials	USA		

Chapter 7

Clothing & Accessories

(**American owned in bold** / *Foreign owned in italic*)

FOOTWEAR

Aarau	USA	Armortex	USA
Aberdeen	USA	Aruba	USA
Acme	USA	Ashton	USA
Active Air	*UK*	*Asics*	*JAP*
Addison	USA	Aspen	USA
Adidas	*GER*	Aston	USA
Aerosoles	USA	*Atomo*	*ITL*
Alden	USA	*Attaccante*	*GER*
Alissa	USA	ATV's by Knapp	USA
Alivia	USA	Avalon	USA
Allen-Edmonds	USA	Avia	USA
Aloe	USA	Aylan	USA
Alphaburly Boots	USA	Badlands Boots	USA
Alphaforce	USA	Bahama	USA
Alphagrange	USA	Bakers	USA
Alphamoc	USA	Balloon	USA
Alphamule	USA	Bandolino	USA
Altama	USA	Barefoot Freedom	USA
Altama	USA	Barley	USA
Always	USA	Barratts	USA
Alycea	*GER*	Barry Comfort Slippers	USA
Amanda	USA	Bass	USA
Amarillo Boot	USA	Basswood	USA
Ambulator	USA	Bavaria	USA
American Eagle	USA	Becca	USA
American Legend	USA	Becky	USA
Amor	USA	Bella	USA
Angela	USA	Bellamo	USA
Ann Marino	USA	Benita	USA
Ann Taylor	USA	Benton	USA
Annapolis	USA	Biarritz	USA
Anne Klein	USA	Big Country	USA
Annie	USA	Big Horn Workboots	USA
Apex	USA	Big Sky Loafers	USA
Apres Ski	USA	Birki's	USA
Arc	USA	Bisou Bisou	USA
Argyll Waterproof	*UK*	Black Cowboy Boots	USA
		Blair	USA

Footwear (cont.)

Blanchi	USA	Carla Cristaldi	USA
Bluemarine	USA	Carlos by Carlos	USA
Boks	*GER*	Carolina	USA
Bongo	USA	Carrera	USA
Bontex	USA	Carrie	USA
Bootalinos	USA	Caruba	USA
Born	USA	Carver	USA
Boss Boots	USA	Casidy	USA
Bostonian	*UK*	Casino	USA
Brady	USA	Catalina	USA
Brandy	USA	Catapult	USA
Brass Boot	USA	Caterpillar	USA
Brazen Boots	USA	Catylan	USA
Brazen XL	USA	Cervo	USA
Breeze	USA	Chaddock	USA
Brenda	USA	Chambers	USA
Bridget	USA	Championship	
Brilliant	USA	Wimbledon W	USA
Britta	USA	Chapman & Moore	USA
Brooks	USA	Charles David	USA
Browsabouts	USA	Charlie	USA
Bullhide Boots	USA	Chase	USA
Buster Brown	USA	Chelsea	USA
Buzz	USA	Cherokee	USA
Cadiz	USA	Chicago	USA
Cailyn	USA	Chippewa Boots	USA
Caliber	USA	Chuck Taylor	USA
Cambrelle	USA	*Cica*	*UK*
Cambria	USA	*Clarks*	*UK*
Cameron	USA	Colby	USA
Cammie	USA	Cole-Haan	USA
Campione II	USA	Coleman	USA
Candice	USA	Colina	USA
Capezio Dance Shoes	USA	Comfort Fit	USA
Caprice	USA	Compass	USA
Caresse	USA	Connecticut	USA
Caribbean	USA	Connie	USA
		Contour Boots	USA

Converse	USA	Drew	USA
Cordura	USA	Drifter Boots	USA
Corvallis	USA	Dryjoys	USA
Cove	USA	Dry-Shod	USA
Cowtown Boots	USA	Du Ri Du Bu	USA
Crankshaft Boots	USA	Ducks Unlimited	USA
Curacao	USA	Duet	USA
Cutie	USA	Dukesa	USA
Dahlia	USA	*Dunlop Boots*	*NETH*
Dalia	USA	Durango Boots	USA
Dan Post Western Boots	USA	Eagle Golf	USA
Danica	USA	Easy Spirit	USA
Danner	USA	Eaton	USA
Daphne	USA	Eden	USA
Davenport	USA	Ego	USA
Davos	USA	Elastichette	USA
DC Shoes	USA	Elevators	USA
Dearfoams	USA	Eliminator	USA
Debut	USA	Endicott Johnson	USA
Decker	USA	Enzo Angiolini	USA
Demi II	USA	Erin	USA
Der-Dau	USA	Esprit	USA
Desert	*UK*	Etonic	USA
Destin	USA	Etre	USA
Dexter	USA	Eurosole	USA
Dingo Boots	USA	EZ Feet Slippers	USA
Dipstick Boots	USA	Fairfax	USA
Discret	USA	Faith	USA
Disney	USA	Fanfares	USA
Diva	USA	Farris	USA
Dogwood Golf Shoes	USA	Fayme	USA
Doll	USA	*Fila*	*ITL*
Donna	USA	Flats Sneaker	USA
Dore	USA	Flirt	USA
Dorian	USA	Florsheim	USA
Double-H Boots	USA	Flower Power	USA
Dove	USA	FootJoy Classics	USA
Dr. Scholl's	USA	Footonic Ultra	USA

Footwear (cont.)		Gypsy	USA
Forever	USA	H.H. Brown	USA
Franki	USA	H.S. Trask	USA
Freddie	USA	Haidee	USA
Freedom	USA	Halle	USA
Fremont	USA	Halley	USA
French	USA	Hallkirk	USA
Froghair Golf	USA	Handbag	USA
Frye Boot Co.	USA	*Hanover*	*UK*
Fulton	USA	Happy Go Lightly	USA
Fur Now	USA	Hartford	USA
G. Wiz	USA	Hartney	USA
Gail	USA	Havana	USA
Gali	USA	Heather	USA
Game	USA	Heidi	USA
Geen	USA	*Hermes*	*FRA*
Genesco	USA	Hippo	USA
Gentle	USA	Hitchcock	USA
Georgia Boot	USA	Hogan	USA
Getaway	USA	Hogue	USA
Giggle	USA	Holbrook	USA
Glasgow	USA	Honour	USA
Glen	USA	Hope	USA
Glenda	USA	Hudson	USA
Glendale	USA	Huki	USA
Glory	USA	Huntress	USA
Glossy	USA	Hush Puppies	USA
Godiva	USA	Hyde	USA
Grace	USA	Hytest	USA
Granada	USA	Iceland	USA
Grand	USA	Infantry Combat Boots	USA
Grasshoppers	USA	Ingrid	USA
Gravel Guards	USA	Irene	USA
Greenwich	USA	Isadora	USA
Grid	USA	J & M	USA
Grimes	USA	J Chisolm	USA
Gucci	USA	Jack	USA
Guthrie	USA	Jackie	USA

James	USA	K	USA
Jane	USA	Kaleidoscope	USA
Jarman	USA	Kaley	USA
Jasper	USA	*Kamik*	*CAN*
Java Coast	USA	Kamila	USA
Jello	USA	Kandy	USA
Jem	USA	Kane	USA
Jenna	USA	Kangaroos Boots	USA
Jennie	USA	Kara	USA
Jessie	USA	Karen	USA
Jet Set	USA	Kari	USA
Jetaime	USA	Karisa	USA
Jezebell	USA	Kat	USA
Jiffy	USA	Kathy	USA
Jill	USA	Katrina	USA
Jiminy	USA	Kayla	USA
Jimmy	USA	Keds	USA
Jo	USA	Keesha	USA
Joan & David	USA	Kelsey	USA
Joanna	USA	Kendal	USA
John Deere	USA	Kendall	USA
John Lobb	*FRA*	Kenneth Cole	USA
Johnston & Murphy	USA	Kensington	USA
Jojo	USA	Kenzie	USA
Joker	USA	Kerry	USA
Jordan	USA	Kevlar	USA
Josephine	USA	Kiki	USA
Journeys	USA	King of the Beach	USA
Joyce	USA	Kite	USA
Joyfull Dots	USA	Knapp	USA
Judy	USA	Kodiak	USA
Julie	USA	Koji	USA
Jumping Jack	USA	Krista	USA
Jumpy	USA	K-Swiss	USA
June	USA	Kute	USA
Juno	USA	L.L. Bean	USA
Justin	USA	L.S. Studio	USA
Justin Boots	USA	LA Gear	USA

Footwear (cont.)		Magnum	USA
Lacey	USA	Malia-R	USA
Lacey's Ballerina	USA	Malio	USA
Lacross	USA	Mandolin	USA
Laddy	USA	Mandy	USA
Lakia	USA	Marcie	USA
Laredo	USA	Marco	USA
Lawrence	USA	Marga	USA
Leanne	USA	Marquise	USA
Lehigh	USA	Maserati	USA
Levi's	USA	Mason Shoe	USA
Licorice	USA	Mauri	USA
Lido	USA	Mayde's	USA
Life Stride	USA	Melon	USA
Lili	USA	Melrose	USA
Lilith	USA	Merced	USA
Lindsey	USA	Meredith	USA
Lipstick	USA	Merida	USA
Lisbett	USA	Merrell	USA
Lita	USA	Michael Kors	USA
Livewires	USA	Mimosa	USA
Logger Boots	USA	Missus	USA
Lola	USA	Mojave	USA
Loreta	USA	Mona	USA
Loreto	USA	Monarch	USA
Lotto Athletic Shoes	ITL	Morgan	USA
Lotus	USA	Motiva	USA
Louissa	USA	Nadia	USA
Love Affair	USA	Napoli	USA
Lucchese Boots	USA	Natalia	USA
Lucy	USA	Natoma	USA
Lugz	USA	Naturalizer	USA
Luskeys Roper Boots	USA	NaturalSport	USA
Luxor	USA	Nature Sole	USA
Luz Da Lua	USA	Negril	USA
Maddy	USA	Neon	USA
Madera	USA	New Balance	USA
Magneforce Golf Shoes	USA	Nice	USA

Night Life	USA	Polo Ralph Lauren	USA
Nike	USA	Pony	USA
Nine West	USA	Pricilla	USA
Nocona Boots	USA	Primrose	USA
Noodle	USA	Pro-Keds	USA
Nora	USA	Propet	USA
Northerner	USA	Provence	USA
Nunn-Bush	USA	Pullman	USA
Nurse Mates	USA	*Puma*	*GER*
Oakley	*ITL*	Quest	USA
Obie	USA	Quiksilver	USA
Oceania Sail CU	USA	Radical Boots	USA
Ofelia	USA	Radnor	USA
Olive	USA	Rainbow	USA
Olympia	USA	*Rainha*	*BZL*
Omni	USA	Ramli	USA
Ongaurd	USA	Ranger	USA
Oomphies Slippers	USA	Rangoni	USA
Opium	USA	Rattlesnake Boots	USA
Oracle	USA	Realities	USA
Orion	USA	Red Goose	USA
Outback Boots	USA	*Red River*	*UK*
Outrage Boots	USA	Red Roads	USA
Pacific	USA	Red Wing	USA
Padua	USA	Redmond	USA
Papillio	USA	*Reebok*	*GER*
Parris	USA	Reena	USA
Pasta	USA	Reese	USA
Patty	USA	Renee	USA
Pauline	USA	Report	USA
Payton	USA	Revere	USA
Pedro Garcia	USA	Rioja	USA
Pepe Moll	USA	Ritzy	USA
Perfection	USA	Riviera	USA
Piedmont	USA	Rockport	USA
Pillowbacks	USA	Rocky	USA
Pluma	USA	Rodo	USA
Polar Boots	USA	Romance	USA

Footwear (cont.)

Rosseti Sport	USA	Slider	USA
Rouge	USA	Snowdonia	USA
Ryon's Boots	USA	Snowdrift	USA
Saba	USA	Sof Shu	USA
Sabel	USA	Sofjoy	USA
Sadie	USA	Soft Spots	USA
Safety Skids	USA	Softwalk	USA
Saga	USA	Solano	USA
Salomon	GER	Sole Ultra	USA
Samoa Sandals	BZL	Sorel	USA
San Marino	USA	South Fork	USA
Sandal Sox	USA	Sphere	USA
Sandpipers Sandals	CAN	Sportocasins	USA
Santa Cruz	USA	Sportwalks	CAN
Sao	USA	Springers	UK
SAS Shoes	USA	Sprock-It	USA
Saucony	USA	Spur	USA
Scada	USA	Spyder	CAN
Scapino	NETH	Stabilite	USA
Scholl	UK	Stacey	USA
Scorcher Boots	USA	Stacker Boots	USA
Scovel	USA	Stacooler	USA
Scribe	USA	Stacy Adams	USA
Sentry Boots	USA	Star	USA
Servus	USA	Starter Switch Boots	USA
Sesto Meucci	USA	Stealth	USA
Sete Leguas	BZL	Steve Madden	USA
Sheepskin	USA	Sting Ray	USA
Sheffield	GER	Stormtracks Boots	USA
Shellys	UK	Strada	UK
Shoe Pavilion	USA	Stride Rite	USA
Sierras Boots	USA	Striker	USA
Signature	USA	Strut Boots	USA
Silph	GER	Stuart's Choice	UK
Simms Keen	USA	Sunjuns	USA
Skechers	USA	Sunshine	USA
Skiff	USA	Superga	ITL
		Surflex	USA

Sylvan	USA	Turin	USA
T.R.E.A.T.S.	USA	Twist	USA
Tacticals Boots	USA	Two Shot Soles	USA
Talley	USA	TX Traction	USA
Tan Lady Boots	USA	Tyler	USA
Tayla	USA	Ugg	USA
Tazza	USA	Unisa	USA
Ted Baker	*UK*	Uplander	USA
Tender Tootsies	*CAN*	Valerie	USA
Tenille	USA	Vanderbilt	USA
Terrasoles	USA	Vaneli	USA
Teva	USA	Vans	USA
Tex Mocs	USA	Vantage	USA
The Endurer	USA	*Vector*	*GER*
The Original Muck Boot Co.	USA	Venezia	USA
		Vero Ve	USA
The Walking Company Collection	USA	Verona	USA
		Vibram	USA
Thermolds	USA	Vienna	USA
Thorogard	USA	*Viking*	*NETH*
Tide	USA	*Viking Boots*	*NETH*
Tiki Beaded	USA	Vineta	USA
Timberland	USA	Vista	USA
Timbermaster	USA	*Wallabee*	*UK*
Tingley Rubber	USA	*Wanderlust*	*CAN*
Toddler Boots	USA	Waterkid	USA
Tod's	*ITL*	Waterman	USA
Tommy Bahama	USA	Weather Tuff	USA
Tracy	USA	Weatherlite Series	USA
Treadeasy	USA	*Weebok*	*GER*
Trekker	USA	Weejuns	USA
Tretorn	*GER*	Weinbrenner	USA
Tribeca Lace Boots	USA	Wellington	USA
Trista	USA	Wendell	USA
Trotters	USA	Whitney	USA
Tucker	USA	Wilbur Coon	USA
Tuffkushion	USA	Wild Rice	USA
Tufflex	*UK*	Wiley	USA

Footwear (cont.)

Williams the Shoeman	*AUS*
Windy	USA
Wolverine	USA
Work Force	USA
Worx	USA
XOXO	USA
Youth Boots	USA
Z-Economy	USA
Zelma	USA
Zeta	USA
Zimmer	USA
Zinnia	USA
Zinnia Wedge	USA
Zoom Soccer Shoes	*THAI*
Zurich	USA

GENERAL APPAREL

A/E Sport & Co.	*CAN*
A5	USA
Abanderado	USA
Abbey Brand	USA
Aberdeen	USA
Addition-Elle	*CAN*
Adidas	*GER*
Adirondack	USA
Adobe Rose	USA
Alacrity	USA
Alive	USA
All American Clothing	USA
All Climate	*CAN*
All That Jazz	USA
Almost Bare	*ITL*
Alpha Chi Omega	USA
Alpha Delta Pi	USA
Alpha Factor Gymnastic	USA
Alpine Guide	USA
Alpine Studio	USA

Always Caroline	USA
Amelia	USA
America Today	*NETH*
American Apparel	USA
American Ballet Theater	USA
American Legend	USA
Amici	*NETH*
Amphi	*JAP*
Amplifier	USA
Amy Byer	USA
Amy Too	USA
Anatelier	*JAP*
Andrea	USA
Andrew Blues	USA
Andrew Fezza	USA
Andrew Marc	USA
Andrew Sports	USA
Angelica	*ITL*
Angelica-Priest	USA
Angels by	
Victoria's Secret	USA
Anisette	USA
Anne Cole Collection	USA
Anne Klein	USA
Annie	USA
Antoinette	USA
Appel	USA
Appella	USA
Applegate	USA
Arapahoe	USA
Arcade America	USA
Areo	USA
Arielle	USA
Aristoc	USA
Arnold Palmer	USA
Arrow	USA
Arrow Classic	USA
Arrow Gold Toe Brand	USA

Artisan	USA	Bike	USA
Arwa	*ITL*	Bill Blass Scarves	USA
Ascentials	USA	Bill Burns Sportswear	USA
Ashley Reed	USA	Blake & Manley Sweaters	USA
Ashton	USA	Blanche	USA
Ashworth	USA	Bobbie Brooks	USA
Aspen Sportswear	USA	Body Beautiful	USA
Astrid	USA	Body Drama Sleepwear	USA
Attitudes Only	USA	*Body Wild*	*THAI*
Audra	*ITL*	Bodyflex	USA
Audrey	USA	Boltons	USA
Austin Reed	*JAP*	Bonds	USA
Authentic Chino Casuals	USA	*Bonfire*	*GER*
Ava	USA	Bongo	USA
Avalanche Sportswear	USA	*Borgofiori*	*ITL*
Avalon	USA	*Boss*	*ITL*
Avenue	USA	Breezin Sportswear	USA
Avenue Rose	USA	Brite Legs	USA
Aztec Sportswear	USA	*BSC*	*THAI*
Azure	USA	BT Kids	USA
Baldessarini	*ITL*	Buddy Lee	USA
Bali	USA	Bugle Boy	USA
Bauer & Black	USA	BVD	USA
Bay to Bay	USA	Byer California	
Beaux Reves	USA	Sportswear	USA
Becky	USA	Cabana Life	USA
Belcor	USA	California Influence	
Belday	*GER*	Sportswear	USA
Berkshire	USA	Calvin Klein	USA
Berluti	*FRA*	Cambridge	USA
Bert Pulitzer	USA	Cameo (Sara Lee)	USA
Bestform	USA	Campus	USA
Better Than Bare	USA	Canyon River Blues	USA
B'Gosh	USA	Cape Cod	USA
Bibo	USA	Capezio Dance	USA
Bice	USA	Capital Sportswear	USA
Big Dog Sportswear	USA	Capri	USA
Big Dogs	USA	*Carla Conti*	*MEX*

General Apparel (cont.)

Carter's	USA	Dickies	USA
Cascade	USA	Dim	USA
Casey & Max	USA	Disney	USA
Catalina Swimwear	USA	Dockers Brand	USA
Cathy Lee	USA	Doncaster	USA
Cattleman Westerwear	USA	*Donna Karan*	*FRA*
Champion	USA	Donnkenny	USA
Chantilly Place Dresses	USA	Dotti	USA
Chaps	USA	Dry Foot Socks	USA
Chaps by Ralph Lauren	USA	Due Date	USA
Cherokee	USA	*Dusol*	*JAP*
Cheryl Tiegs	USA	Ease Sport	USA
Chloe	USA	*East West Clothing Co.*	*CAN*
Chorus Line	USA	Ebony Rich	USA
Christian Aujard	USA	Ebony Supreme	USA
Christian Lacroix	*FRA*	Eddie Bauer	USA
Claiborne	USA	Elderado	USA
Coaster Gear	USA	Elisabeth	USA
Colesta	USA	Emily	USA
Coliseum Boys	USA	Enro	USA
Coppley	USA	Enticements	USA
Country by Jax	USA	Especially You	USA
Country Touch	USA	Evan-Picone	USA
Cricket Lane	USA	Eve Byer	USA
Cross Creek	USA	Eve Too	USA
Crowntuft	USA	Excalibur	USA
Dana Buchman	USA	*Excellency*	*THAI*
Danier Leather	*CAN*	*Exquisite Form*	
Danskin Legwear	USA	*(AGP Industrial)*	*PHIL*
David Dart	USA	Exquisite Form	
Deb	USA	(VF Corp.)	USA
Delta	USA	Eyecatchers	USA
Demetre	USA	Farah	USA
Designers Originals		Fashion Galaxy	USA
Sweaters	USA	Fashion Nautigue	USA
Destination Maternity	USA	Fern Bratten	USA
Diams	USA	Field & Stream	USA
		Field & Stream Socks	USA

Fila	*ITL*	Hanes	USA
Filodoro	USA	Hardwick Clothes	USA
Finals Swimwear	USA	Harley-Davidson	USA
Finery by Freeman	USA	*Harmony*	*THAI*
Finish Line Blue Label	USA	Harper	USA
Flight Deck U.S.A.	USA	Hart Schaffner & Marx	USA
Flyer's	USA	Heet	USA
Footnotes	USA	Helen of Troy	USA
Forever New Shirts	USA	Herbcraft	USA
Foxcroft	USA	Hickey Freeman	USA
Fred Meyer	USA	High Grade Western	
Frederick's		Wear	USA
of Hollywood	USA	*Hilfiger*	*CHN*
Freeway	*THAI*	Horace Small	
Fruit of The Loom	USA	(occupational)	USA
Gant	*SWE*	Hot Coles Swimwear	USA
Gantner of California	USA	*Hue Legwear*	*ITL*
Gantner Swimwear	USA	*Hugo*	*ITL*
Garan	USA	*Hugo Boss*	*ITL*
Garanimals	USA	Hunt Club	USA
Genuine Article	USA	Huntley of York	USA
Genuine Blues	USA	I. Appel	USA
Genuine Girl	USA	I.C. Isaacs	USA
Geoffrey Beene	USA	Identity	USA
Gildan Activewear	*CAN*	In Control	USA
Girbaud	USA	Ingeo Underwear	USA
Girls Club	USA	Innsbruck Socks	USA
Gitano	USA	International Male	USA
Gloria Vanderbilt	USA	Intima Cherry	USA
Golden	*THAI*	In-Vest Outerwear	USA
Gore-Tex Rainwear	USA	Irvine Park	USA
Grand Monarch	*JAP*	Isoclean	USA
Grandoe Dress Gloves	USA	It Fits, It Fits!	USA
Grove Avenue	USA	*Itokin*	*THAI*
Guess?	USA	Ivy	USA
Guy Laroche	*THAI*	Izod	USA
H. Freeman	USA	J. Chuckles	USA
Haggar	USA	J. Crew	USA

General Apparel (cont.)

J.J. Cochran Boys	USA	King Louie	USA
Jack Nicklaus	*JAP*	King of the Beach	USA
Jaclyn	USA	Koret	USA
Jaclyn B.	USA	*Kullastri*	*THAI*
Jacques Moret	USA	L.A. Intimates Sleepwear	USA
Jag Beachwear	USA	L.A. T Sport	USA
James B. Fairchild	USA	L.E.I. Swimwear	USA
Jansport	USA	*La Femme*	*THAI*
Jax	USA	LA Gear	USA
Jazzertogs	USA	*La Seine*	*THAI*
Jean Arnou	*IRE*	Lady Hardwick	USA
Jerzees	USA	Lady Supreme	USA
JH Collectibles	USA	Land-N-Lakes	USA
Joan Leslie Sportswear	USA	Lands' End	USA
Jockey	USA	Lanz of Salzburg	USA
Joe Boxer	USA	*Laura Ashley*	*UK*
John Henry	USA	*Lebole*	*ITL*
John Peel Ltd.	USA	Lee	USA
John Weitz	USA	L'eggs	USA
Jones & Co. Sportswear	USA	Les Jeunes Sportswear	USA
Jones New York	USA	Leslie Fay	USA
Jones Wear	USA	Levi's Brand	USA
Jordache	USA	Lily of France	USA
Jos. A. Bank	USA	Little Big Dogs	USA
Juicy Couture	USA	Little L'eggs	USA
Just For You	USA	Little Me	USA
Just My Size	USA	*Little Wacoal*	*THAI*
Justice Sportswear	USA	Liz	USA
Kasper Suits	USA	Liz And Me	USA
Katherine	USA	Liz Claiborne	USA
Kathie Lee Dresses	USA	Liza	USA
Kathy Lee Gifford	USA	Lizsport	USA
Kathy White Sportswear	USA	Lizwear	USA
Kenneth Cole	USA	Loco Blue	USA
Key Bib Overalls	USA	Lofteez	USA
Kicks	USA	London Fog	USA
Kids "R" Us	USA	Long Gone Banlon	USA
		Lord Isaacs	USA

Lord West Formalwear	USA	Company	USA
Lost River Outerwear	USA	**Newport Blue**	USA
Louis Feraud	*THAI*	**Newport News**	USA
Louis Joone	*THAI*	**Next to Nothing Briefs**	USA
Louis Vuitton	*FRA*	*Nicklaus*	*JAP*
Lycra Socks	USA	**Nicole Miller**	USA
Maggie Barnes	USA	**Nike**	USA
Major League Baseball	USA	**Nines by Southwick**	USA
Manhattan	USA	*No Nonsense Pantyhose*	*ITL*
Mariner	*THAI*	*Nona Ladies Wear*	*JAP*
Mayer Pantyhose	USA	*Nonstop*	*ITL*
McKid's	USA	**North Face**	USA
Me-2 Loungewear	USA	**Norton McNaughton**	USA
Megaplay	USA	*Nudie*	*THAI*
Melody	*THAI*	**Nur Die**	USA
Melrose	USA	**Olga**	USA
Members Only	USA	*OMSA*	*ITL*
Men America	USA	**Onesies**	USA
Michel Klein	*THAI*	**Oscar de La Renta**	USA
Minna	*THAI*	**OshKosh**	USA
Miss Elaine Sleepwear	USA	**OshKosh B'Gosh**	USA
Mix Self	*THAI*	**Our Girl by Healthtex**	USA
Mizuno	*JAP*	**Outer Banks**	USA
Montagut	*THAI*	**Oxford Sportswear**	USA
Monte	USA	**Oxygen**	USA
More Intimate Sleepwear	USA	**Page & Tuttle**	USA
Mossimo	USA	**Paquette**	USA
Mountain Lion	USA	**Park Street Dress Shirts**	USA
Movie Star	USA	**Patagonia**	USA
Munsingwear	USA	**Paul Frederick**	USA
My Michelle	USA	**Paul Stuart**	USA
National Football League	USA	**Payhalf**	USA
Natural Baby	USA	**Performance**	USA
Nautica	USA	**Perry Ellis**	USA
Neatgards	USA	*Perry Sport*	*NETH*
New Balance	USA	**Philippe Matignon**	USA
New Man	*THAI*	**Pierre Cardin**	USA
New York Clothing		**Pim**	USA

General Apparel (cont.)

Pizzazz	USA	Russell Athletic	USA
Plains Westernwear	USA	Rustler	USA
Plaza South	USA	Ruth	USA
Poco Briefs	USA	Saber	USA
Polar King	USA	Sag Harbor	USA
Polar-Therm Activewear	USA	Saltaire	USA
Polo by Ralph Lauren	USA	*Saltallegro*	*ITL*
Pony	USA	*Salute*	*JAP*
Portraits by Northern Isles	USA	*Salvatore Ferragamo*	*ITL*
		Samantha	USA
Pretty Polly	USA	*Sandalo*	*ITL*
Primanatural Socks	*ITL*	Sandcastle Swimwear	USA
Principe	*ITL*	Sandia	USA
Pucci	*FRA*	Sandpiper	USA
Quiksilver	USA	*Sangallo*	*ITL*
Radcliffe	USA	*Sanpellegrino*	*ITL*
Ralph Lauren	USA	Sante Fe	USA
Ralph Lauren Polo	USA	Sara	USA
Raven	USA	Sarah	USA
Razzamatazz	USA	Saratoga	USA
Reebok	*GER*	Sassy	USA
Reed St. James	USA	Scaasi	USA
Rena Rowan For Saville	USA	*Scapino*	*NETH*
Resilience	USA	Scarlett	USA
Resistol Hats	USA	Scentblocker Rainwear	USA
Revelation	USA	Scentrex	USA
Riders	USA	*Scherrer*	*JAP*
Risque Undergarments	USA	*Schiesser*	*SWI*
Rob Roy	USA	Schoeller	USA
Robby Len	USA	*Scholl Flight*	*UK*
Robert Terry	USA	School Days	USA
Ross & Cromarty	USA	*Sciarpa*	*ITL*
Rossignol	*FRA*	Scirocco	USA
Roust-A-Bout	USA	Scoopy	USA
Route 66	USA	Scorpions	USA
Roxy Girl	USA	Scott McClintock	USA
Royal Palm	USA	Scottie	USA
		Scout	USA

Screamers	USA	Sigma Kappa	USA
Scrim	USA	Signature II	USA
Scudi Ties	*ITL*	Sigrid Olsen	USA
Sea Dog	USA	Silent Rain	USA
Sean John	USA	Silk Reflections	USA
Seaside	USA	Silka Micro	USA
Seaton	USA	Silkweight	USA
Sedona	USA	Silver Swim	USA
Seductive Wear	USA	Simplicity Patterns	USA
Seek Out	USA	*Sisley*	*ITL*
Seminole	USA	Sister Moon	USA
Senator	USA	*Sixty*	*ITL*
Seneca	USA	SJ	USA
Sensual Curves	USA	Skippi	USA
Serena	USA	Slates	USA
Sewfree	USA	Sleek	USA
SH Plus	USA	Sleepy Sleepwear	USA
Shadmore Jacket	USA	Slim Polo	USA
Shanghai Tang	*SWI*	Slumber Sleepwear	USA
Shannon	USA	Slumber Sox	USA
Shapely Silhouettes	USA	Smart	USA
Sharp	USA	Smart Comfort	USA
Shavonne	USA	*Smart Pink*	*JAP*
Sheer Elegance	USA	Smart Pocket	USA
Sheer Endurance	*ITL*	Smart Shirts	USA
Sheer Therapy	USA	Smart Time	USA
Sheerware	USA	Smith+Noble	USA
Shevron Shell	USA	Smooth Silhouettes	USA
Shield	USA	*Soare*	*SWE*
Shimmer	USA	Sofia	USA
Shooter	USA	Sof-T	USA
Shopper	USA	Soft Supplex	USA
Shrug	USA	Softones	USA
Shrunken	USA	Soiree	USA
Sideline	USA	Sol Y Oro	USA
Sideout	USA	Solarmax	USA
Siena Studio	USA	Sonoma Genuine	USA
Sierra	USA	Sope Creek	USA

General Apparel (cont.)

Sophia	USA	Static Outerwear	USA
Sophie	*ITL*	Staticsorb	USA
Soup	*JAP*	Statshield	USA
Southerly Buster	USA	Stedman For Her	USA
Southwest Canyon	USA	Steel-Built	USA
Southwick	USA	*Stefanel*	*ITL*
Spartan Rainwear	USA	Steph	USA
Spearmint	USA	Stepz	USA
Speedo	*UK*	Stetson Hats	USA
Spencer	USA	*Stimulus*	*JAP*
SP-Glitz	USA	Stonebridge	USA
Spiewak	USA	Storm Champ	USA
Splading	USA	Stormfleece Jacket	USA
Splash	USA	Stormflex Jacket	USA
Split	USA	Storybook Heirlooms	USA
Sporicidin	USA	Stratus	USA
Sporte Parts	USA	Strawberry	USA
Spring And Mercer	USA	Streetgear	USA
Spring Fling	USA	Stretch Lace Bikini	USA
Sprint	USA	Stripe Cap	USA
SS-Shrug	USA	Stripe Tank	USA
St. John's Bay	USA	Structure	USA
St. Looey	USA	Studio B	USA
St. Tropez	USA	Studio Ease	USA
Stacy	USA	Studio Jax	USA
Staflex	USA	Style & Co.	USA
Stain Resister	USA	*StyleJam*	*JAP*
Stan Herman	USA	*Subito*	*JAP*
Stan Smith	*GER*	*Sugar*	*THAI*
Standard Rainwear	USA	Summer Girl Swimwear	USA
Standfield's Underwear	*CAN*	Sun Blush Swimwear	USA
Stanley Blacker	USA	*Sunauna*	*JAP*
Stanton	USA	Sunblock	USA
Star Spangled	USA	Sunburst	USA
Star Struck	USA	Sunclava Outerwear	USA
Stardust Sleepwear	USA	Sunflower	USA
Starlet	USA	Sunny	USA
		Sunscreen	USA

Sunset	USA	Teamsock	USA
Sunshield	USA	Teamwear	USA
Super Tube	USA	Tech 60/40	USA
Superbuilt	USA	Tech Twill	USA
Supermacy	*JAP*	Tech Vent	USA
Supershell Outerwear	USA	Tekware	USA
Superstar	*GER*	Ten Mile Jacket	USA
Super-Tuff	USA	Tencel	USA
Supreme	USA	*Tende Imperiali Ties*	*ITL*
Surla Plage	*JAP*	*Tende Volanti Ties*	*ITL*
Susutseso	*JAP*	Tepee	USA
Sutseso	*JAP*	Teresa Tee	USA
Sutton	USA	Terry Cover Up	USA
Suzelle Skirt	USA	Terry Redlin	USA
Sweet Innocence	USA	*Tex*	*FRA*
Sweetheart	USA	The American Collection	USA
Swim Systems Swimwear	USA	*The Emporium*	*JAP*
Swimming To The Moon	*JAP*	The Flying Jacket	USA
Swing	USA	The Iron Eagle Jacket	USA
Swoosh	USA	The Original Tee	USA
Sylvia	USA	The Ritz Winter Gloves	USA
Sympho	USA	*The Shop TK*	
Symphony	USA	*Takeo Kikuchi*	*JAP*
Synchro X Crossing	*JAP*	The Territory Ahead	USA
Syncro X	*JAP*	Thermal Pro Outerwear	USA
T.L.C.	USA	Thermolite	USA
Tactel	USA	Thinsulate Rainwear	USA
Tahoe	USA	*Thomas Pink*	*FRA*
Tailors Row	USA	Thorlos	USA
Takeo Kikuchi	*JAP*	*Thyme Maternity*	*CAN*
Tallia	USA	Tia	USA
Tallulah	USA	Tiera	USA
Tanner	USA	Tiki Toile	USA
Tara	USA	Timber Creek	
Tayla	USA	by Wrangler	USA
Tea Rose	USA	Timber Falls	USA
Teak	USA	Time Out	USA
Team Realtree Rainwear	USA	Timeout	USA

General Apparel (cont.)

Tingley Jacket	USA	Tucumcari	USA
Tiny	USA	Tuff-Enuff Coats	USA
Titanium	USA	Tulip	USA
TKS Basics	USA	Turkish	USA
Toastie II Mittens	USA	*Tutti*	*ITL*
Tog Shop	USA	Twain	USA
Toledo	USA	*Twinwall Rainwear*	*CAN*
Tom James	USA	Two of Hearts	USA
Tom Sawyer	USA	Two Pepper	USA
Tommy Bahama	USA	Tychem	USA
Tommy Hilfiger	*CHN*	Tyvek	USA
Tony Lambert	USA	U.S. Clothing Company	USA
Top Man	*UK*	Ulani	USA
Top Stitch	USA	Ultimax	USA
Topshop	*UK*	*Ultracil Sweater*	*MEX*
Topsville	USA	Ultragard Jacket	USA
Tosca	USA	Ultra-Tech	USA
Town & Country	USA	*Una Parte*	*JAP*
Tracks Mittens	USA	Under Gear	USA
Tracolla Con Paillettes	*ITL*	Under The Sea	USA
Trail	USA	Underoos	USA
Transparent Control	*ITL*	Union	USA
Trapeze	USA	Union Underwear	USA
Trappings	USA	UnionBay	USA
Travelers Worsted Suits	USA	*Uniqlo*	*JAP*
Travelsmith Outfitters	USA	*United Colors of Benetton*	*ITL*
Treadeasy	USA	University Club	USA
Trefle	*JAP*	Univogue	USA
Trellis	USA	Uniwear Outerwear	USA
Trillogy	USA	Unno	USA
Trimfit	USA	Unno Underwear	USA
Trina	USA	*Untitled*	*JAP*
Trinidad	USA	UO & Design	USA
Trojan	*JAP*	*UOMO*	*ITL*
Trudy	USA	Urban Renewal	USA
Trusoft	USA	*U-Safety*	*GER*
TSV	USA	Utility	USA
		Vacation	USA

Val	USA	Violet	USA
Val Mode Sleepwear	USA	Violets & Roses	USA
Valdez	USA	*Virgola Ties*	*ITL*
Valkarina Jacket	USA	Vista	USA
Value Supplex	USA	Vogue Patterns	USA
ValuGards	USA	*Voicemail*	*JAP*
Van Heusen	USA	*VP*	*JAP*
Vansport	USA	*Wacoal*	*JAP*
Vaporsport	USA	*Wallis*	*UK*
Varilind	*BGM*	Walls	USA
Vassarette	USA	Ward Jacket	USA
Vee Vee	USA	Warn Ware	USA
Vega	USA	*Warsteiner*	*GER*
Veloce 500	USA	*Waruni*	*JAP*
Velocity	USA	Water Girl Int'l	USA
Vena Pareo	USA	Watercolor	USA
Venice Blvd	USA	Watergirl	USA
Ventilator	USA	Water-Pruf	USA
Venus Return	*JAP*	Wave	USA
Venus Swimwear	USA	Wearfirst	USA
Vera	USA	Weather Tuff	USA
Vera Mont	*GER*	Weathergear	USA
Vera Wang	USA	Weather-Tech	USA
Veronique	USA	WebDri	USA
VertX	USA	*Weebok*	*GER*
Vestito	*ITL*	*Wellbeing*	*JAP*
VF	USA	Wendy	USA
Via Della Spiga Ties	*ITL*	*West Win*	*JAP*
Via Max	USA	Westbound	USA
Via Tornabuoni Ties	*ITL*	*Westbury*	*BGM*
Vicky	USA	Western Apparel	USA
Victorinox	*SWI*	Whisper Soft	USA
Victory	USA	Wickers	USA
Villager	USA	Wigwam	USA
Ville Dazur	*JAP*	Wild Flower	USA
Vineyard Vines	USA	Wild Heart	USA
Vintage Blue	USA	William	USA
Vintage Studio	USA	Willow	USA

General Apparel (cont.)

Wilma Jacket	USA
Wind Pro	USA
Windstopper	USA
Wing	*JAP*
Winnie	USA
Wonderbra	USA
Wondermaid	USA
Wonder-Wick	USA
Woodbridge	USA
Wooden Ships	USA
Worklon	USA
WorkPro	*CAN*
Workwear	*NOR*
Worthington	USA
Wrangler	USA
Wrap	USA
Wrapture Body Tights	USA
WrenchWrinsr	USA
Yapre	USA
Yara	*NOR*
Yasmine	*ITL*
Yogatard	USA
Yolanda	USA
York	USA
You Babes	USA
Young Eastsider	USA
Young Stuff	USA
Your Sixth Sense	*BGM*
Youth Outlast	USA
YS Sport	USA
YS Studio	USA
Zariah	*CHN*
Zarzarrosa	*JAP*
Zeke	USA
Zenith	USA
Zerotondo	*ITL*
Zero-Zone	USA

Ziggurat Neckware	USA
Zip Polo	USA
Zippin	USA
Zoccoli	*ITL*
Zorba	USA
Zoya Skirt	USA
Zucca Allegra Ties	*ITL*
Z-Wrap Jacket	USA

INTIMATE APPAREL

Berkshire Intimates	USA
Berlei	USA
Bestform	USA
Body Chic	USA
Body Drama	USA
Body Tease	USA
Bolero	USA
Bra Toppers	USA
Cacique	USA
Charter Club	USA
Cinema Etoile Lingerie	USA
Comfort Casuals	USA
Cross Your Heart	USA
Escapades Lingerie	USA
Everyday Basics Bra	USA
Exquisit Bras	USA
Fits Your Mood	USA
Frederick's of Hollywood	USA
Fresh Expressions	USA
Fruit of the Loom	USA
Gemma	USA
Gossard	USA
Intimate Attitudes	USA
Je T'Adore	USA
Jockey	USA
La Difference Bra	USA
Lily of France Bras	USA

Lilyette Bra	USA	Lafayette	USA
Lorraine	USA	Land's End	USA
Lou	USA	Lee	USA
Maidenform Bra	USA	Lei	USA
Majestic	USA	Levi's	USA
Mara Intimates	USA	Liz Claiborne	USA
Miracle Bra	USA	Lost River	USA
Night & Day Intimates	USA	Maverick	USA
Playtex	USA	Mudd	USA
Self Expressions	USA	Nautica Jeans Co.	USA
Smooth Performance	USA	Perry Ellis America	USA
Subtract	USA	Pointer	USA
Sweet Nothings	USA	Polo Jeans Co.	USA
Teenform	*JAP*	Posted Jeans	USA
Vanity Fair	USA	Riders	USA
Variance	USA	Rustler	USA
Vassarette Bra	USA	Sergio Valente	USA
Wacoal	*JAP*	*Tommy Jeans*	*CHN*
		Wrangler	USA

JEANS

7 For All Mankind	USA	**LEATHER GOODS**	
All American Clothing	USA	*Alfred Dunhill*	*SWI*
Andrew	USA	American Belting	
Antik Denim	USA	Leather	USA
Arizona	USA	Amity	USA
Brittania	USA	*Berluti*	*FRA*
Bugle Boy	USA	Big Sky	USA
Calvin Klein	USA	Bistor Belt	USA
Chic	USA	Bleu	USA
Denver	USA	Blush	USA
East West	*CAN*	Bonwelts	USA
Guess?	USA	Bosca	USA
Harley-Davidson	USA	Botany 500 Belts	USA
Joe Jeans	USA	Brighton Bay	USA
Jones Jeans	USA	Bugle Boy	USA
Jordache	USA	Buxton	USA
Juicy Couture	USA	Canterbury	USA
Just My Size	USA	Canyon Belt	USA

Leather Goods (cont.)

Chapparel	USA	Revelations	USA
Clarino	*JAP*	Riserva	USA
Classique II	USA	Rolfs	USA
Coach	USA	Saddler	USA
Crossroads	USA	*Salvatore Ferragamo*	*ITL*
Danier	*CAN*	Spokes Belts	USA
Don Loper	USA	*Stefanobi*	*FRA*
El Toro Bravo	USA	Swank	USA
Ellington Wallet	USA	T. Anthony	USA
Emilio Pucci	*FRA*	Tandy	USA
Enger Kress	USA	Textan	USA
Fendi	*FRA*	Tiger Belts	USA
Frontier	USA	*Tilley*	*CAN*
Geoffrey Beene	USA		
Givency	*FRA*	**LUGGAGE**	
Guess?	USA	American Tourister	USA
Guy Laroche	*THAI*	Andiamo	USA
Harley-Davidson	USA	Atlantic	USA
Heritage Leathers	USA	Attache-Mate	USA
Hermes	*FRA*	*Aurora*	*TWN*
Insignia	USA	Borneo	USA
Kenzo	*FRA*	Commuter	USA
Leather Artisan	USA	Dynasty	USA
Leathersmith	USA	Emerald	USA
Loewe	*FRA*	Galaxy	USA
Lone Star Wallets	USA	Golden-Pacific	USA
Louis Fontaine	*THAI*	Hartmann	USA
Louis Vuitton	*FRA*	Holiday	USA
Marc Jacobs	*FRA*	JanSport	USA
Matt Tyler Saddles	USA	Land's End	USA
Movado	USA	Lark	USA
Mundi	USA	Lucas	USA
Pierre Cardin	USA	Mercury	USA
Prince Gardner	USA	Millenium	USA
Princess Gardner	USA	Monarch	USA
Private Label	USA	Rimowa	USA
Radiance Plus	USA	Samsonite	USA
		Sarano	USA

Sasson	USA
Sierra Madre	USA
Skyway	USA
Tough Traveler	USA
US Luggage	USA
Wetpak	USA
Widetracker	USA
Wings by Hartman	USA

SUNGLASSES

Alias	USA
Arnette	*ITL*
Blublocker	USA
Bolle	USA
Caddy	USA
Chopstick	USA
Claiborne	*ITL*
DKNY	*FRA*
Eddie Bauer	USA
Fluid Metal	USA
Foster Grant	USA
Guess	USA
Juke	USA
Killer Loop	*ITL*
Liz Claiborne	*ITL*
Oakley	*ITL*
Persol	*ITL*
Polaroid	USA
Ray-Ban	*ITL*
Revo	*ITL*
Serengeti	USA
Sferoflex	*ITL*
Suncloud	*ITL*
Tangle	USA
Vogue	*ITL*

WATCHES & CLOCKS

Accutron	USA
Allia	USA
Andre Giroud	USA
Armitron	USA
Aspen	USA
Astor	USA
Athlite	*GER*
Attesa	*JAP*
Baltimore	USA
Barcelona	USA
Bareleto	USA
Basel	USA
Baume & Mercier	*SWI*
Biltmore	USA
Black Fanned Southwest	USA
Black Leather Band	USA
Blade	USA
Braun	USA
Brea	USA
Bristol	USA
Bull Rider	USA
Bulova	USA
Campanola	*JAP*
Capeland	USA
Capelo	USA
Caravelle	USA
Carriage	USA
Casio	*JAP*
Casiotron	*JAP*
Celestina	USA
Cellini	*SWI*
Certina	*SWI*
Charleston	USA
Chaumet	*FRA*
Citizen	*JAP*
CK Watch	*SWI*

Watches & Clocks (cont.)		Movado	USA
Classic Montana	USA	Museum Automatic	USA
Classima	USA	MW Michele	USA
Concord	USA	Orpheum	USA
Cross Haven	USA	Oyster	SWI
Croton	USA	Patek Phillippe	USA
Crush 2.0	ITL	Piaget	SWI
Dalton	USA	Pierre Balmain	SWI
Dresden	USA	Portico	USA
Elgin	USA	Premier	JAP
Eliro	USA	Printpro	USA
Elliptica	USA	Promaster	JAP
Esperanza	USA	Pulsar	JAP
ESQ	USA	Quiksilver	USA
Faceto	USA	Rabbit Skins	USA
Flik Flak	SWI	Rado	SWI
Franck Muller	USA	Reliance	USA
Gruen	USA	Reverso	SWI
Hamilton	SWI	Ridgeway	USA
Hampton	USA	Riviera	USA
Harmony	USA	Rockford	USA
Hartford	USA	Rolex	SWI
Hermes	FRA	Rush	USA
Howard Miller	USA	San Remo	JAP
Jaeger-LeCoultre	SWI	Sapphire	USA
Krystal	USA	Saratoga	USA
Lassale	JAP	Savoy	USA
Laureate	USA	Seiko	JAP
Linden	USA	Serenade	USA
London	USA	Sharp	USA
Longines	SWI	Silhouette	JAP
Mariner	USA	Skyhawk	JAP
Marquee	USA	Solotempo	ITL
Medalist	USA	Soundesign	USA
Metropolitan	USA	Spoon	JAP
Meza	USA	Sport	USA
Mihewi	USA	Sport Tek	USA
Montserrat	USA	Sportura	JAP

Sprita	USA	**Trembrili**	USA
Stanley	USA	**Triax**	USA
Stiletto	JAP	*Trika*	ITL
Stuart Austin	USA	*Union*	SWI
Style De Chaumet	FRA	*Universo*	SWI
Stylo Mantal	USA	*Vacheron Constantin*	SWI
Suisse	USA	*Valdar*	SWI
Swatch	SWI	**Valor**	USA
Sweda	USA	**Veneto**	USA
Swiss Army	SWI	*Vivace*	JAP
Tag Heuer	FRA	**Vizio**	USA
Tecknik	USA	**Waltham**	USA
Theo	USA	**Watch Gear**	USA
Timekeeper	SWI	**Weight**	USA
Timema	USA	**Welea**	USA
Timex	USA	**Wittnauer**	USA
Tissot	SWI	**World Timer**	USA
Tourbillon	ITL	**York**	USA
Tourneau	USA	*Zenith*	FRA
Travel Lite	USA	**Zodiac**	USA

Chapter 8

Electronics

(**American owned in bold** / *Foreign owned in italic*)

AUDIO/VIDEO PLAYERS & RECORDERS

Aiwa	JAP
Alpine	JAP
Altec Lansing	**USA**
Audiovox	**USA**
Bang & Olufsen	DEN
Blaupunkt	GER
Bose	**USA**
Bose Wave Radio	**USA**
Boston Acoustics	**USA**
Cambridge Soundworks	SNG
Canon	JAP
Casio	JAP
Clarion	JAP
Compaq	**USA**
Creative	SNG
Emerson	**USA**
Fisher	JAP
Fuji	JAP
GE	**USA**
General Electric	**USA**
Goldstar	KOR
Go-Video	CHN
Harman Kardon	**USA**
Hitachi	JAP
JC Penney	**USA**
Jensen	**USA**
JVC	JAP
Kenwood	JAP
Kodak	**USA**
Konica	JAP
Konka	CHN
Koss	**USA**
Kyocera	JAP
Leica	GER
Magnavox	NETH
Marantz	JAP
Memorex	**USA**
Minolta	JAP
Mitsubishi	JAP
Nikon	JAP
Olympus	JAP
Onkyo	JAP
Optimus	**USA**
Otari	JAP
Panasonic	JAP
Pentax	JAP
Philco	NETH
Philips	NETH
Pioneer	JAP
Pro Wonder	FRA
Quasar	JAP
Radio Shack	**USA**
RCA	FRA
Ricoh	JAP
Samsung	KOR
Sanyo	JAP
Scaleo	GER
Sears	**USA**
Sharp	JAP
Sony	JAP
Soundesign	**USA**
Sylvania	JAP
Teac	JAP
Technics	JAP
Toshiba	JAP
Vaddis	**USA**
Vaio Music Clip	JAP
Vibratto	**USA**
Yamaha	JAP
Yashica	JAP
Zenith	KOR

AUDIO & VIDEO RECORDING

3M	USA
Bell & Howell	USA
Fuji	JAP
FujiFilm	JAP
JVC	JAP
Kodak	USA
Maxell	JAP
Memorex	USA
Polaroid	USA
RCA	FRA
Scotch	USA
Sony	JAP
TDK	JAP

BATTERIES

AC Delco	USA
America	USA
Bulldog	USA
DieHard	USA
Dorcy International Batteries	USA
Duracell	USA
East Penn Manufacturing	USA
Energizer	USA
Eveready	USA
Exide	USA
Exide Stowaway	USA
Fulmen	USA
Gold Peak Industries	CHN
Hytron	USA
Kodak	USA
Marathon	USA
Marine Master	USA
Mastercell	USA
Maxell	JAP

Maxguard	USA
Motorcraft	USA
NAPA	USA
Omnipack	JAP
Optima	USA
Orbital	USA
Panasonic	JAP
Panther	USA
Photolife	USA
Polygon	USA
Prestolite	USA
Pro Line (Hearing Aid)	USA
Pro Master	USA
Pro Pac	USA
Procell	USA
Radio Shack	USA
Rayovac	USA
Real Time	USA
Sanyo	JAP
Smarthog	USA
Smartpack	USA
Snaphat	SWI
Sonnenschein	USA
Sony	JAP
Spiracell Technology	USA
Sprinter	USA
Superhog	USA
TDI	BMD
Thin Cell	USA
Toshiba	JAP
Trailblazer	USA
Trimpac	USA
Truck Tough	USA
Tudor	USA
Ultralife Polymer	USA
Unigy	USA
Varta	GER
VR Solar	USA

Willard	USA	*JVC*	*JAP*
Wirtz	USA	**Kodak**	USA
Workhog	USA	*Konica*	*JAP*
Zeropower	*SWI*	*Kyocera*	*JAP*
		Leica	*SWI*
CALCULATORS		**Linhof**	USA
Canon	*JAP*	**Maxxuum**	USA
Casio	*JAP*	*Minolta*	*JAP*
Hewlett Packard	USA	*Nikon*	*JAP*
Olivetti	*ITL*	*Olympus*	*JAP*
Sharp	*JAP*	*Panasonic*	*JAP*
Signalstorm	USA	*Pentax*	*JAP*
Texas Instruments	USA	**Polaroid**	USA
		RCA	*FRA*
CAMERA FILM		*Ricoh*	*JAP*
AGFA	*BGM*	*Samsung*	*KOR*
Centuria	*JAP*	*Sharp*	*JAP*
Fuji	*JAP*	*Sony*	*JAP*
Kodak	USA	**Spectra System**	USA
Konica	*JAP*	**Suprema**	USA
Polaroid	USA	*Sure Shot*	*JAP*
Scotch	USA	*Televid*	*GER*
		Toshiba	*JAP*
CAMERAS		*Trinovid*	*GER*
AGFA	*GER*	*Trip*	*JAP*
Alphacam	USA	*Ultravid*	*GER*
Arca Swiss	*UK*	**USBcam**	USA
Cambo	USA	**Varifocal**	USA
Canon	*JAP*	*Variocam*	*GER*
Casio	*JAP*	*Varioscan*	*GER*
Chinon	USA	*Variotherm*	*GER*
Concord	USA	*Vectis*	*JAP*
Epson	*JAP*	**Vivicam**	USA
Fuji	*JAP*	**Vivitar**	USA
FujiFilm	*JAP*	**Willoughby's**	USA
Hasselblad	*SWE*	**Wista**	USA
Hewlett Packard	USA	**Wormcam**	USA

Cameras (cont.)
Xacti   JAP
Yashica   JAP
Yaucono Coffee   **USA**

COMPUTERS & PRINTERS
Acer   TWN
Apple   **USA**
Brother   JAP
Canon   JAP
Compaq   **USA**
Dell   **USA**
Epson   JAP
Gateway   TWN
Hewlett Packard   **USA**
HP   **USA**
Konica   JAP
Lexmark   **USA**
Macintosh   **USA**
Microline   JAP
Micron   **USA**
Minolta   JAP
Oki   JAP
Olivetti   ITL
Panasonic   JAP
Printronix   **USA**
Samsung   KOR
Savin   **USA**
Smith Corona   **USA**
Sony   JAP
Sun Microsystems **USA**
ThinkCentre   CHN
ThinkPad   CHN
Tianjiao   CHN
Toshiba   JAP
Typhoon   JAP
Vaio   JAP

VideoJet Focus   **USA**

COPIERS, SCANNERS & FAX MACHINES
Brother   JAP
Canon   JAP
Casio   JAP
Epson   JAP
Hewlett-Packard   **USA**
Kenwood   JAP
Konica Minolta   JAP
Lanier   JAP
Lexmark   **USA**
NEC   JAP
Okidata   JAP
Olivetti   ITL
Panasonic   JAP
Quasar   JAP
Radio Shack   **USA**
Samsung   KOR
Savin   JAP
Sharp   JAP
TRM   **USA**
UniMessage   JAP
Xerox   **USA**

PDAs
Casio   JAP
Compaq   **USA**
Handspring   **USA**
Hewlett Packard   **USA**
Kyocera   JAP
Palm   **USA**
Palm Pilot   **USA**
Sony   JAP

SPEAKERS

Altec Lansing	USA
AMT	USA
AR (Acoustic Research)	USA
Bang & Olufsen	DEN
Belle Klipsch	USA
Bose	USA
Boston Acoustics	USA
Cambridge Soundworks	SNG
Cerwin-Vega	USA
Companion	USA
Concerto	USA
Creative Labs	SNG
Crown	USA
ESS Laboratory	USA
Fisher	JAP
Harman Kardon	USA
Iso Drive	JAP
JBL	USA
Jensen	USA
JVC	JAP
Kenwood	JAP
Klipsch	USA
La Scala	USA
McIntosh Laboratory	USA
Neoset	USA
NHT	USA
Nutone Sensonic	USA
Phase Linear	USA
Pioneer	JAP
Polk	USA
Polk Audio	USA
Promedia	USA
Quam-Nichols	USA
Reference	USA
Select Circle	SNG
Sensonic	USA
Sony	JAP
Soundbird	GER
Taurus	USA
Technics	JAP
Tower by Henry Kloss	SNG
Triad	USA
Tripole	USA
Vogue	USA
Yamaha	JAP

TELEVISIONS

Audiocolor	JAP
Audiovox	USA
Bang & Olufsen	DEN
Casio	JAP
Daewoo	KOR
Emerson	USA
General Electric	USA
Goldstar	KOR
Hitachi	JAP
Honeywell	USA
JVC	JAP
Konka	CHN
LG	KOR
Magnavox	NETH
Marantz	JAP
Mitsubishi	JAP
Panasonic	JAP
Philips	NETH
Pioneer	JAP
Proscan	FRA
Quasar	JAP
RCA	FRA
Samsung	KOR
Sansui	CAN
Sanyo	JAP
Sears	USA
SHARP	JAP
Sony	JAP

Televisions (cont.)

Soundesign	**USA**
Sylvania	*JAP*
Toshiba	*JAP*
Vizio	**USA**
Zenith	*KOR*

Chapter 9

Recreation

(**American owned in bold** / *Foreign owned in italic*)

BACKPACKS

Dana Design	USA
Eastpak	USA
Jansport	USA
Ridgeway	USA
Tough Traveler	USA

BICYCLES

Aragon	USA
Aurora	USA
BMW	*GER*
Boss Cruiser 7	USA
Capri	USA
Coda Comp	USA
Coda Elite	USA
Coda Sport	USA
Columbia	USA
Comet	USA
Commuter	USA
Contessa	USA
Dakar	USA
Dakota	USA
Dragon	USA
Huffy	USA
Jamis	USA
K2 Roflex	USA
Litespeed	USA
Mongoose	USA
Peugot	*FRA*
Roadmaster	USA
Sassy	USA
Satellite	USA
Schwinn	USA
Shimano	*JAP*
Shock Wave	USA
Sierra Madre	USA
Slammer	USA
Sora	*JAP*

Spectra	*SWE*
Spectrum	USA
Springdale	USA
Starlite	USA
Street Metal	USA
Summer Breeze	USA
Super Doodlebug	USA
Taboo	USA
Tangier	USA
Taxi	USA
Teen Talk	USA
Tejas	USA
Tiagara	*JAP*
Tomac	USA
Torker	USA
Tourney	*JAP*
Trek	USA
Trilogy	USA
Ultegra	*JAP*
Ventura	USA
Xenith	USA
Zero Gravity	USA

BINOCULARS

Aerolite	USA
Audubon	USA
Bausch & Lomb	USA
Bell & Howell	USA
Bobcat	USA
Bushnell	USA
Canon	*JAP*
Eaglet	USA
Eddie Bauer	USA
Egret	USA
Jaguar	USA
Kestrel	USA
Legacy	USA
Leica	*GER*

Micron	USA	**Robalo**	USA
Minolta	*JAP*	**Savannah**	USA
Nightstar	USA	**Sea Ray**	USA
Nikon	*JAP*	**Seacraft**	USA
Olympus	*JAP*	**Serenity**	USA
Plover	USA	**Simaron**	USA
Powerview	USA	**Sis W**	USA
Redfield	USA	**Smoker Craft Boats**	USA
Sea Hawk	USA	*Solas*	*FRA*
Sea King	USA	**Sorrento**	USA
Serengeti	USA	**Sportster**	USA
Simmons	USA	**Striper**	USA
Skymaster	USA	**Suncruiser**	USA
Swift	USA	**Sundancer**	USA
Tasco	USA	**Sundeck**	USA
Timber HD	USA	**Sundowner**	USA
Traveler	USA	**Sunscape**	USA
Travelview	USA	**Sunsetter**	USA
Trekker	USA	**Sun-Sport**	USA
Trophy	USA	**Suntracker**	USA
Ultima	USA	**Super Fisherman**	USA
Ultralite	USA	**Sylvan**	USA
Upclose	USA	**Tahoe**	USA
Viceroy	USA	**Thunder**	USA
Vistapix	USA	**Tornado**	USA
Voyager	USA	**Tournament**	USA
Warbler	USA	**Trophy**	USA
Weaver	USA	**Vision Sailboats**	USA
Wilderness	USA	**V-Wing**	USA
		Wakeboard	*JAP*
BOATS		**Wakesetter**	USA
Alumacraft	USA	**Wimil**	USA
Aquasport Fishing	USA	**Windrush**	USA
Four Winns	USA	**Windsor Craft**	USA
Hydra-Sports	USA	**Wow**	USA
Javelin	USA	**Xcite Sailboat**	USA
Lund	USA	*Yamaha*	*JAP*

Boats (cont.)

Yukon	USA
Zodiac	*FRA*
Zoom	*FRA*

FIREARMS

American Classic Rifle	USA
Benjamin Sheridan Rifle	USA
Bolt Action 695	USA
Browning Rifles	*BGM*
Camo Rifles	USA
Contender Pistol	USA
Crosman Rifles	USA
Fieldmaster	USA
Hornady Rifle	USA
Hunter Rifles	USA
Lazermark Rifles	USA
Magnathin	USA
Mark V Rifle	USA
Marlin Golden Rifle	USA
Maverick	USA
New England	USA
Package Rifles	USA
Purdey	*SWI*
Rattlesnake	USA
Red Label Shotgun	USA
Remington	USA
Ruger	USA
Sauer	*SWI*
Savage	USA
Shur Shot	USA
Sierra	USA
Sig-Sauer Sporting Gun	*SWI*
Single Six	USA
Smith & Wesson	USA
Snailtraps	USA
Special Purpose 500	USA

SSI-One	USA
Stevens	USA
Stoeger	*ITL*
Striker	USA
Super Bearcat Revolver	USA
Super Shadow Shotgun	*BGM*
Target Grey Shotgun	USA
Targetmaster	USA
Thompson Center Arms	USA
Tribomatic	USA
Uberti	*ITL*
Vaquero	USA
Variair	USA
Varitem	USA
Varmint	USA
Versa-Spray	USA
Viper	USA
Winchester Ammunition	USA
Winchester Shotgun	*BGM*
Wolverine 209	USA
Woodside Shotgun	USA
Yellow Jacket	USA

MOVIE THEATERS

AMC Theaters	USA
Lowe's Theaters	*JAP*
Marcus	USA
National Film Theater	*UK*
Odeon	*UK*
Regal Cinemas	USA
United Artists Theatre	USA
Village Theatre	USA

MUSICAL INSTRUMENTS AND EQUIPMENT

Ambassador Drumhead	USA
Americana	USA

Armstrong	USA	Ludwig	USA
Artley	USA	Mark Knopfler	
Avante	USA	Stratocaster	USA
Baldwin	USA	Matador	USA
Bebop Drum Set	USA	Nady Amplifiers	USA
Billy Martin Guitars	USA	Nashville Guitar	
Bodhran Drums	USA	Amplifiers	USA
Bongo	USA	Orgatron Organs	USA
Boston Pianos	USA	Ovation Guitars	USA
Briarwood Acoustic		Parker Guitars	USA
Guitar	USA	Paul Reed Smith Guitars	USA
Brownsville Guitars		Pearl	USA
& Amplifiers	USA	Peavey	USA
Champion Guitar		Powerstroke Drumhead	USA
Amplifier	USA	Princeton Guitar	
Charvel Guitars	USA	Amplifier	USA
Chickering Pianos	USA	Protégé Organs	USA
Combo	USA	PRS Guitars	USA
Cyclops	USA	Remo	USA
Ebony Drumhead	USA	Renaissance Classic	
Echoplex	USA	Organs	USA
Edge Cymbals	USA	Renaissance Drumhead	USA
Ellington Pianos	USA	Rhythmix	USA
Emerson Flutes	USA	Robert Cray Stratocaster	USA
Emporer Drumhead	USA	Rodriguez Classical	
Eterna Pianos	JAP	Guitars	USA
Fender Guitars	USA	Rosewood Guitars	USA
Galaxy	USA	Santana Guitars	USA
Gibson	USA	Selmer	USA
Guild Guitar	USA	Signature Organs	USA
Hamer Guitars	USA	Silent Series Pianos	JAP
Hamilton Pianos	USA	Silhouette Guitars	USA
Hawk	USA	Slinky Guitars	USA
Jimmie Vaughan Guitars	USA	Sonor Drums	GER
Kanjira Drums	USA	Spirit	USA
Kawai Pianos	JAP	Squier Guitars	USA
Korg Pianos	JAP	Steinberger	USA
Leblanc France	USA	Steinway	USA

Musical Instruments & Equipment
(cont.)

Steinway & Sons Pianos	USA
Sterling Guitars	USA
Stingray Guitars	USA
Stratocaster	USA
Studio King Drums	USA
Surdo Drums	USA
Swamp Ash Guitars	USA
SWR Guitars	USA
Tambora	USA
Tamborim Drum	USA
Tan-Tan Drum	USA
Telecaster	USA
Timbale	USA
Timbau Drum	USA
Tobias	USA
Toca Drums	USA
Valley Arts Guitars	USA
Vesicare	*JAP*
Victory	USA
Vito	USA
W. Schreiber & Son	*UK*
Washburn Guitars	USA
Wes Montgomery Guitars	USA
Wolfgang Guitars	USA
Wurlitzer	USA
Yamaha	*JAP*
Yanagisawa	USA
Yngwie Malmsteen Stratocaster	USA
ZBT Cymbals	USA
Zildjian	USA

OUTDOOR GRILLS

Barbecue King	USA
Broilmaster	USA
Char-Broil	USA
Ducane	USA
Genesis	USA
Jenn-Air	USA
Kenmore	USA
Marshallan	USA
Phoenix Grill	USA
Santa Fe	USA
Signature Grills	*ICE*
Smokey Joe	USA
Smokey Mountain Cooker	USA
Summit	USA
Swinger II	USA
Uniflame	USA
Vortex	USA
Weber	USA

GENERAL RECREATION

Airzone Trampolines	USA
Almost Heaven Hot Tubs	USA
American Heritage Billiards	USA
Anthony & Sylvan Pools	USA
Apex Snowmobiles	*JAP*
Arctic Cat Snowmobile	USA
ATV Sport	USA
Avalon Pool Tables	USA
Bearcat Snowmobile	USA
Britton Pool Table	USA
Brunswick Billiard Tables	USA
Cambridge Pool Tables	USA
Carlton Pool Table	USA
Cypress Pool Table	USA
Esther Williams Pools	USA
Fairfax Pool Tables	USA
Great Lakes Hot Tubs	USA
Jacuzzi	USA

Jet Ski	JAP	**Symphony Series Pools**	USA
Jumpking Trampolines	USA	**Tacoma Pool Tables**	USA
King Cat Snowmobile	USA	**Tiger River Spas**	USA
Kingston Pool Table	USA	*Trail Performance*	
Lasalle Pool Tables	USA	*Snowmobiles*	JAP
Lynx Snowmobiles	USA	**Tuscany Pool Tables**	USA
Merrillville Pool Tables	USA	**Twin Otter Kayak**	USA
Mirage Outback Kayak	USA	**Ultralite Scooter**	USA
Murrey Pool Tables	USA	**Vail Pool Tables**	USA
Muskin Pools	USA	**Valencia Pool Tables**	USA
Odyssey Kayaks	USA	**Versailles Pool Tables**	USA
Old Town Canoes		*Vespa Scooter*	ITL
And Kayaks	USA	**Victory Scooter**	USA
Otter Kayaks	USA	**Vienna Pool Tables**	USA
Palermo Pool Tables	USA	*Vino Classic Scooter*	JAP
Pantera Snowmobile	USA	*Vk Professional*	
Pursuit Kyaks	USA	*Snowmobiles*	JAP
Putt-Putt Golf Course	USA	*Wave Scooter*	IND
Redline Snowmobiles	USA	**Wave Sport Kayaks**	USA
Revolt Snowmobiles	USA	*Waverunner*	JAP
Sabercat Snowmobiles	USA	**Weatherking Pools**	USA
Sante Cruz Pool Tables	USA	**Wellington Pool Tables**	USA
Sea Blue Pools	USA	**Wilderness Kayaks**	USA
Seneca Pool Tables	USA	**Winslow Pool Tables**	USA
Sidekick Scooter	USA	*Wolverine All-Terrain*	
Signature Pools	USA	*Vehicle*	JAP
Silver Wing Scooter	JAP	*Yamaha Snowmobiles*	JAP
Ski-Doo Snowmobiles	USA	**ZR Snowmobiles**	USA
Sno Pro Snowmobiles	USA	*Zuma Scooter*	JAP
Sonic Scooter	USA		
Sterling Pool Tables	USA	**SPORTS EQUIPMENT**	
Stiga Table Tennis	USA	**444 Lazerline Fly Line**	USA
Strathmore Pool Tables	USA	**Abu Garcia Fishing Reels**	USA
Summer Fun Pools	CAN	**Abu-Matic Casting Reels**	USA
Sundance Hot Tubs	USA	**AC Golf Gloves**	USA
Sundancer Scooter	USA	**Accudart**	USA
Superjet Watercraft	JAP	**Acushnet**	USA
Sxvenom Snowmobiles	JAP	**Adams Golf**	USA

Sports Equipment (cont.)		Bill Cook Saddles	USA
Adidas	GER	Black Gold Reels	USA
Adio And Hawk	USA	Blackburn Bicycle	
Adirondack	USA	Accessories	USA
Aero Strike	USA	Blue Streak Fly Bait	USA
Air Cel Fishing Lines	USA	Body Pump	USA
Air Neville Pro		Boomerang Helmet	USA
Water Skis	USA	*Bridgestone Golf*	JAP
All Star	USA	Brine	USA
Allstar Water Skis	USA	Browning Fishing Reels	USA
Ally Golf Clubs	USA	Brunswick	USA
Al's Goldfish Lure	USA	Burton Snowboards	USA
Altawand Golf Clubs	JAP	Callaway Golf	USA
Alumagold Track		Cardinal Spinning Reels	USA
& Field	USA	*Careca*	JAP
Ambassadeur Reels	USA	Casemaster Dart Cases	USA
American Angler	USA	Castelli Bicycle	
AMF	USA	Accessories	USA
Amigo Helmet	USA	Cherrywood Fishing	
Amigo Water Skis	USA	Rods	USA
Apex	USA	*Cleveland Golf*	FRA
Arcade Ball	USA	*Cliché Skateboards*	GER
Aristocraft	USA	Cobra Skates	USA
Arnold Palmer	USA	Cognito Helmet	USA
Asics	JAP	Concept Fishing	USA
Athletic Works	USA	Contact Water Ski	USA
Atlas Inline Skates	USA	Cooper Hockey	USA
Atmosphere	CAN	Cosmic Bowling	USA
Ayrtime Golf	USA	Cosom	USA
Banzai	USA	Crown II Fly Reel	USA
Barrecrafters	USA	D.B. Dun Fishing Rod	USA
Bauer Sports	USA	Daiwa Rods And Reels	USA
Bean's	USA	Darby Golf Club	USA
Bell Helmets	USA	*Davis Cup*	JAP
Ben Hogan Golf	USA	DCI Golf Clubs	USA
Big Bertha	USA	Discoverer Sporting	
Big Shot	USA	Scope	USA
Bike	USA	Doc Golf Clubs	USA

Dry-Ur-Fly	USA	Grip-Rite	USA
Dynastar Alpine Skis	*FRA*	GTO	USA
Easton	USA	Gymnastik	USA
Ebonite Bowling Balls	USA	Hammer Snowboard	USA
Elite Fitness Products		Hannay Reels	USA
(York Barbell)	USA	Heaton Ice Hockey	USA
Elite Sporting Scope	USA	Hercules Fitness	
Europa	USA	Products	USA
Eurotape	USA	Huffy Sports	USA
Everlast	USA	Idea Golf Clubs	USA
Externo Hockey Skates	USA	Indian Archery	USA
Eye 2 Golf Clubs	USA	Iquana Skates	USA
Eye-O-Matic Golf Clubs	USA	J Bag Golf Bag	USA
F2 Youth Baseball Bats	*FIN*	Jack Nicklaus	USA
Fair Play Fishing Line	USA	Jansport Backpacks	USA
Fair-Court	USA	Jantzen Swimsuits	USA
Featherlight Fishing	USA	J-Blade Golf Club	USA
Federal Sporting		Jet Blaster	USA
Ammunition	USA	Jr. Celebrity Water Skis	USA
Field & Stream	USA	K2	USA
Firefly Riflescope	USA	Karsten Golf Clubs	USA
Flak Hockey	USA	Kerboom Fly Line	USA
Flight Tested Gymanstic	USA	Killer Bee Golf	USA
Fortune Golf	USA	King	USA
Franklin Sports	USA	Koho Hockey	USA
Fred Bear Archery	USA	Kushin Golf Clubs	USA
Free Kick	USA	L/E Golf Clubs	USA
Frontier Golf Bag	USA	*Laddie Golf Balls*	*JAP*
Future Chaps	USA	Leopard Sporting Scope	USA
G2 EZ Golf Clubs	USA	Lightning Rod	
Gator Knives	USA	Fishing Rod	USA
Giro Helmets	USA	*Los Andes Skis*	*JAP*
Gold Medal	USA	Louisville Slugger	USA
Golden Bear Golf	USA	Lynx Sporting Scopes	USA
Golf Pride	USA	MacGregor	USA
Grand Monarch	*JAP*	Magneforce	USA
Grand Slam	USA	Mammoth Basketball	USA
Green Dot Softballs	USA	Mapple Water Skis	USA

<u>Sports Equipment (cont.)</u>

Mark of A Pro	USA	Penthouse Ski Wear	USA
Marker Ski Bindings	USA	Performance Water Skis	USA
Martin Fishing Reels	USA	Ping Golf	USA
Matrix Water Skis	USA	Pinnacle Golf Balls	USA
Maxfli	GER	Planet Earth	
Miller Soft Ski		Skateboards	USA
Equipment	USA	Porter Pro	USA
Mister Twister		Precision I-Fly Rods	USA
Fishing Lures	USA	*President XD Golf*	
Mizerak Pool Cues	USA	*Clubs*	JAP
Mizuno	JAP	Pro Commander	USA
Morrow Snowboards	USA	Pro Flex	USA
Multigrip Fitness		Pro Hummer	USA
Accessories	USA	Pro Tac Water Skis	USA
Musky Master Fishing		Promark Sports Gloves	USA
Line	USA	*Proto Forged TI Clubs*	JAP
Nancy Lopez	USA	Pusuit 400 Skates	USA
Neptune Skates	USA	Quantum Fishing Tackle	USA
NFL	USA	Racer X Skiing Gloves	USA
NHL	USA	Radial Loc Gym	
Nicklaus	USA	Equipment	USA
Nighthawk Sporting		Rail Wakeboard	USA
Scopes	USA	Rainguard Riflescope	USA
Nitrous	USA	Rainmaker Paintball	
No Balls No Glory	USA	Guns	USA
NSS Performance	USA	Ram Golf	USA
Olin Skis	USA	Rawlings	USA
Orbit Skates	USA	Red Wolf Fishing Tackle	USA
Orvis	USA	Redfield Riflescopes	USA
Ovation Golf Clubs	USA	Redline Golf Clubs	USA
Oxygen Snowboards	FIN	Riddell	USA
Pack It Fishing Rods	USA	Ride Snowboards	USA
Pal Golf Clubs	USA	Rimfly Fly Reel	USA
Palm Springs Golf	USA	Rite-In Golf Clubs	USA
Pangaea Camping Gear	USA	Rocket Power Skating	USA
Panther Spotting Scopes	USA	Roller Derby Roller	
Penn	NETH	Skates	USA
		Rossignol	FRA

Russell	USA	**Sportsman Riflescope**	USA
Salomon	*GER*	**Sportsmans Choice**	USA
Saltiga Spinning Reels	*JAP*	*SS Tournament*	
Sanfords Fishing	*NZ*	*Spinning Reels*	*JAP*
Santa Fe Golf	USA	**Static Skateboards**	USA
Science Wakeboard	USA	**Stearn Outdoors**	USA
Scorcher Golf	USA	**Stearns**	USA
Scottsdale Anser Golf		**Step**	USA
Club	USA	**Stiga**	USA
Scotty Cameron Golf		**Storm**	USA
Club	USA	**Strata Golf Balls**	USA
Sealine BR Spinning		**Strategy Golf**	USA
Reels	*JAP*	*Strikeforce Casting*	
Secondwind	USA	*Reels*	*JAP*
Serious Play	USA	**Super Dot Softball**	USA
Shakespeare	USA	**Supermaq Bows**	USA
Shareline Bodyboard	USA	*Suunto*	*FIN*
Shoot 'N Score	USA	*Sweepfire Spinning*	
Shortys Skateboards	USA	*Reels*	*JAP*
Siege Water Skis	USA	**Swift**	USA
Silver Slugger	USA	*Swix*	*NOR*
Silverback	USA	**Synchro Water Skis**	USA
Simmons Riflescopes	USA	**SZ Golf**	USA
Slazenger	*UK*	**Tamega Bodyboard**	USA
Slovin Bodyboard	USA	**Taos Ski & Boot**	USA
Snake Eyes Golf	USA	**Targa Water Skis**	USA
Soft Sport	USA	*Taylormade*	*GER*
Spalding	USA	*Team Daiwa*	*JAP*
Spectron Fishing Line	USA	**Teardrop Golf**	USA
Spectrum Bodyboard	USA	*Techfire Bat*	*JAP*
Speedo	USA	**Tenseconds**	USA
Spin Milled Golf	USA	**The Rock**	USA
Spinmatic Spinning		**The Trump**	USA
Reels	*JAP*	*Thommo Golf Balls*	*MAL*
Spinstar Spinning Reels	*JAP*	**Throbot Bowling**	USA
Sportcraft	USA	*Tiger*	*JAP*
Sports Experts	*CAN*	**Ti-Plosion Golf**	USA
Sports Lady Golf Balls	*JAP*	**Tisi Golf Club**	USA

256 How Americans Can Buy American

Sports Equipment (cont.)

Titleist	USA	VFX	USA
TNT2 Strings	USA	Vision Wakeboard	USA
Tommy Armour Golf	USA	Vixen Wakeboard	USA
Top-Flite Golf Balls		Viz-A-Ball Bowling	USA
& Clubs	USA	Voit	USA
Torch Golf	USA	Vokey Design Golf Club	USA
Tornado Bowlng	USA	Volkl	USA
Torq-Flex	USA	Vortex Water Skis	USA
Tour Select Golf	USA	Wakestar Skis	USA
TPS Series Baseball		Warrior Lacrosse	USA
Glove	USA	Wave Rebel Bodyboard	USA
Traditional Water Skis	USA	Weatherrite Outdoor	USA
Traffic Wakeskate	USA	Weaver Riflescopes	USA
Transfer Water Skis	USA	Wetgear	USA
Tretorn Tennis Balls	*GER*	White Hot Golf	USA
Triad	USA	*Wilson*	*FIN*
Triax Paintballs	USA	Wolverine Sports	USA
Tribal Sport Golf Shoes	USA	World Team Water Skis	USA
Trident	USA	Worr Games	USA
Triforce I Casting Reels	*JAP*	Worth	USA
Trihot Golf	USA	Worth Copperhead	USA
Trilene Fishing Line	USA	XDimension Golf Shoes	USA
Tubbs	USA	X-Tra Bows	USA
Tyrolia	*NETH*	*Yamaha*	*JAP*
T-Zoid Golf	*JAP*	Zebco	USA
Unicorn Darts		Zevo Golf	USA
Equipment	USA	Zing Golf Club	USA
Uppercuts Boxing	USA	Zo Strings	USA
US Weight	USA	Zone Bowling	USA
Valley Bowling	USA	*Zoom Soccer Shoes*	*THAI*
Valley-Dynamo Bowling	USA		
Vantage Water Skis	USA		
Vega 500 Roller Skates	USA		
Verdict Water Skis	USA		
V-Foil Golf Club	USA		
VFT Golf	USA		

TOYS & GAMES

Below is a list of American-made toys you can buy in just about any toy store:

- **Battleship**
- **Bicycle Playing Cards**
- **Boggle Jr.**
- **Candyland**
- **Chutes and Ladders**
- **Clue**
- **Connect Four**
- **Life**
- **Louisville Slugger**
- **Monopoly**
- **Mouse Trap**
- **Operation**
- **Parcheesi**
- **Pop-O-Matic Trouble**
- **Radio Flyer Discovery Wagon**
- **Scrabble**
- **Sorry**
- **Stratego**
- **Tri-ominos**
- **Trivial Pursuit**
- **Yahtzee**
- **Melissa and Doug U.S.A. Floor Puzzle**
- **Most puzzles are made in the USA!**
- **Crayola Crayons**
  (Not all packages of Crayola Crayons are made in the USA - please check the label.)

Also, anything you buy from the American Plastic Toy Company (www.americanplastictoys.com) is made in America.

You can find more American-made toys on these websites:

- www.ShopForAmerica.com
- www.ZebulonUSA.com
- www.usmadetoys.com
- www.holgatetoy.com
- www.maplelandmark.com
- www.kathyskreations.com
- www.lauritoys.com
- www.scalemodeltoys.com
- www.tigercandyarts.com
- www.fingazinga.com
- www.turnertoys.com
- www.knex.com
- www.step2.com
- www.fractiles.com
- www.zometool.com
- www.marxtrains.com
- www.bokainc.com
- www.channelcraft.com
- www.woodentrain.com
- www.unclegoose.com
- www.ez2love.com
- www.froebelgifts.com
- www.storyboardtoys.com
- www.tagtoys.com
- www.taurustoy.com
- www.underthegreenroof.com
- www.buyamerican.com
- www.yackleball.com

5 Alive Card Game	USA
A.G. Gear	USA
Accudart	USA
Advanced Dungeons & Dragons	USA
All In One Nursery	USA
Amanda Star	USA

<u>Toys & Games (cont.)</u>

Amazing Amy Dolls	HK
Ambassador	USA
American Bandstand	USA
American Flyer Electric Trains	USA
American Girls Collection	USA
American Reels	USA
American Spirit	USA
American West	USA
Americana	USA
Angles	USA
Aqua Jump	USA
Arena	USA
Army Men	USA
Around Kitchen	USA
Auditrack	USA
Austin Powers	USA
Avalanche	JAP
Avenger Hockey Table	USA
Aviator Playing Cards	USA
Aztec Adventure	USA
Babble-On	USA
Baby Born Dolls	GER
Baby Bright Eyes Doll	CHN
Baby Gear	USA
Baby University	USA
Babygund	USA
Baha	USA
Barbie	USA
Bath Time Color Blast	USA
Battle Box	USA
Battleship	USA
Beach Wagon	USA
Beanie Babies	USA
Beanie Buddies	USA
Bee Playing Cards	USA

Beet Boop	USA
Bethlehem Toy Rain	USA
Betty Spagetty	USA
Bible Trivia	USA
Bicycle Playing Cards	USA
Big Ben Puzzles	USA
Big Burst	USA
Bitty Baby Collection	USA
Bitty Bear	USA
Blondie	USA
Blue Angel	USA
Bone-To-Pick	USA
Booloon Busters	USA
Bosun Sailboats	USA
Brain Puzzler	USA
Brass Eagle Paintball	USA
Bratz Dolls	USA
Buddy L	USA
Candy Land	USA
Capitol	USA
Care Set	USA
Cart Fury	USA
Cash King Checkers	USA
Castle Pail of Toy	USA
Caterpillar Trains	USA
Century	USA
Chair Assortment	USA
Chubby Auto Hauler	USA
Chubby Hook And Ladder	USA
Chutes & Ladders	USA
Clifford	USA
Clue	USA
Connect Four	USA
Cootie	USA
Coppertone Kids	USA
Corsair	USA
Croxley Puzzles	USA

Curious Cross Puzzles	USA	*Frisbee*	*CHN*
Curtiss	USA	Fun In The Sun	USA
Deal	USA	Funglasses Card Game	USA
Deluxe Boat	USA	Funnoodle	USA
Deluxe Runabout Stake	USA	Gallon Pale And Shovel	USA
Deluxe Skip-Bo	USA	*Game Boy*	*JAP*
Deluxe Uno	USA	Game of Life	USA
Disney Classics	USA	Games Arcade	USA
Doll Care Center	USA	Gearbox	USA
Don't Break the Ice	USA	Girl Talk	USA
Down And Out	USA	Gliders	USA
Duncan	USA	*Glowzone Hockey*	*CHN*
Dungeons & Dragons	USA	Go To The Head of	
Duplo	*DEN*	Class	USA
Easybake Oven	USA	*Golf 150G*	*CHN*
Eden	USA	Guess Who?	USA
Ello Fashion Dolls	USA	Hacky Sack	USA
Elvis	USA	Hands Down	USA
Emax	USA	Hard Body	USA
Emily Doll	USA	Hearsay	USA
Etch-A-Sketch	USA	Hearts N' Home	USA
Extreme Ride In	USA	Heroes In A Half Shell	USA
Fab Fish Puzzle	USA	Horsey Ride On	USA
Fairiees	USA	Hot Wheels	USA
Faith Kidz	USA	Hoyle Playing Cards	USA
Falcon	USA	*Hula Hoop*	*CHN*
Family Jewel Puzzle	USA	Hungry Hippos	USA
Fashion Magic	USA	Hydrostrike	USA
Fat Cat Table Soccer	USA	Iceburgs	USA
Fighting Falcon	USA	*Impact*	*CHN*
First Games	USA	*Infinity*	*CHN*
Fisher Price	USA	International Game	
Flexible Flyer Snow		Technology	USA
Sleds	USA	Isoflex	USA
Flip-It	USA	Jenga	USA
Floam	USA	Jumpin' Monkeys	USA
Flying Colors	USA	Junior Puzzles	USA
Four Square Puzzles	USA	Koosh Ball	USA

Toys & Games (cont.)

Lamaze	USA	Nursery Rhyme Games	USA
Leapfrog	USA	Off Road Set	USA
Lego	DEN	On The Level Puzzles	USA
Let's Go Fishing	USA	One Man Jam	USA
Liar's Maze	USA	Operation	USA
Life	USA	Optical Conclusions	USA
Light And Sound		Original Memory	USA
Kitchen	USA	Othello	USA
Li'l Miss Dress Up	USA	Ouija	USA
Lionel Trains	USA	Paperboy	USA
Lite Brite	USA	Parcheesi	USA
Little People	USA	Parker Brothers	USA
Little Pretty Doll	USA	Pastel Pets Puzzles	USA
Little Tikes	USA	Pictionary	USA
Luck Plus	USA	Pillsbury Toy Trains	USA
Magic Nursery Dolls	USA	Play-Doh	USA
Magna Doodle	USA	*Playmates Toys*	HK
Mastermind	USA	Playskool	USA
Matchbox	USA	*Playstation*	JAP
Mattel	USA	Pocket Simon	USA
Maze Pen Puzzles	USA	Pokemon	USA
Mega Bloks	USA	Polly Pocket	USA
Merry Rider Tim Mee	USA	Poof	USA
Mig Killer	USA	Pop-O-Matic Trouble	USA
Milton Bradley	USA	Portable Bible Trivia	USA
Mini Extreme	USA	Powerballs	USA
Monopoly	USA	Pressman	USA
Mortal Kombat	USA	Pride	USA
Mousetrap	USA	Primal Rage	USA
Mr. Bubbles	USA	Proto Model Trains	USA
Mr. Mouth	USA	Rage Card Game	USA
Mr. Potato Head	USA	Remco	USA
My First Uno	USA	Rex Puzzles	USA
Nerf	USA	Risk	USA
Nesquik Trains	USA	Roadmaster	USA
Nintendo	JAP	Rock'Em Sock'Em	
Nitrocity	USA	Robots	USA
		Rocking Hippo	USA

Rolling Case	USA	Self-Esteem	USA
Rubbermaid	USA	Senator	USA
Rubik's Cube	USA	Sesame Street	USA
Ruggie Bear	USA	Shapes	USA
Rummikub	USA	*Shark Hunter*	*JAP*
Rummy Rumble	USA	Shield Blaster	USA
Rummy-Up	USA	Shining Stars	USA
Runabout	USA	Shout About Movies	USA
Sand	USA	Showdown Sports	USA
Sand Fish	USA	Signeture	USA
Sand Sack	USA	Silly Putty	USA
Sand Storm	*CAN*	Silly Silly Sea	USA
Santa's Workshop	USA	Silly Soccer	USA
Sarin Playground		Sillysports	USA
Equipment	*DEN*	Simon	USA
Scattergories	USA	Simpson Sez	USA
Scene It	USA	Sing With Me Magic	
School Bus	USA	Cube	USA
School Days	USA	Sippin Sue Doll	USA
School Daze	USA	*Sirius Playground*	
School Desk	USA	*Equipment*	*DEN*
Sciscan Technology	USA	Sit 'N Spin	USA
Scorpion	*JAP*	*Skannerz*	*HK*
Scrabble	USA	Skateboard Shannen	USA
Scrambled Egg Puzzle	USA	Skip-Bo	USA
Scrambled States		Sky Racer	USA
of America	USA	Sky Raider	USA
Screw Breaker	*JAP*	Sky Star	USA
Sea Dragon	*CAN*	*Skyline Playground*	
Sea Wasp	USA	*Equipment*	*DEN*
Seaborg	USA	Slam-A-Rama	USA
Seascapes Puzzles	USA	Slapdragon	USA
Seaside	USA	*Slim Line Hockey*	*CHN*
Secret Central	USA	*Slim Line Soccer*	*CHN*
Secret Message Pop	USA	Slingchute	USA
See 'N Say	USA	*Slingshot*	*CAN*
See-Thru Swap	USA	Slinky	USA
Sega	*JAP*	Slinky Science & More	USA

Toys & Games (cont.)

Slip 'N Slide	CHN
Slotsky	USA
Small Stuff	USA
Smart Bomb	UK
Smart Mouth	USA
Smilebit	JAP
Smokin Stunt Speedway	CAN
Snap	USA
Sneaky Puzzles	USA
Snowboarding	JAP
Soccer Billiards	CHN
Soft Spokes	USA
Softina Doll	USA
Solitaire	USA
Solitaire Master	USA
Solitaire Tiles	USA
Something For Nothing	USA
Sony	JAP
Soothing Lavender Doll	USA
Sorry!	USA
Soul of The Ultimate Nation	KOR
Soul Reaver	UK
Sounds On The Go	USA
Space Colony	USA
Space Racer	JAP
Space Voyagers	USA
Spark Knight	USA
Spear's Games	USA
Special Forces	FRA
Special Pine Playsets	USA
Spectromagic	USA
Spectrum	USA
Speedeez	HK
Speedstars	USA
Speedy Eggbert	USA

Spellmaster	USA
Spike Spike	USA
Spin Pop	USA
Spin The Beetle	USA
Spinning First Friends	USA
Spirit Playground Equipment	DEN
Spirograph	USA
Spit	USA
Spite And Malice	USA
Spitfire	USA
Splash & Stack Island	CAN
Split	USA
Sports Trivia	USA
Sportster Ride-In	USA
Sproing	USA
Spy	CAN
Spybotics	DEN
Squeeze & Squeak Doll	USA
Stacking Shopping Cart	USA
Stage of Riches	USA
Stampede!	USA
Stand 'N' Swing	USA
Star Fox	JAP
Star Sisterz	USA
Starburst	USA
Starfish Playground Equipment	DEN
Stargazer Playground Equipment	DEN
Statesman	USA
Step Start Walk N' Ride	USA
Stick-Ons	USA
Stick-Ums	USA
Stone Soup	USA
Storytime Game With Mother Goose	USA

Stratego	USA	*Talking Bingo*	*HK*
Streamer Tag	USA	**Talking Stix**	USA
Street Fighter	*JAP*	*Tamagotchi*	*JAP*
Stride-To-Ride Walker	USA	**Tangley Oaks**	USA
Strife	*CAN*	**Taradiddle**	USA
Stuff The Stockings	USA	**Tea Cart**	USA
Stun Card Game	USA	**Tear-Opens**	USA
Sugar Planet	USA	**Tec Blue**	USA
Summer Fun	USA	*Technic*	*DEN*
Summit Playground		**Teeny Doll**	USA
Equipment	*DEN*	**Terra 2000**	USA
Summoner	USA	**Texas Hold'Em Poker**	USA
Sundowner	USA	**The Big Money**	
Sunrise	USA	**Cheese Caper**	USA
Sunset Glow	USA	**The Concord Swing Sets**	USA
Super Electronic		**The Dover Swing Sets**	USA
Ker Plunk	USA	**The Fairfax Swing Sets**	USA
Super Mario	*JAP*	**The First Years**	USA
Super Pail Set	USA	**The Hampton Swingsets**	USA
Super Scrabble	USA	**The Math Game**	USA
Super Soaker	USA	**The Phonics Game**	USA
Super Wacky Stick	*JAP*	**The Scrambled States**	
Supernova Playground		**of America**	USA
Equipment	*DEN*	**The Three Stooges**	USA
Superplexus	USA	**The Warriors**	USA
Sure Shot	USA	*Theme Playground*	
Surf's Up	USA	*Equipment*	*DEN*
Surprise!	USA	*Thief*	*UK*
Surprize	USA	**Third Dimension Puzzle**	USA
Swap	USA	**Thomas And Friends**	USA
Swingerz Golf	*UK*	*Thomas The Tank*	
Swingin' In The Green	USA	*Engine*	*HK*
Tab	*AUS*	*Thor*	*JAP*
Tabaret	*AUS*	**Thrasher**	USA
Table And Chair Set	USA	**Three Card Poker**	USA
Table Master	USA	**Three Throws**	USA
Taboo	USA	**Throw Me A Bone**	USA
Tabsportsbef	*AUS*	**Thumb Thing**	USA

Toys & Games (cont.)

Thunderbird	USA
Thunderbolt	USA
Tiger Games	USA
Tiger Gertie	USA
Tilt N' Tumble	USA
Timeless Moments Doll	USA
Timeless Treasures	USA
Tiny 'N Tuff	CAN
Tiny Tins	USA
Tip-It	USA
Toast of The Town	USA
Tomb Raider	UK
Tomcat	USA
Tomy	JAP
Tonka	USA
Tool Bench	USA
Top Banana	USA
Top Performance	USA
Top That	USA
Top Trumps	USA
Toppleball	USA
Torch	CAN
Toss Across	USA
Toss Up	USA
Total Meltdown	HK
Toughest Mighty Dump	USA
Tower	HK
Tower of Doom	USA
Toy Organizer	USA
Toy Story	USA
Toymax	USA
Tracball	CHN
Trace Memory	JAP
Trackside	AUS
Trainmaster	USA
Transformers	USA
Transforming Blok Bots	CAN

Travel Sparkle Light	USA
Treasury Collection Doll	USA
Trendmasters	USA
Tri Ominos	USA
Tribes	FRA
Trinity:Battleground	USA
Triple It	USA
Tripoley	USA
Triton Playground Equipment	DEN
Trivaoke Music Trivia	USA
Trivial Pursuit	USA
Triviatron	USA
Tropico	USA
Trouble	USA
Trump The Game	USA
Trygle	USA
Trypio	USA
Tumblin' Monkeys	USA
Turbo Rally Racer	CAN
Turbopaddle	USA
Turnabout	USA
Tut's Tomb Puzzle	USA
TV Gamecube	USA
TV Guide	USA
Twinkleberries	HK
Twinkletwirls Dance Studio	USA
Twister	USA
Tyco	USA
U-122 Striker	CAN
U-240 Assault	CAN
Ultimate Pinball	HK
Ultimate Stratego	USA
Ultimate Texas Hold' Em	USA
Unbelievably Soft Baby Doll	USA
Uncle Wiggily	USA

Underground Online	USA	*Water Golf*	*USA*
Unicornucopia	USA	*Water Symphony*	*JAP*
Unimax	USA	*Waterfall Playground*	
Uno	USA	*Equipment*	*DEN*
U-Pik-Em	USA	**Watertrotter**	USA
Upwords	USA	**Waterworks**	USA
Valle Nevado	USA	*Wavebird*	*JAP*
Valor Vs. Venom	USA	**Wealthy Wizard**	USA
Vampire Hunter	USA	**Weapons & Warriors**	USA
Vampire: The		**Weebles**	USA
Masquerade	USA	**Whac-A-Mole**	USA
Vega Playground		*Wham-O*	*CHN*
Equipment	*DEN*	*Wham-O-Rang*	*CHN*
Vegas Nite	USA	**What Am I**	USA
Vermont Teddy Bear	USA	**What Do Animals Say**	USA
Vertex Playground		**What's Her Face**	USA
Equipment	*DEN*	**Wheel of Fortune**	USA
Vertical Challenge		**Wheels On The Bus**	USA
Playground		*Whiplash*	*UK*
Equipment	*DEN*	**Whirl-A-Way**	USA
Victor	USA	**Who Dunnit?**	USA
Videonow	USA	**Wiggle 'N Giggle**	USA
Vietcong	USA	**Wiggly Giggly**	USA
View-Master	USA	*Wiki*	*KOR*
Vina Del Mar	USA	**Wild 2's Poker**	USA
Virtua Fighter 4	*JAP*	**Wild Climbers**	USA
Visions	USA	**Wild Metal**	USA
Vorgan Attack	*CAN*	**Wild Streak**	USA
Vorgan Stronghold	*CAN*	**Wild Wheels**	USA
Vorgan War Chest	*CAN*	**Wild Wilderness**	USA
Voyager Adventure		**Willy Water Bug**	USA
System	*HK*	**Win A Million**	USA
Vroom Vroom Vehicles	USA	**Windsocks**	USA
Wagon Set	USA	**Wing Attacker**	USA
Warioworld	*JAP*	**Wing Defenser**	USA
Warp	*CAN*	**Winners Choice**	USA
Warriors	*CAN*	**Winning Bid**	USA
Water Babies	*HK*	*Wizard Water Games*	*JAP*

Toys & Games (cont.)

Wizards of The Coast	USA	X-Tra Hot Sevens	USA
WNBA	USA	Xtreme Poker	USA
Wolborg	USA	Yahtzee	USA
Woodkits	USA	*Yo Stick*	*HK*
Woody Woodpecker	USA	*Yoshi*	*JAP*
Word Connect	USA	Yu-Gi-Oh	USA
Word Scramble	*HK*	Yukon Gold	USA
Workshop	USA	Zamboni	USA
World of Darkness	USA	*Zelda*	*JAP*
World of Shapes	USA	*Zibal Playground*	
Worm	USA	*Equipment*	*DEN*
WWJD The Game	USA	Ziggy	USA
X-Box	USA	Zingo	USA
X-Pod	*DEN*	Zip-Ity Do-Dolly Doll	USA
Xtender	*JAP*	Zoam Turbine	USA
		Zoe	USA

Chapter 10

Services

(**American owned in bold** / *Foreign owned in italic*)

BANKS

Advest	*FRA*
Alliance Bank	**USA**
American Community Bank	**USA**
Anchor Bank	**USA**
ASB Bank	*AUS*
Banc One	**USA**
Banc One Wisconsin	**USA**
Banco Popular	**USA**
Bancomer	*MEX*
Bancwest	**USA**
Bank Brussels Lambert	*NETH*
Bank Hapoalim	*ISR*
Bank of America	**USA**
Bank of Bermuda	*BMD*
Bank of Boston	**USA**
Bank of Canton (Ga.)	**USA**
Bank of China	*CHN*
Bank of Commerce	**USA**
Bank of Communications	*CHN*
Bank of Hawaii	**USA**
Bank of Lake County	**USA**
Bank of Montreal	*CAN*
Bank of New Hamphire	*CAN*
Bank of New York	**USA**
Bank of North Dakota	**USA**
Bank of Pennsylvania	*IRE*
Bank of Smithtown	**USA**
Bank of The Hudson	**USA**
Bank of The West	**USA**
Bank of Tidewater	**USA**
Bank of Yokohama	*JAP*
Bank Plus	**USA**
BankAmerica	**USA**
Banknorth Connecticut	*CAN*
Banknorth Massachusetts	*CAN*
Banknorth Vermont	*CAN*
Barclays	*UK*
BNP	*FRA*
Canadian Western Bank	*CAN*
Carrollton Bank	**USA**
Chase Manhattan	**USA**
China Merchants Bank	*CHN*
Citibank	**USA**
Citizens Financial	*UK*
Colonial	**USA**
Columbia River Bank	**USA**
Comerica	**USA**
Dundee Bancorp	*CAN*
Evergreen Bank	*CAN*
First American	**USA**
First Arizona Savings	**USA**
First Chicago/NBD Bancorp	**USA**
First Citizens	**USA**
First Consumers National Bank	**USA**
First Federal Bank	**USA**
First Federal Savings	**USA**
First Hawaiian	*FRA*
First Interstate	**USA**
First Interstate Bank of California	**USA**
First Interstate Bank of Oregon	**USA**
First Interstate Bank of Washington	**USA**
First Mariner Bank	**USA**
First Maryland Bancorp	*IRE*
First Midwest	**USA**
First National Bank of Florida	**USA**
First National Bank of St. Louis	**USA**

First Northern Savings	**USA**	*Standard Bank*	*SAF*
First Omni Bank	*IRE*	*Standard Chartered*	*UK*
First Security	**USA**	**State Farm Bank**	**USA**
First Tennessee	**USA**	**Suntrust**	**USA**
First Union	**USA**	**Sunwest Bank**	**USA**
First Virginia	**USA**	*TD Bank*	*CAN*
Firstar	**USA**	**The Provident Bank**	**USA**
FloridaFirst	**USA**	**Third Federal**	**USA**
Hancock	**USA**	*Toronto-Dominion*	*CAN*
Hibernia National	**USA**	**USB**	**USA**
Home Star	**USA**	**USBank**	**USA**
ING	*NETH*	**Wachovia**	**USA**
J.P. Morgan	**USA**	**Washington Mutual**	**USA**
La Salle	*NETH*	**Wells Fargo**	**USA**
Liberty Bank	**USA**	**Winter Hill**	**USA**
Mercantile Bank	*CAN*	**Yes Bank**	**USA**
Napa Valley	**USA**	**Zions Bank**	**USA**
National Bank of Alaska	**USA**		
National Bank		**HOTELS**	
of Arizona	**USA**	*Accor*	*FRA*
National Bank		**Adam's Mark**	**USA**
of South Carolina	**USA**	*All Seasons*	*FRA*
Northern Trust	**USA**	**Amerihost Inn**	**USA**
Oceanfirst Bank	**USA**	**AmeriSuites**	**USA**
Pacific Century Bank	**USA**	**Atlas**	**USA**
Peoples Heritage (Maine)	*CAN*	**Aztar**	**USA**
Pittsburgh National	**USA**	**Baymount**	**USA**
Port Financial	*UK*	**Best Suites**	**USA**
Provident	**USA**	**Best Western**	**USA**
RegionsBank	**USA**	*Candlewood Suites*	*UK*
Reliance Federal Savings	**USA**	**Clarion**	**USA**
Riggs	**USA**	**Comfort Inn**	**USA**
San Diego National	**USA**	**Country Hearth Inn**	**USA**
Sandy Spring Bank	**USA**	**Country Inn & Suites**	
SCB	*JAP*	**by Carlson**	**USA**
Shore Bank	**USA**	**Courtyard by Marriott**	**USA**
SouthTrust	**USA**	*Crowne Plaza*	*UK*
Stanbic	*SAF*	**Days Inn**	**USA**

<u>Hotels (cont.)</u>

Daystops	USA	Quality Inn	USA
Doubletree	USA	Radisson	USA
Econo Lodge	USA	Ramada Inn	USA
Embassy Suites	USA	Raphael	USA
ExecuStay	USA	*Red Roof Inn*	*FRA*
Fairfield Inn	USA	Residence Inn	USA
Fairmont Hotels	USA	Rodeway Inn	USA
Family Inns of America	USA	Royal Orleans	USA
Four Points	USA	Sands Regency	USA
Four Seasons	USA	Sheraton	USA
Hampton Inn	USA	Shoney's Inns	USA
Harrah's	USA	Signature Inn	USA
Hilton	USA	Sleep Inn	USA
Holiday Inn	*UK*	Sonesta	USA
Holiday Inn Express	*UK*	Springhill Suites	USA
Homewood Suites	USA	*Stamford*	*SNG*
Hotel Indigo	*UK*	*Staybridge Suites*	*UK*
Howard Johnson	USA	*Studio 6*	*FRA*
Hyatt	USA	Studioplus Deluxe	
InnSuites	USA	Studios	USA
Inter-Continental	*UK*	Suiteamerica	USA
James K. Polk	USA	*Suitehotel*	*FRA*
Knights Inn	USA	Super 8	USA
La Quinta	USA	*Taj*	*IND*
Little America	USA	TownePlace Suites	USA
Loews	USA	*Travel Inn*	*UK*
Mainstay Hotels	USA	Travelodge	USA
Marriott	USA	Utell	USA
Microtel	USA	Vagabond Inn	USA
Motel 6	*FRA*	*Village Leisure*	*UK*
Novotel	FRA	W Hotels	USA
Omni	USA	Wellesley Inns & Suites	USA
Orbis	USA	Westgate Hotel	USA
Park Inn	USA	Westin	USA
Park Plaza	USA	Wingate Inn	USA
Parker House	USA	Woodfield Suites	USA
Prime Suites	USA	Woodfin Suite Hotels	USA
		Wyndham	USA

INSURANCE

AAA	USA
Aetna	USA
Aflac	USA
Alico	USA
Allied Group	USA
Allstate	USA
Altis Life	USA
American Family Mutual	USA
American Hardware Mutual	USA
American National	USA
American United Life	USA
Americare	USA
Amerisure	USA
Ameritas	USA
Anthem Life	USA
Ark Life	*IRE*
Atlanta Life	USA
CAN	USA
Catawba	USA
Central Mutual	USA
Central United Life	USA
Centurion	USA
Citzens	USA
Consolidated American	USA
Coverdell	USA
Deerbrook	USA
Empire	USA
Farm Bureau	USA
Farmers & Traders Life	USA
Farmers Mutual	USA
First Colony Life	USA
First Maryland Life Insurance	*IRE*
Franklin Life Insurance	USA
GEICO	USA
Glenbrook Life	USA
Golden State Mutual	USA
Guardian Life	USA
Homebiz	USA
Horace Mann Educators	USA
Horizon	USA
Integrity Mutual	USA
Lutheran Brotherhood	USA
Meridian	USA
Metropolitan Life	USA
Modern Woodmen of America	USA
Mutual of Omaha	USA
Nationwide	USA
New England	USA
Nippon Life	*JAP*
Northbrook Life	USA
Old American Life	USA
Pacific Life Insurance	USA
Partners In Progress	USA
Principal Financial Group	USA
Protective Life	USA
Sapiens	*ISR*
SGIC	*AUS*
SIS	*AUS*
Standard	*SWI*
State Farm	USA
State Insurance	*AUS*
Sunamerica	USA
Texas Mutual	USA
The Cooperators	*CAN*
The Derbyshire	*UK*
The Franklin	USA
The Medical Mutual Group	USA
Transamerica	*NETH*
Transition	*CAN*
Travelers Life	USA

Insurance (cont.)

Unimerica	USA
Universal Underwriters	*SWI*
USA Life Insurance Company	USA
Vero	*AUS*
Wausau	USA
Whole Life	USA
Woman's Life Insurance	USA
Woodmen Accident & Life	USA
WRL	*NETH*
Yellow Key	USA
Zurich	*SWI*

MAIL DELIVERY SERVICES

Airborne	*GER*
DHL	*GER*
Federal Express (FedEx)	USA
Overnite	USA
U.S. Postal Service (USPS)	USA
UPS	USA

MOVING SERVICES

Allied Van Lines	*UK*
Atlas Van Lines	USA
Global Van Lines	USA
National Van Lines	USA
North American Van Lines	USA
Ryder	USA
U-Haul	USA
United	USA

OIL CHANGE CENTERS

Jiffy Lube	*NETH*
Mobil	USA
Quick 10	USA
Valvoline Instant Oil Change	USA

PHONES & PHONE SERVICES

AT&T	USA
Audiovox	USA
Bell South	USA
Cobra	USA
Ericsson	*SWE*
General Electric	USA
Kenwood	*JAP*
Lucent	*FRA*
Motorola	USA
NEC	*JAP*
Nokia	*FIN*
Panasonic	*JAP*
Phonemate	*JAP*
Radio Shack	USA
Razr	USA
Samsung	*KOR*
Sanyo	*JAP*
Sony	*JAP*
Sprint	USA
Telus Mobility	*CAN*
Toshiba	*JAP*
Verizon	USA
Vmix	*HK*

RESTAURANTS

A & W	USA
Abdow's Restaurants	USA
Abe & Louie's	USA
Acapulco Mexican	USA
Alcatraz Brewing	USA
Amarillo Mesquite Grill	USA
Ambria	USA
America	USA

American Bandstand		Black Eyed Pea	USA
Grill	USA	Blackhawk Grill Eatery	USA
American Park	USA	Blimpie Subs	USA
Angelo & Maxie's		Bob Evans	USA
Steakhouse	USA	Bojangles	USA
Antico Posto	USA	*Bombay Bicycle Club*	*NZ*
Applebee's		Bonanza	USA
Neighborhood Grill		Bonefish Grill	USA
& Bar	USA	Boston Market	USA
Arby's	USA	Boulder Creek	USA
Aribica Coffee House	USA	Brasserie Jo	USA
Arthur Treachers	USA	Braum's	USA
Artic Circle	USA	Braxton	USA
Ashley's Cafe	USA	*Brewsters*	*UK*
Atlantic Fish Co	USA	Bridgeman's	USA
Atlas	USA	Bristol Bar & Grill	USA
Austins Steaks & Saloon	USA	Brown's Chicken	USA
Avado	USA	Buca Di Beppo	USA
Azteca	USA	BuddyFreddy's	USA
B&Burger	*FRA*	Buffalo Wild Wings	USA
Back Street Brewery	USA	Bugaboo Creek	USA
Back Yard Burgers	USA	Burger King	USA
Bahama Breeze	USA	Burton & Doyle	USA
Bailey's	USA	Café Ba-Ba-Reeba	USA
Bamboo Club	USA	*Café Chicago*	*UK*
Barnie's Coffee & Tea Co.	USA	*Café Route*	*FRA*
Baskin-Robbins	USA	*Café Spaggia*	*UK*
Beefeater	*UK*	California Café	USA
Ben Pao Chinese	USA	California Pizza Kitchen	USA
Benihana Grill	USA	Canyon Road	USA
Bennigan's	USA	Cape Del Ray	USA
Bertolini's	USA	Captain D's	USA
Bickford Grille	USA	Carl's Jr.	USA
Bickford's	USA	Carraba's	USA
Big T	USA	Carrows	USA
Bishop's Buffets	USA	Casa Bonita	USA
Bistro 110	*UK*	Casa Gallardo	USA
BJ's	USA	Casa Ole	USA

Restaurants (cont.)

Center Café	USA	Daily Grill	USA
Cesario	FRA	Dairy Queen	USA
Charley Horse	USA	Dakota	USA
Charley's	USA	Damon's	USA
Charley's Crab	USA	D'Angelo Sandwich Shops	USA
Charrito's	USA	Dante's Seafood Grill	USA
Chart House	USA	Darryl's	USA
Chat Noir	USA	Dash-In Grill	USA
Checkers	USA	Del Frisco's Steak House	USA
Cheese Cellar	USA	Denny's	USA
Chef's Express	UK	Devon	USA
Chequers	USA	Dick Clark's	USA
Chesapeake Bagel Bakery	USA	Dixie House	USA
Chi Chi's	USA	Domino's Pizza	USA
Chick-Fil-A	USA	Don & Charlie's	USA
Chili's Grill & Bar	USA	Don Pablo's Mexican Kitchen	USA
Chimayo Grill	USA	Donatos Pizza	USA
Chop House	USA	Doolittles	USA
Chuck E Cheese's	USA	Doraku	USA
Church's	USA	Dos Hermanos	UK
Cinnabon	USA	Drivers Diner	USA
Coach Grill	USA	Dunkin' Donuts	USA
Coco's	USA	Durango's	USA
Collin Street Bakery	USA	Eadie's Kitchen & Market	UK
Colorado Steakhouse	USA	Eat 'N Park	USA
Columbus Bakery	USA	Einstein Bros.	USA
Cookietree Cookies	USA	El Chico	USA
Corky's	USA	El Pollo Loco	USA
Corner Bakery Café	USA	El Rio Grande	USA
Country Buffet	USA	Elmer's	USA
Country Market	USA	Ernie's	USA
Country Roadhouse Buffet & Grill	USA	Everest	USA
Cousin's Submarines	USA	Family Inns of America	USA
Cracker Barrel Old Country Store	USA	Famous Dave's	USA
		Fat Boys Bbq	USA
Cutter's Bayhouse	USA	Fazoli's	USA

Fleming's Prime Steakhouse	USA	Hooter's	USA
		Hops	USA
Fox & Hound	USA	Horatio's	USA
Frankie's Italian Grille	USA	Horizon's Eatery	USA
Fresh Choice	USA	Hot Sam Pretzels	USA
Friday's Front Row	USA	Houlihan's	USA
Friendly's Restaurants	USA	Howard Johnson	USA
Frisch's	USA	Hungry Howies	USA
Frisch's Big Boy	USA	Hunter's Steakhouse	USA
Fuddruckers	USA	IHOP	USA
Furr's Cafeterias	USA	Iron Skillet	USA
Gallagher's	USA	J. Gilbert's Wood-Fried Steaks	USA
Garcia's Mexican	USA		
Garfield's Restaurant & Pub	USA	J.B. Winberie	USA
		Jack Baker's Lobster Shanty	USA
Gattiland	USA		
Gattis'-To-Go	USA	Jack In The Box	USA
Gattitown	USA	Jack Rose	USA
Giraffe	*JAP*	JB's Restaurants	USA
Gloria Jean's Coffee	USA	Jerry's	USA
Godfather's Pizza	USA	Jerry's Famous Deli	USA
Golden Corral	USA	JJ North's	USA
Gonzalez Y Gonzalez	USA	Joe Muggs	USA
Good Times	USA	Joe's American Bar & Grill	USA
Grandy's	USA		
Granny's Buffets	USA	Joe's Crab Shack	USA
Grisanti's	USA	Joe's Seafood	USA
H. Salt Seafood Galley	USA	Johnny Rockets	USA
Haagen-Dazs	*SWI*	Karmelkorn Shoppes	USA
Hamburger Hamlet	USA	Kenny Rogers Roasters	USA
Hard Rock Café	UK	Kentucky Fried Chicken	USA
Hardees	USA	KFC	USA
Harry's Bar & American Grill	USA	*Kirin City*	*JAP*
		Koo Koo Roo California Kitchen	USA
Harvey's	*CAN*		
Hearty Platter	USA	Krispy Kreme	USA
Hibachi Grill	USA	L Woods	USA
Hometown Buffet	USA	La Rambla	USA

Restaurants (cont.)

La Salsa	USA
La Senorita	USA
Lamp Post Pizza	USA
Landry's Seafood House	USA
Le Peep	USA
Lettuce Entertain You	USA
Little Caeser's	USA
Lobster Shanty	USA
Long John Silver's	USA
Longhorn Steakhouse	USA
Luby's Restaurants	USA
Lyons	USA
Maggiano's Little Italy	USA
Mama Fu's Asian House	USA
Mamma Ilardo's Pizza	USA
Manchu Wok	CAN
Manhattan Bagel Co.	USA
Maui Tacos	USA
Max & Ermas	USA
Mazzios	USA
McCormick & Schmick's Seafood	USA
McDonalds	USA
Medieval Times	USA
Mein Street Wok	USA
Miami Grill	USA
Miami Subs	USA
Mity Nice Grill	USA
Mitzel's American Kitchen	USA
Mom N Pop's Buffet & Bakery	USA
Monterey's	USA
Morton's The Steakhouse	USA
Mr. Gatti's Pizza	USA
Mr. Hero	USA
Mrs. Baird's	MEX
Mrs. Field's	USA
Mrs. Powell's Bakery	USA
Nappa Valley Grill	USA
Nathan's Famous	USA
National Sports Grill	USA
New World Coffee	USA
Noah's New York Bagels	USA
Noble Roman's Pizza	USA
Numero Uno Pizza	USA
O'Charley's	USA
Old Chicago	USA
Old Country Buffet	USA
Olive Garden	USA
Omcar	USA
On The Border	USA
Ondine	USA
Orange Julius	USA
Outback Steakhouse	USA
Owens Family Restaurants	USA
Paco's Pizza & Taco	USA
Palomino	USA
Panera Bread	USA
Papa Gino's	USA
Papa John's	USA
Papa Razzi	USA
Papagus	USA
Parkers' Lighthouse	USA
Parkers Blue Ash Grill	USA
Pasta Central	USA
Pat & Oscars	USA
Penny Curtis Bakeries	USA
Pepperoni Grill	USA
Perkins	USA
Perry's	USA
Petterino's	USA
Piccadilly Cafeterias	USA
Pick Up Stix	USA

Pier W	USA	Rubio's	USA
Pizza Del Arte	*FRA*	Ruby Tuesdays	USA
Pizza Hut	USA	Rusty Scupper	USA
Pizza Inn	USA	Ryan's Family Steakhouse	USA
Pizza King	USA	Saloon Bar & Grill	USA
Pizza Mart	*CAN*	Saltgrass Steak House	USA
Pizza Parlor Sandwich	USA	Samurai	USA
Pizzeria Uno	USA	*San Marzano*	*UK*
PJ's Coffee & Wine Bar	USA	Savannah Chop House	USA
Planet Smoothie	USA	Sbarro	USA
Player's Grill	USA	Schlotzsky's Deli	USA
Pollo Tropical	USA	Scoozi!	USA
Ponderosa Steakhouse	USA	Sea Lion Cafe	USA
Popeye's	USA	Seasons 52	USA
Poppies	USA	Seattle's Best	USA
Potowmack Landing	USA	*Second Cup*	*CAN*
Pretzel Time	USA	Sequoia	USA
Pretzelmaker	USA	Shane's Rib Shack	USA
Prime Sirlion	USA	Shaw's Crab House	USA
Pump Room	USA	Shoney's	USA
Qdoba Mexican Grill	USA	Silver Diner	USA
Quincy Steakhouse	USA	Sirloin Saloons	USA
R.J. Grunts	USA	Sizzler	USA
RA Sushi	USA	Skates On The Bay	USA
Ragazzis	USA	Skyline Chili	USA
Rainforest Café	USA	Smokey Bones	USA
Red Lobster	USA	Smoothie Island	USA
Red Robin	USA	Solleys Bakery	USA
Redfish Cajun	USA	Sonic Drive-In	USA
Richard's Deli & Pub	USA	Sonny's Real Pit Bar-B-Q	USA
Risoterria	USA	Sorrento Grille	USA
Rock Bottom Restaurant		Soup 'N Salad Unlimited	USA
& Brewery	USA	Spectrum	USA
Rockfish Seafood Grill	USA	Spoons Bar & Grill	USA
Rock-Ola	USA	*Spratt's Kitchen & Market*	*UK*
Romano's Macaroni Grill	USA	Steak And Ale	USA
Roxy Café	USA	Steak 'N Shake	USA
Roy's	USA	Subway	USA

Restaurants (cont.)

Sullivan's Steakhouse	USA
Sweetwaters	USA
Swiss Chalet	CAN
T.G.I. Friday's	USA
Taco Bell	USA
Taco Bueno	USA
Taco Cabana	USA
Taco John's	USA
Taco Time	USA
Taco Villa	USA
Tahoe Joe's Famous Steakhouse	USA
Tastee Freez	USA
Tavola Baccano	JAP
TCBY Yogurt	USA
Texas Burger	USA
Texas Land & Cattle Co. Steak House	USA
TGI Friday's	USA
The Black-Eyed Pea	USA
The Border Grill	USA
The Capital Grille	USA
The Chart House	USA
The Cheesecake Factory	USA
The Crab House	USA
The Grill Room	USA
The Metropolitan Cafe	USA
The Ocean Club	USA
The Original Cookie Co.	USA
The Salon	USA
The Times	USA
Thunder Grill	USA
Tim Hortons	USA
Togo's	USA
Tony Roma's	USA
Top of The Hub	USA
Tortuga's Coastal Cantina	USA
Triggerfish	USA
Tropigrill	USA
TRU	USA
Tsunami Grill	USA
Tucci Benucch	USA
Turano	USA
Tutto Mare	USA
Twin City Grill	USA
Uno Chicago Bar & Grill	USA
Village Inn	USA
Vinny T's of Boston	USA
Vong's Thai Kitchen	USA
Waffle House	USA
Wall Street Deli	USA
Wendy's	USA
Western Sizzlin	USA
Whataburger	USA
White Castle	USA
Who-Song & Larry's	USA
Wienerschnitzel	USA
Wildfire	USA
Willoughby's Coffee & Tea	USA
Winchell's Donut House	USA
Wow Bao	USA
Zio's Italian Kitchen	USA
Zoopa	USA

Chapter 11

Appliances

(**American owned in bold** / *Foreign owned in italic*)

AIR CONDITIONERS

Amana	USA
American Standard	USA
Armstrong	USA
Bard	USA
Carrier	USA
Carrier	USA
Casement	USA
Coleman	USA
Colman	USA
Comfortmaker	USA
Compact-Aire	USA
Delonghi	*ITL*
Edenaire	USA
Fedders	USA
Fraser Johnston	USA
Frigidaire	*SWE*
Frost Sentry	USA
General Electric	USA
Goldstar	*KOR*
Governair	USA
Heil	USA
Intertherm	USA
Johnson	USA
Kelvinator	USA
Kenmore	USA
Koppel	USA
KP	USA
Lennox	USA
LG	*KOR*
Mammoth	USA
Miller	USA
Moducci	USA
Panasonic	*JAP*
Payne	USA
Philco	USA
Powermiser	USA
Quasar	*JAP*
Rheem	*JAP*
Ruud	*JAP*
Sharp	*JAP*
Silensys	USA
Smoke Eliminator	USA
Super Power-Aire	USA
Superior	USA
Tappan	*SWE*
Tempstar	USA
Train	USA
Trane	USA
Vectra	*IND*
Verdant	*IND*
Vert-I-Pak	USA
Vertis	*IND*
Viper	USA
Webco	USA
Weldy 2000	USA
Whitfield	USA
York	USA

HOUSEHOLD APPLIANCES

Allure	USA
Altus	*TUR*
Amana	USA
Amazing Chef Chopper	*CAN*
Arcelik	*TUR*
Aroma	*ITL*
Arthur Martin	*SWE*
Astro Popcorn Machine	USA
Atlantis	USA
Bagel Perfect Toaster	USA
Bauknecht	USA
Best	USA
Betty Crocker	USA
Bionaire	USA
Bissell	USA
Black & Decker	USA

Blendor	USA	**Fiesta**	USA
Bosch	GER	**Filter Queen**	USA
Braun	USA	*Fisher & Paykel*	NZ
Bravo! Boss	SWE	**Flavor Duo**	USA
Bread Box Breadmaker	USA	**Flavorcell Food Processor**	USA
Breadman	USA	*Frigidaire*	SWE
Broan	USA	**Frydaddy Deep Fryer**	USA
Brother	JAP	**Futura**	USA
Bunn-O-Matic	USA	**Gay 90's Popcorn**	
Carpetriever	USA	**Machine**	USA
Carpetwin	USA	**GE**	USA
Chef-Aire	USA	**General Electric**	USA
Citation Popcorn		*Genie Garage Door*	
Machine	USA	*Openers*	JAP
Conair	USA	**George Foreman Grill**	USA
Corner Bakery	USA	*Gibson*	SWE
Crock-Pot	USA	**Glo-Ray Foodwarmer**	USA
Cuisinart	USA	*Goldstar*	KOR
Delonghi	ITL	**Grindmaster**	USA
Deluxe Whiz Bang		*Haier*	CHN
Popcorn Machine	USA	**Hamilton Beach**	USA
Designer Dry	USA	**Hardwick**	USA
Dirt Devil	USA	*Hitachi*	JAP
Dixie-Narco	USA	*Hoover*	CHN
Dogeroo	USA	**Hotpoint**	USA
Douglas	USA	**Inglis**	USA
Drinkmaster	USA	**In-Sink-Erator**	USA
Dyson	UK	**JC Penney**	USA
Econo-Pop Popcorn		**Jenn-Air**	USA
Machine	USA	**Jetzone**	USA
Electrolux	SWE	*Kelvinator*	SWE
Emerson	USA	**Kenmore**	USA
Empress	USA	**Kirby**	USA
Encore	USA	**KitchenAid**	USA
Estate	USA	*Kobold*	GER
Eureka	SWE	*Krups*	FRA
Fantom	CAN	*LG*	KOR
Farberware	USA	**Little Pro Food Processer**	USA

Household Appliances (cont.)			
Litton	USA	Pollenex Air Purifiers	USA
Magic Chef	USA	Pop-A-Lot	USA
Majestic	USA	Popcornnow	USA
Matador	*DEN*	Popeil Products	USA
Matsushita	*JAP*	Popeil's Pasta Maker	USA
Maytag	USA	Poplite	USA
McCall	USA	Powerpop Multi-Popper	USA
Melitta	*GER*	Presto	USA
Miele	*GER*	Presto Pride	USA
Mighty Mite	*SWE*	Princess	USA
Mini Chill Ice Cream		Proctor-Silex	USA
Maker	USA	Prolite	USA
Mirro	USA	Pure Air	USA
Mixmate	USA	Quanitcut Food Machine	USA
Mr. Coffee	USA	*Quasar*	*JAP*
Nautilus	USA	Rainbow	USA
Nesco	USA	Rangemaster	USA
Nespresso	*SWI*	*RCA*	*FRA*
Nilfisk	*DEN*	Readivac	USA
Norcold	USA	Red Goat Waste	
Norelco	*NETH*	Disposers	USA
Norge	USA	*Redco Food Slicer*	*GER*
Nutone	USA	Regal	USA
Nutri-Blender	USA	Regal Ware	USA
Onion King Vegetable		*Regina*	*NETH*
Slicer	USA	Revco	USA
Oreck	USA	Ridgid	USA
Oster	USA	Rival	USA
Outlaw	USA	Roper	USA
Pacer	USA	*Rowenta*	*FRA*
Panasonic	*JAP*	Royal	USA
Pasta Chef	USA	Saladshooter	USA
Perfection	USA	Salton	USA
Philips	*NETH*	Salton/Maxim	USA
Pinto Pop Popcorn		*Samsung*	*KOR*
Machine	USA	*Sangiorgio*	*ISR*
Pitco Frialator Fryer	USA	*Sanyo*	*JAP*
		Sauter	*ISR*

Savory	UK	*Thermo King*	BMD
Scandinavian Design	USA	*Thermomix*	GER
Sears	USA	*Thomson*	ISR
Sears Craftsman	USA	*Tiger*	GER
SEB	FRA	**Titan Popcorn Machine**	USA
Sebo	GER	**Toast King**	USA
Selectvac	USA	**Toastmaster**	USA
Shark	CAN	**Toast-Qwik**	USA
Sharp	JAP	**Toast-Rite**	USA
Shop-Vac	USA	**Tomato Paste Food**	
Shortcut	USA	**Processor**	USA
Silhouette	USA	*Toshiba*	JAP
Simplicity	USA	*Tricity Bendix*	SWE
Singer	NETH	**Trivection**	USA
Slowcook'N More	USA	**Turbo Chef**	USA
Smartbrew	USA	**Tyler**	USA
Smarty	ITL	*U.S. Range*	UK
Smooth Edge	USA	*Vedette*	ISR
Snackster	USA	**Versamatic**	USA
Sona	IRE	**Versamix**	USA
Sonicweb	USA	*Vienna*	ITL
Sprite Air Scoop	USA	**Viking**	USA
Steamxpress	USA	*Vita-Mix Blender*	CAN
Steelcoat Griddle	USA	**Wafflemaster**	USA
Stepsavor	USA	**Waring by Cuisinart**	USA
Stratos	ITL	**Waste King**	USA
Super Pot Electric Cooker	USA	**Weitech**	USA
Superidea	ITL	**West Bend**	USA
Supreme Air Series	USA	**Whirlpool**	USA
Symphony	USA	**Whispaire**	USA
Tailgater Blender	USA	**Whisperflo**	USA
Tappan	SWE	*White Westinghouse*	SWE
Tefal	FRA	**Whitemagic**	USA
T-Fal	FRA	**Wisconsin Oven**	USA
The Boss	SWE	**Wolf**	USA
The Vibra-Blender	USA	*Wood Stone*	CAN
Thermador	GER	*Zerowatt*	ITL
Thermo Cafe	USA	*Zoppas*	SWE

HUMIDIFIERS/
DEHUMIDIFIERS

April-Air	**USA**
Aqua	**USA**
Delonghi	*ITL*
Emerson	**USA**
Frigidaire	*SWE*
General Electric	**USA**
Gibson	*SWE*
Hunter	**USA**
Kenmore	**USA**
Lennox	**USA**
Magic Chef	**USA**
Thermo-Mist	**USA**
Toastmaster	**USA**
Vapac	**USA**
Vicks	**USA**
Wheelair	**USA**

SEWING MACHINES

Activa 220	*SWI*
Artista	*SWI*
Aurora	*SWI*
Bernette	*SWI*
Fales	**USA**
Husqvarna Viking	*SWE*
Singer	*NETH*

WATER HEATERS

A.O. Smith	**USA**
Amptec	*UK*
Aurora	**USA**
Bradford White	**USA**
Burkay	**USA**
Conservationist	**USA**
Copper-Pak	**USA**
Everhot	**USA**
FBM	**USA**
Glascote	**USA**
Intelli-Fin	**USA**
Lochinvar	**USA**
Lock-Temp	**USA**
Multipoint	**USA**
PK Compact	**USA**
Power Shot	**USA**
Power-Fin	**USA**
Powermite	**USA**
Quickdraw	**USA**
Rheem	*JAP*
Richmond	*JAP*
Ruud	*JAP*
Sandblaster	**USA**
Santon	*UK*
Scott & English	*SNG*
Sets-Systems (tankless)	**USA**
Statesman	**USA**
Streamline	*UK*
Sure Shot	**USA**
UTC 99	*UK*
Vitraglas	**USA**

Chapter 12

Beverages

(**American owned in bold** / *Foreign owned in italic*)

BOTTLED WATER

Aberfoyle	*SWI*
Aberfoyle Springs	*SWI*
Acqua Panna	*SWI*
Aqua Minerale	**USA**
Aquafina	**USA**
Arrowhead	*SWI*
Ashborne	*SWI*
Aura	*ITL*
Baraka	*SWI*
Blaue Quellen	*SWI*
California Mountain Water	**USA**
Calistoga	*SWI*
Canada Dry	*UK*
Clearfruit	**USA**
Clearly Canadian	*CAN*
Crystal Spring	*FRA*
Crystal Springs	*FRA*
Culligan	**USA**
Dannon	*FRA*
Dasani	**USA**
Deer Park	**USA**
Deja Blue	*UK*
Diamond Water	**USA**
Emporer's Fountain	**USA**
Evian	*FRA*
Font Vella	*FRA*
Glaceau	**USA**
Glacier Valley	**USA**
Great Bear	*SWI*
Hinckley & Schmitt	*JAP*
Ice Mountain	*SWI*
Johannis Quell	**USA**
La Croix	**USA**
Labrador	*FRA*
Lanjaron	*FRA*
Lindoya	*SWI*
Midnight Springs	**USA**
Minere	*SWI*
Mont Dore	*FRA*
Montclair	*SWI*
Mountain Valley Water	**USA**
Oasis	*SWI*
Ozarka	*SWI*
Penafiel	*UK*
Perrier	*SWI*
Petropolis	*SWI*
Poland Spring	*SWI*
San Benedetto	*UK*
San Pellegrino	*SWI*
Sangemini	*ITL*
Saratoga Splash	**USA**
Saratoga Springs	**USA**
Schweppes	*UK*
Smartwater	**USA**
Spa City	*BGM*
Spa Marie-Henriette	*BGM*
St. Michaels	*DEN*
Strathmore	**USA**
Switezianka	**USA**
The Ultimate Refresher	*JAP*
Toppur	**USA**
Tyler	**USA**
Valser	**USA**
Vermont Pure	**USA**
Vita Di Sangemini	*ITL*
Vitalis	*POR*
Vitaminwater	**USA**
Vittel	*SWI*
Viva	**USA**
Viva!/First	*PHIL*
Wissahickon	**USA**
Zephyrhills	*SWI*
Zero Calorie	**USA**

COCOA

Ambrosia	USA
Café Delight	USA
Carnation	*SWI*
Chipits	USA
De Zaan	USA
Fry's	*UK*
Guest House	USA
Hershey's	USA
Kayo	USA
Nestle	*SWI*
Old Dutch	USA
Rowntree's	*SWI*
Swiss Miss	USA

COFFEE

Alta Rica	*SWI*
Apffel	USA
Aroma	*SNG*
Beantown	USA
Beyond Gourmet	USA
Birdy	*JAP*
Bokar	*GER*
Bonjour	*SWI*
Brussels Blend	USA
Cabana Blends	USA
Cadillac	USA
Café Karuba	USA
Café Ristretto	*SWI*
Café Verde	USA
Café Vermont	USA
Cain's	USA
Caribou	USA
Caro	*SWI*
Carte Noire	USA
CDM	USA
Chase & Sanborn	USA
Chat Noir	USA

Chock Full O' Nuts	USA
Colcafe	USA
Community	USA
Costa Rica	USA
Custom House	USA
Dark Magic	USA
Diedrich	USA
Donut Shoppe	USA
Douwe Egberts	USA
Fire	*JAP*
First Colony	USA
Flor De Apanas	USA
Folgers	USA
Friele	USA
General Foods International	USA
Georgia Coffee	USA
Gevalia	USA
Ghirardelli	USA
Gold Label	USA
Golden Blend	USA
Golden Brazil	USA
Goodhost	*SWI*
Grand Mere	USA
Green Mountian	USA
Harris	USA
Harvest Peak	USA
High Mountain View	USA
Hills Bros.	USA
Icebreaker Canned Ice Coffee	*SWI*
Jack	*JAP*
Jacobs	USA
Jacques Vabre	USA
JFG	USA
Justin Lloyd	USA
Kanis & Gunnick	USA
Kauai	USA

Coffee (cont.)		Roaster's Pride	USA
Kenya	USA	*Rombouts*	*UK*
Keystone	USA	Rowland Coffee Roasters	USA
Laurentis	USA	Royal Kauai	USA
Lola's Shop	USA	Royal Maui	USA
Luzianne	USA	RT	USA
Maison Du Café	USA	Sabro	USA
Marcilla	USA	Sanka	USA
Master Choice	*GER*	Seattle	USA
Maxim	USA	*Select Varietal*	*COL*
Maxwell House	USA	Sello Dorado	USA
Melitta	*GER*	*Serena Organic Blend*	*SWI*
Mellow Bird's	USA	Sical	USA
Merrild	USA	*Sierra Dorada Blend*	*CAN*
Metropolitan	USA	Signature	USA
Millstone	USA	Snickerdoodle	USA
MJB	USA	Sonero	USA
Mr. Bean	USA	Southern Pride	USA
Nabob	USA	Starbucks	USA
Nescafe	*SWI*	Sulawesi-Kalosi	USA
Nescore	*SWI*	*Sumatra*	*CAN*
Nespresso	*SWI*	Sunshine Joe Coffee Co.	USA
New England	USA	Superior	USA
New Guinea	USA	T. Henry	USA
Out Island Java	USA	Tapestry Blend Dark	USA
Paradiso	*CAN*	*Taster's Choice*	*SWI*
Peet's Coffee & Tea	USA	*Tchibo*	*GRE*
Perfect Balance	*SWI*	The Coffee Bean And	
Philly Roast	USA	Tea Leaf	USA
Pilon Blends	USA	Top Blend	USA
Postum	USA	*Toppets*	*GER*
Private Label	USA	Torrefazione Italia	USA
Rain Forest Nut	USA	Tully's Coffee	USA
Red Bag	USA	Vermont Country Blend	USA
Red Circle	*GER*	Victor	USA
Ricoffy	*SWI*	Viennese Blend	USA
Ricore	*SWI*	Waialua	USA
Roasted Kauai	USA	Water St.	USA

Wiener Melange Blend	USA	**Bubble-Up**	USA
Winslow's Gourmet	USA	**Buffalo Rock**	USA
Yauco Selecto	USA	**Cabana Life**	USA
Yuban	USA	*Calistoga*	*SWI*
Yukon Blend	*AUS*	*Calorie Mate*	*JAP*
Zumtobel Mild	USA	**Campbell's**	USA
		Canada Dry	*UK*
GENERAL BEVERAGES		**Capri Sun**	USA
4C	USA	**Care Tree**	USA
7 Up	*UK*	*Carnation*	*SWI*
A & W Root Beer	*UK*	*Champomy*	*UK*
Accelerade	USA	**Chaser**	USA
After The Fall	USA	**Cherry Coke**	USA
All Sport	USA	**Cherry Cola Slice**	USA
Alpro	*NETH*	**Cherry Ski**	USA
AME Fruit Drink	*UK*	**Chiquita**	USA
American Cola	USA	**Choco Lyne**	USA
Amigo	*UK*	**Choco-Cream**	USA
Aperio Health Drink	*JAP*	*Chocolate Cow*	*UK*
Apple Dandy	USA	**Citra**	USA
Arctic Blast	USA	**Citro Pure**	USA
Ardmore Farms	USA	**Citrus Belle**	USA
Asante	USA	*Clamato*	*UK*
Athlon	*FRA*	**Clearfruit**	USA
Aylmer	USA	*Clearly Canadian*	*CAN*
Balesca	USA	**Clover Farm Apple**	USA
Banania	*UKN*	*Club Yogurt Drink*	*SWI*
Barq's Ro t Beer	USA	**Coastal Breezes**	USA
Bean Stalk Organic	*JAP*	**Coca-Cola**	USA
Beatrice	*ITL*	**Coke**	USA
Benco	*UKN*	**Copella**	USA
Big Shot	USA	*Cotee's*	*UK*
Big Tex	USA	*Cott*	*CAN*
Birds Eye	USA	*Country Harvest*	*CAN*
Blackthorn Cider	USA	**Country Time**	USA
Bluebird	USA	*Cresta*	*UK*
Bournvita	*UK*	*Crush*	*UK*
Breckenridge Farms	USA	**Crystal Bay**	USA

General Beverages (cont.)

Crystal Light	USA	Frui'Vita	USA
Dad's Root Beer	USA	Fuze	USA
Daily's Fruit Juices	*NETH*	Gatorade	USA
Daisy Fresh Apple	USA	Gaymers Old English Cider	USA
Danactive	*FRA*	Gear Up	USA
Del Monte	USA	Gentle Juice	USA
Demisoda	USA	Georgia Peach	USA
Diamond White Cider	USA	*Gini*	*UK*
Diet Rite	*UK*	Ginseng Rush	USA
DNA	USA	Grab-N-Go Lemonade	USA
DNL	*UK*	Green Spot	USA
Dole	USA	Growers Fancy	USA
Donald Duck	USA	Growers Pride	USA
Double-Cola	USA	Hansen's	USA
Double-Dry	USA	Hansen's Natural Sodas	USA
Dr. McGuillicuddy's	USA	Hansen's Super Smoothie	USA
Dr. Pepper	*UK*	*Hawaiian Punch*	*UK*
Dr. Wells	USA	Heidelberg	USA
Eckes	*GER*	Heine's	USA
Everfresh	USA	Herbalife Weight Control Drink Mixes	USA
Fanta	USA	Hershey Chocolate Drink Box	USA
Farleys Hard Cider	USA	Hi-C	USA
Faygo	USA	*Hires Root Beer*	*UK*
First Tee	USA	Home Juice	USA
Five Alive	USA	Horchata	USA
Flavia	USA	Hygeia	USA
Flavor-Aid	USA	*I.B.C. Root Beer*	*UK*
Florida's Natural	USA	*Ice Break*	*ITL*
Farmer's Market	USA	*Indian Summer*	*JAP*
Fresca	USA	Jake's Diet Cola	USA
Frostie Root Beer	USA	JC Meier	USA
Fruco	*UKN*	Jolly Good	USA
Fruit 2 0	USA	Jolt Cola	USA
Fruit of The Vine	USA	*Juicy Juice*	*SWI*
Fruitland	USA	Jumbo	USA
Fruitopia	USA		
Fruitworks	USA		

Junior Juice	CAN	*Mistic*	UK
Ju's	USA	*Mocha Cooler*	SWI
Just Pikt	USA	Morning Blend	USA
K Cider	USA	*Mott's*	UK
Kayo Hot Chocolate	USA	Mountain Dew	USA
Kent	USA	Mountain Dew Code Red	USA
Kern's	SWI	Moxie Soft Drink	USA
Kickapoo	USA	Mr. Pibb	USA
Kinley Club Soda	USA	Mr. Pure	USA
Kist	UKN	Mt. Shasta	USA
Klix	USA	Mug Root Beer	USA
Knudsen	USA	Naked	USA
Koko Blanco	UK	Nantucket Nectar	USA
Kool-Aid	USA	Natch Cider	USA
Kristian Regale	USA	*Natura*	SWI
Lacroix	USA	*Nature's Best*	CAN
Lady Carolyn	USA	Nature's Own	USA
Lady's Choice	UKN	*Nehi*	UK
Lake Niagra	USA	Nesbitt's	USA
Lamb-Weston	USA	*Nescafe Iced Coffee*	SWI
Langer	USA	*Nescao*	SWI
Langers	USA	*Nescau*	SWI
Libby's	SWI	*Nesquick*	SWI
Lincoln	USA	*Nesquik*	SWI
Lion Brewery Root Beer	USA	*Nestea*	SWI
Lipton	UKN	*Nestle Quick*	SWI
Looza	USA	New England MacIntosh	
Mad River Traders	USA	Cider	USA
Marlin	USA	Nice & Natural	USA
Martinelli's	USA	Northland	USA
Mason's	USA	*Nubasics*	SWI
Mauna La'i	UK	Nugrape	USA
McCain	CAN	Nutrament	USA
Meiers Non-Alcholic		*Oasis*	UK
Sparkling Grape	USA	Obi	USA
Mello Yello	USA	Ocean Spray	USA
Milo Chocolate Drink	SWI	Odwalla	USA
Minute Maid	USA	Ogura Punch	USA

General Beverages (cont.)

Old New England	
Egg Nog	USA
Old South	USA
Old VA	USA
Olde Brooklyn	USA
Olde Philadelphia	
Black Cherry	USA
One A Night	JAP
Orange Dream Soda	USA
Orange Driver	USA
Orangina	UK
Orchard Fruit Drink	SWI
Orchard Park Drink Mix	USA
Ovaltine	UK
Party Club	USA
Party Nogg	USA
Party Treat	USA
Pepsi	USA
Pepsi One	USA
Pepsi-Cola	USA
Picnic	USA
Pilkil	JAP
Pirate's Keg	USA
Poker	USA
Polar	USA
Postum	USA
Powerade	USA
Propel Sports Drink	USA
Quench	USA
R Whites Lemonade	USA
Raging Cow	UK
Raison Cider	FRA
Ravin' Red Soda	USA
Razzle Berry	USA
RC Cola	UK
Realemon	UK
Realime	UK

Red Bull	AST
Red C Cider	USA
Red Pack	USA
Refreshers	USA
Robert Corr	USA
Rose's	UK
Royal Crown Cola	UK
Ruby of The Cape	USA
Rubykist	USA
Russhian	USA
Sabra	USA
Sacramento	USA
Samurai	USA
Sanagola	UK
Santal	ITL
Saranac	USA
Sarsi	USA
Saudia Junior Drink	SAUD
Scheid Vineyards	USA
Schlossgold	SWI
Schwan's	USA
Schweppes	UK
Scrumpy Jack Cider	UK
Seagram's	FRA
Seawatch	USA
Sella & Mosca	ITL
Seneca	USA
Sensational Soy	ITL
Seven Up	UK
Shasta	USA
Sherbets	UK
Shivery Shake	USA
Shochikubai	JAP
Sierra	USA
Sierra Mist	USA
Siggi	AUS
Simply Citrus	UK
Simply Nutritious	USA

Simply Orange	USA	*Stress-B*	USA
Sinvino Java Tea Straight	JAP	*Strongbow Cider*	UK
SIO	GER	*Sunboost*	UK
Slice	USA	*Suncrest*	USA
Slimdown	USA	*Sundrop*	UK
Slim-Fast	UKN	**Sunfill**	USA
Slurpee	JAP	*Sunkist*	UK
Slush Puppie	UK	**Sunny Delight**	USA
Snapple	UK	*Superbomba*	UK
Snappy	POR	**Surge**	USA
Sobe	USA	*Susi*	GER
Softfruits	UK	*Suzy*	GER
Sokenbicha	USA	**Swerve**	USA
Solo	UK	**Tab**	USA
Southbeach	USA	*Tackidex Energy Drink*	FRA
Soy	USA	**Tahitian Noni**	USA
Soy2O	CAN	*Taksi*	NETH
Sparkies	UK	**Tamipco**	USA
Sparkle	USA	**Tang**	USA
Sparkletts	USA	*Taz*	UK
Speas Farm	USA	*Tempo*	UK
Special Harvest	USA	*Tesalia*	COL
Special Vat Cider	USA	*Tete*	THAI
Spicewood	USA	**Texan**	USA
Sport Plus	UK	**Thornwood**	USA
Spree	USA	**Tian Tey**	USA
Spring Valley	UK	*Tigro Fruit*	GER
Springtime	USA	**Tiky**	USA
Sprite	USA	*Tizer*	UK
Sprite Remix	USA	**Toddynho**	USA
Sqeez	UK	*Tofita*	UK
Squeeze	THAI	*Tofy*	UK
Squeeze Six	USA	**Toma**	USA
Squirt	UK	*Tomoe Tea*	JAP
Ssips	USA	*Topi*	UK
Stamina	USA	**Total Balance**	USA
Stars & Stripes	CAN	*Traubensaft*	GER
Stewarts	UK	*Tre' Limone*	CAN

General Beverages (cont.)			
Tree Ripe	USA	Westpac	USA
Tree Sweet	USA	White House	USA
Tree Top	USA	White Lightning Cider	UK
Treefresh	USA	White Rock	USA
Trek Energy Drink	CAN	Wink	UK
Trendic Eistee	DEN	Woodchuck Cider	USA
Trip	GER	Woodpecker Cider	UK
Tropic	GER	XTC	USA
Tropicana	USA	Yonique	USA
Tropicana Twister	USA	Yoo-Hoo	UK
Trueblue	CAN	Zedda Piras	ITL
Tru-Val	USA	Zingerade	USA
Tutti Frutti	UK	Zip	PHIL
Tuttorosso	USA	Zipfer	SWI
Ultimate Juice	USA	Zumm	COL
V8	USA	Zunectar	COL
Valle	MEX		
Vault	USA	**TEA**	
Veggie Magma	USA	4C	USA
Vernors	UK	Alvita	USA
Very Veggie	USA	Amaretto	USA
Veryfine	USA	Arizona	USA
Vess	CAN	Aroma	SNG
Vibrant-C	USA	Bigelow	USA
Vida	UK	Celestial Seasonings	USA
Vimto	SAUD	Douwe Egberts	USA
Vintage	CAN	Earl Grey	USA
Virgin Drinks	ITL	Fruitopia	USA
Vita	USA	Grab-N-Go	USA
Vita Gold	USA	Guest House	USA
Vita Juice	USA	Harris	USA
Vital-T	USA	Kirin Lemon	JAP
Voodoo Rain	USA	Lipton	UKN
Welchade	USA	Luzianne	USA
Welch's	USA	Mighty Leaf	USA
West Bend	USA	Nestea	SWI
		Our Own	GER
West Coast	FRA	Paradise	USA

Peet's Coffee & Tea	**USA**	*Tea Kravings*	*SNG*
Pickwick	**USA**	*Tejava*	*JAP*
Premium Reserve	*UK*	*Temptation*	*IND*
Private Label	**USA**	*Tetley*	*IND*
R.C. Bigelow	**USA**	*Twinings*	*UK*
Red Rose	*GER*	**Twinlab**	**USA**
Ryokucha	*JAP*	**Typhoo**	**USA**
Salada	*GER*	**Victor**	**USA**
Santal	*ITL*	*Vita Light*	*CHN*
Sir Winston	*GER*	**Zingerade**	**USA**
Suntipt	**USA**		

Chapter 13

Alcohol & Tobacco

(**American owned in bold** / *Foreign owned in italic*)

BEER & ALE

Abbey Triple	USA	Blitz Weinhard	UK
ABC Golden Lager	SWI	Blue Moon Belgian	
Accel	USA	White	CAN
Adirondack	USA	Boddington's	BGM
Alfa	SWI	Bourbon	SWI
Almaza	SWI	Brau	JAP
Amber Bock	USA	Bruck	USA
Amber Lager	USA	Buckler	NETH
Amber Weizen	USA	Bud Dry	USA
American	USA	Bud Ice	USA
Amstel	SWI	Bud Light	USA
Anchor	SWI	Budweiser	USA
Ancre	SWI	Busch	USA
Antarctica	BGM	Busch Light	USA
Asahi	JAP	Busch NA	USA
Augustiner Lager	USA	Caramel Porter	USA
Avalanche	USA	Carling	CAN
Barbican	BGM	Carling Black Label	USA
Bartels	USA	Castle Lager	UK
Bass	BGM	Castle Mill Stout	UK
Bavaria	USA	Champale	USA
Baviera	USA	Chill	UK
Beamish	AUS	Colt 45	USA
Beck's	BGM	Coors	CAN
Berghoff	USA	Coral	USA
Birch	USA	Corona	USA
Birell	USA	Country Club	USA
Bitburger	GER	Crazy Horse Malt Liquor	USA
Black	JAP	Dave's	CAN
Black & Tan	USA	Diebels	GER
Black Amber Ale	USA	Dixie	USA
Black Bavarian	USA	Dreher	UK
Black Label	JAP	Esslinger Premium	USA
Black Stout Draft	JAP	Extra Old Stock	CAN
Blanche De Chambly	USA	Falstaff	USA
Blatz	USA	Fischer	SWI
Bleacher Blonde	UK	Foster's Lager	AUS
		Gambrinus	UK

Beer & Ale (cont.)

Genesee	USA	**Lionshead**	USA
George Killian's	SWI	**Little Kings**	USA
Get Down Brown	UK	**Lone Star**	USA
Gibbons	USA	*Lowenbrau*	BGM
Grolsch	NETH	**Loyal Hannah Lager**	USA
Guinness	UK	**Lucky Lager**	USA
Hamm's	USA	*Maes*	UK
Harp Lager	UK	*Magnum*	UK
Harpoon	USA	*Mahler Oil Soap*	FRA
Heartland	JAP	*Matilda Bay*	AUS
Hefe Weiss	USA	*McEwan's*	UK
Heineken	SWI	**Meister Brau**	USA
Henry Weinhard's	UK	*Melbourne Bitter*	AUS
Hoegaarden	BGM	**Michelob**	USA
Hofbrau	USA	**Michelob Light**	USA
Hokkaido	JAP	*Mickey's*	UK
Huber	USA	*Mickey's Malt Liquor*	UK
Hurricane Malt Liquor	USA	*Miller*	UK
I.C. Light	USA	*Miller Genuine Draft*	UK
Icehouse	UK	*Miller High Life*	UK
India Pale Ale	USA	*Miller Lite*	UK
Iron City	USA	*Miller Molson Ice*	UK
Jed's Hard Lemonade	USA	*Miller Reserve*	UK
Keystone	CAN	*Milwaukee's Best*	UK
Kilkenny	UK	*Milwaukee's Best Light*	UK
Killian's Irish Red	CAN	**Mississippi Mud**	USA
King Cobra	USA	*Molson*	CAN
Kingsbury	USA	*Molson Canadian*	CAN
Kirin	JAP	*Molson Golden*	CAN
Kronenbourg	FRA	*Molson Ice*	CAN
Kylian	NETH	*Moretti*	SWI
Labatt	BGM	**Mustang**	USA
Lasko	USA	**National Bohemian**	USA
Leinenkugel	UK	**Natural Light**	USA
Liebotschoner	USA	*Newcastle Brown Ale*	UK
Lingen's Blond	NETH	**Nik Gold**	USA
Lion Brewery	USA	*OB-Lager*	UK
		O'Doul's	USA

Old Dutch	USA	*Santiago*	*JAP*
Old German	USA	*Sapporo*	*JAP*
Old Milwaukee	USA	**Saranac**	USA
Old Style	USA	**Schlitz**	USA
Old Vienna	*UK*	*Schohoffer Weizen*	*UK*
Olde English 800	USA	*Schooner*	*BGM*
Olde Philadelphia	USA	*Schwarzer Steiger*	*DEN*
Olympia	USA	*Serramalte*	*BGM*
Opale	*SWI*	*Shanghai*	*UK*
Pabst	USA	*Shanta Super Shandy*	*PHIL*
Pabst Blue Ribbon	USA	*Shaohsing*	*TWN*
Pacific Ridge Pale	USA	*Sharp's*	*UK*
Pacifico	USA	*Sheaf Stout*	*UK*
Pale Ale	USA	**Shea's**	USA
Pale Lager	USA	*Shenyang*	*CHN*
Pearl	USA	**Shiner**	USA
Pelican	*SWI*	*Skol*	*BGM*
Perlina	USA	*Sleeman Cream Ale*	*CAN*
Peroni	*UK*	*Smithwick's Ale*	*UK*
Pilsner Urquell	*UK*	*Snow Beer*	*UK*
Pocono	USA	**Snow Cap**	USA
Presidente	*UK*	*Snowflake*	*CHN*
Pub Ale	USA	*Soberana*	*SWI*
R.J.'s Ginseng	USA	*Spiess*	*UK*
Rainier	USA	**St. Ides Malt Liquor**	USA
Rally Red	*UK*	*St. Omer*	*SWI*
Red Dog	*UK*	**St. Pauli Girl**	USA
Red Horse	*PHIL*	**Stag**	USA
Red Stripe	*UK*	*Star*	*SWI*
Red Wolf	USA	**Stargazer**	USA
Redhook	USA	**Stegmeier**	USA
Rhumba	USA	*Steinbock*	*UK*
Ridder	*SWI*	**Steinlager**	USA
Rolling Rock	*BGM*	*Stella*	*SWI*
Sagres	*POR*	*Stella Artois*	*BGM*
Samuel Adams	USA	*Stella Export*	*SWI*
San Miguel	*PHIL*	*St-Hubert*	*CAN*
Sans Souci	*SWI*	**Stroh's**	USA

Beer & Ale (cont.)

Suol	DEN
Super Bock	POR
Super Malt	JAP
Talleros	SWI
Tanrei	JAP
Tapeto Volante	**USA**
Taquina Export	LUX
Tarta	SWI
Tauras	DEN
Tecate	BGM
Tennant's	BGM
Tequiza	**USA**
Tetleys Bitter	DEN
The Glenrothes Vintage Malt	UK
The Winter's Tale	JAP
Thomas Kemper	**USA**
Thor	DEN
Tian Shan	SWI
Tiger	SWI
Tornade	**USA**
Toronto's Own	**USA**
Trois Pistoles	CAN
Trumer Pils	**USA**
Tsingtao	**USA**
Tuborg	DEN
Turboking	SWI
U	CAN
U2	CAN
Valima	SAM
Valor	PHIL
Vita Malta	SWI
Vitamalz	DEN
VOS	SWI
Warka	SWI
Warsteiner	GER
Warthog Cream Ale	CAN

Webster's Bitter	UK
Windansea Wheat	**USA**
Winterhook	**USA**
Wisconsin Club	**USA**
Yebisu	JAP
Younger's Pale Ale	UK
Yubisu	JAP
Zillertal	LUX
Zima	**USA**
Zlaty Bazant	SWI
Zolotaya Bochka	UK
Zywlec	SWI

CHAMPAGNE

Andre	**USA**
Armstrong Ridge	**USA**
Baby Piper	FRA
Ballatore	**USA**
Bollinger	**USA**
Brut Imperial	FRA
Champagne Perrier Jouet	UK
Charles Heidsieck	FRA
Chateau Chardon	**USA**
Chateaulet	**USA**
Cooks	**USA**
Cook's American	**USA**
Dom Perignon	FRA
Dom Ruinart	FRA
Korbell	**USA**
Krug	FRA
Mercier	FRA
Moet & Chandon	FRA
Mumm	FRA
Piper Heidsieck	FRA
Private Label	**USA**
Ruinart	FRA
Stanford	**USA**

Veuve Clicquot	*FRA*	*Jan III Sobieski*	*UK*
		John Player	*UK*
CIGARETTES		**Kent**	**USA**
Alpine	**USA**	**Kool**	**USA**
Amadis	*JAP*	**L&M**	**USA**
Arsenal	*JAP*	**Lark**	**USA**
Aspen	*JAP*	*Lucky Strike*	*UK*
Barclay	*UK*	*MacDonald Select*	*JAP*
Basic	**USA**	*Magna*	*JAP*
Belair	**USA**	**Marlboro**	**USA**
Belomor	*JAP*	*Matinee*	*UK*
Benson & Hedges	**USA**	**Max**	**USA**
Berkeley	*UK*	*Mayfair*	*UK*
Bristol	**USA**	**Merit**	**USA**
Brooklyn	*SP*	*Mild Seven*	*JAP*
Bucks	**USA**	**Misty**	**USA**
Cabin	*JAP*	*Monte Carlo*	*JAP*
Cambridge	**USA**	*More*	*JAP*
Camel	**USA**	*Mustang*	*JAP*
Capri	**USA**	**Newport**	**USA**
Carlton	**USA**	*Now*	*FRA*
Caro	**USA**	**Old Gold**	**USA**
Carrolls	*UK*	**Pall Mall**	**USA**
Cartier	**USA**	*Parisienne*	*UK*
Chesterfield	**USA**	**Parliament**	**USA**
Collector's Choice	**USA**	*Peace*	*JAP*
Commander	**USA**	*Peter 1*	*JAP*
Craven "A"	*UK*	**Peter Jackson**	**USA**
Derby	*UK*	*Peter Stuyvesant*	*UK*
Doral	**USA**	**Philip Morris**	**USA**
Dunhill	*UK*	**Players**	**USA**
Embassy	*UK*	*Prima*	*JAP*
English Ovals	**USA**	**Private Stock**	**USA**
Eve	**USA**	**Pyramid**	**USA**
Golden American	*UK*	**Raleigh**	**USA**
GPC	**USA**	*Red Kamel*	*JAP*
Hollywood	*UK*	*Richmond*	*UK*

Cigarettes (cont.)		Avanti	USA
Rothmans	UK	Avo	USA
Royale	SP	AYC Grenadiers	UK
Salem	USA	Backwoods	UK
Saratoga	USA	Buckwoods Smokes	UK
Satin	USA	Bances	SWE
Seasons	KOR	Ben Franklin	UK
Senior Service	UK	Big Butt	UK
Sopianae	UK	Black Hawk	USA
St Moritz	USA	Bolivar	USA
Stallions	JOR	Broadleaf	USA
State Express 555	USA	Canaria D'Oro	USA
Superkings	UK	Captain Black	USA
Superslims	USA	Caribbean	USA
Sweet Afton	UK	Carnegie	USA
Tareyton	USA	Castella	USA
The One	KOR	Charles Bdenby	USA
Time	ISR	Charles The Great	USA
True	USA	Cohiba	UK
Value For Money	UK	Cruzeros	UK
Vantage	USA	De Nobili	USA
Vegas	JOR	Domaine Avo	USA
Viceroy	USA	Don Diego	USA
Virginia Slims	USA	Don Miguel	UK
Vision	KOR	Don Tomas	USA
Vogue	UK	Ducados	UK
West	UK	Dutch Masters	UK
Winfield	UK	Dutch Treats	UK
Winston	USA	El Dorado	UK
Zest	KOR	El Macco	USA
		El Producto	UK
CIGARS		El Trellis	USA
Angler	USA	El Verso	USA
Antonio Y Cleopatra	UK	Erik	UK
Ashton	USA	Evermore	USA
Aston	USA	Explorer	USA
Astor	USA	Farnam Drive	USA
Astral	SWE	Finck	USA

Flamenco	*UK*	*Ninas*	*UK*
Florida Queen	**USA**	*Only Reserve*	*UK*
Fonseca	**USA**	**Optimo**	**USA**
Garcia Y Vega	*SWE*	**Padron**	**USA**
Gargoyle Lanza	**USA**	*Panama*	*UK*
George Burns Vintage	*UK*	**Parodi**	**USA**
Gispert	*UK*	**Petri**	**USA**
Gotham	**USA**	*Playboy by Don Diego*	*UK*
H. Upmann	**USA**	*Pleiades*	*UK*
Habana 2000	**USA**	*Por Larranaga*	*UK*
Halstead	**USA**	*Primo Del Rey*	*UK*
Hamlet	*JAP*	**R.G. Dun**	**USA**
Hampton	**USA**	**Ramrod**	**USA**
Hanover	**USA**	**Red Dot**	**USA**
Harrington	**USA**	*Reinitas*	*UK*
Harvesters	*UK*	*Romeo And Juliet*	*UK*
Havana	**USA**	**Romeo Y Julieta**	**USA**
Havanitos	*UK*	*Rothmans*	*UK*
Henri Wintermann	*UK*	*Rustlers*	*UK*
Henri Winterman's	*UK*	**San Felice**	**USA**
Henry Clay	*UK*	*Santa Damiana*	*UK*
Hobart	**USA**	**Siglo 21**	**USA**
Hunter	**USA**	*Supre Sweets*	*UK*
Huron	**USA**	**Swisher Sweets**	**USA**
King Edward	**USA**	*Tampa Nugget*	*UK*
La Coronas	**USA**	*Tampa Sweet*	*UK*
Las Cabrillas	*UK*	*Te Amo*	*UK*
Longchamps	*UK*	*Tijuana Smalls*	*SWE*
Macanudo	**USA**	*Tiparillo*	*SWE*
Maduro	**USA**	**Toscano**	**USA**
Marsh Wheeling	**USA**	**Travis Club**	**USA**
Masters Collection	*UK*	**Union**	**USA**
Matacan Bundles	*UK*	**University**	**USA**
Metropolitan	**USA**	*Villiger*	*UK*
Monte Cristo	**USA**	*White Owl*	*SWE*
Montecristo	*UK*	*Willem*	*SWE*
Morgan	**USA**	**Winchester**	**USA**
Muriel	*UK*	*Wings*	*SWE*

Cigars (cont.)		
Wolf Bros.	**USA**	
Zigfeld	**USA**	

LIQUOR

100 Pipers	*FRA*
99 Bananas	**USA**
Aberlour	*FRA*
Absolut	*SWE*
After Shock	**USA**
Albert Robin	**USA**
Alberta Springs	**USA**
Alexi	**USA**
Alize	**USA**
Allen's Liqueur	**USA**
Altai	*FRA*
Amaretto Crème Di Amore	**USA**
Amaretto De Sabroso	**USA**
Amaretto Del L'Oroso	*GER*
Amaretto Di Amore	**USA**
Amaretto Di Padrino Liquer	**USA**
Amaretto Liquore	**USA**
Amaro Montenegro	*ITL*
Amaro Ramazzotti	*FRA*
Ambassadeur Aperitif	*FRA*
Amber Cream Liquer	**USA**
Americano 505 Aperitif	*FRA*
Amontillado Valdespino Sherry	**USA**
Anejo	*PHIL*
Ansac	**USA**
Aperol Aperitif	*UK*
Arak Razzouk	**USA**
Archer's	*UK*
Ardbeg	**USA**
Argent	**USA**

Armadale	*UK*
Arrow Cordials Mixers	**USA**
Artic	**USA**
Artic Italian Liqueur	**USA**
Ashbourne	*UK*
Avalanche	**USA**
B&B	*BMD*
B. J. Holladay	**USA**
Bacardi	*BMD*
Baffert's	**USA**
Bailey's	*UK*
Baileys Liquer	*UK*
Baja Cream Liqueur	**USA**
Baker's	**USA**
Balblair	**USA**
Ballantine's	*FRA*
Bally	*FRA*
Balvenie	*UK*
Banff Ice	**USA**
Bankers Club	**USA**
Bar Tenders Cocktail Mix	**USA**
Barclay	**USA**
Barristers Scotch	**USA**
Bartini's Cocktail	**USA**
Bartissol Apertif	*FRA*
Barton	**USA**
Barton's QT Premium	**USA**
Basilica	*UK*
Beefeater	*FRA*
Bells	*UK*
Benchmark	**USA**
Benedictine Liquer	*BMD*
Bisquit Cognac	*FRA*
Black & White	*UK*
Black Bush	**USA**
Black Heart	*UK*
Black Russian Liqueur	**USA**
Black Velvet	**USA**

Blanton's	USA	**Carnaby's**	USA
Blenders Pride	FRA	**Carnaval**	USA
Bols	FRA	**Carstairs' White Seal**	
Bombay	BMD	**American**	USA
Boodles British Gin	UK	**Casalini**	USA
Booker's	USA	**Centinela**	USA
Booth's	UK	**Chambord**	USA
Borzoivodka	UK	*Chantre Cream*	GER
Boston	USA	*Chaska*	UK
Bowman's	USA	**Chinaco**	USA
Braemer	ITL	*Chivas Regal*	FRA
Brennan's Irish	USA	*Cinzano Vermouth*	FRA
Brokers	USA	*Ciroc*	UK
Bulleit	UK	**Claymore**	USA
Bundaberg	UK	**Cognac Davidoff**	USA
Burnett's	USA	*Cointreau*	FRA
Bushmills	UK	**Colonel Lee**	USA
Byrrh Apertif	FRA	**Conquisatdor**	USA
Cabin Still	USA	**Copa De Oro Liqueur**	USA
Cactus Jack	USA	**Corby's**	USA
Caldwell's	USA	*Cork Dry*	FRA
Calvert	USA	**Cossack**	USA
Calvert Extra	USA	**Country Club**	USA
Calypso	USA	*Courvoisier Liqueur*	UK
Campari Aperitivo	USA	*Crown Royal*	UK
Canadian Bay	USA	**Crown Russe**	USA
Canadian Club	UK	**Crystal Palace**	USA
Canadian Gold	USA	*Cutty Sark*	UK
Canadian Host	USA	**Cynar Apertif**	USA
Canadian Lord Calvert	USA	**Cyrus Noble**	USA
Canadian Mist	USA	**Czarinavodka**	USA
Canadian Supreme	USA	**De Keizer Bitter**	USA
Canadian Woods	USA	**Dekuyper**	USA
Capitan	USA	*Denaka*	UK
Captain Morgan	UK	**Dental**	USA
Cardhu	UK	**Destinee Line**	USA
Carmichael's Cream		**Devon's Shandy**	USA
Liqueur	USA		

Liquor (cont.)				

Liquor (cont.)

Devonshire Cream Liqueur	USA	Five Star American	USA
		Fleischmann's	USA
Dewar's	*BMD*	Forty Creek	USA
Di Saronno Amaretto Liquer	*UK*	Four Queens Blend	USA
		Four Seasons	USA
Dimitri	*FRA*	Fris	USA
Dita Liqueur	*FRA*	G.M. Tiddy's Liqueur	USA
Dobra	USA	*Galliano Liqueur*	*FRA*
Don Cossack	USA	Gautier	USA
Don Eduardo	USA	Gentleman Jack	USA
Don Julio	*UK*	*George Dickel*	*UK*
Dos Gusanos	USA	Georgi	USA
Dos Tiranos	USA	*Glen Grant*	*ITL*
Dr. McGillicuddy's	USA	*Glendronach*	*FRA*
Drambuie	*UK*	Glendrostan	USA
Drie Sterren Genever	*FRA*	Glenfarclas	USA
Du Bouchett Cordial	USA	*Glenfiddich*	*UK*
Duggan's Dew	USA	*Glengoyne*	*UK*
Dunbar	*FRA*	Glenmore	USA
Duncans	USA	*Glenturret*	*UK*
Dunheath	USA	*Gloag's*	*UK*
Eagle Rare	USA	Gold Crown	USA
Early Times	USA	Golden Wedding	USA
Eckes Liquer	*GER*	Goldring	USA
El Charro	USA	*Gordon's*	*UK*
El Condor	USA	Gosling's Black Seal	USA
El Conquistador	USA	*Gran Sambuca Liqueur*	*UK*
El Jimador Anejo	USA	Grand Cardinal Sparkling	USA
El Mayor	USA	*Grants*	*UK*
El Toro	USA	*Grey Goose*	*BMD*
Elijah Craig	USA	Hancock's Reserve	USA
Evan Williams	USA	Harlequin Liqueur	USA
Fighting Cock	USA	Hartley & Parker	USA
Finlandia	USA	Harvey's	USA
Fire Water	USA	Harwood	USA
Fireball Cinnamon	USA	*Havana Club*	*BMD*
Five O'Clock	USA	Heather Cream Liquer	USA

Heather-Glo Liquer	USA	Karimba	USA
Heaven Hill	USA	Karl Marx	USA
Hedges & Butler	USA	Kasser	USA
Henry McKenna	USA	Keke Beach Liqueur	USA
Herbsaint Liqueue		Kennedy's	USA
D'Anis	USA	Kentucky Dale	USA
Herradura	USA	Kentucky Gentleman	USA
Highland	*UK*	Kentucky's Tavern	USA
Highland Mist	USA	Kessler	USA
Highland Park	*UK*	Kimnoff	USA
Hine	*FRA*	Kings Crown	USA
Hiram Walker Liquer	*FRA*	Knob Creek	USA
House of Stuart	USA	Kranberi	USA
Hpnotic Liqueur	USA	La Prima	USA
HRD Distilled Spirits	USA	Lady Bligh	USA
Hudson's Bay	USA	Laird's	USA
Hussong's	USA	*Laphroaig Islay*	*UK*
Huzzar	*FRA*	*Larios*	*FRA*
Ice 101 Liquer	USA	LaSalle	USA
Imperial	USA	Lauder's	USA
Imperial Blue	*FRA*	Legacy	USA
Inver House Scotch	USA	LeRoux	USA
Irish Mist Liqueur	*UK*	Little John	USA
J&B	*UK*	*Lodowa*	*FRA*
Jack Daniels	USA	*London Hill Gin*	*UK*
James Foxe	USA	*Long John*	*FRA*
Jameson	*FRA*	*Longmorn*	*FRA*
Jaya Liqueur	*FRA*	Lord Calvert	USA
Jenkins	USA	*Louis Royer*	*JAP*
Jim Beam	USA	M.S. Walker	USA
John Barr	USA	*Macleod's Malts*	*UK*
John Handy	USA	MacNaughton's	USA
Johnnie Walker	*UK*	Majorstea	USA
Jose Ceurvo	*FRA*	*Maker's Mark*	*FRA*
Kahlua Liquer	*FRA*	*Malibu*	*FRA*
Kamachatka	USA	*Malliac Armagnac*	*FRA*
Kamora	USA	Marimba	USA

Liquor (cont.)			
Martell	FRA	Old Crow	USA
Marys Devil Cocktail		Old Fitzgerald	USA
Mix	USA	Old Forester Kentucky	USA
Massenez	USA	Old Grand Dad	USA
Master Blend	FRA	Old McCall	USA
Maui	USA	Old Pulteney	USA
Mazzetti Grappa	USA	*Old Saint Croix*	UK
McCalls	USA	*Old Smuggler*	ITL
McCarthy's	USA	Ole Tequila	USA
McColl's	USA	*Olifant Genever*	FRA
McCormick's Irish		*Olmeca*	FRA
Cream	USA	O'Mara's Irish Cream	
Melone Liquer	UK	Liquer	USA
Midori	FRA	*Opal Nera*	FRA
Miles	USA	*Orloff*	FRA
Millwood Whiskey		*Oxford London Dry*	PHIL
Cream	FRA	*Pacific*	FRA
Miltonduff	FRA	Paddy	USA
Mims	USA	Padilla	USA
Mohawk	FRA	Pai Dang	USA
Mojito Club	USA	Pallini Lemoncello	USA
Monogram Blend	USA	Paramount	USA
Montana Silver	USA	*Passoa Liqueur*	FRA
Montebello	USA	*Passport*	FRA
Montego Bay	USA	Pepe Lopez	USA
Montezuma	USA	Peychaud's Bitter	USA
Montilla	FRA	Pig's Nose	USA
Mount Gay	FRA	Pike Creek	USA
Mr. Boston	USA	Pikeman Gin	USA
Myer's	FRA	*Pimm's*	UK
Natu Nobilis	FRA	Pines Brook Vintners	USA
Newport	FRA	Pisco Capel Liqueur	USA
Nikolai	USA	*Plymouth*	SWE
Noilly Prat	USA	Poland Springs Liquer	USA
Normandin	UK	Ponche Kuba Liqueur	USA
Northern Light	USA	*Popov*	UK
Old Charter	USA	Praline Liqueur	USA
		Press Club Blend	USA

Prestige	USA	**Silver Wedding**	USA
Private Stock	USA	*Single Highland Malt*	UK
Puerto Nuevo	UK	*Six Isles*	UK
Pusser's Navy	USA	**Skol**	USA
Raffles	USA	*Skyy*	ITL
Rainbow Spirits	UK	*Smirnoff*	UK
Rebel Yell	USA	*Soju*	KOR
Red Heart	FRA	**Sourz**	USA
Remy Red	FRA	**Southern Comfort**	USA
Renault	FRA	**Spudka**	USA
Rhum Dillon	USA	*Star*	SWI
Rich & Rare	FRA	**Staub Cognac**	USA
Rock Hill Farms	USA	*Stewarts*	IND
Romanoff	UK	*Stolichnaya*	UK
Ron Pontalba	USA	*Strathisla*	FRA
Ron Rio	USA	*Tamdhu*	UK
Ronrico	USA	*Tamnavulin*	IND
Rosita	UK	**Tangle Ridge**	USA
Royal Canadian	FRA	*Tanqueray*	UK
Royal Gate	USA	*Tapio*	SWE
Royal Reserve	FRA	**Teachers**	USA
Royal Salute	FRA	**Tempo**	USA
Royal Stag	FRA	**Ten High**	USA
Royal Stewart	FRA	**Tequila Herradura**	USA
Ruble	USA	*The Black Douglas*	AUS
Sabroso Liqueur	USA	**The Dalmore**	USA
Salignac	FRA	*The Glenlivet*	FRA
Schenley	USA	*The Macallan*	UK
Schwegmann's	USA	*The Original Mackinlay*	IND
Scots Grey	IND	*The Real MacKenzie*	IND
Scots Poet	IND	**Thor Hammer**	USA
Sea Dog Old Fine Jamaican Rum	UK	**Three Olives**	USA
Seagram's	FRA	*Tia Lusso*	UK
Senators Club	USA	*Tia Maria*	UK
Shiso-Budoushu	JAP	**Tijuana**	USA
Sidekick	UK	**Tina**	USA
Silver Ice	SWE	*Tolstoy*	UK
		Tom Moore	USA

Liquor (cont.)		TOBACCO	
Tomintoul	*FRA*	*Amber Leaf*	*UK*
Tondena Manila Rum	*PHIL*	*Amphora*	*UK*
Tortilla	**USA**	**Apple Jack**	**USA**
Trave	**USA**	**Argosy**	**USA**
Triple Crown	**USA**	**Barking Dog**	**USA**
Tuaca	**USA**	**Big Twist**	**USA**
Tullamore Dew	*UK*	**Black Maria**	**USA**
Two Fingers	**USA**	**Bourbon Street**	**USA**
Tyrconnell	**USA**	**Briggs**	**USA**
Usher's	**USA**	**Bull of The Woods**	**USA**
V.S	*FRA*	**Buttercup**	**USA**
V.S.O.P	*FRA*	**Cannon Ball**	**USA**
Very Old Barton	**USA**	**Cappucino**	**USA**
Villa Massa	**USA**	**Captain Black**	**USA**
Virginia Gentleman	**USA**	**Chattanooga Chew**	**USA**
Vladimir	**USA**	*China Black*	*SP*
Vlaldivar	*IND*	**Chocolate Cream**	**USA**
VO	*UK*	*Clan*	*UK*
Vox	**USA**	**Classic Cavendish**	**USA**
Watson's	*UK*	**Clover Bloom**	**USA**
Whaler's	**USA**	*Condor*	*UK*
White Fang	**USA**	**Copenhagen**	**USA**
White Pack	*JAP*	**Cotton Boll**	**USA**
Whyte & Mackay	*IND*	**Country Blend**	**USA**
Wild Turkey	*FRA*	**Country Doctor**	**USA**
Wincarnis	*UK*	**Cumberland**	**USA**
Windsor	**USA**	**Douwe Egberts**	**USA**
Wiser's	*CAN*	**Dr. Rumney's**	**USA**
WL Weller	**USA**	*Drum*	*UK*
Wolfschmidt	**USA**	*Dunhill*	*UK*
Woodford Reserve	**USA**	**Erinmore**	**USA**
Yazi Ginger	**USA**	**Field & Stream**	**USA**
Yukon Jack	*UK*	**Garrett**	**USA**
Zubrowka	*FRA*	*Golden Virginia*	*UK*
		Happy Jim	**USA**
		Hawken Wintergreen	**USA**

Hines Mixture	USA	**Sir Walter Raleigh**	USA
Honest	USA	**Skoal**	USA
Honey	USA	*Southern Pride*	SWE
Kentucky	USA	**Spiced Rum**	USA
Kentucky King	USA	**Standard**	USA
Kite	USA	**Starcured**	USA
Kodiak	USA	**Stonewall**	USA
Lancaster	USA	*Sweet Afton Ryo*	UK
Levi Extra	USA	**Tabac Sherman**	USA
Levi Garrett	USA	*Taxi*	SWE
Lieberman's	USA	**Taylor's Pride**	USA
Long Cut Cougar	USA	*Timberwolf*	SWE
Mail Pouch	USA	*Traveller's Joy*	UK
Mammoth Cave	USA	**Tube Rose**	USA
Mapleton	USA	**Union Leader**	USA
Mellow Virginia	UK	**Union Workman**	USA
Midnight Special	USA	*Velvan*	UK
Model	USA	**W.E. Garrett**	USA
Moore's Red Leaf	USA	**Warren**	USA
Navy Sweet	USA	*Warrior*	UK
Old Mill	USA	**WB Cut**	USA
Old Taylor	USA	**Winters Clippings**	USA
Peach Sweet	USA	*Yachtsman*	UK
Peachey	USA		
R.T. Junior	USA	<u>**WINE**</u>	
Rail Road Mills	USA	**Allen's**	USA
Rainbow Sweet	USA	**Almaden**	USA
Red Rose	USA	*Amselkeller*	GER
Red Seal	USA	**Andre**	USA
Redwood	USA	*Andres*	CAN
Revelation	USA	*Antinori*	FRA
Rooster	USA	**Antonelli**	USA
Rough Country	USA	*Ararat*	FRA
Samson	USA	**Arbor Mist**	USA
Samson's	USA	**Argiano**	USA
Seal	USA	**Aristocrat**	USA
Singletons	SWE	**Armstrong Ridge**	USA

Wine (cont.)		*Callaway*	*UK*
Asti Mondoro	*UK*	**Camelot**	**USA**
Asti Spumante Banfi		**Canandaigua Lake Niagra**	**USA**
(Castello Banfi)	**USA**	*Canei*	*FRA*
Atlas Peak	*UK*	**Canyon Road**	**USA**
Attache	*GER*	*Cape Mentelle*	*FRA*
Aura Cabernet Sauvignon	*UK*	**Captain Applejack**	**USA**
B&G	*UK*	**Carlo Rossi**	**USA**
Bach	*SP*	*Carrington*	*FRA*
Banfi Brut	**USA**	*Carta Nevada*	*SP*
Bareboat	*FRA*	*Castell Blanch*	*SP*
Bartles & Jaymes	**USA**	*Castellarin*	*UK*
Batasiolo	*UK*	**Castello Banfi**	**USA**
Beaulieu Vinyard Wines	*UK*	**Cedar Creek**	**USA**
Bel Arbor	**USA**	*Champagne Mumm*	*UK*
Belnero-Pinot Noir	**USA**	*Chandon*	*FRA*
Beringer	*SWI*	*Chantre*	*GER*
Black Tower	**USA**	**Charles Krug**	**USA**
Blackstone	**USA**	**Chase Limogere**	**USA**
Blanc De Fruit	*FRA*	**Chateau Chardon**	**USA**
Blansac	**USA**	*Chateau Clarke*	*FRA*
Blossom Hill	*UK*	**Chateau D'Arch**	**USA**
Blue Pyrenees	*FRA*	*Chateau D'Yquen*	*FRA*
Bodegas	*UK*	**Chateau La Couronne**	**USA**
Bolla	**USA**	*Chateau Liversan*	*UK*
Bollinger	**USA**	**Chateau Palmer**	**USA**
Bols	*FRA*	*Chateau Souverain*	*SWI*
Bonterra Vineyards	**USA**	**Chateau Ste. Michelle**	**USA**
Boone's	**USA**	**Chistian Moreau**	**USA**
Boston 5 Star Brandy	**USA**	**Cisco**	**USA**
Bouchard Pere & Fils	*UK*	*Clos De Bois*	*FRA*
Brancott	*UK*	*Clos Du Bois*	*UK*
Brut Nature	*SP*	**Coastal Ridge**	**USA**
Buena Vista	*UK*	**Coastal Vintners**	**USA**
Busnell	*FRA*	**Colour Volant**	**USA**
Café De Paris	*FRA*	**Columbia Crest**	**USA**
California Cellars		**Cook's Captain Reserve**	**USA**
of Chase-Limogere	**USA**	*Coolabah*	*FRA*

Coronet	USA	*Haras De Pirque*	*FRA*
Costa Do Sol Rose	USA	**Hartley**	USA
Cribari	USA	*Harveys*	*UK*
Criss	*GER*	**Henkell Trocken**	USA
Cruse	*FRA*	*Hennessy*	*FRA*
Deschaux	USA	*Hillebrand Estates*	*CAN*
Dom Perignon	*FRA*	*Hine*	*FRA*
Domaine	USA	*Hiram Walker*	*FRA*
Domaine St. Michelle	USA	*Hochtaler*	*CAN*
Don Pedro	*FRA*	**Hogue**	USA
Dorville	*FRA*	*Inca Pisco*	*UK*
Dunnewood	USA	**Inglenook**	USA
E. & J. Brandy	USA	**Inniskillin**	USA
Eckes	*GER*	**ISC**	USA
Eden Valley	USA	*Iverus*	*FRA*
Elk Ridge Vineyards	USA	*J Garcia*	*FRA*
Eoliki	*FRA*	**J. Roget**	USA
Etchart	*FRA*	**Jackson-Triggs**	USA
Fetzer Vineyards	USA	*Jacob's Creek*	*FRA*
Fiddlers Creek	*FRA*	**Jacque Bonet**	USA
Folonari	USA	**Jean Danflou**	USA
Forestier	*FRA*	*Jean Dorsene*	*FRA*
Foxhorn Vineyards	USA	**Jekel Vineyards**	USA
Franciscan	*CAN*	**Jenkins**	USA
Francois Labet	USA	**Joseph Victori**	USA
Franzia Winetaps	USA	**Justino**	USA
Gallo	USA	*Kaiser Stuhl*	*AUS*
Gallo of Sonoma	USA	**Karl Von Stetter**	USA
Gandia	USA	**Kendall-Jackson**	USA
Gerhard Schulz	USA	*Kirsberry*	*SWE*
Geyser Peak	USA	**Kitchens Best (Cooking)**	USA
Gibson Vineyards	USA	**Kobrand**	USA
Glen Ellen		*Krizia*	*UK*
(The Wine Group)	USA	**Krug**	FRA
Graffigna	*FRA*	**La Chablisienne**	USA
Grandin	*FRA*	*La Ina (Sherry)*	*FRA*
Graziosi	USA	**La Terre**	USA
Great Estates	USA	**Laird's**	USA

Wine (cont.)

Lake Niagra	USA	*Old Tblissi*	*FRA*
Lancers	*UK*	**Olivier Leflaive**	USA
Le Domaine Champagne	USA	*Orlando*	*FRA*
Leo Buring	*AUS*	*Ozeki-Sake*	*JAP*
Leonard Kreusch	USA	**Panther Creek Cellars**	USA
Leonardini	USA	**Pascal Jolivet**	USA
Livingston Cellars	USA	*Pasquier Desvignes*	*FRA*
Long Mountain	*FRA*	**Paul Jaboulet Aine**	USA
Lucien Deschaux	USA	**Paul Masson**	USA
Manischewitz	USA	*Peller Estates*	*CAN*
Marcus James	USA	*Perrier Jouet*	*FRA*
Marega	USA	*Piemontello*	*FRA*
Marques De Arienzo	*FRA*	*Pionero*	*GER*
Martinez Ports	*FRA*	*Piper Sonoma*	*FRA*
Martini & Rossi	*BMD*	**Placido**	USA
Mazzoni	USA	*Poet's Corner*	*FRA*
McPherson	USA	**Premiat**	USA
MD 20/20	USA	**Premium Canadian**	USA
Meiers	USA	**Principessa Gavi**	USA
Melini	USA	*Queen Adelaide*	*AUS*
Meridian	*SWI*	**Racho Zabaco**	USA
Michel Picard	USA	**Ravenswood**	USA
Mogen David	USA	**Redwood Creek**	USA
Moletto	USA	*Renault*	*FRA*
Mommessin	*FRA*	*Richmond Grove*	*FRA*
Monarch	USA	**Robert Mondavi**	USA
Mondoro	USA	*Robert Stemmler*	*GER*
Monsieur Henri	USA	**Rocche Castagmagna**	USA
Monterra	USA	**Romano**	USA
Mumm Napa	*FRA*	*Rosemount*	*AUS*
Mumm Vsop	*FRA*	**Rougemont**	USA
Muscat	USA	*Ruinart*	*FRA*
Napa Ridge	*SWI*	*Saint Remy*	*FRA*
Nardi Brunello	USA	*Samazeuilh*	*FRA*
Noilly Prat Vermouth	USA	**San Angelo**	USA
Old Brookville	USA	**San Rocco**	USA
Old England	USA	**Sangiowese**	USA
		Santa Anita	USA

Santa Carolina	USA	Stature	USA
Santa Isabel Argentina	USA	Ste. Chapelle	USA
Santa Margherita	*ITL*	*Sterling Vineyards*	*UK*
Santa Sofia	USA	Stival	USA
Sartori	USA	Stonehaven	USA
Sauvignon Blanc	USA	Stonehaven Vineyards	USA
Scala Dei	*SP*	Stone's	USA
Scharlachberg	*GER*	Stowells	USA
Schloss Johannisberg	USA	Stowells of Chelsea	USA
Schwegmann's		*Sumac Ridge*	*CAN*
(Burgandy)	USA	*Sunrise*	*CHL*
Seagram's Coolers	*FRA*	*Superior*	*AUS*
Selaks	USA	Sutter Home	USA
Selection Estate Series	*CAN*	*Suze Tonic*	*FRA*
Septima	*SP*	Syrah	USA
Sequoia	USA	*Taft Street*	*UK*
Sequoia Grove	USA	Talus	USA
Serena Sauvignon Blanc	USA	*Tamada*	*FRA*
Sergio Gattinara		Tavernelle	USA
Gattinara	USA	Taylor	USA
Seventh Moon	USA	Taylor New York	USA
Shochu	*JAP*	*Terra Nova*	*SP*
Showcase Collection	*CAN*	*Terrazas De Los Andes*	*FRA*
Sierra Club	USA	Terre Nere	USA
Signature	USA	*Terrunyo*	*CHL*
Signature Cuvee	USA	*The Bend In The River*	*UK*
Silverstone Cellars	USA	The Dynamic Duo	USA
Simi	USA	The Fab Four	USA
Similkameen	*CAN*	*The Hess Collection*	*SWI*
Sinnya	USA	The Jibe	USA
Smashed Grapes	USA	The Singular Sensation	USA
Snoqualmie	USA	The Terrific Trio	USA
Sonoma-Cutrer	USA	Three Monkeys	USA
Sparkling-Sec	USA	Tintara	USA
St James	USA	*Tio Pepe*	*FRA*
St. Francis	USA	Tio Soto	USA
Stars And Stripes	*FRA*	*Toasted Head*	*CAN*
Starvedog Lane	USA	*Tocornal*	*CHL*

Wine (cont.)

Toro Nero	CAN
Torresella	ITL
Triangle Shochu	JAP
Trilogy	FRA
Trinchero	USA
Trinity Oaks	USA
Trio	CHL
Trius	CAN
Trivento	USA
True North	CAN
Tualatin Estates	USA
Turner Road	USA
Twin Fin	USA
Two Dogs	FRA
Ultimus	USA
Ureshii	JAP
Valdivieso	USA
Valley Oaks	USA
Vendagne	USA
Veramonte	USA
Veuve Clicquot Ponsardin	FRA
Veuve Du Vernay	FRA
Via Firenze	USA
Viala	GER
Vicchiomaggio	USA
Victor Cream Sherry	USA
Viette	FRA
Vigne Regali	USA
Villa Aba	FRA
Villa Cerna	USA
Villa Jolada Italy	USA
Villa Mt. Eden	USA
Vina Pomal	SP
Vina Santa Carolina	USA
Vineyard	AUS

Vinfenas	UK
Vinho Verde	POR
Vino Kulafu	PHIL
Vintage	USA
Vintner's Reserve	USA
Vitae	GER
VP	UK
Walking Tree	USA
Weber	USA
West Coast Coolers	FRA
Whidbeys Liqueur & Port	USA
Whole Cluster	USA
Widmer's	USA
Wild Horse	USA
Wild Irish Rose	USA
Willamette Valley Vineyards	USA
William Hill	USA
Wincarnis	USA
Woodbridge by Robert Mondavi	USA
Wyndham Estate	FRA
XY Zin	USA
Yardstick	AUS
Yarra Burn	USA
Yates Original Australian	UK
Yellow Tail	AUS
Yves Roche	USA

"We finally found the American dream by working for the Japanese in Mexico."

Chapter 14

Life, Liberty, and the Pursuit of...Competition?

Wake up and smell the competition. It's good for America. Well, that is if you choose to believe what we are told by the champions of globalization. Competition's beneficial presence is all around you, unless you live near, or were employed by, one of the 33,600 U.S. factories that have closed in the last decade.

Competition can be a good thing, but sometimes too much of a good thing ends up not being so good (remember all those Halloween stomachaches brought on by all that "good" candy?) Competition can be a single-edged sword, cutting what might otherwise be inefficient production down to a size that might have existed or continued because of its absence. Or it can be a double-edged sword, transforming itself into cutthroat competition, needlessly cutting American jobs by unfairly pitting high wage-earning workers in America with low wage-earning workers in Asia or elsewhere.

There is a real difference between competition and cutthroat competition, and we need to recognize that difference. But to know where we are going in today's super-competitive global economy, perhaps we should look back and see where we have been so we learn from history and do not repeat past mistakes all over again.

Abraham Lincoln, the founder of the Republican Party, said that we should "Trade where it is necessary and avoid it where it is not." And the fact is that today much of world trade is simply not necessary. It is actually detrimental, not only to our economy as well as others, but also in ways that simply cannot be measured in economic terms.

Excessive world trade is not just responsible for the loss of good paying American jobs and the increase in sweatshops in China and other foreign countries. According to an April 2, 2007, *Business Week* article, global warming can be added to the list of negatives that come from excessive world trade. Over 90,000 commercial vessels crossing the oceans are responsible for more carbon dioxide than 29 industrialized nations combined. These vessels emit more sulfur dioxide than all the earth's cars, trucks, and buses and are responsible for one-sixth of the atmosphere's nitrogen oxide.

The outsize emissions at sea reflect the limitations of world politics. While national governments have forced giant reductions in discharges from vehicles and smokestacks, the U.N.'s International Maritime Organization has maintained looser limits on ships, in part because 139 countries are involved in crafting controls. Some ships contain an average of 27,000 parts per million of sulfur, where American standards don't allow diesel fuel to have over 15 parts per million.

Before the North American Free Trade Agreement (NAFTA) was passed in 1993, we were told that only about 25 percent of the American workforce would be negatively affected by free trade policies, presumably those who worked in manufacturing. We were also told that an intended increase in imports that would ultimately displace those manufacturing jobs was a good thing since the other 75 percent who did not work in manufacturing, and who wouldn't be losing their jobs, would actually reap rewards of imported goods they could buy at cheaper prices and would be better off. In other words, there were to be more winners than losers.

But is the whole idea behind sending manufacturing jobs overseas and not protecting American workers really a good idea and a fair strategy? Well, no, not if you look at it like this:

Let's say you have three kids, and you give each child ten dollars in weekly allowance. Is it a good idea to take away one child's ten dollars and give the other two kids five extra bucks each? Two of your children— a majority—are better off, but one is worse off. As a parent, would you just write off that third kid as an *"Oh, well!"* I do not think any parent would do that to their children, and I do not think any country should do that to their workers!

Baseball, for instance, works as a game, a pastime, and a passion for Americans because it's a level playing field. The same rules apply to both teams. The same number of strikes, balls, and outs are used for both teams.

This is not true with *"free trade"* where different rules apply to foreign producers than American producers. Before the American workers even "take the field"—to use a baseball analogy—they're already behind in the game! We never even give our own manufacturers the home field advantage. We grant foreigner producers cheaper, and therefore easier, access to our market since they do not "ante-up" the same amount as domestic producers.

President George W. Bush was greeted with stony silence in Mexico at a Latin American summit in January 2004 when he claimed to the leaders of over 30 Latin American countries that "trade is the most certain path to lasting prosperity." But politicians are discovering that it is even more painful politically to continue to defend free trade and increased foreign competition. In the 2006 election, states like Iowa, Missouri, and Kansas that had a history of rejecting anti free trade rhetoric, handed victories to candidates who based their campaigns on exposing the negatives of free trade. It was not the negative trade statistics necessarily that drove these Congressional candidates to adopt the outlook on trade that they did but rather the anxious voters that were being negatively affected by trade.

When many of us learned about the meaning of trade growing up, it meant an exchange for something we didn't already have. I can remember trading baseball cards as a youth, and when I did, I always offered a card to someone else in trade for something I didn't already have in my collection. But now trade usually means offering something to another nation that they already have in exchange for something we already have. Even if you make the argument that other nations can supply something to us that we already have for cheaper than we can supply it to ourselves, which isn't really fair to our own producers, it makes no sense to import something from Germany that could be imported from a lower-wage country. Germany pays higher wages and consequently has higher production costs than we do in America. So there isn't a lot of logic to be found in our trade policies today. But one thing is for sure. America usually gets the short end of the stick in trade negotiations.

For example, both Germany and the United States produce all kinds of apparel, including socks. It is of no extra economic advantage to either country if we buy Germany's socks and they buy our socks rather than if we just buy our own and they buy their own. Yet we waste energy and pollute the environment needlessly running ships back and forth across the ocean in the false belief that trade is the sure path to prosperity. But that cannot be true, especially for the United States, since our trade volume has never been greater, and our trade deficit has never been worse. By the end of the twentieth century, world trade—as measured by the value of goods that cross borders—was 22 times what it had been in 1950. This is important information since globalization advocates repeatedly cite statistics detailing increases in trade volume as proof that trade in and of itself is beneficial by default.

THE BROKEN RULES OF COMPETITION

The United States has trade deficits with almost every country on earth. The United States practices free trade with a protectionist Japan, and Japan has a trade surplus with us. The United States practices free trade with a protectionist China, and China has a trade surplus with us. Before the U.S. signed NAFTA with neighboring Canada and Mexico, we had a trade surplus with Mexico of about $1.6 billion, which has turned into a trade deficit of $60 billion as of the end of 2006. And we had a small deficit with Canada when NAFTA was signed, which has steadily gotten worse and risen to $73.2 billion by the end of 2006.

Part of the reason is the negative impact NAFTA has had on our southern neighbors and their ability to buy American products. The minimum wage in Mexico lost over 75 percent of its purchasing power between 1994 and 2000 alone. Nearly 8 million middle class Mexicans fell into poverty. Mexico's growth rate after NAFTA has dipped far below the level where it was in the 1960s and 1970s under previous protectionist policies.

In the battle of NAFTA in 1993, the uncompromising free trade team of Clinton, Gore, Dole, and Gingrich steadfastly maintained that our existing trade surplus with Mexico would become larger, the Mexican economy would prosper, and the burden of illegal immigration would be lighter. They were wrong on all accounts.

Maybe you have already seen or heard the many statistics detailing the effects of trade on employment in America. But the problem is that free trade proponents have muddied the waters with these statistics in an attempt to assure us that the creative destruction of American manufacturing is but a necessary disturbance on the road to a better life for all of us. We need to revisit the most basic trade statistics and re-analyze what they mean.

According to the U.S. government, every $1 billion in trade deficit translates into 13,000 lost American jobs. Conversely, every $1 billion in trade surplus adds 13,000 American jobs. Simply put, the measure by which we determine whether a trade policy is beneficial for America is whether it causes a trade surplus or a trade deficit. Therefore, trade for the sake of trade is not necessarily a positive for the United States, and an increase in trade volume isn't, either.

The problem is not with competitive trade per se, but rather with the rules of competition, which have been transformed into what can be called cutthroat competition. Our current policies do not dictate that the laws of trade apply evenly to all countries. In other words, trade originating from all countries is not regulated the same way. If it was, the possibility of one company gaining a competitive advantage over another would be eliminated. I am sure the workers of these companies would find it heartening and encouraging that all players in the world economy were playing by the same rules. It is alluring to win in a competition in which you are the underdog, swimming upstream against the tide and prevailing anyway, but there is no sensible reason to intentionally stack the deck against ourselves to begin with like we have with our current trade policies. Everyday working Americans pay the price. Those who lose manufacturing jobs may have made out okay in the end, finding another job, but just because they made it through does not mean it was right to take them through it in the first place.

Today, American producers are at a production-cost disadvantage simply because they are subject to several laws and regulations, which have consequently worked to raise our standard of living in this country. What is conspicuously absent from our Constitution, as well as other founding national documents like the Declaration of Independence, is the mere mention of "free trade" or the "free market" in any sense of the terms. Even leaders of America's modern day capitalist institutions recognize the need for regulation. In an interview with the *Financial Times*, NASDAQ CEO, Robert Greifeld, said, "Good regulation is good business," adding that he believed the costs of the Sarbanes-Oxley Act of 2002, also known as the Public Company Accounting Reform and Investor Protection Act of 2002, were far less than the costs of not having good verification. William Greider, author of *The Soul of Capitalism*, said, "Financial fraud costs investors and creditors $400 billion a year, according to one industry estimate that, based on the recent scandals, appears to understate the true losses." As Rudolph Giuliani put it in an April 30, 2007, interview with *Business Week*, "We have a tendency to underregulate. Then we have scandals, and we swing wildly in the other direction."

Barbara Roper, Director of the Investor Protection Consumer Federation of America, says that the scandals stemming from corporate America the past few years resulted in more regulation for which the purpose was to expand and improve protections for investors. Free traders, of course, have no reason to be against protection for Americans who strive to make money or a living investing. They are only against protections for those Americans who actually try to make their money working for a living.

Former Federal Reserve Chairman, Alan Greenspan, once said, "Capital gains do not finance capital investment," because they only exist on paper. Since Americans apparently aren't able to save enough to finance new investment, the U.S. is forced to sell American assets to foreigners or borrow from foreigners. The assets might stay in the U.S., but an increasing share of the income generated from those assets will go to foreigners—not Americans. The United States has to borrow $2.6 billion every day to finance consumption since we save very little and occasionally spend more than we earn.

But is it necessary that we rely on foreign investors, or is it possible to have a national economic system where foreign investment is not necessary? Korea and Japan are stark examples that prove it is possible. For over three decades, Korea has experienced outstanding economic growth by relying on the national savings of their own people and their own firms managed by their own people. They are aware of what has happened to America due to poor regulation, starting with the Savings and Loan crisis of the 1980s, which cost American taxpayers $125 billion to clean up after 1,000 thrifts went out of business. In Japan, foreign investment continues to play a negligible role in their economic success.

Even though free market advocates believe that we should "get the government out of it" and let the market dictate the terms of competition, free traders have never been too ashamed to ask the U.S. government to go to bat for them in pushing their agenda to break down trade barriers in foreign countries so they can gain greater market access. It hasn't worked in Japan, and to a large extent it has not worked in China, as both countries protect domestic industries behind high tariff walls.

Free market advocates say government isn't the answer to the question of how to make America's marketplace run better in the eyes of corporate America. Yet by default they are saying that government *is* the answer by advocating government intervention to urge other countries to lower their import tariffs and create government (taxpayer) funded re-training programs for Americans until they do.

THE BAD OLD, GOOD OLD DAYS

Despite the continued criticism of free market advocates about the Great Depression, which of course is usually littered with accusations of high U.S. tariffs as the cause, there can be no question that globalization has wreaked it's own havoc on the global economy. According to a May 23, 2005, *Business Week* article, the U.S. economy wasted trillions of dollars as an end result of the stock market bubble of the 1990s and conflict of interest scandals on Wall Street. Tens of billions of dollars invested in just optical fiber was spent that will never generate a return—a consequence of flawed demand projections and corporate balance sheets.

Also according to *Business Week,* the greatest destruction of shareholder wealth in our country's history may have occurred between the boom years of 1995 and 2001, not during the Great Depression.

According to Robert Gordon, a Northwestern University economist who has studied trends in productivity for years, "All the elements of the good years of the '90s have now turned around," as published in the *Wall Street Journal* on March 31, 2007.

Productivity grew 2.6 percent a year for the more-protectionist quarter century following World War II (between 1946 and 1973, when U.S. wages increased by an average of 80 percent) and then declined to 1.5 percent year on average from 1973 to 1995. The reasons for the slowdown are still being debated, but in my opinion it is pretty clear. In 1973 we essentially switched from a more closed economy to a much more open economy, and this is when the belief in free trade dominated U.S. trade policy.

From 1995 to 2000 the growth in productivity accelerated to 2.6 percent. This is generally believed to have been triggered by widespread advances and changes in technology.

Then productivity growth accelerated even more, surprising most economists, even though the economy fell into recession. By 2004, productivity growth was more than 4 percent. Productivity growth has since fallen steadily, declining to just 1.4 percent at the end of the fourth quarter of 2006.

According to the *Wall Street Journal,* the most significant development in our economy—and the most under-rated as well—in 2005 was that the U.S. had a negative personal savings rate. This means that as consumers we spent more than we earned, which hasn't happened since the Great Depression.

PHANTOMS AND OTHER MYSTERIES OF GROWTH

The disconnect between estimated productivity growth and what's really happening in the economy (soaring productivity growth during the recession earlier in this decade) can be explained at least in part by a creative and informative *Business Week* analysis from their June 18, 2007, issue describing what they call phantom GDP (Gross Domestic Product). This "phantom GDP" is represented or defined by gains in productivity that were thought to be a result of, and counted as, domestic production but were actually a result of foreign production. In other words, the practice of outsourcing has caused the Bureau of Economic Analysis (BEA), the U.S. agency that estimates GDP, to over-estimate the amount that comes from U.S. production. The BEA has also acknowledged that phantom GDP is real, they just aren't sure of the enormity of the problem. *Business Week* estimates that phantom GDP represents $66 billion in gains that were from outsourced production to foreign countries, eliminating 40 percent of the productivity thought to be a result of domestic production.

In any case, phantom GDP explains why companies are producing more efficiently, but American workers employed by them are not seeing many benefits from it. It explains why we read about layoffs in the newspapers day after day, but we are constantly told the economy is growing and expanding. It explains why wages have stagnated or fallen, but free trade leaning government officials remark that this is the best economy they have seen in their lifetimes. It explains why anyone who is skeptical of globalization and excessive foreign competition is labeled a protectionist, defeatist, isolationist, or just plain afraid to compete. It explains why we were told not to worry about the trade deficit, because as long as we could show economic growth, foreigners would forever want to invest here. It explains the "blame the victim" mentality of free traders when Americans are laid off from their jobs because of foreign competition. It explains why furniture imports nearly doubled between 2000 and 2006 (almost completely from China). The American furniture industry lost over one-fifth of its jobs, yet domestic productivity was estimated to have gone up a whopping 23 percent between 2000 and 2005.

Other studies have shown that what is known as the American dream—the widely held belief that each generation should be better off than the previous one—is in jeopardy. An analysis by The Pew Charitable Trusts seeking answers on the questions of increasing income inequality, as well as economic volatility and insecurity, found that there has been a significant decline in household income growth for today's generation when compared with the generation of thirty years ago. Not surprisingly, it was little more than thirty years ago when America began to fully embrace the philosophy of free trade as the generator of American growth and prosperity.

The report concedes that high economic growth cannot be depended upon to solve the problems of increasing income inequality. Since 1820, America's economy has averaged 52 percent growth for each generation. But since 1973 (again, the year that free trade policymakers began wielding their influence over our economy), America's economy has averaged a 17 percent growth rate for each generation allowing the median family income to grow by only 0.6 percent per year. This means that our standard of living is increasing at one-third of the rate today compared to the historical average since 1820.

For nearly three decades after World War II, a rise in productivity growth was accompanied by a rise in median household income, but since the mid 1970s, the gap between the two has widened and even more so since the year 2000. The key reason for rising family incomes has been more women entering the workforce. And more and more today, it is by necessity and not by freedom of choice.

Most of us know that the days when a family could depend on one income to supply its needs are long gone, but most don't know that the income for the youngest generation of Americans is 12 percent less than when their fathers were their age.

A July 2007 Pew Global Attitudes survey found that only 31 percent of Americans think their children will be better off than they are. For Europeans, the percentage is even lower. Eighty-one percent of the Chinese, however, think their children will be better off than they are.

WHEN PAYING MORE IS GOOD FOR AMERICA

It is no surprise that Americans are becoming more suspicious of foreign competition. A September 5, 2007, poll as reported by the *Associated Press* showed 58 percent of Ohioans favor more restrictions on foreign imports, and they believe that it would make Ohio's economy better. Free trade republicans should take note, for no republican has ever won the presidency without winning Ohio.

And what about the risk of higher prices because of those increased restrictions? Remember that August 7, 2007, Zogby poll I mentioned in the first chapter that showed that one in three Americans would be willing to pay *four times* as much for American-made toys, and 63 percent were willing to join a boycott of Chinese-made goods in general? The point is that paying higher prices may sound difficult at first, but if Americans come to understand that it is generally for the greater public good, I believe most will agree to go along.

Some politicians stand on principle and don't mind proclaiming their protectionist leanings. One such politician is New Jersey State Senator, Shirley K. Turner, who wrote a letter in response to the *Wall Street Journal* after being blasted in an April 15, 2005, editorial railing against her apparent protectionist Senate bill that would disallow state contracts that utilize foreign labor. In her letter, she claimed that sending U.S. tax dollars to foreign lands to pay for services back home is not good public policy. By transferring tax dollars overseas, Senator Turner says, both New Jersey and the U.S. lose many economic benefits since no income or sales taxes will be collected, no local goods or services will be bought, and no mortgage payments will be made from the foreign-paid wages. She also calls it hypocrisy to criticize welfare recipients for being jobless and then transfer jobs for which they would qualify to other countries. Finally, she makes no apology for her admittedly protectionist bill, claiming it is her job to fight for secure jobs for the people within her state.

Capitalism consists of private or corporate ownership of production, but the government clearly plays a role in regulating private industry as well as trade policy. If everyone simply did as they pleased for their own self-interest without any oversight or regulation, our capitalist system would quickly switch to a cannibalistic, winner-take-all system that would result in anarchy. The U.S. Constitution says Congress shall regulate trade with foreign nations. Regulation is not anti-capitalist and neither are tariffs. Abraham Lincoln once said, "By the tariff system the whole revenue is paid by the consumer of foreign goods...the man who contents himself to live upon the products of his own country pays nothing at all." I have never heard anyone accuse Abraham Lincoln, George Washington, Thomas Jefferson, or Theodore Roosevelt of being anti-capitalist. All of these men, whose presence is forever memorialized on Mount Rushmore, were all protectionists, not free traders. And for the false charge that raising tariffs is anti-capitalist? We are Americans first and capitalists second.

DEFINING OUR TERMS

Everybody deserves a safe place to work as well as adequate controls for pollution and other environmental issues. Other laws and regulations that impose costs on domestic producers that producers in foreign countries are not subjected to include various labor laws and tax laws, minimum wage, unemployment compensation, vacation and sick leave, property taxes on factories, Social Security, Medicare, national defense, and the Family and Medical Leave Act. Clearly, we do not live in a "free market" or "laissez-faire" economy.

Webster's dictionary defines "laissez-faire" as "letting people do as they please, especially non-interference in matters of economics and business; letting the owners of industry and business fix the rules of competition, the conditions of labor etc as they please, without government regulation or control."

Webster defines "free" as "not under control of some arbitrary power; not constrained, hindered or hampered; without cost or payment; having a government that does not impose arbitrary restrictions, etc."

The terms "laissez-faire" and "free market" both imply a state of being "unregulated." The U.S. Constitution makes no provision whatsoever for commerce to be transacted without regulation. Instead, Paragraph 3 of Article I, Section 8 specifically delegates to Congress the power and responsibility to "regulate" commerce with foreign nations and between the states. Paragraph 1 of Article I, Section 8 says Congress has the power "to lay and collect taxes, duties, imposts and excises [which shall be] uniform throughout the United States."

Taxes of any kind represent a "cost or payment," are an "arbitrary restriction imposed by government," and contravene "letting business fix the rules of competition." Any form of taxation is a violation of a "free market" system, so it is obvious that our Constitutional system is opposed to a "laissez-faire" system. Since our government imposes taxes and regulations in literally hundreds of ways, which results in costs to businesses that can often end up in the prices of American-made consumer products, we cannot seriously believe we live in a "free market" society.

THE COST OF AMERICAN VALUES

American laws and regulations reflect American values and principles, such as protection for the environment; the health and safety of the American worker and consumer; our contempt for child labor and violation of human rights; and support for Social Security, the elderly, and the disadvantaged. Values and principles such as these are not cost free.

Free trade is not possible without free markets, and free markets are not possible with laws and regulations. If free trade is defined by allowing various goods to be imported from countries with few or no laws and regulations to compete with American producers that are forced to operate under a different and more costly set of rules that reflect

American values and principles, then there should be no apology for putting an end to "free trade."

However, if we are serious about continuing such an unfair trade policy that is also obviously founded upon double standards (hence the double-edged sword), then we should do away with all laws and regulations that hold us back from producing American products at the lowest possible cost. On the other hand, if we are serious about adhering to our professed principles and values, then we ought to raise tariffs on the imports of any nation that has fewer laws and regulations, and therefore fewer principles and values, than we do in America. The tariffs should be raised on each nation to a level that works to "equalize" the cost burdens between the country we are trading with and our own.

Costs that hold our nation back from producing goods at the lowest possible price include things like requirements for American companies to make workplaces more accommodating to Americans with disabilities. According to a 2007 government and industry study, the number of American workers with disabilities is accelerating. Especially since the retirement savings for Americans is staggeringly low and many plan to keep working past age 65 and even into their 70s, companies operating in the U.S. will need to expand special accommodations in their workplaces if they plan to keep their workers productive.

The Council of Disability Awareness found that in 2006 the number of Americans receiving long-term disability payouts from firms that are members of the council went up 4.4 percent from 2005 to over 500,000 individuals.

So the question concerning free trade and the emphasis on keeping America competitive is this: should we turn our backs on Americans with disabilities and allow companies operating in the United States to refuse to spend money accommodating this growing segment of the American workforce? Companies operating in foreign countries like China are allowed to avoid these production-cost burdens, so if we are to stay "competitive" we would have to allow companies producing here to avoid these cost burdens as well. Examples like these are the only way we could level the playing field without imposing equalizing tariffs on foreign countries to equalize production-cost burdens.

To be fair, if we recommend that companies producing in America bear the cost burdens of accommodating disabled Americans and other cost burdens that reflect our principles and values, we would clearly be out of line if we were to bad-mouth American producers for not being competitive enough when these costs are reflected in higher prices for American-made goods. When we buy identical alternatives from China that do not have these production-cost burdens included in the price of their goods, we are choosing not to fund or pay for the principles we apparently uphold and expect American producers to adhere to as well. If we expect to stick to our principles and values in this country, it means buying American-made products when they are higher priced because of these extra production-cost burdens. We should not look at this as paying more in the store but rather investing in America and the principles and values in which we profess to believe.

BULLY FOR OUR WAGE EARNERS

President Theodore Roosevelt once said, "duties must never be reduced below the point that will cover the difference between the labor cost here and abroad. The well-being of the wage-worker is a prime consideration of our entire policy of economic legislation."

This quote reveals two very important points. First, Roosevelt advocates what we would today call equalizing tariffs or tariffs that level the playing field and ensure equality in accessing markets. Second, he states that the purpose of equalizing tariffs is to consider the well-being of the wage-worker, not the stock market investor. You can make the point that we are more dependent on the stock market now than ever, but that doesn't mean it's a good thing. After all, people live their day-to-day lives on wages, not dividends and capital gains.

Wall Street continually views rising American wages as bad and inflationary, although Federal Reserve Chairman, Ben Bernanke, has said that rising wages are not a bad thing as long as they are matched by higher productivity and do not have corresponding price increases.

Such statements reflect the attitude that the American worker is not seen as a contributor to the glory and progress of the nation but rather a labor-cost problem to be dealt with. We can only be affluent as consumers to the degree that we are wage earners. Higher wages, which are consistent with a higher standard of living, are a cost to production along with other principles and values like safeguarding our water supplies and implementing toxic cleanups.

Sometimes circumventing our safety laws and regulations and the associated costs they impose can be fatal to our fellow American workers. An independent panel chaired by former U.S. Secretary of State, James Baker III, found on January 17, 2007, that an explosion at a Texas City, Texas oil refinery operated by foreign-owned British Petroleum was responsible for killing 15 American workers in 2005. This was because British Petroleum had "not adequately established process safety as a *core* value across all its five U.S. refineries." If human life isn't the primary American value, I don't know what is. Again, if we want free markets and free trade so badly, then we should eliminate costly regulatory agencies like the Occupational Safety and Health Administration (OSHA) and the U.S. Chemical Safety and Hazard Investigation Board that both worked to identify specific cost-cutting and safety shortfalls and directly played a role in causing the deadly explosion.

ALL WORK, ALL THE TIME

Even with the laws and regulations we do have on the books, one could argue that we haven't gone far enough, if only to at least match other "wealthy" nations. A 2007 study by researchers at Harvard and McGill Universities found that the U.S. trails almost all high-income countries in family-friendly workplace policies like paid sick days and support for breast feeding. The United States was found to be one of five countries, along with Papau New Guinea, Swaziland, Liberia, and Lesotho, out of 173 surveyed, that did not offer the promise of paid maternity leave. According to the Families and Work Institute, an October 13, 2005, survey showed that only 18 percent of employers grant their employees full pay during maternity leave.

The problem with many of our leaders today is that they seem to advocate a system that keeps family-oriented policies out of the workplace. The *Wall Street Journal* reported on June 26, 2007, that New York City Mayor, Michael Bloomberg, recently proposed in a college commencement speech that if you want to beat the competition, you should be the first one to work and the last to leave, "never take a sick day," and skimp on vacation. Mayor Bloomberg commended his father for working every day of the week until the day he "checked himself into the hospital to die."

Certainly Mr. Bloomberg and other leaders can praise their parents for running their families that way, but it is wrong to attempt to legislate or encourage such work-yourself-to-death policies for the rest of us and ignore the fact that excessively long work hours can cause serious social and health problems. Such policies can also cause problems at home and contribute to the climbing divorce rate since women mostly favor more work flexibility. Free trade and cutthroat competition work against families who value having dinner together at home, attending their kids' soccer games and parent-teacher conferences, or having enough free time to go on picnics and to parades.

FUNDING OTHERS, UNDER-FUNDING OUR OWN

The state of Alabama is an excellent example of how creative destruction of existing jobs in favor of heavily subsidized new ones is not successful and only works to lower our tax base and put us deeper into debt. Beginning in the late 1990s, Alabama gave away almost $1 billion in tax subsidies to foreign-owned companies like Mercedes-Benz, Honda, Hyundai, and Toyota. But Alabama later found out that funding corporate favor with taxpayer dollars revealed a financial crisis of underfunded schools and other public priorities. The state also discovered that at least 600 corporations paid zero taxes on an estimated $800 million in profits.

Part of the problem is that corporations play one state against the other in pursuit of the highest tax giveaways possible. One wonders how the process of attracting private companies with public dollars can be classified as economic development. How will we ever be able to educate American workers for the so-called jobs of the future if our public schools have to go begging for adequate education funding? Alabama's pride temporarily swelled while they basked in the presence of famous foreign-owned corporations, but after the novelty wore off, the state realized that they remained at the bottom in educational achievement and forty-third among other states in per-capita income.

Perhaps the worst part is that all these tax giveaways were used to replace good paying textile jobs that were intentionally allowed to be destroyed. Alabama even spent $60 million in state tax dollars to send fellow state citizens to Germany for training to be used at the Mercedes-Benz plant built in the late 1990s. Total tax incentives topped $300 million. On one hand, we allow a flood of Chinese apparel and other textile imports to displace existing American jobs, and on the other we pay hundreds of millions of dollars in public tax dollars for re-training the same workers for new jobs to replace the ones we intentionally destroyed. You would think that at the very least we would not advocate the destruction of old jobs until the new ones were actually created.

What eventually happened? In September 2003, Alabama voters overwhelmingly rejected a proposed $1.2 billion tax increase, sending a strong message to the state that it needed to control spending rather than orchestrate what would have been the largest tax increase in the history of the state.

Robert S. McIntyre, Director of Citizens for Tax Justice, a group that serves as a watchdog of tax loopholes, estimated that business investors benefited by the disbursement of $195 billion in tax subsidies in fiscal 2000 alone that subsidized their business products. He says that both the corporate and the personal tax rate are 20 percent higher than they should be simply because of these business and investment tax preferences.

Before we purposely destroy any more jobs thinking that education and re-training are the answers to our economic challenges, we should consider that the average wages of those with a four-year college degree have not kept pace with inflation in recent years. Only those who obtain graduate degrees have been lucky enough to beat inflation.

It's doubtful that this is what Congress had in mind back in 1962 when they fist committed to training the unemployed. "For too long a time we have paid lip service to our nation's manpower problems without doing anything significant to solve them," President Kennedy said. "Now we have a potent tool which can be used effectively against unemployment and for the promotion of a highly skilled labor force throughout the entire nation."

It's one thing to re-train the unemployed who lose work for jobs that naturally no longer exist anywhere, like manufacturing slide rules or eight-track tapes, but it's another thing to re-train them because we intentionally saw to it that these jobs no longer existed in the United States.

The hundreds of thousands of jobs we have lost in apparel and textiles were dead-end jobs to free traders, but those who lost them didn't feel that way. According to Pat Buchanan in his book *Where the Right Went Wrong*, U.S. apparel jobs pay 23 percent more than retail sales jobs, and textile jobs pay 59 percent more. The only thing left for a large number of Americans to do if we won't allow them to manufacture certain goods here in America anymore is to sell the manufactured goods they used to make that are now imported.

If free traders point to increased productivity as the answer to rising wages and prosperity, then they should also advocate keeping American workers in the jobs of their choice since they will be happiest, and therefore, more productive in those jobs. And a more productive worker is a worker who is more competitive in a world economy.

A *Business Week* poll on March 28, 2005, showed that 25 percent of American workers "are just showing up to collect a paycheck." And only 14 percent say they are very satisfied with their job. Surely the answer to America's competitiveness problem is not to displace more workers from the career of their choosing and force them to re-train for jobs they never wanted in the fist place, which would only increase the first percentage in the poll and decrease the second one. How can America's future be more secure if its workers are more insecure about their jobs?

CAREER VERSUS PAY CHECK

Job searching is not a cost-free endeavor. When you are looking for work without any income and trying to juggle (and pay for) subsidized college courses or worrying about what might happen if you get sick because you just lost your health insurance along with your old job, it does not necessarily put you in the best frame of mind to learn what might be your best shot at a new career that might provide some stability. But then again, using the word "career" might not be the best choice of words since it is hard to actually have one as excessive competition mandates that we change jobs so often. These chosen careers do not just represent jobs, they represent livelihoods.

In an April 7, 2004, interview, U.S. Commerce Secretary, Donald Evans, said, "The President and I will not rest and we will not tire until we know that everyone who wants a job has a job." Well, it's certain that neither Mr. Evans nor the President have gotten much rest since that quote.

Most Americans like to comment that America is still the world's sole superpower, and everyone loves a "Go USA" rallying cry, but America isn't going to stay number one just because we think we are number one. We would be foolish to think the world works that way.

An August 5, 2003, paper by Katharine Bradbury of the Federal Reserve Bank of Boston suggested that there may be up to 5.1 million Americans who don't show up in the unemployment rolls but who might re-enter the work force if work was "more forthcoming." She estimates the real unemployment rate to be over 8 percent instead of 5 percent and the number of those unemployed to be 12.6 million instead of 7.5 million.

If we're going to have a diverse economy and employ an increasingly diverse population, we should have as many job and industry options for American job seekers as possible. Yet we seem to want to intentionally destroy our manufacturing jobs and funnel everyone into some type of service job, which can only work to lower the wages of those existing service jobs as we are increasing the number of those seeking the same positions. It's simple supply and demand. Surely free trade economists recognize that.

WHO ARE WE REALLY COMPETING WITH?

According to *Business Week*'s September 25, 2006, issue, since 2001 there have been 1.7 million jobs created in America in the health care industry. Guess how many other private sector jobs have been added in the same time frame? None. Clearly, America is intent on flying on only one engine—services. If the stock market has taught us anything over the past few years, it's not to put all of our eggs in one basket. Any nation that tries to create wealth in just health care and services is going to need lots of luck. A well-balanced American economy needs a balanced variety of American jobs, not just health care positions like medical technicians, doctors, and nurses.

But what kind of service jobs are really available, and what do these jobs pay? According to November 2005 Bureau of Labor Statistics information, only 6 of the top 25 hottest jobs needed by 2014 require as much as an Associate Degree, and all 25 are service jobs. It is estimated that the demand for these top 25 positions, which on average pay less than manufacturing jobs, will employ 2,286,000 Americans between November 2005 and 2014, or an average of 254,000 jobs per year and 21,667 per month. The average pay for these 25 jobs is $35,983.68, which is well below the yearly average wage of manufacturing jobs. The average annual manufacturing job pays 33 percent more than the average service job, according to Charles W. McMillion, PhD, who is president and chief economist at MBG Information Services. There are a few bright spots in the top 25 list, like higher-wage annual salaries for service occupations such as registered nurse ($55,680.00), post-secondary teacher ($62,032.00), general and operations manager ($93,580.00), and computer applications software engineer ($78,570.00), but the average is seriously dragged down by jobs like food preparation/serving worker ($17,850.00), personal and home care aide ($17,560.00), and teacher assistant ($20,750.00).

When a $47,000.00-a-year manufacturing job is replaced by a $33,000.00-a-year service job, the buying power of the American consumer diminishes. Competition for the existing service jobs intensifies, putting downward pressure on existing wages. Cutthroat competition begins, but we're all competing with ourselves since many service jobs—like the high-demand ones identified in the Bureau of Labor Statistics above, such as retail salesperson, waiter/waitress, home health aide, janitor, and office clerk—can't be outsourced to other countries. The only thing worse than cutthroat competition from abroad is cutthroat competition at home where we cut our own throats and destine ourselves to a future low-wage, low-production, and low-consumption economy. I've yet to hear from any free trader just how a nation is better off with declining incomes.

Service jobs also come with benefit packages that are typically less generous than manufacturing jobs. But then again, isn't that part of the strategy in moving toward a free market where we can free people from the manufacturing job of their choice, transfer those jobs to a third world country, and free ourselves of costly employee benefits, which only makes the price of American-made products higher? Surely if we allow the trashing of our pensions, health care, and retirement costs, we would again be able to justify buying American-made products since these benefit costs wouldn't be factored into the American-made price. But surely no one believes that this is the road we should take, do they?

Although committed free traders like Princeton University Professor of Economics, Alan S. Blinder, have changed their message, they remain opposed to tariffs or other barriers to trade. This is a classic case of attempting to take credit for identifying the problem without offering a solution. The truth is, free traders have no solutions other than the old and easily discredited calls for higher education, which I have already shown is not going to significantly change the situation we find ourselves in, or some form of taxpayer-supported wage insurance to subsidize those who have lost their jobs while they go back to school or look for another job.

Since the average American worker is making the same amount of money today as they were in 1972, standard-of-living increases have mainly been obtained by forcing more family members to leave home and enter the work force as well as having them retire later in life.

You cannot successfully legislate a high standard of living through consumer, investor, and worker-protection legislation and simultaneously allow free trade to encourage companies to avoid the cost consequences of such legislation by moving offshore.

SITTING AT THE POKER TABLE

American producers who have made the "mistake" of keeping production in the United States and obeying more costly U.S. laws and regulations should not be put at a disadvantage against those companies who choose to fire their American workers and move elsewhere for the purpose of avoiding American laws and regulations and their associated costs.

Because foreign producers are not subject to, or burdened by, these various laws and regulations, they enjoy a production-cost advantage over domestic producers, which can easily result in lower prices of goods you see in the store or on the Internet (if the company decides to pass the savings on to you rather than increase their own profits). We end up cheating ourselves if we happily take advantage of the many benefits we get from our tax dollars but then fail to pay for them when their costs are manifested in the prices we are asked to pay for American-made products. We cannot have it both ways. If we avoid buying American-made products when their prices are higher, we are advocating the destruction of the very benefits that have created our high standard of living in this country.

Simply put, if you want to sit at the poker table and share in the pot like everyone else, you have to ante-up just like everyone else. The pot in this case is the lucrative U.S. market. No one at a poker table is going to ante-up ten dollars and let someone else at the poker table ante-up two dollars and allow them to compete for the same pot. The fact is that foreign producers do not ante-up their fair share to be granted access to our market. In fact, we grant them preferential access to our market over our own domestic producers simply because they are not required to abide by the same laws. We have granted "most favored nation" status to plenty of other countries in various trade deals. It is time we granted it to ourselves.

The National Association of Manufacturers, which by the way favors a free trade policy for the United States, reported that various taxes and regulations (including energy, litigation, and heath care costs) add 22.4 percent to the costs of operating in this country compared to our nine largest trading partners. If taxes are tariffs, that represents a 22.4 percent tariff on ourselves. Meanwhile, the average import tariff—taxes foreign producers must pay in order to access our lucrative U.S. market—is only about 3 percent. That means that we charge American producers over 7 times as many taxes for the privilege of selling to American consumers as we do foreign producers. We do this even as lawmakers continue to add more and more regulations on domestic production while simultaneously advocating even further cuts in import tariffs.

The cost of access to compete for the pot at the poker table should be the same for everyone, and the cost to access and compete for the U.S. market should be the same for everyone. That way, the winner of the competition and the one who is rewarded with the most profits is likely to be the best competitor, not the one who pays the least to enter the competition.

What this means is that our trade policy is based on double standards. There is one set of standards for producing in America and another completely different set of standards for producing elsewhere. World trade is likely the only competitive activity where the rules are not the same for all competitors.

So it becomes apparent that with free trade we are subsidizing imports. Any time one producer is exempt from costs from which another producer in the same industry is not exempt, that constitutes a subsidy.

But wait a minute. Free traders tell us that imposing import tariffs shields domestic factories from competition, unfairly subsidizes them, causes them to lack incentives to innovate, and causes them to become lazy and unproductive. Free trade, we are told, eliminates subsidies and puts pressure on companies to innovate and seek ways to become more productive through greater competition.

DEFINING OUR TERMS: PART TWO

But again, we must remember to differentiate between fair competition and unfair cutthroat competition. We must also define the terms "free trade" and "protectionism" since they are so often used but never defined, although many people have their own ideas about what they mean. In simplest terms, free trade is any policy that puts America at a competitive disadvantage with other nations, at least those with lower standards of living. Protectionism, on the other hand, is a policy that puts no nation at a competitive advantage or disadvantage because import tariffs, when applied properly, can equalize production cost-burdens so that no one competing nation has easier or lower cost access to consumers. You would think that those advocating more and more trade would also advocate fairness in the system for all, but they don't.

There is more at stake here than just numbers and statistics. We are talking about the livelihood of the American people. When an American worker has to take a pay cut because of the downward pressure put upon wages in this country, they have to lower their standard of living. The monthly mortgage payment does not go down along with rates of pay. Neither do tuition rates go down for parents who are sending their kids through college.

TWO PRODUCTS, TWO COUNTRIES, TOO UNFAIR

It is not that free traders do not talk about their desire to level the playing field, it is just that their polices will never achieve it, because their focus is on breaking down barriers overseas while keeping barriers to American market access low at the same time. But trying to level the playing field by eliminating tariffs worldwide will not work.

For example, let's examine two similar products produced in two different countries. American-owned New Balance makes shoes in four factories in the United States where they pay at least $13.00 per hour in wages. They are also burdened with all the laws and regulations

Constitutionally passed by our U.S. Congress, including benefits like health care and pensions, which could easily raise the total hourly cost burden to say $32.00 per hour. German-owned Reebok, on the other hand, produces strictly in low-wage countries like China where wages combined with other production-cost burdens such as factory maintenance and operations (there are few if any employee benefits) may result in a total cost of say $8.00 per hour. For the sake of argument, let's say that it takes one hour to completely make a pair of tennis shoes from start to finish, which would mean the declared value of those shoes would be $8.00 when it enters one of our U.S. ports. Since the United States tariff rate averages about 3 percent, total revenue collected by the U.S. Treasury would be just twenty-four cents ($8.00 x 0.03 = $0.24), raising Reebok's cost to $8.24, compared to New Balance's cost of an American-made pair of shoes at $32.00.

The only way to level the playing field in this example would be to apply an equalizing tariff to Reebok's imported shoes in the neighborhood of 400 percent ($8.00 x 400 percent = $32.00). A 400 percent tariff may sound high, but we should put aside any temptations to think about political correctness. Forget how it sounds. Forget how it looks. What does it accomplish? That is the question we should be asking ourselves. This may not be in the best interests of Reebok, but then again free trade and minimal tariffs aren't in the best interests of New Balance.

We shouldn't be so concerned with the interests of those who want to outsource and destroy American jobs and the American standard of living. We should be more concerned with the well-being of an American-owned company like New Balance that has proven it wants to stay in America than we are with a foreign-owned company like Reebok that has proven that it does not care either about staying in America or being an American-owned company. Reebok was American-owned until August 3, 2005, when it announced it was being acquired by German-owned Adidas.

WHAT HISTORY DOESN'T TELL US:
THE GREAT DEPRESSION

High tariffs aren't going to bring worldwide trade to a grinding halt, regardless of how many horror stories you have heard about the Great Depression. For an in depth study into what really caused the Great Depression, I devoted an entire chapter to the subject in the second edition of How Americans Can Buy American. But since I wrote that chapter, I have discovered even more proof through the statements of even more prominent people that the Great Depression was a result of many factors other than tariffs.

For instance, a December 7, 2005, *Wall Street Journal* article about current Federal Reserve chairman, Ben Bernanke, revealed that he is a self-described "Great Depression buff" much like the way others interested in American history are Civil War buffs. The article talked about a book Bernanke was going to write about the Great Depression, including the factors that caused it. The word "tariffs" was nowhere to be found in the article, although it did mention how Bernanke's research revealed how the catastrophe that was the Great Depression was confounded by mistakes by the Federal Reserve. Bernanke also contends that he learned about the threats that weakened banks and declining asset prices can pose to the economy. But most significantly, he learned about the damage the Federal Reserve can do when it follows "wrongheaded ideas," which could not have included the idea of increased tariffs since setting tariff levels clearly is not a function of the Federal Reserve.

Joseph Stiglitz, in his book *The Roaring Nineties*, said that the Great Depression was caused by insufficient government regulation rather than excessive government regulation. Tariffs, of course, are a form of government regulation. The legislation in the aftermath of the Great Depression included the creation of the Securities and Exchange Commission in 1934 to issue in a new era of regulation to address problems of insider trading and cornering the market, among other market abuses.

If you visit the Rockefeller Center in New York, you may read this about the Great Depression:

"On Black Tuesday-October 29, 1929-the stock market crashed. Boom turned dramatically to bust, triggering the Great Depression, the worst economic collapse in the history of the modern industrial world.

New York was hit especially hard, with three-quarters of a million people out of work. "Hoovervilles" sprang up in Central Park and along the East River.

Rockefeller, by creating over 75,000 jobs, helped keep many people afloat during those dark days."

Here again, there is no mention of tariffs or protectionism as a contributor to the cause of the Great Depression.

Nobel Prize winner and free trade advocate, Milton Friedman, also blamed the Federal Reserve for bringing on the Great Depression. In *Monetary History in the United States, 1867-1960,* he and Anna Jacobson Schwartz argued that an "inept" Federal Reserve was foolish to raise interest rates in 1928, which sparked a recession in 1929, triggering the stock market crash. Then, thinking a hands-off approach to allowing thousands of weak banks to fail was the right approach, the money supply was allowed to shrink. Milton Friedman's assessment is particularly significant because Friedman was the one who began pushing free trade theories in the 1970s claiming that everyone would benefit. Friedman believed the poor countries would become richer and the rich countries even richer. We are still waiting for both of those predictions to come true.

The 1955 book *The Great Crash 1929* by John Kenneth Galbraith reinforced the view of several policy makers and economists who had the opinion that the Great Depression was inevitable given the speculation of the 1920s, excess investment, and unsound corporate governance. The unwise application of tariffs, of course, could only be described as unsound legislative governance. Former Federal Reserve chairman, Alan Greenspan, after studying the Great Depression, said that it was brought on largely from mistakes the Federal Reserve made in tightening credit after the stock market crash of 1929. George Soros, author of several books and founder of the Open Society Institute, put the blame on the monetary system for the Great Depression. And George Soros is certainly no protectionist.

Of course, you don't have to agree with the opinions of these influential people. The influential Steve Forbes, Editor-in-Chief of *Forbes Magazine* and former presidential candidate, does not agree, but surely he knows better than to believe in the well-known lie that the passage of the Smoot-Hawley Tariff Act gave rise to 1) the stock market crash; 2) the Great Depression; and 3) World War II. In his 2005 book *Get Movin' on Trade—or Else!*, Mr. Forbes subscribes to such foolish fallacies in an attempt to somehow demonstrate how tariffs can result in catastrophic events. But the undeniable historical fact is that the stock market crash, which occurred in October 1929, could not have been caused by the Smoot-Hawley Tariff Act, which was signed in June 1930 and did not take effect until 1931.

Oregon Republican Willis C. Hawley, who co-sponsored the Smoot-Hawley Tariff legislation accurately pointed out that the bill didn't "exclude foreign products from our markets, but does propose that such products shall not come into this country to the detriment of the American producers and wage earners."

The Great Depression was so devastatingly "great" because the Federal Reserve allowed 1,300 banks to go under, wiping out millions of Americans' life savings. Complaints over the Smoot-Hawley Tariff Act which were officially registered from only four foreign countries, had very little to do with any decrease in the buying power of Americans compared to the millions who saw every dollar they had saved in bank accounts literally evaporate. And how could the Smoot-Hawley tariffs have caused such a depression when, as Pat Buchanan has noted, imports represented only about 4 percent of the Gross National Product (GNP), and 66 percent of all imports entered the U.S. duty-free, comprising only 1.3 percent of our GNP. How could a modest tariff increase on 1.3 percent of our GNP cause 5,000 banks to fail, erase 56 percent of the stock market, decrease the GNP 46 percent, and cause the unemployment rate to reach 25 percent?

WORLD TRADE AND HIGH TARIFFS

For further evidence that high tariffs don't negatively impact worldwide trade, we need only look at the tariff rates of other countries as well as some of our own. As late as 2000, India had a 120 percent tariff on automobiles. In March 1995, Brazil raised tariffs on automobiles from 32 percent to 70 percent and then decreased them in December to 35 percent—but only for companies that built automobiles in Brazil. Malaysia applies 100 percent tariffs on imported vehicles to protect national champion Proton, which has a 74 percent Malaysian market share. In 2004, the United States imposed tariffs of over 50 percent on Mexican-owned Cemex's cement imports.

In 2003 the U.S. joined the European Union in imposing duties on computer memory chips of 44.29 percent and 34.8 percent respectively. Japan followed in January 2006 with 27.2 percent tariffs of its own, charging the South Korean banks (affiliated with the South Korean government) with subsidizing the production of the computer chips with low-interest loans. In December 2006, Poland imposed 34.2 percent tariffs on Chinese frozen strawberries to protect their strawberry producers. The United States places an average of 12 percent tariffs on imported food, but that is much lower than the worldwide average tariff of 62 percent. China applies a 45 percent tariff on tile imported from the United States even though they can obviously manufacture tile much cheaper than we can, even if the tariff rate was zero. Even though Brazil is the world's second largest maker of ceramic tile, it still applies a 17 percent tariff on imported ceramic tile, plus a value-added tax of 29 percent.

In October 2002, a U.S. trade panel endorsed tariffs up to 369 percent on steel-wire rod imports. America's garlic producers were able to get a 367 percent tariff imposed on Chinese fresh garlic for a short time, but the flood of garlic imports only slowed. Japan imposes tariff rates of up to 700 percent on imported rice to protect Japanese rice farmers. In June 2004, the U.S. Commerce Department reported making progress on reducing Egypt's clothing and other textile import tariffs, some of which were as high as 51,296 percent. In fact, the Commerce Department was working to reduce high tariffs and other excessive labeling requirements that effectively blocked exports of U.S. tile to China, Brazil, India, Argentina, and Indonesia. And Ronald Reagan started a trade war with Japan when he slapped a 50 percent tariff on Japanese motorcycles to protect Harley-Davidson from foreign competition for five years so they could become more productive and efficient. Before the five years was up, Harley-Davidson was exporting to Japan.

Vijay Mallya, the Indian tycoon who's United Breweries Group Ltd., recently bought Scotch Whiskey maker Whyte & MacKay to become the world's third-largest spirits company, built an entire empire on protectionism and continues to shield it with Indian tariffs as high as 550 percent. The enormous profits and shareholder wealth his company has created through annual revenues of $1.2 billion was all made possible through limiting competition from big-time spirits makers based outside of India, like France's Pernod Ricard, Britain's Diageo PLC, and America's Fortune Brands. These three companies have united to convince the World Trade Organization (WTO) to question India's sky-high tariffs, but Mallya doesn't care. His top-selling whiskey brand Bagpiper sells for far less than imported whiskeys at $5.00 a bottle.

And even if the WTO decides India should lower tariffs, it could take three more years to happen. Has the United States retaliated against India for their sky-high tariffs? Of course not. Retaliation is something free traders conjure up as a reason to continue ruinous free trade that rarely happens, and it is even rarer coming from the United States. The world already knows that America's threat of retaliation is about as scary as walking through a zoo of caged animals. Even if the WTO consented to American retaliation against high foreign tariffs, the foreign companies that benefit from it have usually already grabbed significant market share at the expense of their competitors, which have provided loads of profits to weather just about any future downturn in business.

LEVERAGING OUR CONSUMER STRENGTH

There is certainly no fear of trade wars among our trade competitors as they threaten to decimate one American industry after another. Americans must realize that we have enormous leverage in today's global economy. Every country wants access to our market. Every country wants to sell to us. The United States is the biggest consuming country the world has ever seen. If we cannot use our leverage and structure the rules of competition to our advantage, then we have proven we cannot compete since competition begins at the negotiating table. The simple fact that we have huge leverage and are seemingly unable to figure out how to create a trade surplus shows how ineffective we are at trade negotiations, and this is truly a national embarrassment. So those who would label protectionists as "defeatists," since they propose raising tariffs, are truly the ones who deserve that label since their free trade policies are those that have brought us defeat year in and year out.

But despite the baseless rantings of free traders about the supposed dangers of American tariffs, it looks as though, as of this writing, the repeatedly introduced 2003 tariff legislation offered by Senators Charles Schumer (D., NY) and Lindsey Graham (R., SC) will finally be passed into law. Continued warnings to China that they must allow their undervalued currency to rise have been repeatedly ignored, and the consequential 27.5 percent tariff on Chinese imports seems likely to be imposed. With China's currency artificially low, critics contend, downward pressure is placed on U.S. wages since Chinese imports are especially cheap in the American market (as if Chinese goods we not cheap enough already), diverting American dollars away from domestically produced goods. According to Senator Charles Schumer, undervaluation of the Chinese yuan (the Chinese ccurrency) makes exports from China to the United States cheaper and exports from the United States to China more expensive. This puts the United States at a considerable price disadvantage.

But currency manipulation doesn't always work when the goal is to narrow U.S. trade deficits. For example, the Chinese often remind us that in 1985, after the Plaza Accord allowed the Japanese yen to appreciate 100 percent against the U.S. dollar for two years, America's trade deficit with Japan did not decrease substantially.

Free traders never criticize China for the high tariffs placed upon American exports. They only criticize the mere thought or proposal of American tariffs on Chinese goods. For example, I have never heard any free trader criticize China for making General Motors pay a 25 percent tariff on every Cadillac they export to China. Free traders cannot seem to connect the dots between China's high exports and high economic growth or America's low tariffs and low economic growth. They dismiss the fact that while a protectionist China experiences double-digit economic growth year after year, America's economic growth continues to languish between 2 and 3 percent.

And there are examples that indicate that the Gross Domestic Products (GDP) had already been overestimated before *Business Week* discovered phantom GDP. What is often reported as growth is often a loss or decline for society since all economic activity contributes to a higher GDP. For instance, combating terrorism and increased crime, as well as the resulting need for hiring more police and security personnel and building more prisons, all translate to higher estimated economic growth.

Illness, sickness, and disease are also positive contributors to economic growth, causing the health care industry to work to discover cures and other medicines and to combat other viruses from other countries that could be introduced here in the future. Even the cost of countering the negative social consequences from poverty, pollution, stress in the workplace, and cleaning up after national disasters like hurricane Katrina is registered as a plus for GDP. Since the U.S. prison population increased to 1.6 million state and federal inmates, or 2.8 percent in 2006, the GDP will undoubtedly register higher compared to 2005 assuming all other things are equal.

THE REAL REASON FOR UNBALANCED TRADE

Free trade politicians have used every excuse in the book as to why we cannot achieve balanced trade. One minute they tell us China is cheating. The next minute they blame other countries for not consuming enough or having the wrong economic policies, or they say that foreign trade barriers are too high, and we can't get our products into foreign markets. At least they are partially correct. China is cheating, but we have the ability to raise tariffs on their imports to encourage them to stop. However we continue to accept the same old lines from China. As Representative Charlie Rangel (D., NY) has said, "In China, there's only one story–give us time, it takes time, we will not yield to pressure, it's win-win." Meanwhile, we keep our markets wide open, waiting for China to change its mind. As I said in a column written by Lou Dobbs in July 2003, "China would have no interest in opening its markets to the United States because they enjoy almost unimpeded and unlimited access to our market while they practice protectionism at home."

Today's free trade economists claim that trade promotes growth, but as shown in the case of Harley-Davidson, growth promotes trade. As American businesses are sheltered from cutthroat and unfair import competition, they are allowed to become more productive and efficient through economies of scale and can offer their products and exports at a lower cost to better compete with foreign products both here and abroad. If the response to the cutthroat competition from Japanese motorcycles in the 1980s had been left to idealistic free traders, Harley would be a historical footnote, and America's trade deficit would be larger than it is now.

If President Reagan had listened to the free trade zealots and "let the market do it's magic," Harley-Davidson would have been the feature in a disappearing act. But Harley prospered instead and became an engine of export growth for America creating thousands of American jobs. Even if you are a fan of foreign investment, you should have been a fan of the tariffs that saved Harley-Davidson. Because foreign motorcycle companies were encouraged to build new factories in the U.S. or expand existing ones, they created even more jobs for American workers, even though they unfortunately have to report to foreign bosses.

In an interesting letter to the editor, a *Business Week* reader wrote about how ironic it was that Harley-Davidson found itself in the magazine's top 50 companies in 2004 despite relentless writing among *Business Week*'s writers about their unshaken faith in free trade and unfettered globalism. The letter writer wondered if they thought America would have been better off if they did not have the ability to enjoy an American alternative to Kawasaki, Yamaha, and Honda. Harley-Davidson was ranked number 45 among the best global brands in 2006 and 2007.

Today, Harley-Davidson stands strong and tall, symbolizing both American patriotism and the American spirit in the belief that there is enormous pride in owning a motorcycle that continues to be made only in America by an American-owned company.

The Harley-Davidson of today is not only wildly popular in the United States, but there is also now a huge following in Europe. As the EU pondered which U.S. exports to use as examples of retaliation for President George W. Bush's 30 percent tariffs designed to protect the U.S. steel industry, many European citizens lobbied hard to keep Harley-Davidson off the list.

THE RETALIATION MYTH

One subject free traders always bring up when protective tariffs for American industries are discussed is the prospect that foreign countries could retaliate with tariffs of their own. This, however, makes about as much sense as refusing to outfit our police to protect themselves against criminals. After all, if the police ever shoot their guns, the criminals might "retaliate" and shoot back.

Tariffs are tools that we have at our disposal, and we should use them more often. Of course, foreign producers aren't criminals, but many times the reason protective tariffs are proposed in the first place is to protect American producers from illegal "dumping," which is defined as selling goods in the U.S. below cost of production.

Protective tariffs in the face of illegal dumping aren't just about fairness for American producers who must obey and absorb the cost of American laws and regulations that strengthen our standard of living in this country. They are also about our reputation in upholding high standards to the rest of the world. It is doubtful that other nations really trust and respect an America that continuously caves in to pressure motivated by the relentless pursuit of profit for select industries that would sacrifice another American industry for the increased prosperity of their own.

Sometimes the biggest threat of retaliation against American industry comes from within the United States. For example, in November 1994, the American Soybeans Association urged the U.S. Commerce Department not to put additional tariffs on shrimp imported from Thailand. I guess they were worried that Thailand might "retaliate" against American soybean exports.

If Vietnam were to raise tariffs against American exports of soybeans, then we could simply raise tariffs on other Vietnamese exports to the U.S. The point we often miss when considering protective tariffs for our American farmers and manufacturers is that we still have the most lucrative market in the world. For this reason, every country desires access to our markets, and this should give us a powerful bargaining tool.

But just like a poker player who does not realize he has the best hand at the table, if we do not realize how powerful our negotiating position is in the global economy, we should not even be in the game. Maybe that is why we have basically surrendered our manufacturing industries to other countries, often under the ridiculous reasoning that "gee, if we try to defend our home market against foreign aggression, other countries might 'retaliate.'" So the answer of free traders is to not defend our market at all. Such a strategy reminds me of a football team that loses every game by allowing the other teams to score a high number of points and whose answer is not to improve their defense but simply to continue to focus on offense and scoring more often.

CUTTHROAT COMPETITION IN ACTION

The situation surrounding the American shrimp industry is one of the most clear-cut issues involving unfair cutthroat competition in recent memory. According to 2004 research from restaurant menu-tracking Food Beat Inc., the price of many shrimp entrees the previous five years increased over 25 percent, even though wholesale shrimp prices decreased over 30 percent. So much for the theory that if we allow more lower cost imports, prices for the American consumer will fall. Today, nearly 90 percent of the shrimp consumed by Americans is imported. And for what purpose? So we could destroy another American industry and pay higher prices to boot?

The myth is not only in the thinking that foreign countries would automatically retaliate and raise tariffs on American exports if we were to raise import tariffs on them, but it is also in the thinking that foreign countries would somehow stop exporting to us. To dispel this myth, I had to do no more than look around me in my home state of Florida, which is widely known to be a tourist state. Florida has no state tax, and it is also widely known in the state of Florida that the reason is because tourists pay what would otherwise be a tax on the citizens of Florida in hotel, car rental, and other fees.

If one believes that foreign producers would stop exporting to the United States if we raised import fees, one could also easily believe that tourists from all over the country, and indeed from all over the world, would stop visiting Florida if we impose all kinds of tourist fees. But, of course, this is not the case as Orlando (where I live) is the world's number one tourist destination. No one believes that tourists would stop coming to Orlando, Florida because of fees, but free traders eagerly believe foreign countries might stop exporting to the U.S. because of fees (tariffs) and repeatedly oppose tariffs for this reason. If all you do is stand around and think about all the things that can happen before you do something, you will never do anything. And that is what we are doing now—nothing—while one American industry after another is decimated. Just more waiting, wondering, and hoping. More free trade.

The example of Harley-Davidson is sufficient to explain just why entering a trade war is not necessarily a bad thing. We have the most to win in a trade war. Everybody wants to sell to us. Let's use tariffs and our leverage. After all, it was Abraham Lincoln who said, "The probability that we may fail in the struggle ought not to deter us from the support of a cause we believe to be just." But it is highly doubtful that America would fail in such a "struggle" given the position it is in. It is interesting to note that Lincoln also said, "Give us a protective tariff, and we will have the greatest country on earth," believing that the tariff was a tool to protect jobs and raise significant revenue. He was not worried about a tax on those willing to pay it to buy imported goods.

When Abraham Lincoln was our President, America considered building a transcontinental railroad. Some suggested we might get the steel for the new rail system from England. But Lincoln decided America was going to build her own steel plants and restricted steel imports from the British. Lincoln then said, "...when we buy manufactured goods abroad, we get the goods and the foreigner gets the money. When we buy the manufactured goods at home, we get both the goods and the money."

President William McKinley once commented, "Open competition between high paid American labor and poorly paid European labor will either drive out of existence American industry or lower American wages." I wonder if McKinley would be shocked to know that today that open competition, also known as free trade as propagated by the false-ly-conceived free market mentality, is working to do both.

There is plenty of evidence that cutthroat competition is working to drive out the existence of American industry. Although tariffs imposed by President Ronald Reagan revitalized the American machine tool industry, that industry should now be placed on the endangered species list. The *Wall Street Journal* reported back in November 2003 that tool-makers are seeing their work vanish before their eyes. At the time, 30 percent of America's toolmakers had shut their doors in the three years prior to the report, while orders for the machines that toolmakers use have dropped about 70 percent during the past six years.

But why does this matter to America? Let's put some real-life meaning behind the percentages. By November 2003 one of the two remaining American companies that fabricated tools that could precisely lay tape and carbon fiber in the patterns required to build stealth aircraft components had recently gone bankrupt. That bankrupt Illinois company was eventually acquired by an Italian-owned company that fortunately decided to keep making the machines. But what if the Italian company had decided that they did not think America needed this technology? Could we then depend on our one remaining American-based company, and would we protect them from cheap imports and production or surrender them to the free market and decide that if they failed it would be just a natural disappearing act resulting from the magic of the marketplace?

To bring the issue even closer to home, toolmakers create tools that produce everything from car doors, sippy cups, and flat-screen TVs to operating room surgical tools and laser-guided bombs used in Iraq. America clearly cannot afford to lose such a vital innovation engine.

When President Harding was challenged by the argument that consumers benefit from cheaper imports, he replied, "One who values American prosperity and...American standards of wage[s] and living can have no sympathy with the proposal that easy entry and a flood of imports will cheapen our cost of living. It is more likely to destroy our capacity to buy." The problem with free trade is that it creates an over-abundance of cheap goods but reduces the ability for the average American to buy them at the same time.

In discussing the cumulative global trade deficits of $2.85 trillion America has suffered between January 2001 and January 2006, former U.S. International Trade Commission chief economist, Peter Morici, said, "The primary effect...was to displace American workers rather than offer Americans lower prices. The trade deficit is reducing U.S. investments in knowledge-based industries and skills and slashing more than one percentage point off economic growth each year."

With free trade, we can only hope that prices fall faster and farther than wages, but we're applying pressure in the wrong direction. Prices can seem to fall close to zero at times, but the same doesn't hold true for wages. If a retail store is overstocked on a particular item, it's not uncommon to see a "buy one get one free" sale, effectively slashing that price 50 percent on one of the products among many, and the consumer benefits slightly. But the impact would be quite a bit greater to the American worker if companies were able to hire two employees for the price of one, effectively slashing wages 50 percent. Companies can't have "hire one get one free" employment arrangements, unless of course you listen to former General Electric CEO, Jack Welch, who along with his wife, writes a weekly column for *Business Week*.

When a 58 year-old middle manager wrote to Mr. Welch for advice explaining that he was forced into "early retirement" and was having trouble finding work after two years of job searching, Mr. Welch told him he still had at least one remaining option—a paid-on-commission job with little or no salary—and urged the man to tell employers, "Give me a shot—I'm free." Surely with this kind of thinking we cannot be headed in the direction of even general prosperity.

THE SAVINGS DILEMMA

If free trade has been so successful in lowering prices so consumers can save more on their purchases, then why is the American savings rate so low? In fact, the savings rate went negative in 2005—since we spent more than we earned—for the first time since the Great Depression. The *Wall Street Journal* called it the "biggest and most underrated development in the U.S. economy." A low savings rate, economist say, is among the most serious of structural weaknesses in the U.S. economy.

If we cannot save as a nation in an era with an emphasis on cheap import prices, in what environment will we ever be able to save? Why were we able to save 10 percent of our income in 1980 with interest rates approaching 18 percent? The reason is that wages are falling along with prices, and we are doing what President Warren Harding warned us about. We are destroying our capacity to buy.

A November 2006 *Business Week* article reported that real wages for graduates with bachelor's degrees dropped nearly 8 percent in the previous three years. Economists are finally beginning to suspect that international competition, or what I have referred to as cutthroat competition, has been part of the reason. Even when we do save, the rate is negligibly small.

For example, in October 2004, we saved at a characteristically low rate of 0.2 percent, which means that if you're earning an annual salary of $40,000.00, you're saving only $1.50 a week. Meanwhile, China's personal savings rate is 40 percent, and the personal savings rate for Germany, France, and Italy is routinely over 10 percent.

If America's problem is its low savings rate in an economy backed by free trade that is supposed to ensure the most efficient allocation of resources, China's biggest problem is its inefficiency in utilizing capital. This is according to Chinese economist Wu Jinglan, who the *Wall Street Journal* has said is an economist "worth listening to." In China, it takes $7.00 worth of investment to yield $1.00 worth of output, where in developed countries like the U.S., the ratio is 1:1. The question here is why are we subsidizing imports from a country that is wasting capital because of its stubbornly high savings rate? Do not free market advocates claim that we are supposed to reward efficiency and not waste?

With a low personal savings rate, how will millions of potential retirees be able to save enough to retire at the same time we are hearing about the dangers of Social Security's viability? The answer to America's Social Security problem, as well as all other financial problems, is right in our own back yard. The secret to saving Social Security and doing right by America's retirees is two-fold.

First, we should raise import tariffs to a point that will level the playing field so all competitors are on equal footing. In doing so, we will ensure adequate protection for companies producing in the United States, thus protecting their profits, so they will have sufficient profits to contribute enough to strengthen their pension funds and fulfill their retirement promises. Older companies have promised over a trillion dollars to retirees. The reason they are under such pressure to compete with newer rivals and are in danger of not fulfilling their promises is because these newer rivals often don't make these same costly promises. Workers for these newer companies are essentially told that they are on their own in funding their retirement.

Second, we need to buy American and support the companies (American companies) that pay the most taxes to the U.S. Treasury. The powerful, positive impact that a smaller trade deficit can have through buying American-made goods—and therefore creating more manufacturing jobs—is staggering.

According to Gus Stelzer, former senior executive of General Motors and author of *The Nightmare of Camelot*, our trade deficits are primarily responsible for our national debt. Based on a conservative ripple multiplier effect of 3-to-1 and taking into account the current federal, state, and local tax rates of 50 percent, if the products represented by only a $600 billion trade deficit had been made in America, $300 billion in tax revenue would have been added to state and local treasuries, and $600 billion would have gone to the federal treasury.

Here's how the math stacks up. The $600 billion in trade deficits that could have been eliminated by a trade balance, through a 3-to-1 ripple multiplier effect, would have generated $1.8 trillion in actual economic activity. The ripple multiplier effect is described as the resulting economic activity that occurs when we spend money in America. For example, when you buy something made in the U.S. from a local store, the American recipient of the money may use it to invest in his or her locally-owned store by either simply performing maintenance or upgrading the store, which would require local carpenters or electricians (ripple number 1). Those carpenters or electricians, in addition to creating demand for lumber, tools, and other things, may decide to take their lunch break at a local restaurant (ripple number 2). Let's say they have a hamburger or chicken sandwich with fries. This causes demand from American cattle farmers or poultry farmers and potato farmers (ripple number 3). And it can continue on and on if we support American products and American companies.

The first time, however, we buy a foreign good or support a foreign-owned company, the money will likely go offshore, and all residual economic activity will be lost unless foreign governments or individuals decide to purchase American products or services with that money. This, of course, is unlikely as evidenced by our large and increasing trade deficit.

Through this example, we could easily pay for America's current economic challenges like saving Social Security and funding pensions so retirees can live in dignity. The answer to saving Social Security is to achieve a trade balance or surplus through import tariffs as well as a Buy American strategy as outlined in Chapter 1. As a reduced trade deficit creates more jobs, more Americans are working and paying taxes, while fewer Americans are receiving unemployment checks—a double positive. America would also collect more revenue from the newly erected import tariffs—a triple positive.

We should be putting upward pressure on wages. People who do not earn more cannot spend more, and the consumer's ability to spend is increasingly more significant in today's economy. Most (including free trade leaning) economists will tell you that consumer spending contributes 66 percent to 70 percent of economic activity in this country.

Henry Ford once said, "There is one rule for industrialists and that is: Make the best quality of goods possible at the lowest cost possible, paying the highest wages possible." This was, of course, prior to the days of outsourcing, and Henry Ford was talking about paying the lowest cost possible within the United States as well as the highest wages in the United States. He certainly was not making a case for transferring the production of his beloved automobiles to lower-cost countries.

Regulations are not bad news for the U.S. economy. According to Nobel Peace Prize winner Joseph Stiglitz, author of *The Roaring Nineties*, "Regulations help restrain conflicts of interest and abusive practices so that investors can be confident that the market provides a level playing field and that those who were supposed to be acting in their interests actually do so."

LEVEL PLAYING FIELD? NOT QUITE

President Bush repeatedly talks about leveling the playing field. According to our president, "When the rules are fair and enforced, and the playing field is level, our workers, farmers, ranchers and small-business owners can compete with anybody in the world." But when factory workers in China can be hired for $2,000.00 a year and we hire factory workers here for $40,000.00 a year, how can we possibly level the playing field? By lowering our wages to theirs? By forgoing paid sick leave, vacations, and pensions along with any other cost burdens for domestic factories so they can get their production costs down?

The problem in President Bush's opinion is, "There are economic isolationists in our country who believe we should separate ourselves from the rest of the world by putting up barriers and closing off markets —they're wrong. Given a level playing field, America will out-perform the competition, and America will continue to be a world leader." But Bush is the one who is wrong. The problem in not the threat of American tariffs. The problem is excessive competition, namely from China, that is driving down wages in America and destroying our capacity to buy.

According to U.S. Commerce Secretary, Donald Evans, in his remarks to Manufacturing Tomorrow in Minneapolis, Minnesota, some members of the Bush administration met with manufacturers to find out what was making it so hard for American companies to be successful both domestically and internationally, and they were told, "The international playing field isn't level." Mr. Evans continued, saying, "On a level playing field, they can beat anyone. So, this Administration is taking aggressive action to level the field." He also stated, "We are aggressively confronting any country that tilts the playing field against American workers. My message is simple: The economic isolationists and their message of defeatism must be rejected."

The problem is that everyone in the Bush administration talks about leveling the playing field, but they all know it is not possible without tariffs, and that option has been soundly rejected. Nothing George W. Bush has done or intends to do will ever level the playing field for American producers, and he knows it. A strategy of breaking down trade barriers overseas will help, although this strategy has proven to be ineffective for decades. The only real way to level the playing field is with import tariffs.

At Condoleezza Rice's confirmation hearing on January 18, 2005, when she was seeking to become Secretary of State, she said, "My role, I think, will be to try and enhance our economic growth and our econom-

Chapter 14: Life, Liberty, and the Pursuit of…Competition?   363

ic strength through our openness in trade, but also by making certain that those with whom we trade are dealing with us on a level playing field, and I'll be completely dedicated to that." If Ms. Rice has told us the truth, her dedication has gotten us nowhere.

Earlier in October 2004, when she was President Bush's national security adviser and was talking about our economic relationship with China, Ms. Rice said in an interview with the *Pittsburgh Tribune-Review*, that "...there are times when we have to enforce our rules so that our people are not unfairly disadvantaged." I'm wondering when are the times we should not enforce our rules?

Republican Representative James DeMint, when he was running for Senator Ernest "Fritz" Hollings' seat in South Carolina in 2004, said he was concerned about China's trade practices and said he would "make sure we are operating on a level playing field." But he hasn't made sure of anything, and he knew that he would not when he said it since he does not support higher American tariffs. Just more smoke and mirrors.

But James DeMint also stated, "The only way we are going to keep textiles and manufacturing in South Carolina is to expand our exports to growing countries around the world." This indicates the flawed thinking of free traders. Many seem to think that since we have been foolish enough to surrender our markets to other nations, they in turn should be required to surrender their markets to us. It does not work that way.

Between January and April 2005 alone, the United States accepted surges in imports from China in the following volumes: 287 percent in man-made fiber trousers, 364 percent in man-made fiber shirts, 293 percent in non-knit shirts, and 78 percent in combed cotton yarn. Surely Senator DeMint is smart enough to know that by not allowing these surges in imports to take place, we could keep the American workers employed in South Carolina from being displaced from their jobs. Surely he cannot think that the *only* way to keep manufacturing in his state is by expanding exports. What country would allow a reciprocal surge of exports from us in that magnitude? Protectionist China certainly will not.

The surge in Chinese textile exports, which followed the lifting of quotas on January 1, 2005, resulted in calls from around the world for new restraints on Chinese exports. Both Europe and the U.S. lobbied for increased protections, and even the Chinese considered putting limits on how low prices could go.

Some think that the United States should pursue a policy that consists of driving down the value of the dollar or pushing China to allow the value of the yuan to rise or a combination of both. This would supposedly help reduce America's ever-expanding trade deficit by making American exports cheaper and by also making imports more expensive. In 1985, President Reagan's Treasury Secretary, James Baker, implemented a worldwide strategy to drive down the value of the dollar to resist protectionist sentiment from the United States Congress. The strategy did eventually help reduce our trade deficit by making imports costlier and exports cheaper. However, the Chinese yuan has risen over 9 percent against the dollar during the past two years, but China's trade deficit with America continues to expand. Even with the dollar at a current 15-year low against the world's major currencies, the United States continues to run trade deficits across the globe.

The problem with this strategy today is that we must get the concurrence of China to let the value of their currency rise further. China resents us meddling in their affairs and trying to tell them how to run their economy, just like we would resent China meddling in our affairs and telling us how to run our economy.

But if part of the goal back then, and also today, as I pointed out when I discussed the Schumer-Graham legislation, is to make imports costlier, why not just simply raise tariffs on Chinese imports since it would accomplish the same thing as an increase in the value of the yuan? By unilaterally raising tariffs, we wouldn't need to meddle in China's affairs or pressure them to manipulate their currency, and if we hadn't transferred the power to protect our economy from cutthroat competition to the WTO, we wouldn't have to get the concurrence of a multinational bureaucracy before we decide to act, either.

THE *UN*-LEVEL PLAYING FIELD: PART TWO

The policy of free trade is based on consumption, so those who advocate free markets oppose tariffs since they discourage consumption and can make imports more expensive. Yet, this is precisely what happens when we devalue the dollar.

On Thursday, February 17, 2005, in his message to Congress, Bush said, "I believe that Americans benefit from open markets and free and fair trade and I am working to open up markets around the world and make sure that the playing field is level for our workers, farmers, manufacturers and other job creators." But you can't have free trade and fair trade at the same time since free trade ends up giving one country a competitive advantage over the other, unless the standard of living and all production costs (including labor rates and regulations) are identical.

But all these are just general ideological statements. Let's look at a concrete example of how the United States has failed to level the playing field that demonstrates why all the rhetoric about commitment to leveling the playing field is getting us nowhere.

In June 2004, then U.S. Trade Representative, Robert Zoellick, stated that the U.S. was going to utilize our WTO rights and seek $143 million in trade penalties against Japan for restricting American apple exports. Zoellick said "American apple growers have been blocked from the Japanese market—that's wrong." He added that Japan and the U.S. have clashed for *decades* (my emphasis added) over the important Washington-state crop. According to Tracy King, export director at the Washington Apple Commission, "We've really never had a level playing field with exports." Japan only imports 110 tons of the 850,000 tons of apples they consume, according to United States Department of Agriculture (USDA).

Although Japan recently eased some of their strict regulations, Zoellick claimed it wasn't enough, saying, "We won't be satisfied until there is a level playing field..." I wonder if Robert Zoellick, now chairman of the World Bank, is satisfied because the playing field is *still* not level. The fact that we have allowed Japan to effectively shut us out of their market without consequence is an atrocity to American apple producers and an embarrassingly defeatist circumstance for the United States.

The problem with working through the WTO dispute process is that even if America wins the dispute, by the time the relief comes the U.S. industry could already be decimated, or the U.S. companies involved could already be out of business. It is a smart strategy that foreign countries utilize in purposely being noncompliant with WTO rules. They gain the upper hand in setting high tariffs or unrealistic regulations on American exports. Then they benefit while they wait for us to act on our WTO rights. After we file the complaint, we wait for the WTO to make a ruling while our market remains open and foreign markets remain closed. Protectionist countries gain by setting high tariffs and then waiting for the WTO to disapprove them no matter how long it takes.

According to Alan Tonelson, author of the book *Race to the Bottom*, victory is not a guarantee of compliance. Even President Clinton acknowledged, "A lot of times when decisions are made, they aren't honored." Countries who know they stand to lose certain WTO rulings can purposely drag out the appeal process inflicting even more damage on U.S. companies and industry until relief from the unfair trading practices comes. In today's world, where businesses must operate at warp speed to stay afloat, a lengthy WTO process can be fatal.

Mickey Kantor, who was President Clinton's original U.S. trade representative, once said. "...We often opened our market to the products of the world without obtaining comparable commitments from others. As the dominant economic power in the world, we could afford to do so. And as part of a strategy in the Cold War, we needed to do so. We should no longer tolerate free riders in the global trading system and we must demand reciprocity in our trade agreements. This would mark a critical change in the way we view both trade policy and foreign policy."

On April 7, 2003, *Business Week* cited America's loss of 13 of the last 15 WTO disputes and stated that some members of Congress were advocating for a U.S. pull-out of the multinational organization. Then in a November 24, 2003, *Business Week* article, a report from the General

Accounting Office found that the U.S. loses the most WTO cases and is slapped with the highest penalties. One may easily wonder how this can be when we are already the most open market in the world.

One possible reason, according to Georgetown University trade law expert Robert Stumberg, is that WTO rules "are vague, and until a panel [of WTO judges] tells you, you don't know what the rules mean." He adds, "Congress has shifted a tremendous amount of power to the WTO." If free traders are concerned about trade wars, they should advocate the U.S. withdrawal from the WTO since our membership seems to mean we are always in a trade war of some sort with other nations over the meaning of WTO rulings. Another possible reason is that the WTO is dominated by countries that regularly subsidize their own industries, create overcapacity, and dump their excess surplus into the wide open United States market. According to Pat Buchanan in his book *Death of the West*, in the international tribunal that is the WTO, America has one vote and the European Union has fifteen.

The case for globalization is that it benefits everyone. Low-cost countries get jobs to make goods for rich countries, and rich countries benefit by being able to buy lower cost goods, which should supposedly raise their standard of living. But if this is true and the United States (one of the rich countries) saves money by buying lower cost goods, then why do we have such a low savings rate? Because even if prices go down, wages are likely to go down as well, so the only way to come out ahead with this strategy is to hope that prices will fall faster and farther than wages. The problem is that we're going in the wrong direction since wages can't fall as close to zero as prices can. In other words, prices will reach their bottom before wages will. Wages can continue to fall after prices have bottomed out. Once prices reach a certain point where lowering them further would eliminate any profits from the sale of those goods at that price, they can't go any lower. With wages, on the other hand, companies almost always have at least a little bit more room to continue to lower them since wages represent a cost to business, and lowering them means more business profits.

We will have to decide for ourselves the extent to which we will accept lower wages in order to get cheaper prices. The best part of the entire situation is that we get to decide. Ultimately, the American people will determine which direction wages and prices will go. But it would be a mistake to believe that either both wages and prices will have to go up together or they will both have to fall together.

From 1870 to 1900, domestic prices for American products made behind high tariff walls fell substantially. Prices for textiles and household furnishings fell 30 percent, prices for metal products fell 49 percent, and prices for chemicals fell 41 percent. The increased efficiency of domestic production protected behind high tariff walls was paying off for both workers who saw their incomes rise and consumers who saw prices drop. The economic connection between high tariffs and low prices was solidified during the golden age of protectionism. In 1900, Secretary of State John Hay proclaimed, "The United States is approaching...a position of eminence in the world's markets due to superior quality and greater cheapness of...its manufactures."

The practice of not protecting American jobs with tariffs and other import restrictions has resulted in the movement of high-wage jobs to low-wage countries, causing American workers to migrate from high-wage employment sectors (like manufacturing jobs) to low-wage employment sectors (like service jobs). This significantly increases the number of workers competing for service jobs, which has a tendency to lower wages in that sector. So now we have not only voluntarily given away the high-wage manufacturing jobs, we have created our own domestic cutthroat competition for the service jobs that remain a double-whammy on the U.S. economy. Once service-sector employers discover that there is an over-supply of Americans seeking or competing for their available positions, they can easily lower the wages they offer those job seekers.

But is it really in America's best interests to offer high wages in the service sector? Absolutely. Here is just one example why. According to the May 24, 2004, issue of *Business Week*, in New York City, security guards for the Empire State Building—possibly one of America's biggest terrorist targets—earn $7.50 an hour checking visitor IDs, X-raying packages, and patrolling the building for any suspicious activity. So in America's priciest city, we employ security guards who have no security for themselves. They have no health care, no pensions, and no paid sick leave.

The same *Business Week* article described that about one-fourth of the workforce between the ages of 18 and 64 make under $9.04 an hour—or $18,800.00 a year—the federally defined poverty line for a family of four.

It is unfortunate that today the jobs that provide the most security are also the least desirable since they are mostly low-wage jobs in the service sector. It appears that only by having a job where one must interact face-to-face with a customer can we have job security.

Clyde Prestowitz, author of *Three Billion New Capitalists: The Great Shift of Wealth and Power to the East*, says that his oldest son, who was working as a software developer and living on Lake Tahoe, gave him a revelation when his son tried to persuade him to invest in a company whose sole business was snow removal. Prestowitz wondered why his son, who was far more familiar with high-tech companies, would want his father to invest in something as low-tech as snow removal. His son explained that the snow couldn't be moved to India. Prestowitz soon began to see the rationality in his son's thinking and wrote about it in his book.

PAYING THE PRICE ONE WAY OR ANOTHER

If workers cannot get health care through their jobs by working for profitable companies, American taxpayers will suffer because the general public ends up making up the difference. Some wind up on Medicaid while others depend on heavily taxpayer-subsidized emergency rooms. Pressure is already growing for the U.S. government to pay for more of America's health care tab. Already at 45 percent of the national total, it is expected to near 50 percent within the next decade. Americans spent $250.6 billion in 2006 out of their own pockets for health care. That figure is expected to rise to $440.8 billion by 2016. So either we protect

American jobs with higher tariffs—which *might* raise consumer prices—or we don't protect them and allow them to go overseas, which *will* raise taxes. This is the choice we have to make. Either *possibly* pay more now, or *definitely* pay more later.

Alexander Hamilton believed in a strong protectionist U.S. economy where American workers were protected from cheap foreign competition. Hamilton didn't worry about whether the United States had the lowest prices in the world. He worried about having enough manufacturing jobs to employ Americans because workers who do not have jobs do not care about low prices because a worker with no job cannot buy anything. If prices go up due to higher-cost American manufacturing, workers secure in their jobs can always cut back on their purchases. Hamilton believed workers would rather have secure jobs with higher pay and higher prices than scarce, insecure jobs with lower pay and lower prices. Under the guidance and protectionist thinking of those like Alexander Hamilton, the United States became the wealthiest nation on the earth.

The *Wall Street Journal* commented on how higher wages helped explain why Japan's economy grew so quickly in the fourth quarter of 2005, for example. Since people were better paid, consumption rose, and so did economic growth.

ASKING THE HARD QUESTIONS

How many pension plans will we allow to be destroyed in the search for ever-cheaper prices on consumer products? Will we sit idly by while industry after industry and company after company eliminate their pensions? Will we not care about it until it personally happens to us? Will we continue to bad-mouth the U.S. auto industry in the midst of their problems claiming that the auto workers are the problem because they are asking for too much? Is it too much to ask to be able to afford a comfortable life with a good wage, adequate health care, an adequate pension, and the ability to send their kids to a good college? Or will we complain that American auto workers make too much money, stop buying the automobiles they make, and let the government take over their health care and their pension costs so we, the taxpayers, can make up the difference? Then will we complain that taxes are too high? Then will we complain that not enough parents are able to afford to send their kids to college in order to "compete" in a global economy after we've effectively advocated the destruction of the very wages that allowed parents access to the financial resources with which to do it?

And what about those big ships involved in making that increase in trade possible? While our Congress (and many Americans) favor raising the mileage standards on passenger vehicles to a point that may well put American automakers out of business, we're willing to turn a blind eye to that while we wasted 2.3 billion gallons of fuel in 2003 alone on our highways due to travel delays. This represents carbon dioxide emissions in excess of 20 million metric tons. The result of this policy is to penalize U.S. automakers for America's inability to pay for adequate infrastructure that includes a transportation system that is not so heavily dependent on the automobile.

If we had a protectionist trading system that encouraged production in the United States instead of a free trade/free market system that encouraged the consumption of goods imported from outside the United States, we would have an adequate tax base to pay for better roads and bridges. Instead, we neglect bridges like the collapsed I-35W bridge in Minneapolis, Minnesota that was overlooked because we didn't have the money to fix it. If the state of Minnesota didn't have the funds, surely they can't look to the U.S. government for help since Congress was too busy considering raising the debt ceiling to nearly $9 trillion so the government could keep its doors open.

Yet the Wall Street elite still has the outlook that as long as the economy keeps growing at a respectable clip, that is sufficient proof that both the middle class and the standard of living in America are "thriving" This is evident in a March 12, 2007, *Wall Street Journal* editorial entitled "Protectionists Never Learn." A more appropriate title would have been "Free Traders Don't Remember." Many fathers, like my own, supported his wife, now of 34 years, and three kids, a very respectable house, and a

mortgage on one income from a job that didn't require a college education. One *Wall Street Journal* reader responded to the editorial identifying himself as a college graduate with a BS and an MBA who could only
afford rent with the help of a roommate in Boston, claiming that the
relationship between salaries and the most basic of living expenses "has
become severely distorted."

He is not alone in feeling like he is merely toiling on a treadmill in
an attempt to get ahead through higher education. Princeton University
economist Alan S. Blinder, who is also a former Federal Reserve Board
vice chairman and former aide to President Clinton who favored and
helped sell NAFTA, wrote in 2001, "Like 99 percent of economists
since the days of Adam Smith, I am a free trader down to my toes." But
today, Mr. Blinder says that telling Americans that they can adequately compete in an increasingly global economy by going to college is
"insufficient."

Blinder also acknowledges that factory workers have known this
for a generation, and it is now being understood by the more highly
educated and politically vocal, "and they're not going to take it." I
would only counter by saying that factory workers have not decided to
"take it," and it is not that they have not been politically vocal. Many
factory workers are unionized workers, and even those who are not in
a union have been telling us in great detail about the detrimental
effects of globalization for years. It is just that those who are not yet
affected did not want to listen.

A February 24, 2003, letter to the editor in *Business Week* magazine
hit the nail on the head. Responding to an earlier cover story article entitled "Is Your Job Next," one blue-collar worker wrote, "We blue-collar
workers have been telling you white-collars for more than 20 years that
we all should be buying American. But no one listened. You white-collars had to have your imports while bad-mouthing American products.
You never looked back until it was too late. Hop into the lifeboat with
us—hope you can find a seat."

It is great that former staunch free traders are now beginning to see
the folly of their support for such policies, but none of them go so far as

to suggest solutions beyond more education for displaced Americans or compensating them with wage insurance to soften the blow of losing their jobs. According to Alan Tonelson, author of *Race to the Bottom*, "most of today's high-wage jobs are already becoming lower-wage jobs, and this trend will continue whether U.S. workers go back-to-school or whether businesses offer them retraining or not."

Former South Carolina Senator Ernest "Fritz" Hollings, who retired in 2004 but who began his service as a U.S. Senator in 1966, explained the fallacy of simply committing to re-train laid off Americans for other jobs. Hollings spoke about a T-Shirt maker in the small town of Andrews, South Carolina that closed and moved to Mexico. The average age of the 487 laid-off workers was 47. Through re-training programs where we spend billions of taxpayer dollars per year for the privilege of laying off Americans in the industry of their choice to "educate" them for jobs they never sought and likely never wanted, Andrews, South Carolina now has 487 highly educated computer operators.

Now would a computer outfit rather hire a 21-year-old highly educated computer operator who is light years away from imposing any retirement or pension burdens on his or her company or the 47-year-old who will be seeking such benefits much sooner, not to mention higher health care support in the near term if not immediately? The computer company would obviously much rather hire the 21-year-old college graduate. "So don't tell me about retraining," Hollings said. Every American has unique talents, and we should both enable them and encourage them to do what they do best. But to the extent that we are spending our tax dollars for job re-training, which is the wrong prescription for America's economic problems, we are shortchanging the American public by not giving them the proper return on their money, and we offer them fewer job options.

Wall Street Journal columnist and free trade advocate David Wessel titled his August 11, 2005, column "Aid to Workers Hurt by Trade Comes in Trickle." He reported that in 2002 when President Bush was re-authorized to negotiate free trade deals, an idea that was supposed to help workers who lost their jobs due to trade called "wage insurance" was signed into law.

But when Julia Hicks of Concord, North Carolina, lost her textile job at Pillowtex Corp., one she held for 38 years, she got one of those fine service jobs as a coffee roaster at S & D Coffee Inc. The new job paid 50 percent less than her old job, and your tax dollars subsidized her new position by $2.00 an hour for many months to help close the gap.

Brenda Miller, a worker at Pillowtex for 15 years and who is now studying marketing at Rowan-Cabbarus Community College, said she thinks about "300 to 400 Pillowtex workers have found jobs out of 4,500. A friend of mine quit school. She just said, 'I'm too old for this.' These people lost their jobs, and they just weren't ready to go back to school." Another former worker said, "I didn't pay 26 years on a house to give it up to someone else. I had but five years left on my mortgage. Now where's my American dream? It's in the garbage."

In 2005, President Bush's new budget called for cutting the funding for the nation's adult education and literacy system by 75 percent, which would include GED classes being sought by those who were laid off from the Pillowtex factories and textile mills in North Carolina. How can a system that intentionally lays off American workers with the promise of re-training funds work for America when the scarcity of tax revenue causes us to entertain cuts that defeat the intent, however misguided, of the proposed solution?

The future significance of any funding proposal will now be overshadowed by the fact that eighty-four cents of every dollar spent by the government has already been committed before the president or Congress even looks at it. We are not going to make it any better by continuing to do what we have been doing, either. I remember that back in 2003, *Business Week* reported that three-fourths of all federal spending goes to defense, education, Social Security, Medicare, highways, parks, farm subsidies, and interest on the national debt. So in just four years, the so-called "untouchables" of federal spending have gone from 75 percent to 84 percent of total spending. At this rate, we don't have much more to go to get to 100 percent of all tax revenue being spent on American benefits that, if taken away, will result in spending cuts that will be viewed as unacceptable to many Americans. Polls show that a majority of Americans react negatively to the term "government spend-ing" but still strongly support these programs. You can be sure that the problem will get much worse when the majority of baby boomers start to retire.

ENTITLEMENTS: WHO PAYS? WHO BENEFITS?

Nobody likes paying taxes, but few people would dare tell the gov-ernment to stop paving their roads, stop regulating their mutual-fund manager, or stop paying for their mother's health care. Yes, of course, free traders come back saying that they don't want to pay for other peo-ple's health care through Medicare taxes and the like. But if not through our tax dollars, who will pay for your mother's or grandmother's health care needs? Wouldn't it be right to assume that if your mother or grand-mother could pay for their own health care, they would be already? Otherwise, they would be hypocritical to be able to do so, but yet put-ting the burden on the government, while complaining about taxes being too high. I think it would be fair to ask anyone who doesn't want the government involved in providing any health care or retirement whatsoever to demand that their government deny them any health care or Social Security in the future. Do free traders realize that the U.S. Government makes available about half of the many billions of dollars provided for drug research and possible breakthrough discoveries?

In March 2006, House Speaker Dennis Hastert received a letter from then Secretary of the Treasury, John Snow, informing him that new investments designed for the Civil Service Retirement and Disability Fund were being suspended and that a portion of the fund's investments were being redeemed to stay under the nation's then-current $8.184 tril-lion national debt limit.

By July 2007, current Secretary of the Treasury, Henry Paulsen, told Congress that the current $8.965 trillion debt ceiling needed to be raised so our country could keep paying its bills into the fall. As President Nixon's economic adviser, Herb Stein, once said, "If something cannot go on forever, it will stop." Our national debt clearly cannot continue to go up forever. The message to those who don't want government involved in entitlements like Medicare and Social Security should be, "if you are against them, then tell the government you do not want to benefit from them."

A 2007 study from the Employee Benefit Research Institute and Mathew Greenwald & Associates revealed that 66 percent of workers say that they have absolutely no retirement savings. And with no retirement savings to live on, how will they be able to afford health care? According to the Fidelity Research Institute the typical American household has only 58 percent of its needed retirement income, including pension and Social Security income. But the executive director of the institute, Guy Patton, warns that if unexpected health conditions or layoffs occur, Americans may not even be able to count on the 58 percent. And layoffs are always possible, especially if our love affair with free trade continues.

I'm not proposing we have a nationalized health care system. I'm saying we should protect middle class jobs that pay middle class wages so the middle class can afford to retire and live in dignity. If American employers were protected from cutthroat competition through equalizing tariffs, they would have the profits to sock away enough into their pension funds to provide an adequate pension for retirees.

Other free traders, and especially libertarians, want to get the government out of as many functions as possible. This has always served as an effective rallying cry since consumers understandably love to hear about ways that could put more money in their pockets. But at what cost could we "get the government out of it," as former Libertarian presidential candidate Harry Brown used to say?

Should we, for example, get the government out of airline safety regulations and allow the airlines to take responsibility for the quality of maintenance on their airplanes? In February 2004, the National Transportation Safety Board pointed to poor maintenance and a lack of federal oversight when determining the cause of a fatal 2003 US Airways crash that killed 21 people. The US Airways flight was operated by Air Midwest. Federal oversight of maintenance was also a factor in 2000 when an Alaska Airlines plane crashed and killed 88 people.

But before you point the finger at the government, the problem is actually that the Federal Aviation Administration (FAA), the government agency that is charged with maintenance oversight for our nation's airline carriers, is drastically under-funded and under-staffed. Couple that with the fact that every major U.S. carrier has outsourced a significant amount of maintenance to low-cost foreign countries, and you have a disaster waiting to happen. Delta saves a reported $250 million a year with moves such as outsourcing maintenance on their planes to a Hong Kong-based company, and United Airlines has outsourced maintenance to a Chinese company. The Transportation Department says 64 percent of the budget for maintenance by U.S. carriers is now outsourced (Air Midwest brought their maintenance in-house after the 2003 crash). That compares to just 37 percent spent on outsourcing in 1996.

FAA inspectors say they that are only able to effectively monitor a handful of 698 overseas contractors, which have been known to employ untrained and unskilled workers in the past. The FAA has also reported that over 500,000 counterfeit parts are used on planes every year, an estimate that Boeing officials have admitted is accurate. When FAA inspectors are able to travel overseas to foreign repair stations, they discover things like improper engine installations and undocumented parts. Out of the dozens of facilities one FAA inspector might be responsible for scrutinizing, they might be able to get to one or two each year at the most. One inspector insisted that if the maintenance facilities were located in the United States, they could easily visit them on a daily basis.

As if the cutthroat competition (which has now affected our airlines) brought on by globalization and the perpetual strategy of lowering prices for U.S. consumers at all costs hasn't been worrisome enough with lead-laced Chinese toys, faulty Chinese tires, and toxic Chinese toothpaste, we're now risking passenger safety by outsourcing aircraft maintenance to China as well.

Airline passenger safety is one safety net we don't need to be destroying, along with the instability that comes with compromising such conventional safety nets like adequate pensions and health insurance in the name of cutthroat competition. Our economy is already subject to too much instability to allow further dependence on the marketplace without strong and effective regulation. It took September 11, 2001, to increase the number of federal air marshals from 33 to over 2,500. Let's hope it doesn't take more fatal crashes to mandate that the maintenance of our national airlines take place within our nation's borders by quality certified mechanics. Competition between airlines should be regulated so that each can turn a profit without having to resort to outsourcing maintenance and compromising safety.

What about other government mandates and intervention like requiring websites like MySpace.com to release information about registered sex offenders who could be exploiting our children online? Or what about the cooperation of federal authorities with local law enforcement in participating in shows like Dateline NBC's "To Catch a Predator" program, which has prevented several possible cases of molestation of young children? As of May 2007, MySpace.com says it has removed nearly 7,000 profiles of registered sex offenders. So is the American government a necessary partner of American industry or merely a hindrance to capitalism that should be avoided to maximize profits?

BUILDING PROSPERITY ON SHAKY GROUND

We have sacrificed too much potential revenue and taken on far too much debt as a result by accepting competition as the cornerstone for prosperity in our economy. By allowing cutthroat competition in America, we have transferred our historic reliance on continuously rising wages as the main propeller of American growth and prosperity to a reliance on stock market gains instead. But is that a wise move?

The *Wall Street Journal* reported how a particular stock market rally in July 2007, which they dubbed a "mystery market," could be described as nothing more than a "lucky streak" and was what made the market so much "fun" and encouraged readers to "roll with it." On that day, the Dow Jones set a new record high and saw the biggest increase in almost four years. But nobody knows why stocks accelerated to those record highs. Market strategist and author Peter L. Bernstein says he's been involved in the market for more than 50 years, and he still doesn't understand why Wall Street suddenly decides to take an optimistic turn for one day.

An August 6, 2007, *Business Week* article says that our economy should be fine, with the exception of a possible U.S. currency crash. But the article also warns that all bets are off if the fallout from the weakening housing market is worse than we have been led to believe and if productivity growth slows. Both are happening now as of this writing. But what should we do while we are waiting for these events to work themselves out? According to the *Business Week* article, we should "just sit back and enjoy the show."

Does it really make sense to stake our economic future on a totally irrational stock market that even 50-year veteran stock traders cannot figure out? Or should we do as we have done in the past and protect American companies from cutthroat competition, and therefore, American jobs that pay middle class wages, ensuring we maintain a healthy and vibrant middle class, allowing those companies to make sufficient profits and provide adequate pensions for their loyal workers? Surely we have more at stake in our lives and with our futures to subject ourselves to a "mystery market" where stock market advocates, while warning of the irrationality and potential crises, simultaneously tell us to "roll with it" and "sit back and enjoy the show." This is America's future we are gambling with, not a few dollars of disposable income at a roulette wheel in Las Vegas.

PAYING NEW ATTENTION TO GLOBALIZATION

Free market advocates have been wrong in their predictions since the U.S. embraced free trade in the early 1970s. Predictions back then estimated that technology would have led to decreasing workloads and more free time for vacations and leisure time. Instead, a decisive majority of Americans don't use their earned vacation time. One-fifth take less than a full week of vacation every year, and 42 percent cancel vacation plans on a regular basis. The Japanese coined the term *karoshi*, which is the act of working oneself to death, but we now take less vacation time than the Japanese. America is the new nation of overwork.

Even when we manage to "get away," we really don't. In the quest to remain competitive, we avoid taking time off, become susceptible to burnout, jeopardize productivity, make more mistakes in the workplace, and resent our co-workers more often. This is according to a survey from the Families and Work Institute.

Even if the number of those who benefit from increasing volumes of trade outnumber those negatively affected by it, as most free trade economists will tell you, more economists are starting to reconsider the strength of those benefits. Paul A. Samuelson, Professor Emeritus of Economics, Massachusetts Institute of Technology and Nobel Prize winner, who, according to a December 6, 2004, *Business Week* article is credited with inventing much of modern-day economics, said on September 9, 2004, that he believes the assumption that "the gains [from trade] of the American winners are big enough to more than compensate for the losers" is "dead wrong..." He also claims, "Being able to purchase groceries 20 percent cheaper at Wal-Mart does not necessarily make up for the wage losses."

Samuelson isn't alone in his new-found skepticism for global trade. Paul M. Krugman, Professor of Economics, Princeton University and New York Times columnist, said in 1996 that globalization critics are "entirely ignorant men, who...are unaware of the most basic principles and facts about the world economy..." Today, however, he is singing at least a slightly different tune, saying in 2005, "If you aren't a little bit tortured by globalization, you're not paying attention."

So-called wage insurance may help by putting a small band-aid on our economic problems, but it is no long-term solution. Alan Blinder believes our education system should prepare Americans for jobs that cannot go overseas, but is not that against free market thinking since the government would have to get involved by mandating standards and policies (and therefore, costs)? Remember, the term "free" is defined by Webster's Dictionary as "without cost or payment," so Blinder is trying to blind us to the fact that he supports free trade (which implies free markets) yet supports policy suggestions that counter those same foundational beliefs.

SUBSIDIZING IMPORTS MEANS MORE IMPORTS

In today's terms, both free trade and protectionism can easily be more clearly defined. For the United States, free trade is basically any trade policy that puts us at a competitive disadvantage compared to other countries. This is especially true if the other trading nation has a lower standard of living and pays lower wages than the United States. Protectionism, however, is a trade policy that puts no country at a competitive disadvantage. This is true since a protectionist policy consists of equalizing tariffs that would equalize the production-cost burdens between the United States and other countries, eliminating subsidies and favoritism.

With free trade, we are actually subsidizing imports since we impose costs on our own producers that other trading nations are not required to bear. As the saying goes, if you subsidize anything, you get more of it. And since we are subsidizing imports, we are getting more than our fair share. In many cases, imports are not merely disturbing the U.S. market, they are destroying the U.S. market. Next time you go shopping for a television, a cordless phone, a DVD player, a VCR, or something as simple as an alarm clock radio, you will see what I mean because we do not make these items in the U.S. anymore. It is also very difficult to find any furniture, toys, or apparel made in the United States unless you know where to look.

The *Wall Street Journal* reported back in November 2004 that the results of various re-training programs have been largely disappointing. When the San Antonio, Texas Levi Strauss factory closed in 2004 (Levi's has since closed all of their American factories), some workers lost jobs they had held for 20 years. One female former Levi's employee received a college grant worth 11,373.00, which she used to combine English classes with training to learn office skills. Upon graduation, she should qualify for a $6.50-an-hour office job. As James P. Hoffa, General President of the International Brotherhood of Teamsters once said, "And how are today's or tomorrow's workers to afford higher education with health care costs soaring and wages stagnant or dropping in the areas where new jobs are being created?"

In January 2007, Webb furniture of Galax, Virginia closed its 80-year-old factory in the Blue Ridge Mountains as a result of intense pressure from Chinese imports of wood furniture. Single mother Tonya Graber lost her job painting furniture as well as her health insurance that not only covered herself but also her son, now 12 years old. Ms. Graber became eligible for government (taxpayer) subsidized health insurance that she couldn't afford. Even though the 2002 Health Coverage Tax Credit bill mandates that the government pay 65 percent of health insurance premiums to Americans hurt by trade deals, only 11 percent of those eligible take advantage of it. The reason? According to Stan Dorn, who studied the wage insurance program as part of the Urban Institute think tank, it's simply not realistic to expect a worker who has been laid off to spring for 35 percent of a health care premium. And that's if you can be so financially sound as to devote your time to understanding the rules in dealing with five federal and state agencies.

If economists and politicians are aware that re-training doesn't work, why do they keep touting it? Put simply, it buys them more time to see if free trade will actually eventually gain the approval of the American public and temporarily gets us off their backs. Instead of free trade politicians, economists, and corporations taking the responsibility of so many lost jobs, sending the laid off American worker back to school is a subtle scenario of blaming the victim. You should have known better. You were in the wrong industry. Be an American. Take responsibility for your situation and get the training you need for a job that is still available. Or in the words of a 2004 Bush campaign worker overheard by a news colleague during the transfer of a reporter's phone call seeking comments about job quality, American workers who are unhappy with the low-quality of their jobs should go get new ones—or pop some Prozac if it will make them feel better.

Would simplifying the bureaucracy and the process of dealing with five agencies help? I suppose. But I have a much better answer to the problem. If we would simply protect the jobs we have (which we often lose due to unfair cutthroat competition) instead of intentionally destroying them and creating another bureaucracy devoted to spending over a billion dollars each year to re-train the laid off workers for new jobs, we would save a lot of taxpayer dollars, have smaller government, a more diverse economy, and a happier American workforce overall.

THERE IS A PROBLEM, AND YES, THERE IS AN ANSWER

Lou Dobbs seems to echo the facts of the negative impact free trade has on our society nightly on his program on CNN, but like Princeton economist Alan Blinder, Lou fails to offer any solutions to the pain free trade is causing us, and none of his guests seem to offer any solutions, either. I admire and sympathize with Lou Dobbs because he is willing to take as much criticism as he has from those who criticize his strong stance against free trade, but when he defends himself by proudly explaining that he has never proposed raising a single tariff, it indicates that he just doesn't have any solutions.

When he had economist Paul Craig Roberts, former Assistant Treasury Secretary to Ronald Reagan, on his show on March 5, 2004, as he has many times, Lou Dobbs asked him point blank for his solution, saying, "What is the solution, Paul? First I'm going to ask you the big questions. What's the solution on outsourcing? What's the solution on a trade deficit that—we now have an accumulated trade deficit in debt of $3 trillion" Paul Craig Roberts responded, "Lou, I'm afraid I don't have a solution. I'm trying to make people aware that there's a problem."

Later Lou Dobbs began promotional spots for his shows saying, "It's time for answers," but it is clear no one rallying against our current free trade/free market policies seems to have any answers, at least until now. The answer to our trade deficit problem and much of our outsourcing problem (there are other types of outsourcing problems I will address later in this chapter) is protectionism.

I realize the term "protectionism" brings to mind negative connotations, but when used appropriately, it brings powerfully positive features to the economy that almost everyone overlooks. I am not incredibly preoccupied with or worried about how it sounds, seems, or looks, and neither should you be. We should all be interested in results that will benefit our economy.

In his book *Exporting America*, Lou Dobbs says, "Corporate enablers are simply out of fresh ideas." Protectionism is not really a "fresh" idea like Lou Dobbs is seeking, but that makes it no less of a solution. You may very well think of protectionism as a fresh idea since America sparingly uses it in the realm of trade policy. Protectionism is a tried and true solution that has been tested by our founding fathers and popular presidents like Theodore Roosevelt.

The first bill in Congress, after the United States Seal was adopted, was a tariff bill, through which a 50 percent tariff was applied on various imports. On the day the bill was passed, July 4, 1789, we ushered in an era of protectionism for the United States. The father of our country, George Washington, was a protectionist. Abraham Lincoln was, too. After Lincoln's presidential nomination in 1860, Lincoln declared he was "a Henry Clay tariff man." It was none other than Senator Henry Clay, who in 1839 proudly declared, "I would rather be right than be president." Protectionism may not be popular today, but to paraphrase Senator Clay, I would rather be a protectionist than be popular. And I have the benefit of the agreement of some of the greatest men our nation has ever known. I would much rather be in agreement with George Washington and Abraham Lincoln than with Bill Clinton and George W. Bush. Who would you count among your supporters?

Apparently free traders feel more comfortable with past writers like Adam Smith who wrote *Wealth of Nations* in 1776. But I feel sorry for Adam Smith since his corpse is constantly exhumed in the support of free trade theory that his written words would hardly endorse.

For instance, in the book *Globalization And Its Discontents*, Nobel Prize winner and author Joseph E. Stiglitz says that Adam Smith was much more aware of market limitations and the imperfections of competition compared to those who today claim to be his free market followers. If competition was perfect, there certainly would be no need for market-correcting antitrust mechanisms. Concerning market failures, Smith said, "I have advocated a balanced view of the role of government, one which recognizes both the limitations and failures of markets and government." Balance, of course, is something we should strive for in our economy just as we strive for balance in our daily lives with work and spending time with our families.

According to Edward Luttwak, a conservative senior fellow at the Center for Strategic and International Studies and author of *Turbo Capitalism: Winners and Losers in the Global Economy*, the devotion of those who look to Adam Smith as their guide depends essentially on not carefully reading his work. Luttwak says Smith was much wiser than his present-day worshippers and highlighted his writings with exclusions, exceptions, and reservations about the ability of free markets to constantly maximize efficiency and the common welfare.

It was Adam Smith who gave us the free market descriptive phrase "invisible hand." In his book, Smith contends that the workings of the market lead to economic efficiency as if it was being guided by an "invisible hand," and it is because of this writing that we now have this free market descriptive phrase that is so often used to defend or advance the cause of free trade. But in the mid twentieth century, Nobel Prize award winners, Kenneth Arrow of Stanford and Gerard Debreu of the University of California at Berkeley, established the circumstances that were required for Adam Smith's "invisible hand" theory to work. These included unrealistic assumptions such as the knowledge of information that was both perfect and unaffected by any current economic events and that everyone in the economy shared the same perfect information. Competition, of course, had to be perfect, and it had to be assumed that anyone could be insured against any number of possible risks. I have often wondered what the risks would be if our free market world, guided by an invisible hand, was so perfect. The propagation of such unrealistic market conditions to provide back up support for free trade is nothing short of verbal voodoo.

Of course, you know if you have read this far that competition is certainly not perfect. And for all the recommendations by free traders and big-business leaders that we need to ever increase competition in every sector of the economy, these same free traders and big-business leaders privately advocate varying degrees of competition for different reasons. If you are a CEO of a multinational firm in the health and beauty business, you are not going to advocate more competition in your own industry since it would only decrease your own company's profits. And one of the first things an entrepreneur does before going into business is determine the amount of competition in that sector. Any entrepreneur would much rather start a business in a sector where there was less competition rather than more competition. So I have to laugh when I hear business or corporate representatives talk about the need for more competition in markets to hold down consumer prices. More often than not they are speaking in generalities, but specifically they only favor competition in every business sector except their own.

For instance, back in December 2003, the *Wall Street Journal* reported that consumers, because of increased competition, had more choices than ever before in making cheap phone calls. But what happened? Despite the competition, long-distance carriers raised prices, and consumers paid 76 percent more for a 20 minute call. Increased competition isn't always everything it's cracked up to be.

I remember attending a seminar years ago about the book publishing business, and one of the speakers at the seminar told a story about a now-successful author who originally wanted to write a book about hunting and capturing different types of mushrooms in the wild. Once the author did some research about the vast number of books already on the market about wild mushrooms, he decided that the competition was too great, and he smartly diverted his writing attempt to a different subject and a different audience. And since there was less competition in the area of his second choice, he has become successful.

Adam Smith himself realized that businesses would strive to suppress competition. That is why we have antitrust laws—to keep businesses from engaging in anti-competitive behavior, gaining too much market power, denying new upstart competitors in their sectors, and exploiting consumers with high prices. Of course, some competition is better than no competition, but the competitive economy cannot be left solely to the market, and our futures cannot be guided by an invisible hand. Any good economy needs good regulation, and one of the reasons our economy has been negatively impacted by excessive cutthroat competition is because we have often left no one at the wheel to steer the global economy in a direction that best benefits America.

With an economy guided by an invisible hand, everyone pursues their own interests to satisfy their own personal greed at the expense of others. Too few have been concerned about whether what is good for them personally is actually good for the nation. Morally motivated questions like, "Is this the right thing to do?" wouldn't exist.

Adam Smith was far less concerned about retaliatory tariffs than his present-day followers, saying, "The recovery of a great foreign market will generally more than compensate the transitory inconveniency of paying dearer during a short time for some sorts of goods." He also said that the invisible hand had the propensity to impose harm on a country and its citizens "unless government takes great pains to prevent it." Smith even contended that investment in a country's domestic producers generates "more revenue and employment" than investment in trade with foreign nations. Indeed, with quotes like these, Adam Smith sounds more like a protectionist than a free trader and more like George Washington than George W. Bush.

America would be fortunate to have a trade policy that reflects a balance between America and other nations. But free market types would have us believe government should have a minimal role, if any, in erecting tariffs to protect American producers from predatory foreign producers. If we had a trade balance with most nations or an actual trade surplus, we would add more jobs in this country (remember the statistic that for each $1 billion in trade deficit we lose 13,000 jobs). It is hard to imagine how free traders can legitimately denounce higher import tariffs when everyone knows the current system is unsustainable.

HEEDING THE SOUND OF ALARM BELLS:
OUR UNSUSTAINABLE SYSTEM

In an April 17, 2006, *Business Week* interview with Tim Geither, president of the powerful Federal Reserve Bank of New York, he was asked about the dual deficits we have in America (the budget deficit and the trade deficit) and if we should be concerned about such imbalances. Mr. Geither said the imbalances in the global economy are not only too large but also clearly unsustainable. The risk of these unsustainable imbalances is that fewer people will be willing to invest in America or raise capital here.

On February 3, 2006, the *Wall Street Journal* said that President Bush, as well as government and non-government analysts, used the term "unsustainable" to describe America's fiscal trend. Again on March 15, 2006, the same paper reported that most economists regard the gap between what the U.S. consumes and what it produces as unsustainable.

In an April 2006 visit between President Bush and Chinese President Hu, Bush said that the trade deficit the U.S. has with China is unsustainable. Of course, it is easier to predict that a system is unsustainable than to predict when the unsustainable system will manifest itself as a defining moment in history on the U.S. economy. But critics of the current system have warned for years that if investors fear that the United States is no longer a stable and safe place to invest their money, the economic shock that follows would include plummeting stock prices and soaring interest rates. The sharp drop in the dollar over the last few years should be sufficient evidence of this.

Back in December 2003, the Congressional Budget Office predicted that unless tax rates in America reached unprecedented levels, present spending policies would likely be unsustainable for the next five decades. But, no one knows when the American economy will reach crisis mode. My contention is that there is no time like the present to act. The longer we wait to turn the corner, the harder it will be to change paths, and the less willing the American people will be to accept painful consequences of several years of wrongheaded, financially unsound, and admittedly unsustainable policies. The real kicker will be that once full crisis mode is reached, we won't be able to say that the alarm bells were never sounded.

One of my favorite analogies is from Larry Burkett's book *The Coming Economic Earthquake*. America, and its love affair with its known unsustainable free trade/free market policies, is just like a cowboy in the wild west frantically riding his horse to get away from the Indians chasing him. The cowboy is fully aware that if he just keeps riding his horse, it will ultimately collapse. But the cowboy is also fully aware that if he makes the horse stop, he will be killed. So he keeps pushing the horse to continue, knowing that only a miracle will save him.

ACHIEVING A TRULY LEVEL PLAYING FIELD

So if free traders from the President through Congress on down know that our current financial policies are unsustainable, why do they keep us on the same path? There are a few possible explanations. As Winston Churchill once said, "The multitudes remained plunged in ignorance of the simplest economic facts, and their leaders, seeking their votes, did not dare to undeceive them." Today, the simplest economic facts are that we cannot continue to consume our way to prosperity. As Gus Stelzer explains in his book *The Nightmare of Camelot*, production creates wealth while consumption dissipates wealth. We can't consume ourselves to greater prosperity. We must produce!

But the best explanation of why our elected leaders seem so unwilling to tackle the issue at hand is because of the negative connotations of "protectionism," when, in fact, a dose of protectionism is exactly what is needed.

For instance, in April 2006, Rick Rubin said, "Nobody I know of who's serious about fiscal matters thinks we're going to be able to deal with the imbalances we have without a combination of spending discipline and revenue increases." Protectionism, or imposing equalizing tariffs on other trading nations so that neither nation has a production-cost advantage, would certainly raise revenue in a couple of different ways.

First, a tariff would raise revenue by the simple fact that we would be collecting more import taxes from those who wish to access America's market. Keep in mind that these increased import taxes would be no more than the direct taxes we impose on our own producers here at home, making trade fair and creating, perhaps for the first time in a long time, a truly level playing field.

Second, an equalizing tariff would encourage production at home since the production-cost advantage for producing in other countries would be eliminated. Since it would be an advantage for producers of various goods and services to be closer to their American customers, producing in America would become even more attractive.

The new factories that would either be built in America or the existing ones that would be expanded would reduce America's burgeoning trade deficit since the products that used to be imported to America would be produced here instead. More jobs in America mean more tax revenue, and therefore, more benefits for everyone in America.

But even Lou Dobbs realizes the problems associated with free trade and complains about them almost nightly on his CNN program, yet he proudly proclaims in his book *Exporting America*, "I certainly have never called for protectionist trade policies, only fair trade policies." What Lou doesn't realize is that protectionist trade polices are fair trade policies! The reason he doesn't realize it and so few others do is because no one has accurately defined protectionism so that everyone, regardless of which side of the debate they are on, may debate its merits fairly.

Dobbs also said in *Exporting America*, "Staunch protectionists believe we can turn back the clock and use high tariffs to protect every industry in this country. Their absolutism forces most of us to dismiss their concerns and even their valid points. But the absolutists who demand free trade should be dismissed every bit as quickly. It's time for all of us to realize that a purely ideological commitment to free trade is as foolhardy as absolute protectionism."

TIME TO GIVE PROTECTIONISM A SECOND LOOK

After Lou Dobbs sent me a complimentary advance copy of *Exporting America* asking me for my comments before the final copy was printed, I complied and wrote him a letter stating that he should have me back on his program (I had already been featured twice on his show) so we could talk about what protectionism really means so it can be accurately discussed in the future. But true to his words I suppose, I have been dismissed for suggesting protectionism as a possible solution to an admittedly unsustainable free trade policy because I have never been invited back on his show. Since then, I have wondered if Lou would also quickly dismiss other proclaimed protectionists like George Washington, Abraham Lincoln, Thomas Jefferson, and Theodore Roosevelt.

One reason protectionism has such a bad reputation is that it isn't judged by the proper standards. "If I were a protectionist," Lou Dobbs said on August 29, 2004, "the first thing I would say is, let's close our borders." But again, Dobbs has it all wrong. Protectionism doesn't mean closing our borders. Did Abraham Lincoln or Teddy Roosevelt, both admitted protectionists, propose closing our borders? No. As AFL-CIO Secretary-Treasurer Richard Trumka once said, "I don't know anybody who wants to stop all trade. The continued references to isolationism does our ability to debate this issue a tremendous disservice."

Dobbs wants to put a wall up on the Mexican border to stop immigration, something I would not be opposed to, and somehow that's okay and is not protectionist but raising tariffs on foreign imports *is*? You can see how much we need a fair and open debate on both the definition and the merits of protectionism.

But even to those who realize that we do have an unsustainable financial situation in this country, protectionism is never even an option. Protectionism would prevent the impending financial crisis from happening, where globalization (which is synonymous with free trade and free market ideology) only ensures that the day of reckoning will eventually come. As I've already detailed in this chapter, even the proponents of globalization admit that. So the question is, do we address the market failure before it occurs (protectionism), or do we just let it happen and attempt to pick up the pieces when it does (globalization)?

STILL WAITING FOR A MIRACLE

Apparently, our leaders are just going to keep riding the horse, hoping for a miracle, until it collapses. On February 7, 2007, Federal Reserve Chairman Ben Bernanke said, "No one should be allowed to slip too far down the economic ladder, especially for reasons beyond his or her control," but yet warned that politicians shouldn't create barriers (tariffs) that might hinder international trade. This is paramount to admitting we have a problem yet also saying that there is no solution or that the only possible solution should not be implemented.

George Soros said in his book *Open Society Endangered*, "...the truth is that market fundamentalism is itself naïve and illogical. To put the matter simply, market forces, if they are given complete authority even the purely economic and financial arenas, produce chaos and could ultimately lead to the downfall of the global capitalist system."

In a 2004 speech, Alan Greenspan said, "It is difficult to imagine that we can continue indefinitely to borrow savings from abroad at a rate equivalent to 5 percent of U.S. gross domestic product (GDP)." But by late 2006, the U.S. was borrowing at the rate of 6.5 percent GDP. Yet Greenspan continued to warn us that protectionism is the primary threat to globalization. I've often wondered how something that threatens a system that is known to be unsustainable can really be a "threat."

A June 2003 study arranged by the National Association of Manufacturers said that if a sufficient number of American factories close, resulting in fewer research and development positions, this would reduce the traditional contribution manufacturing makes to our country's economic growth. Upon the release of the report, National Association of Manufacturers' president Jerry Jasinowski said, "We're not going to suggest anything protectionist," even though he admits that the study shows "loss of pricing power in manufacturing, largely as a result of this international competition."

A PLAN TO SAVE SOCIAL SECURITY

In its June 13, 2005 issue, *Business Week* discussed the "hard choices" facing the reality of public pension underfunding. The proposed options were limited to higher taxes, more borrowing, more risk (with the investment of pension funds), 401 (k)s (shifting investment risk to workers), or default (breaking pension promises). Yet protectionism, which would impose higher taxes on foreigners as opposed to higher direct taxes on Americans which *Business Week* listed as a suggestion, was not mentioned.

But even if *Business Week* writers don't want to acknowledge import tariffs as a valid option, some of their readers do. In a letter printed in the February 20, 2006, issue, a reader explained that for every American job that is outsourced, fragile funds like Social Security lose thousands of dollars, causing the tax bill of every American to increase. Let's say an American worker makes $40,000.00 per year, through which the Social Security fund collects $6,000.00 (based on a combined 15 percent tax—7½ percent from the worker and 7½ percent from the employer) Then the job is outsourced to a foreign country paying lower wages. The employer not only saves money on labor costs, but also $3,000.00 in Social Security costs since workers in foreign countries don't get Social Security nor do they pay into the fund like American workers do. Plus, the company no longer has to worry about the health care costs of the newly laid off American.

But let's deal only with the 7½ percent the company used to pay to the Social Security fund in support of the American worker, which saves the company $3,000.00 based on a $40,000.00 per year salary. Then let's say we outsource 3.3 million workers by 2015 as estimated by the Forrester Research study I outlined in the Chapter 1. Three point three million lost jobs times $3,000.00 equals a huge $990 million in lost revenue for Social Security. The way to save Social Security, or prevent virtually any other funding shortfall, is to require the employer to continue to pay their 7½ percent into Social Security even when they outsource American jobs. Call it a tax on every outsourced job, or call it a 7½ percent tariff. It doesn't matter what you call it. If we want to save Social Security, now we know how. If we don't want to save Social Security, then we can simply continue to keep our heads in the sand, continue demonizing protectionism, continue ranting about our problems without offering any substantial solutions, or all of the above.

Plus, considering the over $4 trillion in cumulative trade deficit we have suffered since 1975 (the last year the United States had a trade surplus), we would have collected in the neighborhood of $1.6 trillion in national revenue based on a 40 percent marginal tax rate, had the lost production responsible for the trade deficit taken place in the United States. Considering a conservative 3-to-1 ripple effect, $4.8 trillion in national income would have been generated, not to mention the hundreds of million of dollars that would have gone to state and local governments who instead have gone begging for lack of funds.

In a February 15, 2007, article, the *Wall Street Journal* described how rising government spending on retirement benefits and health care will almost certainly require tax increases within the next ten years or so. The only undecided issue is who will pay for the tax increases.

The free trade/free market solution, which rejects tariffs on imports since they supposedly raise consumer prices (I proved this not to be true in many cases in Chapter 1), we end up a poorer nation as a result since we:

- Suffer huge trade deficits which destroy American jobs.
- Lose precious tax revenue since workers in foreign countries (to whom the jobs are outsourced) don't pay taxes to America.
- Lose even more tax revenue since companies employing workers in foreign countries can avoid their $7^{1}/_{2}$ percent contribution to Social Security.

Even more amazing than the outright rejection of a more protectionist solution to protect jobs (and therefore precious tax revenue), we casually accept other protectionist solutions for Americans when they are not working through a variety of ways such as:

- Unemployment compensation to protect us if we lose our job.
- Workers compensation to protect us if we get injured on the job.
- Education vouchers to help us get one of those "new economy" jobs.
- Medicare and Medicaid to protect us from getting too sick.
- Disability payments if we are not physically able to work.
- Social Security to protect us when we're beyond retirement.
- Food Stamps and welfare to protect us if we are poor and unable to find a job.

How amazing it is that in various ways we will protect Americans who have lost their jobs or are no longer working through no fault of our own, but we refuse to protect Americans *before* they lose their jobs through no fault of their own!

PROTECTING THE RIGHT TO AVOID AMERICAN LAWS

Then there are the ways that we afford free traders their own sort of protectionism and their right to avoid more costly American laws through outsourcing, avoiding American laws that reflect our standards and values. We protect the rights of multinationals to skirt American laws to produce in third-world, cheap-labor countries and then import their products in direct competition with American companies producing in America that abide by American laws.

According to Senator Sherrod Brown (D., OH) in his book *Myths of Free Trade*, "Even though protection for business interests—repatriation of profits, intellectual property rights, patents—are all done in the name of free trade, free traders label standards for labor rights, food safety, and the environment protectionism."

Even if you attempted to argue that transferring American jobs to third-world, low-wage countries would help raise living standards and wages in those countries, you would be disappointed to know that a 2002 study by the World Bank showed that even during the boom of the 1990s, the number of people who live on less than $2.00 a day rose by almost 100 million. And according to Joseph Stiglitz, the annual growth rate in Latin America (a group of countries that unfortunately follow the free market model of the United States) was 2.9 percent in the 1990s—much slower than the 5.4 percent yearly growth rate in the 1960s when they practiced trade protectionism.

How has a protectionist America fared in the past? According to Pat Buchanan, real wages in America rose 53 percent in the protectionist era between 1869 and 1900. Commodity prices decreased 58 percent. Our Gross National Product quadrupled, and our national debt was reduced by 66 percent. And by what means did we collect over 50 percent of our national revenue? Import tariffs!

Yet there are still those like conservative economist Daniel Mitchell of the Heritage Foundation, who in March 2005 complained about the perceived protectionist stance of Lou Dobbs, saying, "There has never been an example in global history where protectionism worked, period." Also in 2005, Morgan Stanley economist Any Xie said, "For trade-oriented economies, bilateral protectionism decreases competitiveness and simply won't work over time." When you start hearing more and more ignorant-of-history comments like these, you know we are in the "last throes of the free trade insurgency."

THE END (OF FREE TRADE) IS NEAR

Not only do I believe that the policy of free trade is nearing its end, but it is only a matter of time until America enters another era of protectionism. More and more Americans are questioning the so-called benefits of what is known today as free trade. As more and more American workers perceive that they are losers in a free market economy, the public's willingness to support more globalization and cutthroat competition will evaporate. Soon after that, the political will to defend free trade will die, and free trade itself will die. It cannot be long before some version of protectionism is once again implemented in the U.S. because American workers will not forever tolerate declining living standards or the loss of health care or retirement protections. Allow me to explain why.

When NAFTA was being debated in the early 1990s, we were told that a high-tech workforce would replace manufacturing jobs that we supposedly did not want and shouldn't want. As I mentioned in the first chapter, it was the "we think, they sweat" mindset. But it must be realized that we cannot give away our manufacturing industries to other countries and let American companies buy complete designs from foreign developers and slap American brand names on them like Dell and Motorola have. After all, there is an industry term for companies that sell products designed and manufactured by others. They're known as "retailers."

But what are these high-tech jobs that are supposed to replace the old manufacturing jobs? According to a July 16, 2007, *Associated Press* article, the United States has now imported $102 billion worth of high-technology products, including computers and other high-tech components, than it exported, mostly from China. But according to free trade advocates, the millions of jobs lost to free trade were supposed to be converted into jobs in the computer industry.

And how can we be sure newly created jobs have any staying power? America's eight-decade dominance as a major chemical exporter ended in 2003, when a 1997 $19 billion trade surplus became a $9.6 billion trade deficit, as indicated by the American Chemistry Council. One hundred and twenty new chemical plants are currently being built worldwide, and only one of those is being built in the United States. Fifty are being built in China. It is obvious that an even higher trade deficit is on the way.

So can free trade really be counted upon to promote and create jobs for the United States? Not according to Alan Greenspan, who once said, "We often try to promote free trade on the mistaken ground, in my judgment, that it will create jobs." But unfortunately when the free traders' facts don't fit free traders' promises, they simply rearrange the facts and make different promises. Let's recall what British economist John Maynard Keynes' comment was when he was asked about why he changed a previously stated position. He replied, "Sir, the facts have changed, and when the facts change, I change. What do you do, sir?"

But American trade barriers certainly can add jobs in the United States. In 2005, Federal Reserve data showed that output at U.S. textile plants actually increased for the first time in ten years after the U.S. put limits on certain Chinese imports. When factory output increases, it is usually accompanied by more work for existing employees, more new hires at the factory, or both. Either way, more American workers benefit.

Apparently a majority of Americans don't believe that the lower prices free trade may bring are necessarily a good thing. A poll taken on Lou Dobbs' program asked viewers whether they approved of lower prices in America if the result is more unemployment. Seventy-two percent said "no."

Americans displayed their rising protectionist sentiment when they overwhelmingly disapproved of the United Arab Emirates-based Dubai Ports World taking over operational control of a number of U.S. ports. The knee-jerk argument of free traders, of course, was that it would stifle investment in America, cause other countries to retaliate and erect their own barriers to trade and investment, and slow global economic growth. Of course, none of this happened.

THE LAST ONES TO KNOW

Free market advocates always try to make us believe that they can put themselves in the shoes of the people of other countries and tell us what they surely must be thinking of our actions. But they're dead wrong in thinking this is possible.

Despite the uproar in the United States, the attitude of other countries was mostly that it was really no big deal. The London-based Arab-language newspaper, *Asharq Alawsat*, which is available throughout the Middle East, never considered the issue important enough for the front page, although it did run the story most days when the event was current. Editor-in-Chief Tariq Alhomayed explained, "It's not a crisis. It's a debate."

The Dubai-based *Gulf News* wrote that Americans didn't like the idea of "cherished institutions" being in control of "foreigners of any persuasion" and that "it must be realized that Americans, in general, are protectionist by nature." If the Middle East recognizes a protectionist America, maybe it's time we recognize it ourselves.

In a recent issue of *Foreign Affairs* magazine, economist Mark Slaughter, who was recently a member of President Bush's Council of Economic Advisers, and Yale political scientist Kenneth Scheve, wrote, "Policy has become more protectionist because the public is becoming more protectionist. And the public is becoming more protectionist because incomes are stagnating or falling."

Former U.S. Treasury secretary and former Harvard president Lawrence Summers recently commented that the gap that is widening between the winners and losers in the economy is "entirely without precedent in the postwar period."

The popular refrain from the Bush camp and other free traders is more education. Education is no quick fix for current problems and can take generations to bring about a significant payoff. According to economist Mark Slaughter, for the percentage of Americans who have college degrees to rise from 6 percent to 30 percent has taken 60 years. All too often, the education solution only provides rhetorical support. For the progress that can be made to prepare Americans for the good-paying jobs of the future, recent history has shown more education is embarrassingly inadequate.

Professor John Russo of Youngstown State University in Youngstown, Ohio says he can no longer tell his students in good faith that getting an MBA or a degree in engineering will be enough to guarantee that they'll have more affluent lives than their parents. He worries that only by accepting a lower standard of living will we be able to compete.

Stephen Roach, chief economist for the investment banking concern Morgan Stanley, says that to finance our huge budget deficit, which he describes as "consumption supported by foreign lending," America has to borrow $2.6 billion every day, which represents 80 percent of the world's entire net savings. Is that sustainable in the long term? Of course not. When the global economy is this lopsided, something will inevitably happen to make it balanced. Harvard economist Gregory Mankiw, former chief economist for the George W. Bush White House, thinks we will come into balance without too much of an economic shock, but he admits that America's continued dependence on foreigners to lend us so much money every single day suggests that America's future will be less prosperous.

THE TIDE IS RISING.
WHERE ARE ALL THE FLOATING BOATS?

So it is no secret that America has a huge savings problem, and I have often wondered if we are to believe free traders when they tell us about how the economy is in such good shape and that if we are unable to save now when we are experiencing a flood of cheaper imports, when will we ever be able to save? Back when President Reagan was in office and we had mortgage interest rates at 14 percent, we still had an average household savings rate of 10 percent throughout the 1980s.

A low savings rate means we depend upon borrowing from foreign investors for consumption and investment. And this foreign dependence can easily turn into vulnerability if foreign investors begin to be concerned about the creditworthiness of the United States. But until then, as the saying goes, there's always MasterCard.

Economist Stephen Roach isn't alone in his bearish attitude about today's economy. A new study as reported by the *Wall Street Journal* on May 25, 2007, showed that America's productivity nearly doubled between 1947 and 1974. Between 1974 and 2000, productivity increased 56 percent while income increased 29 percent. Between 2000 and 2005, productivity increased 16 percent while income decreased 2 percent. This, of course, challenges the favorite refrain of free traders that "a rising tide will lift all boats," according to the study. This conventional wisdom, according to David Audretsch, director of the Max Planck Institute for Economics in Germany, is overly optimistic. And in my opinion, the fear of protectionism is overly pessimistic.

Increased competition is supposed to make us more productive, and this can be true—to a point. But once we cross the line into excessive or cutthroat competition, things begin to change. Unrestricted and unregulated competition becomes a competition that the United States is unable to win.

But America is not the only country to protect its own national champion industries. Economic patriotism is not a new phenomenon in Europe either. France chased away Pepsi when it was rumored to be targeting French-owned Dannon for a takeover. Madrid thwarted a German buyout of one of Spain's energy companies, and Poland blocked a takeover by an Italian bank. But America's rejection of a foreign-owned company bidding for her ports is much more about national security than any of these other examples. But Americans should know that we cannot trade economic and national security for freedom, and we cannot trade ownership of our industries for prosperity.

It is only a matter of time before America becomes a majority protectionist nation once again. Far from the days of NAFTA when a mere 25 percent of America's working population stood to be negatively affected, we will eventually get to a point where that percentage is over 50 percent of the population. When it is (and people realize what is happening and what is doing it to them), people will rise up or band together one way or another and demand protection for American industry. Let's just hope we still have a significant amount of industry left to protect. Those hurt by globalization are not going to continue to "take one for the team" forever.

Again, this is not some type of isolationist protectionism but a simple policy that stops discriminating against domestic producers. With free trade, other countries pay substantially fewer taxes to do business in the United States than our own producers. A quick analysis of most domestic companies will reveal that federal and state withholding taxes as well as corporate income taxes equal 30 percent of company or corporate sales. Yet if we imported the same exact products from China that domestic producers are making and selling here, our U.S. Treasury would collect an average of 3 percent of the sale of such goods in the form of an import tariff.

It's ridiculous that we collect only 3 percent from foreign countries so they can benefit from our legal system, commercial codes, and other privileges of participating in our economic system, and we have the audacity to require our own companies to pay ten times as much for the privilege of using the same system! Yet an attempt to make the system equal and fair for all players is labeled "protectionism" and promptly rejected.

BRINGING IT HOME

Profits are the lifeblood of any successful capitalist economy, and when we allow too much competition, especially in the form of too many foreign imports, existing American businesses may see their profits drop dramatically. This does not necessarily happen because these domestic operations are mismanaging their companies or doing anything wrong or destructive to the business climate. It may simply be because every competitor in a given industry takes their slice of the pie, and there are only so many slices to go around from the same pie. With more and more competitors, the size of the slices, and therefore the profits, become smaller and smaller. Economics teaches that as too many competitors enter into a given competition, the situation has a way of working itself out as some of the competitors exit the competition because they can't win. But in today's excessively competitive global economy, the competitors likely to exit will be the ones producing in the United States.

Local and state governments suffer from manufacturing job losses as well. A local manufacturer that is forced to close its doors is many times the largest taxpayer in the community. A declining local tax base ultimately results in higher taxes on local citizens to cover the lost tax revenue of the manufacturer so as to avoid cuts in popular services we take for granted, like public schools and libraries, firefighters, and police officers.

Competition can be a good thing, but we only need so much of it. America, as big and diverse as it is, has enough competition within its economy to keep our American companies on their toes in most sectors. If we do not have enough American competition within our domestic economy, we have much bigger problems than we realize, which likely exist because we have gone from an era of friendly, inspiring, motivating competition to cutthroat competition. And since the lower-cost foreign competition will be the likely winner, it is our throats that end up getting cut.

Cutthroat competition from imports can drastically lower output and sales from domestic factories, drastically reducing local, state, and federal tax collections. Tariffs are needed to restore the lost revenues in the short run and to preserve our existing tax base as well as restore domestic manufacturing capacity in the long run. We have to look into the future and wonder what will happen to our tax base if we continue to lose tax-generating manufacturing operations.

We are not even doing a good job collecting the tariff revenue we are supposed to be collecting. In 2004, a group of crawfish processors from Louisiana had to resort to filing a lawsuit to get the U.S. Customs and Border Protection (CBP) to release information on over $250 million in duties they failed to collect since fiscal year 2003.

Documents released in 2005 by CBP under the Freedom of Information Act showed that they received $33 million worth of fake bonds to guarantee anti-dumping duties on Chinese imports, meaning the money is likely to never be collected. The CBP received these fraudulent bonds from ten importers and as of this year was still struggling to collect duties from them.

According to the U.S. Chamber of Commerce, American companies get cheated out of $250 billion a year from (mostly Chinese) pirated goods. U.S. Immigration and Customs Enforcement (ICE) agents and U.S. Customs and Border Protection officials seized 7,255 counterfeit goods in 2004, adding to the over $600 million in counterfeit goods seized between 1998 and 2004.

The intellectual property alliance has said that international digital piracy represents a cost to America's copyright industry of up to $22 billion every year, not including illegal Internet downloads.

Trademarks, copyrights, patents, and other intellectual property protections are of no use if our government does not enforce them due to the absence of adequate funding or otherwise.

In a *Business Week* review of the book *Illicit*, which discusses the pirating of global trade, illegal trade is nothing new, but if left unchecked compromises effective law and order, leads to other crimes and violence, and finances terrorism.

It seems that the quote from Sam Ewing is correct. "The government deficit is the difference between the amount of money the government spends and the amount it has the nerve to collect."

On Wednesday, May 9, 2007, almost three months before the August 1, 2007, collapse of the I-35W Bridge in Minneapolis, Minnesota, the *Wall Street Journal* reported on an eye-opening report entitled "Infrastructure 2007: A Global Perspective." The report argues that there is an emerging mobility crisis that, if left unaddressed, will diminish America's ability to compete internationally. How so? Roads, rail, airport, *bridges*, and other forms of transit infrastructure are gradually deteriorating across the country. Why? Because of inadequate investment. And why do our investments in our nation's infrastructure seem insufficient? Because we are a debtor nation. We spend more than we earn. How does a country become richer by spending more than it earns, anyway? We consume more than we make. We import more than we export. We avoid buying American and supporting workers that pay tax revenue to the U.S. Treasury in favor of foreign workers that do not. Why? It is supposed to be cheaper, or so we thought.

We not only allow our manufacturing base to shrink and erode, we seem to demand that it continue to happen and firmly defend the free market, free trade thinking that says it must and should continue, and we would be better off if it did. The longer we adhere to the unrealistic promises of a free market, the more we will be immersed in a debt market. Any attempt to balance a known unsustainable economic policy is, you guessed it, labeled protectionism and rejected. As long as we are foolish enough to finance the industrialization of other countries by leaving our doors wide open to their exports and exercise perpetual patience in asking them to dismantle trade barriers to our exports, then our tax base, and our ability to finance national infrastructure, will continue to diminish.

Maybe protective and revenue-generating tariffs would be more acceptable if we referred to them as "user fees" for the privilege of using and maintaining our infrastructure. We certainly cannot continue to maintain our current legal, social, and economic institutions with tax-base destroying free market policies. We learned a long time ago there was a lot of truth in the theory that says there is no such thing as a free lunch. It is time we stopped trying to disprove it.

So what are some of the specific infrastructure needs, and how much are they going to cost us? Six billion dollars to repair Chicago subways. Fourteen point five billion dollars to repair or replace New York's Tappan Zee Bridge. If the only thing we maintain in Atlanta is the status quo, drive time during rush hour (which in most big cities is much longer than just an "hour") could increase 75 percent by the year 2030. How's that for sapping productivity, wasting gasoline, polluting the environment, reducing quality time with our families, cutting into our social lives, and general aggravation (not necessarily involving road rage)?

Back in 2005, a report from the American Society of Civil Engineers rated the condition of our country's transit infrastructure, as well as drinking water and wastewater systems, dams, and power grids, as "poor." Add it all up, and the United States of America has a $1.6 trillion deficit in necessary infrastructure spending for maintenance and repairs between now and 2010. Where is all that money going to come from? Not from the millions of toy makers in China who don't pay a dime in taxes to the United States. Now more than ever, we need to bring it home to the United States, or home will never be the same.

Ah, but free traders respond by telling us that if we continue to "engage" China, capitalism will ultimately trump communism, and a democratic China will be good for the global economy and global stability. Maybe we need to pay closer attention to what China's self-professed intentions are. In February 2007, Chinese Premier Wen Jiabao declared that the Communist Party would (not *might*) "unswervingly adhere" to its current course for the next century. He made promises of economic development but no promises of democracy. It is time to stop pandering to China, letting them have their way, enduring their threats to America, and end this game of "Do you like us yet?" When push comes to shove and vital American interests are at stake, we are not going to be able to remind China of all the times we let them have their way in the interest of Sino-U.S. relations and reason that they should support us on this one because of all the times we were nice and cordial to them. Beijing is not going to let us cash in on any perceived popularity points.

A July 23, 2007, *Business Week* article claimed that we may not realize that several buildings on our country's campuses are crumbling due to old age and poor maintenance. Terry W. Ruprecht, director of energy conservation at the University of Illinois at Urbana-Champaign, says dollars are being used for new facilities and not older ones, making an existing problem even worse. Over half of the U.S. campus buildings were erected in the 1960s and 1970s, so most are now at least 40 years old. Many are in need of repair.

A conservative estimate says that the nationwide college campus repair bill might reach $40 billion. Students and their parents are likely to pay the bill, particularly at state schools, which have tighter funding. So is free trade, which causes outsourcing of production to workers in foreign countries who don't pay taxes, really the cheaper way out? Or should we keep production here, where we are able to collect tax revenue, and be able to pay for the things we used to take for granted?

It is doubtful that the most ardent of free trade economists, who have dedicated their professional lives to ridiculing import tariffs as a valuable tool to raise revenue, will ever see the fallacy of their theories. Yet they still are not able to resolve what's happening in the real economy with the theories they have defended so passionately. But in the end, it is the good-paying jobs and the American middle-class that need to be protected, not economic textbook theory.

Competition must be regulated for it to be beneficial for the United States. America must abandon free market policies and apply proper import tariffs to equalize production-cost burdens. When this happens and the playing field is truly level and trade is truly fair, America will rediscover two things that our founding fathers knew. Protectionism equals prosperity, and free trade equals failure.

"The key to productivity? It's Fred, down
in the shop. He makes stuff."

Chapter 15

Auto Explanations

The automotive industry is one of the most recent (and most important) American industries that is in danger of extinction. Because the survival of this industry is so vital to our country, I was motivated to devote an entire chapter to it. Since I have been writing articles about the struggles of the American auto industry since 2005 in the form of e-mails and eventually a newsletter entitled *Auto Explanations*, I decided that composing this chapter with these articles would give the reader a chronological account of the events and issues surrounding the automotive industry since that time.

The reader should keep in mind that because these articles were not originally intended to be part of the book you are holding, there are some quotes and arguments you will find in Chapters 1 and 14 as well as this chapter.

I will continue to write more *Auto Explanations* articles in the future, and these future articles may be viewed on my website at www.howto-buyamerican.com. You may also subscribe to my Buy American e-mail list and receive these articles automatically as they are written, usually every other month.

In Defense Of General Motors
May 7, 2005

Defense, defense, defense. That's all that General Motors, and Detroit in general, can play these days. Many American car and truck buyers, and many of those in the media who write about their buying habits, should know better than to spew their venom at GM for their recent financial troubles. It might be different if the reasons that GM continues to lose market share weren't largely beyond their control, but they are. As an increasing number of Americans spend their money on and drive around in Toyotas and Hondas, the answer to the question "Why doesn't GM have the money to build a car more to my liking?" seems to evade them.

As if the impending health care crisis in America was no clue at all, some even bring up the fact that GM spends over $1,500 per automobile just to provide health care to their employees, retirees, and their dependents. By comparison, Toyota and Honda spend only a few hundred dollars per automobile, mainly because GM has been operating in the United States since the invention of the automobile, and Toyota, for instance, only built their first plant here in 1987. Yet they still say that GM is "living in the past" even though Cadillac now outsells Mercedes, The Chevy Impala beat the Toyota Camry in initial quality, and *Consumer Reports* detailed how Buick now beats BMW in reliability.

But in these times where low-wage Wal-Mart has now replaced high-wage General Motors as the number one employer in the U.S., most Americans get a pass for not having the time to dig deeply enough to understand what is really going on since a large portion of America is working longer hours for lower wages and is just trying to put in enough time at work to make ends meet.

It may seem that your car-buying decision would have no effect on your personal prosperity or that of your country, but it does. It really does matter if you buy an American-made Chevrolet instead of an American-made Toyota.

When you buy an American-made Chevy, you not only support more American workers, you also support American investors, owners, and stockholders. When you buy an American-made Toyota, you may help your Uncle Bob if he's on Toyota's payroll, but you're hurting Uncle Sam since American companies pay about three times as many taxes to the U.S. Treasury as do foreign-owned companies. That's something to think about the next time you hear that we have to cut benefits or raise the retirement age simply because the U.S. Treasury doesn't have enough funds to meet its obligations to Social Security or other benefit programs. General Motors doesn't have enough money to meet its obligations, either. And it's for the very honorable reason that they have promised adequate health care and pensions to workers who gave their lives to a company that has in turn supported so many American livelihoods for so long. If we stop buying GM products, we de-fund American retirees and prevent them from contributing to the American economy. Sure, you have a choice in buying a foreign car over an American one, but if you buy the foreign car, you will likely cause a retiree to make a choice between food and medicine. That very choice is a daily one for many senior citizens in this country right now.

Think it's not possible? Think again. The Pension Benefit Guaranty Corporation (PBGC) has already taken over several pensions from failed American companies in the steel and airline industries and beyond. When these companies declare bankruptcy and fail to meet their obligations, this government-funded agency, which is also running in the red, takes over and gives seniors roughly half of what they were promised by the now-bankrupt company.

This results in a hidden cost to taxpayers since any shortfall in government revenue must be made up eventually in higher taxes or benefit cuts or both. So there you have it. Failure to find a GM (or other American) automobile you can stand will negatively affect your standard of living in one way or another. And you thought that since you didn't work in the car industry it didn't affect you. Think again.

The *Detroit News* recently published the facts, daring to go against the deceiving "foreign cars are built there, and American cars are built there" rhetoric that implies it makes no difference if you buy an American-made Honda instead of an American-made Pontiac. The newspaper reported that American and foreign automakers alike were playing the "Made in USA" card to attract buyers. And you thought consumers didn't care. Poll after poll has shown Americans are willing to pay more to buy American, even when quality and price are similar or equal to foreign automobiles. Most Americans advocate fair play and equality, but eventually they will find out, possibly the hard way, that neither of these attributes apply in the automobile marketplace unless those Americans who should know better start buying American cars again. I'm not asking or expecting the die-hard import buyer crowd to stop their silly griping and buy American. GM's future doesn't depend on them. It depends on those Americans who really should know better.

As the *Detroit News* article boldly pointed out, GM has 82 major plants in the United States, while Toyota, Honda, and Nissan combined have only 24. GM has more American salaried workers than Toyota has total American workers. With 194,000 employees in America, even after hard times, General Motors still employs six times as many Americans as Toyota, seven times as many as Honda, and twelve times as many as Nissan. As *Business Week* pointed out in 2002 (the last data I have seen on the subject), each auto-assembly job created by an American company also creates 6.9 other American jobs, where each auto-assembly job created by a foreign company creates only 5.5 other American jobs. This is true simply because American automobile companies get more of their parts from America.

And what about those foreign transplant factories? A 1995 United Auto Workers study concluded that these foreign automobile companies operating in the United States caused at least 500,000 Americans to lose their jobs. I would hate to think of what that total is today.

The new May 9, 2005, issue of *Business Week* details how GM contributes to the pockets of their assembly workers to the tune of $8.7 billion a year and either directly or indirectly supports the employment of 900,000 Americans. *Business Week* also claims it is "undeniable" that what is bad for GM is bad for America, pointing to a 54-day strike in 1998 that cut that quarter's economic growth for the entire country a whole percentage point.

Many point to bad management decisions in the past to justify their reasoning for not supporting GM, claiming it is "widely known" that they made horrible cars in the 1970s. It's amazing that people who weren't even of driving age in the 1970s (this author wasn't) want to penalize GM for mismanagement as they overlook any mismanagement by other car companies they anxiously spend their money with instead. I have never heard anyone vehemently refuse to buy a Nissan since they almost went bankrupt in the late 1990s. Nor do I hear people planning to penalize Japanese car makers for the (widely known) junk they imported in the 1960s.

In 1999, the *Wall Street Journal* reported that Nissan lost millions of dollars in five of the last six years. Nissan's debt stood between $22 billion and $30 billion, which dwarfed that of any other auto maker. The *Wall Street Journal*, which is no huge supporter of GM, claimed that Nissan would be bankrupt if it happened to be an American company.

The claim that GM made inferior cars in the 1970s is suspect to me, anyway, not because of my patriotic motivation, but because of my personal experience. The 1976 Buick Riviera I owned was outstanding as far as quality and longevity was concerned, and 1976 is right in the middle of the supposed quality-challenged decade for American cars. An *Auto Week* magazine article even call it a "boat with no tail" in a piece they did about the history of the Riviera.

Shortly after the car passed 200,000 miles, I drove it from Florida to Illinois and back to demonstrate to some skeptical friends that the car would make it up, down, and through the Smokey Mountains of Tennessee just fine, as I was getting my own share of comments about how terrible American cars supposedly were. The car had over 250,000 miles before I had it hauled off to the junkyard, but not before a co-worker bought the engine for his airboat. The engine was so quiet that no one knew (by listening) that I warmed it up for five or ten minutes before I drove home from work as my co-workers walked past it in the parking lot to get into their own cars to drive home. People would walk by my '76 Riviera, stop for a second, and ask me, "Is that car running?" The body had rusted out by the late 1990s, but the car never had the advantage of a garage to protect it from the Florida sun and the Atlantic Ocean's salty air.

General Motors spent $5.2 billion on health care for their workers and retirees in 2004. The 2005 figure will be higher. The figure for Toyota, for instance, is certainly less since they didn't build their first American factory until 1987. The Georgetown, Kentucky factory, which assembles the Toyota Camry, was built with Japanese steel by a Japanese steel company. Toyota was given 1,500 acres of free land. To attract this Japanese company to America, we even established a "special trade zone" so they could import parts duty-free from Japan. Financing was handled by Mitsui Bank of Japan. Total federal, state, and local tax incentives (read giveaways) reached $100 million—courtesy of your tax dollars and mine. These are some of the hidden costs few think about when selecting their next car. Before the first Toyota in America was ever assembled, the American steel industry, parts industry, and finance industry took it on the chin. American tax obligations were also raised. Today's Camry has a 55 percent domestic parts content, which is down from 75 percent just a few years ago. American alternatives like the Chevy Impala have a 98 percent domestic parts content, and the aging Ford Taurus, which used to be the number one selling car in America before the Camry took the top spot, has a 95 percent domestic parts content.

In the end, it doesn't matter how you slice it. General Motors pays more taxes; employs more workers; has more domestic plants; supports more families, retirees, and their dependents; and has a higher overall domestic parts content than the foreign competition—hands down. American quality is on the rise. Efficiency has increased. GM kept America rolling by donating millions of dollars in cash and vehicles in the aftermath of September 11, 2001. Where was the foreign competition in America's time of need? They were busy reeling in record profits and sending them home to reward foreign owners at the expense of an American company that built the foundation of prosperity that America as a whole enjoys.

Profits are the lifeblood of any successful company or economy. General Motors makes only a few hundred dollars of profit per vehicle compared to over a thousand dollars for their foreign rivals because GM supports such a wide and diverse number of Americans. They've shown their loyalty to America by extending zero percent financing for several years, and through their history they've done more good for America than any foreign car company ever dreamed of doing. It's time for America to show its loyalty to an American company whose increased prosperity will result in greater American prosperity as well.

So if you want General Motors to be more aggressive and on the offensive in terms of marketing and bolder car designs, among other things, stop spewing your venom at them, which makes them constantly play defense instead. It's unfair, unwarranted, and unproductive. GM wants to keep America rolling, as we all should, so let's let it and help make it happen.

De-Junking The American Auto Industry
June 4, 2005

Since the writing of the May 2005 article "In Defense of General Motors," I have received several responses regarding several of the points made in that article. These responses, along with the subsequent announcement that Standard & Poor's Corp., downgraded both General Motors and Ford to junk status, have proven useful in determining the issues that should be addressed in my future articles related to the automotive industry.

General Motors was the primary focus of the May 2005 article since they were perceived to be in worse financial shape than Ford, although it is certainly vital that both of the two remaining American-based automakers survive and prosper.

The majority of the responses were positive and supportive. Of the negative responses, most of the points made were arguments already diffused and disproved as baseless in the article itself. This only reinforced my belief that most Buy American opponents only read what they agree with and conveniently skip over that with which they disagree—even as, and especially when, their positions are being invalidated.

Some foreign car lovers proclaimed that they would only start to buy American when GM decided to build high-quality cars. Setting aside for a minute the fact that various quality surveys prove they already do, the point I made already was this. Since GM is saddled with at least a $1,000 per automobile cost disadvantage to pay for honorable obligations like pensions and health care for thousands of Americans, that is why they have at least $1,000 less (per automobile) to spend on snazzier dashboards and other creature comforts.

These Buy American bashers are decidedly off base in claiming that GM and Ford don't make cars that Americans want since both companies have higher market shares than their closest foreign rival. General Motors, for instance, has over twice the market share in the U.S. than does Toyota. GM's problem is not necessarily low market share (although a return to the higher market shares of the past would surely be beneficial), but it is the lower profit margins they are able to generate in light of their honorable obligations to their current and former workers and their dependents.

The media hasn't always been forthcoming with the facts, but certain news anchors do expose the truth. On "Your World with Neil Cavuto," a program on which this author has appeared five times, Neil Cavuto promptly corrected one of his frequent guests who just couldn't resist trashing American automakers in knee-jerk fashion. When Mr. Cavuto asked Tom Adkins of www.commonconservative.com why GM and Ford were being downgraded to junk status, Mr. Adkins spewed the typical and tired old venom proclaiming that it was because American car makers only made American junk. Kudos to Neil Cavuto for pointing out some of the quality and efficiency gains American automakers have made over the years in response to such garbage.

Other tired refrains Buy American haters use include the accusation that GM and Ford have misguided objectives and have repeatedly missed the boat by concentrating on more profitable, larger vehicles rather than smaller, more efficient ones. This argument is easily diffused taking into consideration the fact that GM and Ford have merely been responding to broad consumer demand for these larger vehicles. Even as gas prices climbed into the $2.00 per gallon range in early 2005, polls taken around that time show that a majority of American consumers remained unde-terred when it came to buying bigger and badder American trucks and SUVs. The Ford F-150, for instance, has been the number one selling truck for several years. Surely even Buy American opponents (usually laissez-faire advocates) recognize and subscribe to the law of supply and demand. Are these people really suggesting that Ford not concentrate on this obvious cash cow?

The anti-Buy American argument also conveniently ignores the fact that foreign-based automakers have been aggressively accelerating their entry into the large vehicle market to compete with American dominance in this area. The 2006 Lexus 470 Luxury SUV, for instance, boasts 275 horsepower, a full 40 hp increase over the 2005 model, not to mention 12 ft. lbs. extra torque. And, of course, no one can deny the various entries of foreign automakers into the big truck and SUV markets such as the Nissan Armada, Nissan Titan, Toyota Sequoia, Toyota Tundra, and Honda Ridgeline, just to name a few. It smacks of hypocrisy to deride Ford and GM for making large American vehicles when all foreign-based automakers are scrambling to introduce even bigger models in an attempt to out-muscle them.

Ironically, within days of the "In Defense of General Motors" article, the Wall Street Journal ran a "Drive Buys" column featuring the Nissan Xterra comparing it to four other mid-size SUVs. The Chevrolet Equinox was not only the only American vehicle in the comparison (no Ford product was profiled), but it was also the least expensive and had the best mileage rating.

The point here is that when it comes to analyzing the automotive industry, hypocrisy often reigns. It would be different if Buy American naysayers had rhetoric to offer that lined up with the facts, but they normally do not. Most are stuck in the 1970s and their questionable belief (also disproved in the "In Defense of General Motors" article) that American cars were inferior then and by default continue to be today.

One "Reader's Report" submission to Business Week's May 30, 2005, issue chided GM for not investing their profits wisely enough, claiming they could have bought Honda outright for 75 percent of the money they spent creating Saturn. Such Monday morning quarterbacking overlooks the fact that Japan rarely allows foreign-based companies a majority ownership in their home-based companies. GM does own 49 percent of Isuzu, who recently announced an annual 9.7 percent net rise in profit ending March 31, 2005. The Business Week letter writer also pointed out that one

Saturn SUV is powered by a Honda engine as proof that GM has gone astray in its strategies. I wonder if he knows that some BMWs use GM-built transmissions. Let's call it a draw then, shall we?

Finally, and perhaps more importantly, many readers of the original article in defense of the U.S. auto industry cited that it was good to see a non-GM employee stick up for GM. It might be different, of course, if I worked on the factory floor of one of the several dozen Ford or GM domestic plants, but I don't. I defend American auto interests because it is in the best interests of America to do so. And even though the anti-Buy American crowd is aggressively undermining American prosperity with hypocritical and baseless views, those of us who stand for what is right for America deserve a prosperous country and should work hard to create that prosperity. That is what should keep us motivated to fight the good fight. We're all in this together, so let's make it work for all of us—together.

Destroying More Anti-American Automobile Industry Myths
July 17, 2005

The opportunities to de-bunk more of the baseless anti-American rhetoric biased against our country's two remaining American-owned automakers never cease to present themselves.

As reported in its Thursday, July 14, 2005, paper, the *Wall Street Journal* details how rising gas prices are triggering the increased production of "minicars." Before I even begin to discuss the information in this article, it must be said that a traditional anti-Detroit refrain has been that the Motor City has always been slow to respond to marketplace realities (such as high gas prices) and has always seemed to simply follow their Japanese competitors rather than set the standard. If you want to continue to believe these things and keep your head in the sand, it's best that you stop reading here.

It seems the Korean-made Chevy Aveo is the best selling economy car in the United States, ranking higher than the Toyota Scion xA, the Kia Rio, and the Hyundai Accent. I purposely mentioned that the Chevy Aveo is made outside the U.S. right up front so the Anti-American crowd could momentarily crow about how this GM car was not made in America. But as it turns out, none of their foreign minicar competitors are made in the U.S., either. American investors, owners, stockholders, and stakeholders can take comfort that they, not their foreign counterparts, will profit from a more successful General Motors, even when those cars are made elsewhere. The same cannot be said about foreign-made cars from foreign-owned companies.

The article continues and says that since Toyota, Nissan, and Honda now see the evident and supposedly unexpected American success story, they are reacting (rather than leading) to grab their slice of the American pie. Toyota is considering launching a U.S. version of the Vitz (available only in Japan) to replace the Toyota Echo. Why is Toyota sending the Echo to the exit? According to the *Wall Street Journal*, it is partly because of "stodgy styling." If the accusation of "stodgy styling" isn't the most consistently launched term aimed at the heart of Detroit over the last few decades, I don't know what is.

Both Honda and Nissan are reported to be considering U.S. versions of their own cars currently marketed only in Japan. One can only wonder what is happening here. Gone are the once seemingly credible accusations of stodgy styling and slow-to-respond mindsets that only applied to American automakers courtesy of their own people. One has to wonder to which country these Americans actually pledge their allegiance.

Another key point made in this *Wall Street Journal* article is that GM scored an "unexpected hit" with the Aveo. *Business Week* even recently devoted its cover to propagating how GM's turnaround plan won't work. Since then, the GM employees' discount plan has been launched and has resulted in the highest market share GM has experienced since the 1990s. The fact that the Chevy Aveo is made outside the U.S. should not deter any patriotic American from supporting GM, and this is not only because their foreign competitors' cars are not made in America, either. Patriotic consumers should not be geared toward only considering any American-made car. For America to truly benefit, we need to recognize that the primary consideration is ownership.

For instance, many supposedly Buy American-conscious consumers bought an American-made Camry or Corolla instead of an American-made Taurus or Bonneville. It seemingly made no difference which company got the profits as long as the assembly workers were in America. It never occurred to us that the salaried workers who designed the American cars were in America. It never occurred to us that the domestic parts content on the American cars were higher than on the Japanese cars. It never occurred to us that profits of American companies are repatriated to America, and the taxes on those profits were paid to the U.S. Treasury. Next time you are reminded how this nation is drowning in red ink, you'll hopefully realize that this is especially important.

Now that it is apparent that had we bought GM and Ford products (like the Korean-made Aveo) even when they were produced overseas, GM and Ford would have raked in the profit and might not be experiencing junk bond status or considering layoffs of thousands of American workers, putting retirees, their families, and dependents at risk of being de-funded. It's more than just about American-made. It's also about American-owned.

Toyota and Honda were certainly profitable enough to not lay off American workers even if fewer of us bought the Corolla made in California or a Honda made in Ohio. Japanese automakers have to keep a factory presence in the United States to be able to play the "made in USA" card, even though it is a fraction of the factory presence American automakers have always had. This likely means that buying an American-made Bonneville instead of any American-made Japanese car would have likely not led to layoffs of American workers of foreign companies but could have prevented planned layoffs of American workers from the Big Two.

Just like buying New Balance shoes made in Indonesia (New Balance makes 30 percent of their shoes in the U.S.) is better than buying Nike shoes made in Indonesia (Nike makes none of their shoes in the U.S.), it's better to buy a foreign-made GM instead of a foreign-made Toyota. General Motors has 82 major plants in the United States—over three times more than Toyota, Honda, and Nissan combined. It is unrealistic to expect GM or Ford to remain as profitable as their competitors with so many factories in high-wage America when Toyota imports more of their cars and parts from low-wage Asia. If New Balance were to announce tomorrow that they were moving their plants offshore (along with Nike, Reebok, and Adidas), would it be corporate greed or because their labor costs were higher since they employ more Americans? It would be unfair and unjust to direct our anger at New Balance. And it is also unfair to direct our anger at GM for closing some factories in the U.S. What are we really revealing that we are angry about? That GM employed too many Americans for too long? Too many of us want GM to be loyal to America while too few Americans care about showing any loyalty to GM. It has to work both ways, folks. No American can rightfully complain that GM is not doing right by America while they drive behind the steering wheel of a foreign car. Let's be Americans and not hypocrites.

Friedrich List, a now-deceased German economist, once said, "The power of producing wealth is...infinitely more important than wealth itself." And by supporting American companies, America retains the power to create wealth. American companies are more subject to American laws and more influenced by American pleas for corporate responsibility. American presidents can, as both President Clinton and Bush have, stress corporate responsibility in America, but foreign companies need not listen. Why? Foreign companies owe no loyalty to America, and when faced with the option to side with their home country or their American subsidiary, nationalism and self-interest will dictate that they side with their home country. Americans must understand that nationalism is not an American phenomenon but is also alive and well in several countries around the globe, as it should be.

The importance of America's power to create wealth is manifested in the recent bid by Chinese-controlled CNOOC to buy American-based Unocal. If the deal goes through to allow a Chinese company (which is 70 percent owned and controlled by the Communist Chinese government) to buy Unocal instead of allowing American-owned Chevron to do so (which stopped exporting oil to Iran at the request of corporate responsibility pleas from the American government), America will have lost the power to create wealth. Sure, some Americans would profit from the sale to the Chinese company, but it would be a net loss for the nation.

The importance of America's power to create wealth is also manifested in Chinese-owned Haier's bid to buy out Maytag. See the now prophetic Buy American Mention of the Week from February 14, 2005, entitled "To Boycott or Not to Boycott Maytag". Had we not penalized Maytag for moving one refrigerator plant to Mexico when 96 percent of its workers were in America and its American competitors' percentage of American workers was even less, they might not be suffering from a lack of profits and might not be susceptible to a Chinese takeover. Again, the ownership of the company is the primary concern.

It is further blatantly hypocritical to be in favor of free trade with China while they practice protectionism at home and then be against China investing in America to buy American assets like Unocal and Maytag. China is merely finding a use for all those American dollars we sent to them in exchange for all those cheaply made goods. We have to realize that China is using our money to buy our companies. That money used to be ours! But we sent it to China thinking we were getting a good deal on cheap products. I am against foreign investment in America, by Chinese companies in particular, probably more than anyone, but I only point out the hypocrisy in the stance of free traders. How can one be for certain policies but against the resulting affects from those same policies? Have we placed our heads that deeply in the sand?

Focusing on just how cheaply we can find consumer products is ruining America. The "cheap" mindset has invaded our culture and seems to have taken a permanent place in the American way of life. How sad. President William McKinley had a few things to say about the word "cheap." He said, "I do not prize the word 'cheap.' It is not a badge of honor. It is a symbol of despair. Cheap prices make for cheap goods, cheap goods make for cheap men, and cheap men make for a cheap country."

It is unfortunate that within our government, hypocrisy often reigns. This does not mean that we should abandon the hope that a properly run government can offer but that we should band together to reform it and make it better. In the meantime, however, we need to band together to

Buy American in the purest sense of the term. That means buying American-made products from American-owned companies whenever possible and even supporting American companies when some of their products are made overseas because their foreign-based competitors usually have an even greater percentage of their products made overseas. The beauty of a Buy American strategy is that while we are telling our legislators how we feel and electing them or ejecting them as appropriate, we can use the influence of our pocketbook all the while.

We as consumers have the power to steer the global economy in a direction that best benefits the United States of America. Let's use it.

Media Bias Against American Automakers
August 28, 2005

In my June 2005 auto-industry article entitled "De-junking the American Automobile Industry," I reported that "the media hasn't always been forthcoming with the facts" when they compare home team players GM and Ford against their foreign competition.

Fortunately, Editorial Director, Mark Bilek, for *Consumer Guide Automotive* not only saw the obvious but was bold enough to report on it. He says the second most popular question he is asked is "When will domestic cars ever catch up with Japanese quality?" The problem with questions like this is that they are no longer thoughtful but have solidified as an eternal system of belief. Even though the Chevy Impala beats the Toyota Camry in initial quality, the Buick LeSabre was awarded the best premium mid-size car, and the Ford Thunderbird was ranked the most dependable entry luxury car, it never seems to matter. And according to the J.D. Power Associates 2005 Vehicle Dependability Study, which focused on three-year-old vehicles, GM and Ford finished first in most areas. It turns out Ford and GM captured record high awards with Chevrolet earning the coveted top spot in no less than seven segments.

But foreign car defenders cannot be counted on to wake up and face reality anytime soon. They tend to store canned, decades-old quotes in their heads and spit them out at a moments notice like a cassette player

(or maybe an eight-track player since it appears to be one continuous loop.)

I say this because the first reader comment to Mr. Bilek's column resorts to meaningless and derogatory jokes we have all heard before, like the one about each letter in FORD standing for "fix-or-repair-daily" claiming they "break down every 15 miles." Is this all foreign car lovers have got before the truth is known far and wide? Is their strategy now funniness over facts? I wonder if the reader ever heard the one about NISSAN standing for "neatly-installed-steel-sheetmetal-around-nothing" or TOYOTA standing for "two-old-Yamahas-on-thin-aluminum?"

But seriously, it would be a disservice to not reveal Mr. Bilek's answer to the most popular question asked of him, which is, "What's the best car you've ever driven?" His answer was the Ford Five Hundred.

The *Consumer Guide Automotive* article also points out what many pro-American enthusiasts have believed for years. Car critics hold American cars to a higher standard and over-scrutinize their details. Then, when flaws inevitably appear as they always will in foreign and domestics alike, it is the domestic that gets the "poor quality" label.

Case in point is the recent comparison of the Ford Freestar to the Honda Odyssey by the very outfit for which Mr. Bilek works. The Ford Freestar and the Mercury Monterey are criticized by claims that their "cabins abound with budget-grade plastic" while ignoring that the only places you'll find padding in the Odyssey are the seats, carpet, and headliner. Mr. Bilek claims that the Freestar has no less plastic and even has a padded dashboard and door panels, which the Odyssey does not. The Ford also has more soft-touch surfaces. But it is the Odyssey that gets the "top notch" label for assembly.

Even when foreign and American cars have similar problems, foreign automakers often get a free pass, catering to the misleading but popular belief that foreign cars are superior by default. When GM's V6 had intake manifold problems and Honda's V6 had transmission problems, the media crucified GM and hardly mentioned Honda. Personally, I'll take an intake manifold defect over a transmission problem any day.

We as Americans should be careful in supporting foreign firms whose primary loyalties are likely to lie outside the U.S. Ford, for instance, is scrambling to replace current, longtime suppliers (which are affiliated with Honda and Toyota of Japan) with domestic suppliers. It seems Ford wants to increase threefold its hybrid SUV lineup over the next three years, but Aisin-Seiko Co. Ltd., in which Toyota has a minority shareholder stake, will only increase transmission output by 20 percent. If you are of the opinion that Toyota is the leader in hybrid technology, situations like this may reveal why American companies aren't even if they want to be.

But little-known information may show that giving Japanese automakers the leadership nameplate in hybrid technology could be misleading. Few people realize that General Motors has delivered hundreds of hybrid public transportation buses to 23 cities across the U.S. since 2003, which offer fuel economy improvements of up to 55 percent over conventional buses. If you still consider Toyota the hybrid leader, consider a statement made by the company regarding their Prius automobile. In describing how the Toyota Prius can offer a 40 percent improvement in fuel economy, they are quick to mention it is about the same improvement found in General Motors hybrid buses. Now which vehicle has the potential to save more on fuel? A gas-guzzling, mass-transit bus or an already reasonably fuel-efficient compact car? But, of course, the everyday consumer is more familiar with the everyday car than a municipal bus. Hence, it's easier to declare Toyota the visible hybrid leader by the media. Americans should applaud Ford for turning to American suppliers to maintain its independence. Ford is employing other American partners for its Fusion and Milan hybrids for 2008 by switching from Japanese-owned Sanyo to American-owned (and financially struggling) Delphi Corp., for battery orders.

Of course, it's easier for American consumers to switch from foreign "suppliers" to reclaim their self-sufficiency and independence than it is for a large American corporation like Ford, but the blue-oval guys are doing it. The more we can all switch to domestic "suppliers" of our own, from basic household goods to big-ticket items like automobiles, the more production, expertise, and innovation capacity will remain within our borders, and the more we can retain control over our own destiny as producers, a country, an economy, and a united people.

The Japanese Dream
October 13, 2005

The chief economist of General Motors, Mustafa Mohatarem, testified before the U.S. House of Representatives on September 30, 2005, accusing Japan of a trade policy that discriminates against American products, automobiles in particular. The silence of the response from Japan was deafening. Even worse was the silent response from our own government. All Representative Bill Thomas, chairman of the House Ways and Means Committee, could do was rant about Japan's protectionist policies. I guess we have to blame somebody for our huge trade deficit. And the fact that we have to blame someone else is evidence that our elected representatives who form and influence U.S. trade policy really believe it's beyond our control, and there is absolutely nothing we can do. So much for founding American virtues such as independence, self-reliance, and self-sufficiency, as well as controlling our own destiny.

But talk is cheap, and all the U.S. government laissez-faire lip service providers like Representative Thomas can do is whine and warn us about the problems of not getting the desired access to overseas markets. Soon after that, they proclaim once again that we need to keep our market wide open to countries like Japan that remain virtually closed to U.S. products, automobiles in particular. I remember a headline to a news article I read not too long ago about how Chevy had broken a new monthly record for the number of cars it exported to Japan. The figure was only in the 500 or 600 range.

Allow me to make it clear that I am not bashing Japan. Far from it. I admire Japan for its intelligent and well thought out trade policy. Why would Japan abandon protectionism at home while enjoying easy access to America's wide open market? It keeps its market for itself and enjoys taking a greater market share from America where people are eager to quickly bash their own home-based automakers and support foreign companies instead, even though they employ fewer American workers.

The ridiculous rhetoric from foreign car lovers should leave any clear-thinking American wondering how they maintain any sense of credibility. They talk about how foreign car companies are building factories in America but ignore the fact that GM and Ford have nearly five times as many major plants here than do Toyota, Honda, and Nissan combined. They talk about how foreign car companies employ workers in the U.S. but ignore the fact that GM has more U.S. salaried workers than Toyota has total U.S. workers. They talk about how foreign car companies use some domestic parts (the Nissan Maxima has a whopping 5 percent domestic content) but ignore the fact that GM and Ford use more American parts on average. They talk about the reliability of foreign cars while accusing American cars of poor quality, but you'll never hear them mention the following about GM:

- The Chevrolet Malibu/Malibu Maxx is the highest ranked entry mid-size car in initial quality.
- The Chevrolet Suburban is the highest ranked full-size SUV in initial quality
- The GMC Sierra HD is the highest ranked heavy-duty full-size pickup in initial quality.
- The Buick LeSabre is the highest ranked full-size car in initial quality.
- The Buick Century is the highest ranked premium mid-size car in initial quality.
- The Chevrolet Malibu is the most dependable entry mid-size car.
- The Chevrolet Silverado HD is the most dependable heavy-duty full-size pickup.
- The Cadillac Escalade EXT is the most dependable light-duty full-size pickup.
- The GMC Yukon/Yukon XL is the most dependable full-size SUV.
- The Buick LeSabre is the most dependable full-size car.
- The Buick Century is the most dependable premium mid-size car.

- The Chevrolet S-10 pickup is the most dependable mid-size pickup.
- The Chevrolet Prizm is the most dependable compact car.

The above rankings are all according to J.D. Power & Associates Quality Surveys. I especially like the statistic about the Chevy Prizm, which de-bunks the myth that GM is only good at making "gas-guzzlers." It just so happens that after it was announced that the Chevrolet Tahoe took the top ranking for dependability in its class, the *Wall Street Journal* confirmed that the Tahoe's 20 mpg rating was three mpg better than the Nissan Armada. In fact, GM already leads the large-SUV segment in fuel economy and is improving their ratings for the 2006 models by an additional mile per gallon (approximately a 5 percent increase.)

When Ford Motor Co. Chairman, Bill Ford, spoke before the U.S. Chamber of Commerce late last year, he suggested government and industry should work in unison to "restore American competitiveness." It makes sense. Since American companies pay more taxes to the U.S. Treasury than foreign companies because they are U.S. based, they should expect some cooperation from their own government. But laissez-faire lovers (who are usually import lovers) who welcome any and all types of foreign, predatory, do-as-they-please competition would probably cry foul. Any policy other than one that gives foreign producers better access to American consumers than American producers is usually fine with them. And should the government intervene to ensure that the rules of competition are the same for all players, or heaven forbid, tilt them slightly in favor of domestic producers, that would be unwise policy.

Even though Chrysler is now foreign-owned, Bill Ford used them to highlight the foundation of the automobile manufacturing sector. Lumping GM, Ford, and Chrysler together, he pointed out that they employ 90 percent of the autoworkers in America. The former "Big Three" make 75 percent of the cars and trucks that are made in the U.S. And in the last 25 years, GM, Ford, and Chrysler are responsible for more than 85 percent of the investment dollars poured into this country. The average domestic content from these three companies is 80 percent, according to Bill Ford, and only 31 percent for Japanese automakers, 5.4 percent for European automakers, and 2.1 percent for Korean automakers.

Free traders advocate open American markets regardless of the circumstances. The thinking is that unless we remain open and accept any volume of imports, we lessen our chances of convincing foreign countries to open their markets to us. But this strategy can only be beneficial when it results in us selling more to them than they sell to us. Even though that hasn't been the case for decades, and free traders know it, they still claim that if we don't buy stuff from foreign countries, then foreign countries won't buy stuff from us. Is it so difficult to see that most foreign countries already aren't buying our stuff? That's why we have a trade deficit instead of a trade surplus.

If free-trade advocates were coaches of football teams, their entire strategy would be formulated upon a strong offense with little regard to defense. Even if they consistently gave up five touchdowns per game and only scored three for themselves, their focus would be an offense that could score more touchdowns. They would probably also reason that if they tried to protect their end of the field by strengthening their defense, it would only encourage the opposing team to do the same, lessening their ability to score more touchdowns.

So in this sort of fantasy free-trade football as it applies to our trade policies, we continue to focus on invading other markets while neglecting to protect our home turf. We are foolishly trying to convince foreigners that they should buy American when it is much easier to convince our own people to do so. If we try to protect our market with tariffs, free traders tell us, then the other side will "retaliate" with tariffs of their own to protect their markets. The import tariff is there and available, but we should never use it. It's almost as if free traders would suggest equipping our police with guns without bullets, because after all, if the police were to shoot their guns then the criminals might "retaliate" and shoot back. The guns are there and available for the police, but they should never use them for fear of retaliation.

Call it the Japanese dream of American free traders. They're making it a reality by advocating continued wide-open American markets while we all hope and pray, someday, Japan will surrender their market like we have hypocritically surrendered ours. Don't look for it to happen anytime soon. Only trade-balancing tariffs advocated by protectionist-leaning politicians and a strategy focused on convincing Americans, not foreigners, of the benefits of buying American can awaken us from the Japanese dream. Only then can we restore what used to be known by Abraham Lincoln, Teddy Roosevelt, and other true protectionist-leaning statesmen as the "American System."

What's Bad For General Motors And Ford Is Bad For America
January 7, 2006

At last December's local union meeting, which I address every month as our local Machinists Union's Communicator, I passed out literature from the Union Label & Service Trades Department of the AFL-CIO listing all the union-made and American-made vehicles. I reminded everyone that supporting domestic manufacturing was one of the best ways to help erase America's trade deficit. After all, how are we to export as much as or more than we import if we allow our own manufacturers to die off? But after the meeting, the all too predictable happened. Someone pulled me aside and asked me just how we were going to help ease America's expanding trade deficit by buying American-made autos when he had heard that foreign cars were of much higher quality than American cars.

Such misconceptions are depressing when they serve to undermine the very automobile companies that are largely responsible for building the middle class in this country. I reminded the gentleman that General Motors, for instance, has recently won more automotive quality awards than you could shake a stick at. And Toyota recently announced the biggest recall on record for a Japanese automaker. This recall involved 1.27 million vehicles.

How sad it is that people run around with virtual tape recorders in their heads, recording what they hear and spitting it out as fact when the time seems appropriate. And it's unfortunate that time isn't something that either GM or Ford have much of to turn things around in the realm of public opinion.

Despite the efforts of many to publicize the true facts, whether it's articles like these or the CEO of Ford Motor Company addressing the National Press Club in Washington, DC, it's anybody's guess whether the remaining two American automakers can survive retaliation of American consumers who are hell-bent on making them pay for perceived sins of the past.

I'm not claiming that GM and Ford haven't made their share of mistakes over the years. All companies make strategic blunders, but I would argue that no company in U.S. history has ever been the recipient of such pure hatred among American consumers as has GM or Ford. And the venom that has been spewed at them is largely undeserved and unwarranted. It's not that I don't think that for every one person who won't buy an American car under any circumstance, there is at least one person who won't buy a foreign one under any circumstance. It's just that there's too many who won't buy the American car. But I'm willing to bet that there is even a larger group of people that know better than to buy foreign but are being swayed by inaccurate information or outright lies.

Bill Ford, addressing the National Press Club on November 22, 2005, noted that GM, Ford, and DaimlerChrysler combined invest more than $16 billion on research and development each year, which eclipses any other industry in the U.S. From that research and development came, among many other things, America's first hybrid SUV, which was engineered, designed, and built in the U.S. by Ford. The Japanese, of course, have their own hybrids, but the Ford Escape stands alone as the only hybrid vehicle that was built from the ground up. All Japanese hybrid vehicles started as non-hybrids and were converted, a much less innovative task.

Bill Ford went on to point out that U.S. automakers pay more than $11 billion in pensions each year to no less than 800,000 retirees and their spouses. Any American who thinks they aren't affected by the recent struggles of Ford and GM since they don't work for either automaker had better think again. Why? Because you can't take literally billions of dollars out of the U.S. economy without it affecting everyone in the country.

Many Americans recall the days when there was only American competition in the auto industry and in doing so reason that they should buy foreign cars to somehow prevent that situation from occurring again. But if Toyota buys GM and Honda buys Ford, these same people may soon realize that foreign competition absent American competition is much worse. Ultimately, the American economy is large enough to provide enough competition by itself without much foreign competition, as long as there is proper government oversight and regulation to prevent collusion between companies in similar industries. It's hard to believe that a nation as big and diverse as ours can't host enough domestic competition to be considered a healthy and competitive economy.

Retiree benefits are being cut in many industries well beyond the auto industry. If the health care coverage for many Americans doesn't disappear completely, costs may increase to the point that premiums will be unaffordable, resulting in millions more dollars being taken out of the U.S. economy. Wal-Mart already has the deserved reputation for offering unaffordable health coverage, yet they are the apple of corporate America's eye. Unions representing workers at General Motors have voted to take on more of the financial burdens of health care that used to be paid by the company, resulting in over $15 billion more consumer dollars taken out of the U.S. economy. The importance of disposable income for American workers/consumers cannot be overstated since two-thirds of economic activity is dependent on consumer spending.

Americans can only be as affluent as spenders as they are wage earners. And since those employed in the auto industry are among the most well paid, some Americans who don't enjoy similar wages or benefits seem to advocate the industry's demise out of jealousy. But all Americans would be wise to support American autoworkers and their American companies to put upward pressure on wages that will cause ripple effects through other industries.

How does the ripple effect from prominent American industries influence other seemingly unrelated industries? Well-paid American automakers may decide to make improvements on their houses in an increasingly attractive housing market, for example. To do this, they support the banking industry where they get a home-improvement loan. They also support the lumber, construction, and possibly furniture industries as well, whose employees in turn spend their money at restaurants, retail stores, or maybe even on college tuition for their kids.

But instead these same automotive workers are having previously unthinkable reality discussions with their kids, with many telling them that they can no longer afford to send them to college. Major companies such as Delphi, which provide a significant number of parts for GM vehicles, are proposing wage cuts of up to 66 percent saying auto parts workers are too well paid. With China now graduating more engineers than America these days, this is a reality concession our nation cannot afford. But still, the anti-American auto industry crowd cheers these developments on thinking that someone is finally going to pay for the perceived auto-management sins of the past. Little do they realize that we will all pay since we're all Americans, and we are not individually immune regardless of the industry of our employment.

If some American consumers can't see the benefits of buying American through the "Made in USA" argument, maybe they can be persuaded to focus on supporting companies that would prevent American taxpayers from picking up the tab for retirees' pensions and health care if these prominent U.S. companies fail. Such a strategy would not include supporting companies like Toyota, which did not build their first U.S. plant until 1987. In other words, an employee hired by Toyota the first day the plant opened would still have less than 20 years with the company and would not yet be eligible for retirement benefits.

Benefit costs like these are at the forefront of several reasons why GM and Ford have a huge cost disadvantage compared to foreign automakers. But instead of being exalted for their contribution to the U.S. economy, they are accused of being bloated, inefficient, and uncompetitive. American consumers should think twice before passing off the demise of the American auto industry as just another acceptance of global reality and instead long for an economy that at least has some of the traits of the 1970s.

In the 1970s, during which General Motors produced the best running car I've ever owned (my 1976 Buick Riviera accumulated over 250,000 miles before I sold the engine, which still powers a Florida airboat to this day), American consumers managed to save an average of 10 percent of their income each year. And they didn't have to borrow against the equity in their houses and risk their future on speculative bubbles to do it. How amazing it is that the American savings rate has recently turned negative while China's savings rate is around 50 percent. I guess they have to do something with all the American dollars we send them if they aren't trying to buy major American oil companies or appliance makers. My made-in-Michigan 1996 Lincoln Town Car may threaten to take my old '76 Riviera's crown someday since it just passed 160,000 miles with no signs of letting up. There are few things that can counter the lies of the anti-American auto industry crowd than personal experience with American vehicles.

As the old adage says, "As GM goes, so goes the nation." Fortunately, GM will soon begin touting the Chevy Tahoe as the most fuel efficient vehicle in its class. The Chevy Tahoe was also the winner of one those quality awards mentioned at the beginning of this article. If GM is guilty of anything, it's for not communicating well enough or fast enough about how valuable they really are to American prosperity. The American people will eventually find out. It may be the hard way, not through television ads or other media attempts, but they will learn. The only good thing that will emerge from the ashes of the demise of the American auto industry, if it happens, is that Americans will finally learn how to vote with their dollars according to the values upon which a prosperous U.S. economy depends. And not just in the auto industry but in all American industries that are vital to the prosperity of the American nation.

If GM and Ford fail, the American tragedy will be that we'll have to take several steps backward in several areas of our lives before we learn how to start taking steps forward again. But as we begin to take those steps forward, we'll also become more aware of how to avoid going backwards like before. Buying American will become more popular than ever before, and I hope an American presence in the auto industry will emerge and benefit from better and smarter buying habits. I'm not predicting failure for Ford or GM, and I'm hopeful that things can still turn around. But if these two American companies are forced to exit the auto industry, literally millions of Americans will be forced to exit the middle class.

Is It Unpatriotic To Not Buy American Cars?
February 11, 2006

As I sat in an Orlando studio on January 24, 2006, waiting to be interviewed on Fox News' Hannity and Colmes for the first time, that seemed to be the question I was going to be asked to answer if the introductory comments were any indication. In the studio in New York was Malcolm Bricklin, founder and CEO of Visionary Vehicles, who plans to import cars from China by 2007. Ford had just announced plans to lay off 30,000 workers, and since even Mr. Bricklin (to his credit) says he doesn't want to see so many Americans join the ranks of the unemployed, it was a good question to ask. But the show started with Mr. Bricklin being asked a different question, and by the time the cameras pointed to me, I was given a different question as well, so I never really got to answer it

But as I continue to think about it since that interview, the answer I would have given to Sean Hannity is the same as my answer today. If it's unpatriotic to destroy the American middle class, then it's unpatriotic to not buy American cars. As a country, we're drowning in a sea of red ink, and as consumers (those who really should know better, anyway) we're drowning in a sea of "what's in it for me."

Since President Bush has all but ruled out any government help for either Ford or GM saying they have to make a product that is "relevant" (did you know Mr. Bush himself owns a Ford pickup truck?), it's up to the American consumer to realize that a bankruptcy for Ford or GM or both is definitely not in the national interest. Not only would hundreds of thousands of workers lose their jobs, but about 450,000 retirees would be de-funded. These retirees on fixed incomes would see smaller pensions and reduced medical benefits. The workers that remained would see massive cuts in benefits as well.

Big deal, you say? At least American companies still offer their workers pensions. According to a recent article in *The Tennessean*, Nissan North America new hires won't be able to count on a company pension when they retire. And if you work for Nissan and didn't happen to reach the age of 65 by the end of last year, you won't be participating in the company sponsored medical plan, either.

If American companies can't remain successful and shoulder the burden of health care for their workers, the rest of us will likely pick up the tab in the form of higher taxes through expanded entitlement programs, which are already growing at a rate of 8 percent a year.

Eighty-four percent of all federal spending of our tax dollars already goes towards the "big three" untouchables, interest on the national debt; national defense (including homeland security); and entitlements such as Medicare, Medicaid, and Social Security. So much for conservatives who wish for smaller government. Generally speaking, few of us want to invite more government into our lives. But a significantly smaller government these days would result in benefit cuts that would ultimately affect all of us. The days of those who want tax cuts because it means more money in their pockets and means benefit cuts only for someone else are over.

So what's your reason for not buying American cars and trucks? I've heard (and disproved) them all, but I'll list a few of the more popular ones here.

1. **Quality**. According to the latest J.D. Power & Associates Long-term Dependability Survey, Lincoln, Buick, and Cadillac all made the top five for 2005. Lexus was number one, and number two was mysteriously not reported by the CNN story highlighting the survey. What's even better (if you are a fan of American automakers) is that the average dependability of all GM and Ford models combined was greater than the average dependability for all the Japanese models combined.

2. **Too much emphasis on "gas-guzzlers."** The hypocrisy in this statement is rampant since most people who make it are ardent supporters of the "free market." The trouble for these hypocrites is that a major free market principle is the law of supply and demand. According to *Seattle Times* columnist, Shaunti Feldhahn, consumer demand for big bad SUVs

has doubled in the last 15 years. So much for the argument that American car companies aren't building what consumers want to buy. Just like American companies have been scrambling to satisfy the one percent of car buyers who want hybrids, Japanese car makers have been scrambling to catch up to Ford and GM by offering bigger and badder behemoths (at even worse gas mileage ratings than American SUVs). GM has more models with over 30 mpg highway (2006 EPA estimates) than any other automaker. Last month I revealed that my 1996 Lincoln Town Car now has over 160,000 miles with no signs of letting up. What I didn't mention is that my car has averaged 24 mpg since September 2001, which is a result of mostly highway driving during the week and mostly city driving on weekends. Not bad for a big luxury car.

3. **Foreign car companies will pick up the slack.** This argument implies that the hiring of American workers by foreign companies would never take place if there weren't layoffs by American companies first. Even if you view foreign investment as a good thing, which it isn't, foreign companies will still invest in America even if we support American companies so they can actually retain our own workers. This argument is almost as bad as the one that implies we need to destroy American manufacturing jobs in general so we can move American workers into high-tech jobs. Why not let the college graduates strapped with tens of thousands of dollars in student loans and other debts take these jobs and protect American workers in the jobs they choose to have now?

4. **American companies can do better.** Better at what? What will it take for more American people to root for the home team again? Do you only root for your hometown sports team when they are winning, or do you root for them even when they are down, no matter what? Let's see. American companies GM and Ford have won numerous quality awards, they have more domestic plants, employ more American workers, support more retirees along with their dependants and families, pay better wages than the non-union foreign-owned plants, have a higher percentage of domestic parts in their automobiles, pay more taxes to the U.S. Treasury, give more to charities for the benefit of this country,

and donate more in the wake of disasters like 9/11. Need I go on?

5. GM and Ford need to make cars Americans want to buy. I saved this one for last since it the most ridiculous statement of all. General Motors has the highest market share of any automobile company. To say the company that currently sells more cars and trucks to more people than any other company in the industry, even if that market share is falling, is truly ridiculous. Yes, I know Toyota is gaining on GM and may overtake them this year (in worldwide market share, not U.S. market share, where GM has roughly twice the market share of Toyota), and GM used to command around 50 percent of the domestic market. But let's be reasonable, shall we? What company in any industry in today's super-competitive economy can command 50 percent of their market? Not even Coke or Pepsi can do that. Which reminds me, Pepsi recently passed Coke to take the top spot in the beverage wars. Is Coke number two now because they aren't making beverages Americans want to drink? I haven't heard that one yet. Only in America and only in the automobile industry could number two be declared a loser brand. And only if it's GM, not Toyota.

The struggle for GM and Ford to regain much needed and much deserved traction has increasingly become a media war. And it's not just a media war as I reported in my September 2005 article entitled "Media Bias Against American Automakers." The bias towards foreign automakers has extended from journalists and other newsmakers to everyday Americans with vendettas against their home team companies in the form of letters to the editor and blogs on the Internet. The *Wall Street Journal* recently ran a story entitled "Are Rumours Hurting Sales" reporting on a Los Angeles resident who started a Web log called "GM Can Do Better." It's not that this individual has not heard the reports of numerous quality awards bestowed upon American automakers. It's that he's skeptical the reports are true.

Foreign car lovers will believe it if Toyota wins an award. But if General Motors' Chevy Impala is documented to have fewer customer complaints than the Toyota Camry, foreign car lovers will grasp at different false reasons to justify their foreign purchases. But the facts are in, and their arguments no longer hold water. I'd be willing to bet that these American car bashers haven't test-driven an American car in years. Right now it doesn't matter that GM has 82 major plants in America and Ford has 35. What matters is that Toyota, Honda, and Nissan have eight plants each. It doesn't matter that Toyota and Honda average 65 percent to 75 percent domestic parts in their U.S. built cars while GM and Ford average 80 percent to 85 percent. If these percentages ever reverse, then it will matter to foreign car lovers. Facts simply don't matter to them when they don't happen to be in their favor. To them, as *Business Week* reported December 12, 2005, "the economy is unstoppable as the...dianapolis Colts," and foreign purchases have no national negative effect. If you watched the Super Bowl last Sunday you probably noticed that the Indianapolis Colts weren't playing.

I'm sure that this article will not sit well with those who automatically receive it as part of their free "Buy American Mention of the Week" subscription and advocate the demise of GM and Ford. And I'm also sure I'll receive many "unsubscribe" requests as a result. But I don't really care. I don't like writing for people I don't like any more than I like giving speeches to groups I don't like. These articles are not designed to make anyone feel like less of an American for their past foreign purchases, rather they aim to persuade American consumers to make the right purchases in the future.

Those who do agree with the facts and the opinions I have presented, I urge you to forward or distribute my auto industry articles to fellow Americans who need to see them. Simply visit www.overthehillcarpeople.com to see the auto industry articles I've written since May 2005. I'm not sure how much time GM and Ford have left to turn things around given the obstacles they must overcome that have been put there for bogus and unpatriotic reasons. And remember, the next time someone accuses you of questioning their patriotism because of their foreign car, tell them that if it's not unpatriotic to destroy the American middle class, then it's not unpatriotic to buy foreign cars!

What GM And Ford Must Do To Stay Out Of Bankruptcy
May 21, 2006

If you've been listening to the debate over the fate of the U.S. auto industry over the past year, or perhaps longer, you've undoubtedly heard the speculation that either General Motors or Ford or both may slide into bankruptcy.

I've avoided for a long time speculating myself whether it will happen since I honestly didn't feel confident that I had the answer. Now I think I do. All patriotism aside, I have the opinion that I don't think either remaining American automaker will file for bankruptcy, or maybe even worse, be acquired by a foreign-owned automaker. But there are two things I think have to happen, or that GM and Ford must do, to avoid the filing.

1. As they both focus more on the American market, they must not lose their focus on vital overseas markets (notably China).

2. Stop listening to the numbers of the American public (the foreign car loving part) that whine and complain about their every decision.

The first suggestion is obviously more challenging than the second, and I realize it almost sounds like something a globalist, free trader, or internationalist would say. Those of you who have read my "Buy American Mention of the Week" articles for long know that I am none of those. I'm a self-described nationalist and protectionist. I don't believe trade for the sake of trade is either necessary, necessarily good, or the engine of prosperity. If it were, we would surely be in utopia by now.

According to the May 1, 2006, issue of *Business Week*, we imported $1.21 trillion worth of foreign-made goods in 2005, and that's excluding Canada and Mexico! That's twice the number of imports compared to 1992 when Ross Perot warned us about NAFTA's giant sucking sound, and it's an 80-fold increase compared to 1960. If trade were the answer to prosperity, both consumer debt and national debt levels would be negligible.

It's perfectly fine to import things like bananas that we can't grow in the United States or certain fruits from other countries in the off-season, but trade for the sake of trade is not only potentially destructive to American jobs, it's also kind of silly when you think about it. Remember, I'm not saying all trade is bad, but trade for the sake of trade is silly. If both the United States and Germany produce socks, for example, of what benefit is it for Germany to buy our socks and for us to buy Germany's socks rather than for each country to simply buy their own socks? Other than needlessly polluting the environment by running ships all over the place and hiring more port workers and coast guard personnel, the answer is "not much." In fact, it's actually a drain on the economy since these are government (taxpayer-funded) jobs. And why would we import anything from Germany we can't make here since their labor costs are higher than labor costs in America?

The only reason would be to help American companies secure a higher market share for their products in the foreign country than they might otherwise. If GM makes some of their Cadillacs in Germany, they stand a better chance of increasing their sales there, just like some Americans reason that it's good for America if they buy a Toyota that is made here.

This brings me back to the two things GM and Ford must do to stay out of bankruptcy. It's kind of silly that the same Americans who spew venom at GM and Ford for investing overseas are the same ones praising Japanese companies for increasing investment in America. That's why GM and Ford should just tune out American auto whiners and strengthen their focus on both America and countries abroad.

Regardless of whether it was a reaction to criticism for not focusing enough on the market here at home, GM has pulled out of quite a few overseas ventures. They sold 17 percent of their 20 percent stake in Suzuki for $2 billion, their 20 percent stake in Fuji Heavy Industries, exited an alliance with Italian-owned Fiat, and on April 12, 2006, they announced plans to sell their 7.9 percent stake in Isuzu for close to $300 million. Their 50.9 percent stake in the formerly struggling car brand Daewoo is turning out to be a smart move.

Although GM paid $2 billion to separate from Fiat (selling Suzuki cancels out that loss), it is questionable whether it makes sense to exit foreign ventures altogether. On May 24, 2005, the *Wall Street Journal* detailed how Isuzu's net profit increased a record 9.7 percent as their sales in Asia skyrocketed. Does it really make sense to sell a stake in a company that is making record profits? I can see why it may make sense for a company to sell a stake in a profitable non-core asset like Kodak did with a profitable Lysol in 1995 (Lysol is now British-owned), but Isuzu is certainly not a non-core asset.

On the domestic front, GM sold their stake in the immensely profitable GMAC real estate business on March 24, 2006, for about $8.8 billion. Will any of this really matter to criticizing foreign car lovers? Probably not. They've shown their hypocrisy in bashing GM for ventures overseas, even profitable ones, while applauding Japan's ventures in our market. A double standard to be sure.

They conveniently ignore the fact that Japan shuts us out of their market while they are allowed to flood ours. If Chevrolet sells 500 cars a month in Japan, it's considered a good month. They also conveniently ignore the fact that foreign nations like Japan pick up the tab for the health care of their citizens rather than have companies like Toyota, Nissan, and Honda do it.

What does matter is that GM is now super-flush with cash (around $36 billion), and if they play their cards right, starting with items number 1 and number 2 at the beginning of this article, they just might make it. China has been a huge success for GM, where GM is the leading seller of automobiles and made an income of $218 million in the first three quarters of 2005. In fact, the best selling car in China is a Buick Minivan. And despite GM's success in China, they have no plans to import entire vehicles into the U.S. from China, although they do, as all automakers do, import parts from China. The first company to announce plans to import completely assembled cars from China happens to be DaimlerChrysler.

Another reason I believe GM and Ford will escape bankruptcy is because both companies are now profitable. True, Ford has warned that this may change in the next quarter, and GM's profit-showing was the result of revised numbers, but hey, it's a start. If Ford can continue to come out with "bold moves" like the re-designed Mustang and GM can come out with more hits like the Buick Lucerne and Chevy HHR, they should be fine.

General Motors is now sitting on $36 billion in cash, which should buy them enough time to convince consumers that their cars are worth a second, third, or fourth look. It's going to take time to convince Americans they don't need to buy so many Toyota Camrys since the Chevrolet Impala won the top spot for initial quality in its segment. But since gas prices are now so high, it should take less time for Americans to realize that the Chevy Tahoe gets 20 mpg, and the Toyota Sequoia only gets 16 mpg (not to mention that the Tahoe won the top spot for quality in its class).

It may be risky to make such "bold moves" (Ford has a winner in that slogan), but I think Ford and GM are going to make it. Maybe they'll even become profitable enough to buy Chrysler back from the Germans, and we can truly have a "Big Three" again. I guess I'll have to hold out hope for that one for another day.

Why GM Shouldn't Become A General Merger
July 25, 2006

The latest example of greed in America doesn't reside within any major American company and their relentless focus on their bottom line but rather with an individual by the name of Kirk Kerkorian. Mr Kerkorian is perfectly willing to turn GM into a "general merger" of American and foreign companies just to get a big enough bump in the stock price so he can sell his shares. The 89 year-old investor, who owns 9.9 percent of General Motors, has proposed GM hook up with French-owned Renault, which owns 44 percent of Japan's Nissan. The proposed alliance could allow Renault and Nissan to buy as much as 20 percent of General Motors.

Mr. Kerkorian had the unfortunate experience of buying his GM shares when it was priced at over $30 per share. Even though GM's stock has improved markedly over the last few months, it appears that a gradual, measured turnaround isn't good enough for him. You'd think that slow and steady would be better than fast and fragile when you're talking about a huge American company that funds increasingly expensive health care for 1.1 million employees, retirees, and their family members.

But before I even delve into the reasons why a merger with a French-Japanese company that is owned 15 percent by the French government is a horrible idea, allow me to explain why the path GM is currently on is the right path and should not be disrupted.

General Motors has significantly improved efficiency in their assembly operations. According to the 2006 edition of the Harbour Report on North American productivity for auto factories, GM only takes 41 minutes longer than Honda to assemble the average model. In 1998, that gap was 14.62 hours. Taking into account that GM relies more heavily on larger models than Honda, it's entirely possible that this gap is because many of their models simply take longer to assemble. GM is also the most efficient of the Detroit automakers, even if you count German-owned Chrysler as an American automaker, which they aren't.

In addition to GM having the highest U.S. market share of any automaker, the company has made huge strides overseas. GM passed Germany's Volkswagen last year to become China's biggest selling automaker, posting 21 percent growth even as China took measures to cool their economy. Even Ford doubled its sales to China for the first half of this year and has also doubled its sales in Brazil, where its Ecosport SUV has garnered an amazing 80 percent of the SUV market there.

Although rising gas prices have cooled sales of large SUVs, GM has seen the smallest sales drops compared to the competition. According to a *Wall Street Journal* article on July 14, 2006, the sales of the Chevy Suburban dropped 24 percent during the first half of this year. But sales for the Toyota Sequoia fell 30 percent, Jeep Grand Cherokee sales fell 32 percent, Ford Expedition sales fell 29 percent, and sales of the Dodge Durango dropped 37 percent.

Now, onto why the Renault/Nissan combination is a bad bet for an investment-style takeover as far as GM is concerned. Despite Nissan's Chief Executive, Carlos Ghosn's, celebration last year over boosting the company's sales by a million plus vehicles, the *Wall Street Journal* reports that no one at Nissan is celebrating these days. Sales in Canada are down 32 percent compared to April 2005, and exports from home-country Japan are down 18 percent.

None of this should overshadow Nissan's missteps in the United States. *Business Week* reported that their pipeline of fresh American-market vehicles has "dried up." April 2006 sales were down 1.7 percent from April 2005, and the re-design of the all-important number two seller Sentra was called "ugly" by several of those who commented on autoblog.com. Even though it was prior to Mr. Ghosn arriving on the scene, the company lost $6.5 billion in their near-bankruptcy year of 1999 when they also accumulated $20 billion in debt. More recently, over 1,300 of their staffers have quit over their decision to relocate their U.S. subsidiary headquarters from Los Angeles, California to Nashville, Tennessee.

Quality problems have plagued their Canton, Mississippi truck and minivan plant. Even anti-American auto industry publication *Consumer Reports* says Nissan's large SUVs are some of the worst autos available in reliability ratings. And on July 25, 2006, the day of this writing, Nissan reported operating income dropped 26 percent while sales in the U.S. and Japan fell by double-digit margins. Is this a company with which GM should engage in attempting to facilitate a short-sighted, greed-based turnaround initiated by an overly-impatient investor? Hardly.

My stance has more to do with the fact that French-owned Renault owns 44 percent of Nissan. It also has to do with the fact that Renault is 15 percent government-owned and not necessarily that it's the French government. Americans should balk at any government ownership of an American company, including U.S. government ownership. This same argument should be employed to support airline carriers that use Boeing rather than partially European government-owned Airbus.

Properly designed and strategic government intervention in industry is acceptable to correct the imperfections of the market, but government ownership is not. Government ownership of private industry distorts otherwise more straightforward diplomatic relations between countries, including trade and foreign policy concerns. The American taxpayer funded U.S. government should represent American strategic industries like Boeing during WTO disputes against unfair European subsidies for Airbus, but government ownership of private industries should be avoided. And allowing a strategic American company like General Motors to fall under even minimal foreign government ownership should be rejected outright.

As it turns out, President Bush is no help concerning the issue of foreign ownership of strategic American industries. According to a July 14, 2006, article in the *Wall Street Journal*, Mr. Bush applauded foreign investment in American-owned firms saying, "I have no problem with foreign capital buying U.S. companies." Bush is even encouraging foreign companies to become owners of our domestic airlines. Democrat Senator Barack Obama of Illinois seems to have a better take on the issue saying, "When you start seeing GM getting into big trouble and the prospect of mergers or buyouts...foreigners, it stirs up anxiety that our relative position in the global economy is slipping."

The United States certainly isn't the first country whose home-based companies have questioned the impact of foreign investment. Businesses in China are pressuring Beijing, which doesn't deny its policies should benefit its own people, to crack down on foreign takeovers. Executive President, Xiang Wenbo, of Sanya Group, China's biggest private manufacturer of construction equipment, is upset that China's largest maker of cranes is about to allow Washington private equity firm Carlyle Group to take an 85 percent stake in the company. Angry that other Chinese companies are falling into the hands of foreigners, he says, "We are selling our signature enterprises to foreigners" and wonders "Are we losing our minds?"

GM CEO, Rick Wagoner, is right to view the proposed 20 percent foreign stake in the company he currently heads as "hostile." The stability of large American companies like GM is essential for a more stable global economy, although I'm sure the fans of foreign cars and foreign investment would have you believe the reverse. That American companies like GM must allow foreign investment for the rest of the world to be stable.

But as you might guess, even if GM did not allow the Renault/Nissan combination to invest in the company, it's not going to cause foreigners to stop wanting to invest in the United States. And even though Beijing has now set up a commission to combat monopolies and drafted rules to limit foreign stakes in many industrial sectors, it's not going to keep non-Chinese companies from wanting to invest in China. Xiang Wenbo says he doesn't want the Chinese economy to "be affected by factors outside our control."

But GM may be affected by factors outside of its control if it allows sizeable foreign ownership in the company. Among the supposed advantages of this type of merger is the idea of cost-savings through parts sharing between similar models of the involved companies. But since GM has the second highest domestic parts content of any automaker, this vision may dilute that percentage and turn away car buyers who consider patriotism among the factors that determine their purchases.

According to Jim Doyle of the Level Field Institute, whose website, www.levelfieldinstitute.com, lists the domestic parts content of every model sold in the U.S. from Acura to Volvo, what you drive still drives America. Once you see the list of domestic parts content for American and foreign cars alike, you'll see that GM and Ford have higher domestic parts percentages on average than any of their competitors.

Using figures for 2004 automobiles, General Motors had a total average domestic parts content of 80.1 percent, the second highest of any automaker, including all GM-owned nameplates like Saab. Seven models came in at 90 percent, with most in the 70 percent and 80 percent range. Ford came in number one when it comes to using domestic parts in their vehicles, scoring an average 87.5 percent, which was dragged down by formerly foreign-owned nameplates like Volvo and Jaguar that have historically used more foreign parts. German-owned DaimlerChrysler came in third with 78 percent, dragged down by Mercedes vehicles that have zero domestic content in most vehicles. Popular American media darling Toyota came in at 42.9 percent, Honda came in at 52.8 percent, and

Nissan came in at 43.7 percent. BMW averaged 10.6 percent, Hyundai (which includes Kia) averaged 3.1 percent, and Suzuki averaged 5 percent. Grouping automakers by nationality, domestic companies average 78.5 percent (which should be over 80 percent since the Level Field Institute calculates DaimlerChrysler as a domestic automaker), Japanese companies average 44.5 percent, Korean companies average 3.1 percent, and European companies average 6.3 percent (DaimlerChrysler should be averaged in here.)

With numbers like these, it's frustrating to see column after column of editorials praising Honda for building factories in the U.S. while chastising Ford and GM for not adding domestic factories at the same pace. Most of these misleading editorials are just that, misleading. But a July 18, 2006, article in the *Wall Street Journal* crossed the line by making a claim that is an outright lie saying, "Turning farm fields into factories, that's what Henry Ford used to do. Today, in the heartland, it's being done by Honda—a company that doesn't manufacture imports but builds American-made cars." Not only are innocent readers left with the impression that Japanese car companies like Honda are the primary power behind America's prosperity with their 8 American factories compared to Ford's 35, but also we are now to believe Honda manufactures zero imports!

But what do all the high domestic content percentages overwhelmingly in favor of American companies as detailed by the Level Field Institute mean? They mean that on average, for every car you purchase from American-owned Ford or GM, you employ twice as many American workers in the parts sector than you would had you purchased a Japanese brand. Believe me, I've heard all the arguments as to why we should support Japanese factories in America. "What if my Uncle Bob works at one of these factories?" the question usually goes. The answer is that if you want to support Uncle Bob's Japanese factory in America, you're helping Uncle Bob, but you're hurting Uncle Sam. America should come first.

The Level Field Institute was founded by retired workers from Ford, GM, and Chrysler, so it's easy to see how German-owned Chrysler is considered a Detroit automaker by the group. But particularly puzzling is a comment made by Jason Vines, head of communications for the Chrysler Group, when he said, "I'm a little offended with Toyota's 'We're American' campaign. They're not. They're a Japanese car company. Baseball, hot dogs, and Toyota? Sorry, it doesn't ring a bell." My apologies to Mr. Vines, but "Baseball, hot dogs, and DaimlerChrysler" doesn't ring a bell, either. I understand that a lot of American workers and retirees in America are now supported by German-owned DaimlerChrysler, but we still have to call a spade a spade. I fail to understand how anyone in good conscience can continue to call DaimlerChrysler a Detroit automaker. If Toyota bought GM, would GM still be a Detroit automaker? If Honda bought Ford, would Ford still be a Detroit automaker? If we could convince Subaru to move its U.S. subsidiary to Detroit, would we have four Detroit automakers? I'm all for playing up America's strength in the marketplace, but only if it's done honestly by labeling all competitors according to their true ownership or nationality.

DaimlerChrysler has even made recent moves to distinguish itself from Detroit with its "AskDrZ.com" ads, seeking to benefit from high-lighting Chrysler not as an American company, but as a German-American company. "Dr. Z" is none other than DaimlerChrysler Chief Executive, Dieter Zetsche, who works out of DaimlerChrysler's Stuttgart, Germany headquarters, the same location from which all Chrysler pay-checks and pink slips now originate.

Still, however, www.levelfieldinstitute.org is a very useful website for proving that the "Big Two" have the highest domestic parts content of any automaker, including Chrysler, and how Ford and GM directly and indirectly support the most U.S. jobs. The only distortion comes when the Level Field Institute includes Chrysler when determining invest-ment and jobs generated by "American automakers." But even if one were to subtract Chrylser's American contribution and properly count the company as foreign, the combined investment by GM and Ford in America would still best all foreign automakers' combined investment in most instances.

GM CEO, Rick Wagoner, has already met with the would-be foreign investors representing Renault/Nissan, and all are keeping quiet about the meeting. Let's hope it ends there. Wagoner is on the right path to keep America's number one automaker rolling, so let's hope it remains wholly American-owned.

American Perception Problems Of The American Auto Industry
November 29, 2006

Ford and General Motors have taken turns besting the Toyota Camry in quality surveys for the past two years, but if you talk to many Americans, especially the ones who would never consider supporting home-based auto companies, you'd never know it.

Last year, the Chevrolet Impala beat the Toyota Camry in initial quality according to J.D. Power & Associates, and *Consumer Reports* just announced that both the Ford Fusion and Mercury Milan scored higher than both the Toyota Camry and the Honda Accord this year.

After the announcement, Ford's Director of Global Quality, Debbe Yeager, commented, "It's a perception gap," referring to the struggle American companies have had overcoming the perceived and seemingly untarnishable reputation of their foreign rivals.

Even as GM and Ford have accumulated award after award on vehicle quality, you'd almost never know about such quality gains made by American companies or quality declines of foreign companies by listening to the media. Did you hear about it when the National Highway Traffic Safety Administration announced that Toyota recalled more vehicles than it sold in the U.S. last year? Probably not. Did you hear about Toyota making an "elaborate apology" for their "worrisome series of recalls" that has "tarnished its reputation for quality?" Probably not. Did you hear about the Toyota senior manager who stated, "We used to do quiet recalls called 'service campaigns' to deal with defects but we're not going to hide anything anymore?" Such a statement suggests Toyota's past recall numbers were probably much higher than we were led to believe, and they profited handsomely by having a perception of higher quality than they deserved. In Japan, prosecutors are looking into possible negligence on the part of Toyota for shirking recalls for the last eight years.

How ironic. You probably didn't hear about that one either because the American media doesn't like to bash foreign auto companies—only American ones.

Then there's the mythical perception that foreign automakers produce the most fuel efficient cars and that Detroit only makes gas-guzzlers when the truth is that all automakers, including Toyota, Honda, and Hyundai-Kia alike, have allowed fuel economy to slide in the past 20 years since they all now sell bigger trucks and more SUVs. One of Toyota's senior executives was even quoted in the *Wall Street Journal* on September 28, 2006, saying that both the Toyota Sequoia and the Toyota Tundra "are big gas-guzzling vehicles" and expressed "concern about the longer-term prospects." These longer-term prospects about their admitted gas-guzzlers are questioned because they know that Ford's F-150 and Chevy's Silverado have led the pack in sales year after year.

Yes, gasoline has been getting more expensive, at least until recently, but the fact that Americans continue to buy it in greater quantities qualifies us as hypocrites for suggesting GM and Ford stop building so many big trucks and SUVs. After all, GM and Ford are only responding to demand as any company would and should if they want to remain profitable in a cutthroat competitive market. According to a *Business Week* survey, we Americans bought 10 percent more gasoline in the first six months of 2006 compared to the first six months of 2000 even though gas prices rose 75 percent in that period. Maybe here I should also mention that the Chevy Tahoe beat the gas-guzzling Toyota Sequoia in quality surveys and gets better gas mileage.

But what has happened since gas prices have been on the decline in recent months? The *Wall Street Journal* reported a "slight" increase in truck sales by American companies, as Ford Expedition sales were up 41 percent and Lincoln Navigator sales were up 44 percent. The American media even tries to restrain its applause for home-based auto companies by referring to gains of over 40 percent as "slight!"

Perhaps the biggest perception problem is that American automobile companies GM and Ford (Chrysler is now German-owned) squander all their money on plants overseas and foreign automakers build their factories in the U.S. Foreign car lovers will surely point to Kia's plans to build its first-ever U.S. plant in Georgia, but they probably won't mention that they received $400 million in tax giveaways to do it, which translates into $160,000 per job. Among the many benefits for the foreign-owned company, your tax dollars are going to be used for road improvements surrounding the complex, complete with flower beds and other beautification features. Hey, as long as we're going to allow states to bid for private jobs with our public tax dollars, we might as well make it look good, right?

And the foreign car lovers will probably also not tell you (or maybe they just don't know or don't want you to know) that GM and Ford pour more money into existing American facilities than foreign automakers spend on new plants, usually with little or no tax breaks. GM has already spent over $500 million upgrading two transmission plants this year and has spent nearly a billion dollars over the last decade, for example, for facility upgrades in Texas. And what do GM and Ford get for making their existing plants more efficient? It isn't tax breaks. Instead, they get accusations of not being "competitive" enough! Maybe here I should also mention that the average domestic parts content for Kia is 3 percent, while the average domestic parts content of Ford and GM is 78 percent and 74 percent respectively. This means that buying an American-assembled (or even foreign-assembled, for that matter) GM or Ford supports more American jobs than an American-assembled car or truck with a foreign nameplate.

Fortunately, for our benefit, the U.S. remains the overall global leader in research and development, and a big reason for that is that American automakers, according to the Level Field Institute, invest $16 billion in research and development annually, which outpaces any other industry one could name. Admittedly, the Level Field Institute counts German-owned DaimlerChrysler as an American automaker, so Ford and GM's combined research and development contribution to America is closer to around $12 billion. But who's counting, right? Certainly not the American auto-bashing media.

Japanese companies do employ 3,600 American workers in research and development, but that still leaves the foreign competition in the dust staring at American rear bumpers. Thirty-six hundred sounds like a big number until you realize that 65,000 Americans work in research and development facilities in the state of Michigan alone. In fact, two of the top four research and development spending companies in America, as reported by the *Wall Street Journal*, are, you guessed it, Ford and General Motors. The other two are also American companies, Pfizer and Microsoft.

Ford has recently made headlines as the American automaker with the most challenges to its future, but these challenges certainly are not because they "aren't making cars people want to buy." Toyota did outsell Ford in July, 2006, but since then, Ford has reclaimed the number two spot and has held it ever since. GM has the highest market share, increasing over two percentage points from a year ago. So apparently they can't be accused of not making cars people want to buy, either. Ford sales are also up in Europe, and Ford doubled their sales in China, where GM has the highest market share of any automaker.

General Motors also reported a 3.9 percent rise in August 2006 vehicle sales despite high gas prices and a supposedly slowing economy. And even though Toyota reported record sales that month, they couldn't match the non-record setting sales volume of Ford. GM's sales rose 17 percent in October 2006 from the same month in 2005, and Ford sales rose 8 percent in the same period. Ford also sits on $23 billion in cash, so they have plenty of money to focus on and fix any problems.

And for all the talk about the lack of fuel efficiency of American automobiles, it seems that three-fourths of all automakers failed to meet Europe's improved fuel-efficiency standards intended to cut carbon dioxide emissions. Japanese and German automakers topped the list of the study's worst performers, but according to an environmental group's study, GM's Opel division and Ford both "come out well."

In closing, I'll leave some encouraging numbers for those of us who actually like to root for and support the home team. The J.D. Power 2006 Vehicle Dependability Survey reports that Mercury, Buick, and Cadillac (in that order) grabbed the number 2, 3 and 4 spots to beat Toyota,

Honda, Nissan, BMW, and everyone else (except Lexus) in having the least number of problems per 100 vehicles.

Perhaps someday the American media will give GM and Ford the credit they deserve. And once they do, perception among the majority of the American public will rightfully change. GM and Ford aren't only doing what they should to make gains in the American market to deserve American consumer loyalty, they're also doing what they should to make gains in the markets of China, Europe, and across most of the rest of the globe.

Thunder On The Tundra: Toyota Trucks Ahead In 2007 Recalls February 18, 2007

If you've merely done a moderate amount of Internet surfing or cracked open a newspaper lately, just about any newspaper, you've undoubtedly seen the news that Toyota has once again passed Ford in worldwide auto sales and may pass GM sometime this year.

But what you may not have seen is that Toyota has already passed both Ford and GM in a different category—automotive recalls.

Although we've barely passed mid-February, Toyota has already recalled 533,417 vehicles this year in a mix that, according to www.AutoRecalls.us, includes Tundras, Sequoias, and Camrys. That puts Toyota on track to recall more than the over 1.76 million autos they recalled in the U.S. and Japan in 2006 and the 2.2 million they recalled in 2005 when they recalled more cars than they built.

What's more, the current recall related to the Tundra trucks and Sequioa SUVs is similar to the same defect in 800,000 of the same vehicles recalled in 2005. Maybe somebody at Toyota isn't paying attention?

I hope that American consumers are. Recall numbers by domestic companies (GM and Ford) so far this year are as follows: Ford, 128,163; Chevrolet, 4,829; and Pontiac, 1,602.

Chrysler, a German company masquerading as an American company with plans to start importing cars from China in 2008, has recalled 77,432 vehicles so far in 2007.

To be sure, high recall numbers are not good. Auto companies would much prefer high sales numbers instead. As I've already mentioned, the media is abuzz that GM may lose its crown this year to Toyota in world-wide auto sales. But for that to ever happen in the U.S. sales category, it's going to take several more years since GM has a U.S. market share of 24.3 percent compared to 15.4 percent for Toyota. Even Ford, despite its recent troubles, has a higher domestic market share than Toyota at 17.5 percent. But if GM loses its worldwide crown this year, it may actually turn out to be a blessing in disguise.

GM spent 17 percent less per vehicle this January, 2006, compared to last January, which means they are more profitable on a per-unit basis. In fact, GM expects to report a profit for the most recent quarter.

Second, it may be good for GM to step aside temporarily, for now, and let Toyota take all the ammunition that is always aimed at the top dog of the industry so there is less pressure and fewer distractions. And when GM combines its more solid profitability and its improved quality together, its public perception will also improve.

Then they can use these admirable qualities to prepare to surge back to the top at the precise time Toyota is in the top slot with its recall surge in the news. Toyota's timing at being number one worldwide would create further skepticism about whether they really deserve their reputation for untarnished quality.

According to *Business Week*'s January 22, 2007, issue, Toyota has recalled 9.3 million vehicles in the last three years, which is nearly four times the number of recalls in the three-year period prior to 2004.

Other recent news that won't sit well with a Camry-conscious public is the class action lawsuit recently settled by Toyota regarding ruinous oil sludge build up covering 3.5 million Toyota and Lexus (yes, Lexus) vehicles.

Optimistic statements by Toyota executives aren't going to cut it for long, particularly when they don't match well with reality. Denial in the Camry company camp seems to be setting in. Toyota's North American president, Jim Press, recently disputed the suggestion that his company no longer enjoys a large lead in reliability over the American competition.

Speculating on the thoughts of American car company well-wishers while speaking at the recent Chicago Auto Show, Press said, "I think there's some hope that the gap in quality is closing, but it really isn't."

Oh, really? That's a pretty strong comment considering Toyota recalled 1.27 million vehicles in one swoop in 2005, recording the biggest ever recall in history for a Japanese car company.

But, recalls notwithstanding, the evidence that the quality gap is closing is pretty indisputable, and the evidence has been piling up for more than just the last couple of years. With the following facts, you can make your argument for American car quality fully bulletproof, even among your most ardent foreign car defending friends.

- A February 10, 2003, *Business Week* article told of how undeniable it was that GM cars are better built than they used to be. The article cited an improved J.D. Power quality ranking and a *Consumer Reports* recommendation for 13 of GM's vehicles (equal to 41 percent of their sales volume) compared to just five recommended GM vehicles for the previous year. The Chevy Impala beat the Toyota Camry in a quality survey, and Buick beat BMW.

- *Business Week* also reported on September 23, 2003, that GM boosted its productivity 23 percent in six years while Toyota's productivity remained flat and that GM's most productive factories now beat Toyota's most productive factories.

- A 2004 *Consumer Reports* ranking selected the Buick Regal as the most reliable car among family sedans, beating the Toyota Camry, Honda Accord, and Nissan Maxima. They also gave recommended ratings for four Ford models, including the Ford Focus.

- J.D. Power and Associates awarded Cadillac's Lansing Grand River assembly center its highest honor, the Gold Plant Quality Award, in 2004.

- An August 4, 2004, *Wall Street Journal* article said that Toyota's lead in quality and reliability has narrowed in some segments and disappeared in others. Quality problems were reportedly "mushrooming."

- The Toyota Camry hasn't been awarded the best in its segment since the year 2000, but many Americans continue to regard it as the number one model in terms of quality. Toyota's Kentucky Camry plant was awarded with high initial quality rankings by J.D. Power from the late 1980s through the 1990s, but it plummeted to number 26 in 2002, improving to only number 14 in 2004, while two GM factories and one Ford factory took the top three spots that year.
- In a J.D. Power Initial Quality Survey of new 2004 cars, Chevy placed second behind Honda, and Toyota sank to number three.
- As far back as at least 2003, *Business Week* has reported that American consumers regard certain foreign cars as better built than American cars, even when facts prove otherwise.
- Fast-forwarding to 2006, J.D. Power shows Mercury, Buick, and Cadillac beat Toyota in a list of dependable cars. Two Buicks and a Mercury took the top three mid-size car awards; Mercury, Ford, and Buick took the top three large car awards; Ford took the mid-size van award and the mid-size truck award; and GMC and Cadillac took the large MAV (multi-purpose activity vehicle) and large premium MAV awards, respectively.
- In an article about trust issues, *Business Week's* December 11, 2006, issue stated "GM's quality nearly equals Toyota's." Perceived quality among the American public is another story, however. The difference between the actual quality of American cars and the perceived quality of American cars is the "perception gap."
- In the same article, J.D. Power's director for retail research said, "Actual quality is so close," discussing the quality rankings of GMC, Chevrolet, and Cadillac placing them on par with both Honda and Toyota.
- And most recently, of course, the Ford Fusion and Mercury Milan beat the Honda Accord and Toyota Camry, according to *Consumer Reports.*

What's needed among automotive senior executives, and much of the media as well, is a return to intellectual honesty. Everyone tends to have their favorites and biases (mine are pretty obvious), but I pride myself in sticking with the facts to back up my comments.

When Toyota's North American president says that the quality gap isn't really closing, he's not being intellectually honest.

Some editorial writers aren't, either. When Douglas Brinkley trumpeted Indiana's success in a *Wall Street Journal* article last year for attracting a Honda plant to their state, even though it took $140 million in tax credits and incentives, he wasn't what you would call "intellectually honest." In an apparent attempt to convince the reader that Honda doesn't send any automobiles to the U.S. from outside the country, he said, "Turning farm fields into factories, that's what Henry Ford used to do. Today, in the heartland, it's being done by Honda—a company that doesn't manufacture imports but builds American-made cars."

Such statements lead the reader to think that some Japanese companies make all of their cars in the U.S. Hardly. In fact, according to a January 8, 2007, *Wall Street Journal* article, the North American Production (NAP) ratio, a ratio that compares how many cars are built in North America versus the number of cars imported, is slipping for Toyota. And according to Toyota internal documentation, the ratio is going to get worse next year.

Occasionally I'll find an editorial writer that dares to step away from the foreign biases of others in the same industry and rates cars objectively rather than relying on the mindset of the question "Will American cars ever match the Japanese cars in quality?"

Editorial Director for *Consumer Guide Automotive*, Mark Bilek, departed from the typical mindset of his colleagues back in June 2005 by declaring that the Ford Five Hundred was the best car he'd ever driven.

That's good news for Ford, since the Five Hundred is being re-named the Taurus and will get several more second looks because of the Taurus' higher name recognition. Bilek said he judged the Five Hundred based on "what it is" and how well it "fulfills its mission." Based on this, his opinion was that the Five Hundred was "simply the best full-size sedan sold in America."

I am confident, however, that people like Toyota's Jim Press can be somewhat honest in their statements about the competition from time to time. He did say that the "car of the show" at the Detroit Auto Show in January 2007 was, for him, none other than the Chevy Malibu. Maybe there's hope for intellectual honesty after all.

What's Wrong With American Automakers: The Real Story
April 25, 2007

The good news is that there are clear and identifiable reasons for the big-time struggles at the "Big Three" automakers. The bad news is that unless the American people and their elected representatives realize it and do something about it, every American, regardless of whether they are directly linked to the U.S. auto industry or not, will pay a significant price.

But before I get to the heart of the article and explain why America's health care needs to pull into the service bay for a check up because its killing our domestic automakers, I want to state where I stand on what defines a "domestic" automaker.

First, I do not subscribe to the popular belief that there is even a "Big Three" anymore. The term "Big Three" traditionally was invented to describe the three American automakers General Motors, Ford, and Chrysler.

Chrysler, however, can no longer be classified as "American" since it is no longer American-owned. Chrysler became a U.S. subsidiary of a German company when it agreed to supposedly "merge" with Germany's Daimler-Benz in 1998. The newly formed DaimlerChrysler was never a "merger of equals" as was claimed by then CEO, Jurgen Schrempp, and everyone should have realized that there can never be two separate corporate headquarters for the same corporation.

When two companies "merge," one will ultimately become a subsidiary of the other.

According to a November 24, 2003, *Business Week* article, Schrempp let a "tasty morsel" slip when he was interviewed by the *Financial Times* in an October 30, 2000, story. Then CEO Jurgen Schrempp told the London newspaper, "If I had gone and said Chrysler would be a division, everybody on their side would have said: There is no way we'll do a deal," so "we had to go a roundabout way for psychological reasons."

Decisions determining Chrysler's fate are not made in Detroit, they're made in Stuttgart, Germany. So even though most of the (Chrysler) workers are in the U.S., Chrysler is not a stand-alone, independent American company.

And I don't care about whatever hogwash was conceived when NAFTA was ratified determining that cars could be classified as "American" only if 75 percent of their parts content was derived from domestic sources.

Ownership equals control, and control equals independence. Unless a company is owned and controlled by American investors, owners, and stockholders, it isn't American. Chrysler isn't an independent American company under German ownership and control any more than our people could have been an independent American nation under British rule and control prior to the Declaration of Independence.

Perhaps a September 23, 2006, *Wall Street Journal* article summed up independent-thinking Americans' feelings best when discussing the new "Dr. Z" commercials. "Patriotic Americans aren't happy that Detroit had to team up with foreigners to remain competitive, and they certainly don't want it thrown in their faces on TV."

There's a big difference between one company (a non-American one—Chrysler) that wants to team up with a Chinese company to import cars to the U.S. from China and another company (an American one—General Motors) that says they can't see importing cars from China for the foreseeable future.

We don't have the "Big Three" anymore. We have the "Big Two." Fortunately, the "Big Two" (Ford and General Motors), when compared to any other auto company, employ the most Americans, have the most U.S. factories in America, invest the most money in America, get more of their parts from America, and pay more taxes to the U.S. Treasury than Toyota or anyone else ever dreamed.

I did, however, leave out one important issue in the above paragraph that returns me to the root of what the title of this article is all about. Health care.

But contrary to the title of this article, health care is more about what's wrong at the American automakers than what's wrong with the American automakers.

General Motors, for instance, spent $5.4 billion last year in health care for Americans that Toyota didn't have to worry about since Japan has a nationalized health care system and America doesn't. I'm not calling for an American nationalized health care system, but when the rules for all competitors aren't the same for all players in any competitive activity, those who merely watch the players aren't justified in shouting down the losers simply because the only reason they're losing is because they're getting stuck with burdens from which their competition is exempt.

And as much as free market advocates dismiss protectionism, since it would supposedly unfairly subsidize domestic producers, they never mention that free trade, as well as our broken health care system, is subsidizing foreign producers. Any time you exempt the cost burdens of one producer that another producer in the same industry must pay, that constitutes a subsidy. So it's easy to see that we are subsidizing Japanese imports and Japanese companies, as well as any other foreign company and their imports whose home country is exempt from any kind of production cost burden from which American companies are not exempt.

General Motors is the biggest single private purchaser of health care in America. The $5.4 billion in health care costs they paid last year was $5.4 billion that the American people (or the U.S. government) didn't have to pay. If GM fails, someone else is going to have to pick up those costs. We will all pay since you can't continue to take several billions of dollars out of the national economy without affecting everybody in it. So if you're not in favor of America inevitably accepting a nationalized health care system, you'd better be in favor of the survival of Ford and General Motors.

General Motors and Ford also pay the price of an American health care that is broken. GM CEO, Rick Wagoner, knows his company spends more on health care for employees and retirees than on steel for cars and trucks. The cost of health care in America is rising at double-digit rates annually and now costs GM over $1,500 for every vehicle they sell.

And GM gets a horrible return on its health care investment in America. According to a February 9, 2005, *Wall Street Journal* article, errors in America's health care system are frequent. Studies show that adults making doctor or hospital visits get what experts define as the best available treatment only 50 percent of the time. As the *Wall Street Journal* article put it, GM and Ford have to deal with both "pockets of excellence" and "wastelands of inefficiency." These are phrases that foreign car lovers use to describe Ford and GM when these phrases would more accurately describe what Ford and GM have to deal with compared to Japanese automakers.

That's why the CEOs of the "Big Three" automakers were so determined to meet with George W. Bush (who finally agreed to meet with them after ignoring them twice) to discuss the sick state of health care in this country. An inefficient, wasteful health care system forces GM and Ford to do more with less.

George W. Bush knows that the United States spends 15 percent of its entire national output on health care while Japan only spends 8 percent. George W. Bush knows that America needs a system that offers better health care at a lower cost. And he knows American companies Ford and GM (and yes, even German-owned Chrysler) don't compete on a level playing field. But he also knows that even though he talks about how American companies can compete with anybody if they have a level playing field, he's never even going to try to do anything to make the playing field level.

But just try to imagine a nation where General Motors, Ford, and Toyota could all start from scratch and where none are saddled with billions more in pension and health care obligations than the other. Well, you don't have to imagine, because that example already exists in China. And what is happening? In China, General Motors is the number one seller of cars. Volkswagen is second, but Ford is way ahead of Toyota.

The biggest reason Toyota is more successful in America than GM and

Ford is because they don't have big health care and pension millstones around their necks. Sure, you can say it's because Toyota is building cars more Americans like (even though GM and Ford have the number 1 and number 2 market share, respectively, in the U.S.), but the reason they can make snazzier dashboards and the like is because they have more cash to play with. And they have more cash to play with because they don't have to deal with America's sick health care system.

Managing director John Hoffecker of AlixPartners LLP says that his firm's research shows that GM and Ford were both nearly as profitable as Toyota as recently as 2004 if you exclude health care costs.

If you build cars in America for 100 years like GM and Ford have, you are going to have to deal with high health care and pension costs. GM and Ford helped create the system we are so foolishly whittling away today that shielded their workers from these costs. The fact that Toyota employs younger workers is not a corporate virtue. They were able to start from scratch in America in 1987 with their first factory, absent any health care or pension costs for many years to come. And according to the AFL-CIO, Toyota has received $371 million is subsidies from the state of Kentucky alone where they assemble the Camry.

Yes, GM and Ford are dealing with flat sales here in the U.S. while Toyota is surging. But few talk about how Toyota is experiencing flat sales in their home market, too. And it's rarely mentioned that protectionist Japan doesn't allow GM and Ford to have an equal chance to penetrate their market like we allow Japanese companies to penetrate ours.

Eventually, however, it will become evident to all Americans that the real problems are being laid out right here in this article. For Toyota now employs workers at its Georgetown, Kentucky, plant who have reached 20 years with the company. They, too, will soon have to deal with America's health care problem as they prepare for bigger health care bills for their aging American workers, although they employ far fewer American workers than does GM or Ford.

China will eventually become the new Japan, and everyone will wonder why Japanese car companies can't compete with Chinese ones. Those who are shouting down American companies for not being competitive enough with Japanese companies now (if they are honest with themselves) will be shouting down Japanese companies for not being competitive enough with Chinese companies.

But eventually we'll all finally realize that we shouldn't have been spewing our venom at Ford and GM for all their struggles for so many years. Maybe we'll finally realize that they were bearing the weight of an honorable burden on their shoulders so we wouldn't have to carry that burden on our own shoulders.

Maybe also by then we'll realize that we should have protected American producers that were required to absorb the high cost of health care from foreign producers that didn't have to absorb those same costs.

Protectionism for American producers doesn't mean subsidizing them, it means protecting them against unfair subsidies granted to foreign producers. It means eliminating subsidies for any nation or producer. Just like in a poker game, if you want to sit at the table and share in the pot, you have to ante-up equally just like everyone else. The pot in this case is the lucrative U.S. market, and if foreign companies want access to it, they need to bear the burdens of the American system equally with American companies.

So Chrysler Is (Mostly) American Again...Now What?
October 1, 2007

Now that the Germans have finally decided to largely undo their former "merger of equals" fraud they perpetrated in the late 1990s and have allowed Chrysler to be (mostly) acquired by the American-owned, private equity fund Cerebus, there are two main questions for Americans who like to be patriotic with their purchases.

1. How "American" is Chrysler?
2. Is it just as patriotic to buy a GM or Ford product as it is to buy a Chrysler product, which includes Dodge and Jeep brands?

The answer to the first question is that Chrysler is now exactly 80.1 percent American-owned and 19.9 percent German-owned. The answer to the second question is it's still better to buy a GM or Ford if you want the most patriotic bang for your buck. Chrysler purchases are for those Americans who positively can't stand supporting an American company that refused to engage in an entangling alliance with a foreign automaker. Both GM and Ford stared bankruptcy and financial collapse in the face yet refused to give up their American independence by submitting to overwhelming pressure to team up with Japanese-owned Nissan, which is also 44 percent owned by the French.

Chrysler purchases are for those who don't mind the fact that Chrysler plans to start importing complete cars from China next year, which would become a Toyota-type nightmare for GM and Ford, who have no such plans.

Why the nightmare scenario? Because the playing field is already seriously unlevel, with everyone playing by the lowest-cost rules they can. GM and Ford, of course, pay the highest premiums to access and sell to the coveted U.S market since they have taken on the task of supporting health care and pensions for their retirees This honorable burden they have chosen to bear, from which most Americans feel no *direct* relief, makes most free market Americans hopelessly and eternally ungrateful since it makes American automakers "uncompetitive."

Yes, I'm aware that Chrysler, like GM and Ford, has to worry about an unlevel playing field. And I'm aware that Chrysler, like GM and Ford, pays more toward funding the health care and pensions for their workers and retirees and their families than Toyota, Honda, and Nissan do.

But GM and Ford aren't taking un-American actions to try to level the playing field. What are some of these un-American actions, other than Chrysler's plans to import cars from China in 2008?

For starters, The Chinese company that Chrysler is teaming up with, Chery Automobile Company, is the same company that fabricated a knockoff of the Chevy Spark, to which it bore a striking resemblance.

GM sued Chinese-government owned Chery in 2004 and settled in 2005 under a cloud of undisclosed terms, but anyone can easily see the obvious similarities between "Chevy" and "Chery" to see what China's intentions are.

But none of that matters, of course, to Chrysler. They weren't even American-owned at the time, as they were still controlled by Germany's DaimlerChrysler.

But that brings us to the next point of Chrysler's un-American ways. It's simply not American to pretend you are something that you're really not. And the whole time Chrysler was German-owned, they still wanted us to believe they were an American company, even to the point of publicly resenting "Toyota wrapping themselves in the American flag," according to one Chrysler spokesman.

How can Chrysler be upset about a foreign company trying to appear American when they're not when they are guilty of the same deceit?

And all the while Chrysler was pretending to be an American company when they were owned by Germany's DaimlerChrysler AG, it didn't bother them that DaimlerChrysler AG was among one of the companies listed (along with German-owned Siemens) that helped Saddam Hussein amass almost $2 billion in illegal kickbacks through exploiting a humanitarian program devised by the United Nations, according to an October 28, 2005, *Wall Street Journal* article.

It didn't matter that DaimlerChrysler owned a 20 percent stake in the European Aeronautic Defence and Space Co., which is the only formidable competition for American-owned Boeing, America's largest exporter.

It didn't matter that in February 2007 DaimlerChrysler announced it would dole out bonuses of 2,000 Euro to their *German* employees, at the very height of their struggle to adequately fund a turnaround of their American subsidiary.

It didn't matter that Dubai International Capital invested $1 billion in DaimlerChrysler in 2005 to become the third-largest shareholder or that in that same year the company spent huge funds to erect a huge Mercedes-Benz museum as tall as our Statue of Liberty and house three times the exhibit space of the Guggenheim Museum in New York.

Chrysler purchases by Americans during the Daimler years are for those Americans who don't care about any of these things or didn't know about them. Well now you know!

And Chrysler purchases today are for those who both didn't care what was happening at the company then *and* don't care about what's happening at the company now.

It doesn't matter to Chrysler now that they've hired former longtime Toyota executive Jim Press, who most recently served as Toyota's North American chief. It was Jim Press who said at the most recent Chicago Auto Show, talking about the perception that the quality gap between Toyota and American automakers might be closing, "I think there's some hope that the gap in quality is closing, but it really isn't." I wonder what he might say now that he has come to represent a company that is actually based in his own country? Will he refute that comment and now tell us about the quality strides of the new American Chrysler company?

You see, GM and Ford may have had their struggles, but they don't try to draw talent from foreign-owned adversaries, like Chrysler has done in drawing Jim Press from Toyota, and then assume their former adversary is now their friend. Yet Jim Press says he relishes the chance to save what he calls an American icon. Too bad he has been busy trying to destroy two or three of them for the last 20 years.

Then there's the hiring of Robert Nardelli, who barely had a chance to verify he had all $210 million of his Home Depot severance package, before being recruited by Chrysler. Nardelli will likely clash hard with the United Auto Workers and cause problems for Chrysler. The new Chrysler clearly has its work cut out for it, and even if investors looking to make a buck by bottom-searching for stocks love Nardelli, when the stakes are so high, as they are now for Chrysler and indeed any other U.S. automaker, you need inspired employees with high moral. Nardelli isn't the one to inspire employees and build worker morale.

In July 2007, at a visit in Beijing, China, speaking about the new combination between China's cheap manufacturing and Chrysler's technology, Chrysler executive, Tom Lasorda, proposed, "I would say there are endless possibilities." My concern is that those possibilities include destroying what's left of General Motors and Ford, which are America's strongest and most American automakers.

Nardelli isn't going to be able to fix Chrysler by doing what he did at Home Depot and replace higher-wage experienced sales clerks with lower-wage inexperienced students, which was a devastating blow to customer service and only drove consumers to rival companies.

It's my opinion that much like in the way GM decided it was time for Oldsmobile to ride off into the sunset, it's time that Chrysler does the same.

Toyota's rise has come at the expense of GM, Ford, and Chrysler, who now have a combined market share of under 50 percent for the first time in their history.

Back in 1992, William Greider warned us in his book *Who Will Tell the People: The Betrayal of American Democracy*, "Factories worldwide have the capacity to produce 45 million cars annually for a market that, in the best years, will buy no more than 35 million cars." The global oversupply situation isn't any better today. China, with its ability to flood the car market even more with its extra-lean manufacturing, only compounds the problem, and if Chrysler teams up with Chevy-cheating Chery Automotive, the problem compounds even more. If I were a betting man, I wouldn't bet that Chrysler can turn itself around without destroying GM or Ford or both in the process. The auto market is just too crowded for GM, Ford, and Chrysler to all be healthy *and* profitable.

So I'm advocating to those who want to do the patriotic thing when buying a car to put their preference on GM and Ford first and then on Chrysler as a distant preferred third choice. I would never advocate buying a Toyota over a Chrysler (even when Chrysler was German owned), and it is my view that a Big Three can't survive, but a Big Two can survive.

I hope that any layoffs of hard-working Americans at Chrylser will result in hiring at a prosperous Ford or GM if Americans focus on this strategy. At this point, Chrysler will do anything to get back on track, and that "anything" could be what brings down GM and Ford.

Different people have different perceptions, of course, about supposed "merger of equals" between Chrysler and Daimler-Benz back in 1998. But according to the famous and former Chrysler CEO, Lee Iacocca, everyone can agree on at least one thing. Chrysler was screwed royally by Daimler.

Mr. Iacocca knows that American auto companies aren't at the edge of the cliff due to lack of efficiency but rather because of health care and pension costs that foreign automakers don't have to carry.

The only way Chrysler is going to make it out of their hole, other than churning out whole cars in China, is to slash those American health care and pension costs.

For GM and Ford to survive within such a competition nightmare scenario they would have to do the same thing, and there the downward spiral spins out of control.

And surely the way to create a mass consumption economy here at home is not to take money directly out of the hands of those most likely to buy your vehicles. There simply isn't a way to remove spendable income from American consumers without negatively affecting the American economy. And that's basically what Chrysler will be doing if they significantly slash company health care and pension costs since Chrysler workers will be picking up the tab that used to be picked up by the Chrysler company.

Chrysler is partly banking on expanding into foreign markets (I guess they assume they can keep their market share from sliding in the U.S.), but this is much easier said than done. Chrysler, like Toyota, has been kind of late in trying to penetrate the Chinese market, in particular, according to a December 2006 *Wall Street Journal* article. It's not going to be easy to make significant, immediate strides in a country where you don't have very much name recognition.

Chrysler may have very well picked the wrong Chinese partner in Chery Automotive if they want a public perception of high quality manufacturing. When Moscow tested Chery's Chinese-made Aumulet in a crash test in 2007, it folded like an accordion. The front door sills crumpled up like newspaper at 40 mph, and one of Russia's car magazines said it was one of the worst performing crash tests ever. Another Russian car magazine scored the Amulet a "zero" out of a possible 16 in 2001.

Russia's *AvtoRevu* magazine said that the Chevy Spark knockoff Chery QQ does worse in crash tests than similar cars since the Chery QQ uses softer metal. Chery, of course, claims it uses metal they describe as "top-quality."

In any case, American car buyers who buy from Chrysler because they want to do the patriotic thing and save an American icon may destroy one or two others in the process. And in my opinion, it's a dangerous consumer strategy and not worth the risk. Let's stay focused on saving GM and Ford, or we may end up with no American auto industry at all.

Chapter 16

American Made/Union Made Database

IAM (International Association of Machinists) Union-Made Products

Air Conditioners
American Standard
Baird Manufacturing
Federal Industries
General Electric
Goodman
    Manufacturing
Perlick
Red T
Research Products
    Corporation
Standex International
Trane
York International

Aircraft
Cessna Aircraft
Textron Aircraft

Ammunition
Winchester

Appliances
Frigidaire
General Electric
Lasko
Maytag
Metal Ware
Nesco & Empire
Peerless
Whirlpool

Beer & Ale
Anheuser-Busch
Mad River
Miller Beer

Seagram's Liquor
Steelhead Fine Ale

**Boat and Stationary
Motors**
Cummins
Dresser
Enpro
Jimmy Diesel
Mercury
Tecumseh
Volvo

Boats
Lifetimer
Merrill Stevens
    Dry Dock
Vic Francks
Weeres Pontoon

Knives
Fiskars
Gerber

Lawn Mowers
Berkman Louis
    Company
John Deere
Simplicity
Toro

Motorcycles
Harley-Davidson
    Motorcycles

Rifles & Shotguns
Browning
    Rifles/Shotguns
Douglas Barrels
    Rifles/Shotguns
Savage Arms
    Rifles/Shotguns

Tobacco
Beechnut Chewing
    Tobacco
Brown & Williamson
    Cigarettes
Philip Morris Cigarettes
Swisher Cigars

Tools
California Saw & Knife
    Works
Channellock
Hydramec
Independent Die Service
Lisle Corporation
Progressive Service
    Die Co.
S-K
Snap-On
Stanley
Warner

Watches & Clocks
American Time
Montgomery
    Manufacturing
Timex

UAW (United Auto Workers) Union-Made Products

Appliances
Frigidaire Washers
    and Dryers
Gibson Washers
    and Dryers
Kelvinator Washers
    and Dryers
White-Westinghouse
    Washers and Dryers
Montgomery Ward
    Washers and Dryers
Sears Kenmore Laundry
    Center
Grassco Refrigeration
    Units
Grassco Air Compressor
    Units
Lennox Home Furnaces
Lennox Air Conditioners
Northland Freezers
Northland Full
    Refrigerators

Auto Parts
Budd Wheels
Budd Wheel Hubs
Budd Discs
Budd Drums
Bundy Tubing Brake
    Products
International Brake
    Brake Kits
EIS Brake Parts
Delco-Moraine Brake
    Shoes
NI Industries Wire
    Wheel Covers
ABEX Brake Shoes
Standard Motors Brakes
Fleetguard Fuel Filters

Fleetguard Oil Filters
Fleetguard Air Filters
Fleetguard Water Filters
AP Mufflers and
    Tail Pipes
Tuffy Mufflers and
    Tail Pipes
Goerlich Mufflers and
    Tail Pipes
Merrit Mufflers and
    Tail Pipes
Delco Points
Delco Starter Coils
Delco Alternators
AC Delco Starters
Service Turn Signal
    Switches
AC Delco Turn Signal
    Switches
Durakon Truck Bed
    Liners
General Motors
    Replacement Tail Lights
Kem Mfg. Points
Kem Mfg. Starters
Kem Mfg. Distributors
MBL USA Fan Belts
Midas Mufflers
Midas Reconditioned
    Brake Calipers
Snap Cleaning Products
Outlaw Cleaning
    Products
Dollar General Cleaning
    Products
Tach One Cleaning
    Products
Mag 1 Cleaning
    Products
Stant Mfg. Gas Caps

Stant Mfg. Radiator
    Caps
Trico Wiper Blades
Wells Ignition Parts
AC Spark Plugs
AC Glo Plugs
Autolite Spark Plugs
Champion Spark Plugs
Motorcraft Spark Plugs
Mighty Spark Plugs
Sears Spark Plugs
Valley Forge Spark Plugs
Wellman Spark Plugs

Automobile Batteries
Amoco
Atlas
BJ's Wholesale Club
Delco Freedom
Dura-Power
Ford
Western Auto
Sam's Club
Sears - DieHard Gold
Shell Service Stations
Trak-Auto - Permacell,
    Lastacell and Ultracell
Voyager Marine Batteries
Goodyear
Kmart
Exide
Champion
Motorcraft
Action Pak
Super Crank
Stowaway
Globe-Union
Firestone
American Hardware
Ames

Kmart
Energizer
Everready
Wal-mart
Price Costo

Automobiles
Buick Lucerne
Cadillac CTS
Cadillac DTS
Cadillac STS
Cadillac XLR
Chevrolet Cobalt
Chevrolet Corvette
Chevrolet Malibu
Chrysler Sebring
Dodge Avenger
Dodge Caliber
Dodge Viper
Ford Focus
Ford Mustang
Ford Taurus
Lincoln MKS
Mazda 6
Mercury Sable
Mitsubishi Eclipse
Mitsubishi Galant
Pontiac G5
Pontiac G6
Pontiac Solstice
Pontiac Vibe
Saturn Aura
Saturn Sky
Toyota Corolla*
Chevrolet Colorado
Dodge Dakota
Dodge Ram Pickup*
Ford Explorer Sport Trac
Ford F-Series*
Ford Ranger
GMC Canyon
Isuzu i-Series
Lincoln Mark LT

Mazda B-series
Mitsubishi Raider
Toyota Tacoma*
Buick Enclave
Cadillac Escalade
Cadillac Escalade ESV
Cadillac SRX
Chevrolet Suburban*
Chevrolet Tahoe/
   Tahoe Hybrid
Chrysler Aspen
Dodge Durango
Dodge Nitro
Ford Escape
Ford Expedition
Ford Explorer
Ford Taurus X
GMC Acadia
GMC Yukon/Yukon
   Hybrid
GMC Yukon Denali
Hummer H1
Hummer H2
Hummer H3
Jeep Commander
Jeep Compass
Jeep Grand Cherokee
Jeep Liberty
Jeep Patriot
Jeep Wrangler
Lincoln Navigator
Mazda Tribute
Mercury Mariner
Mercury Mountaineer
Mitsubishi Endeavor
Saturn Outlook
Ford E-series
Chevrolet Express
Chevrolet Uplander
GMC Savana
Chevrolet Silverado*
GMC Sierra*
Chrysler Town & Country

Dodge Caravan
Chevrolet TrailBlazer
GMC Envoy
GMC Envoy Denali
Isuzu Ascender
Saab 9-7X

Beer
Miller Lite
Miller Genuine Draft
Miller Genuine Draft
   Light
Miller High Life
Miller High Life Light
Milwaukee's Best
Milwaukee's Best Light
Milwaukee's Best Ice
Leinenkugel's
Sharp's (non alcoholic)
Mickey's Malt
Mickey's Ice
Hamm's
Hamm's Draft
Hamm's Light
Icehouse
Miller Lite Ice
Red Dog
Olde English 800
Henry Weinhard's
Private Reserve
Henry Weinhard's Blue
Boar Pale Ale

Factory-Built Homes
Active Homes Modular
   Homes
Active Homes Panel
   Houses

Food Products
Merita Bakery Goods
Old Fashioned Bread

Food Products (cont.)
Land O' Lakes Butter
Land O' Lakes
Margarine
Mar-Ja Peanut Butter
Planters Honey Roasted
Cocktail Peanuts
Planters Caribbean
Peanuts
Dairy Pak Champion
Milk Containers
Folgers Instant Coffee
Folgers Brick-Pack
Coffee
Pruden Ham
(Mail Order)
Sunshine Biscuits
Cheese Crackers
Universal Foods Corp.
Red Star Yeast

Home Repair
Advance Pressure
Castings Corp
Aluminum Sinks
Bradford-White Water
Heaters
Jetglas Water Heaters
Central Brass Faucets
Central Brass Plumbing
Products
Gerber Plumbing
Fixtures
Guaranteed Specialties
Sink Strainers
Guaranteed Specialties
Plumbing Products
Kohler Bath Tubs
Kohler Plumbing
Fixtures
Kohler Small Engines
Kohler Generators
Kohler Toilets

Kohler Stainless Steel
Sinks
Polar Stainless Steel Sinks
Polar Ware Stainless
Steel Sinks
Moen Faucets
Moen Stainless Steel
Sink Accessories
Taylor Building Products
Garage Doors
Taylor Building Products
Entry Doors
Trane Heating Units
Trane Air Conditioning
Units
Acorn Window Systems
Replacement Windows
Acorn Window Systems
Sliding Glass Patio
Doors
Acorn Window Systems
Entrance Doors
Acorn Window Systems
Specialty Windows
American Welding &
Tank (Harsco) LP
Gas Tanks
Armstrong Air
Conditioners
Armstrong Heating
Systems
Andersen Windows
Stanley Doors
C&A Hand-Screened
Wall Paper
Dare Products Corp.
Fence Supplies
EMCO Forever Storm
Doors
GTE Sylvania
Floodlights
GTE Sylvania Halogen
Lights

Hydrotech (Purex) Pool
Lights
Hydrotech (Purex) Pool
Pumps
Hydrotech (Purex) Pool
Heaters
Tube-Lite Doors
Tube-Lite Curtain Walls
NuTone Security
Systems
NuTone Central Vacuum
Systems
NuTone Ventilation Fans
NuTone Bathroom
Cabinets
NuTone Food Blender
Systems
Versa Ladders
Warner Wood Ladders
Warner Attic Ladders
Warner Step Ladders

Housewares
Rice Hold-Fast Shades
Embassy Industries
Baseboard Heaters
Eagle Electric Extension
Cords
Eagle Electric Plugs
Eagle Electric Sockets
Eagle Electric Fuses
Eagle Electric Decorator
Lamps
Green Manufacturing
Outdoor Gas Grill
Burner Kits
Green Manufacturing
Replacement Parts
Kirsch Drapery
Hardware
Kirsch Curtain Rods
Kirsch Traverse Rods
Kirsch Decorator Rods

Lloyd Flanders Wicker Furniture

Nestaway (Axia) Dish Drainers

Nestaway (Axia) Oven Racks

Penn-Plax Fish Tanks

Penn-Plax Bird Cages

Pressure Castings Union Mugs

Pillowtex Pillowcases

Pillowtex Bed Spreads

Pillowtex Sheets

Lysol Toilet Bowl Cleaner

Lysol Basin Tub & Tile Cleaner

Lysol Antibacterial Kitchen Cleaner

Por-Rok Concrete Mix

Polar Ware Pitchers

Polar Ware Trays

Polar Ware Pans

Polar Ware Cookware

Ronson Lighter Fluid

Ronson Lighters

Ronson Multi Lube

Ronson Glosstex Igniters

Sew What Embroidery

Silvatrim Corp. Picture Frames

Wisco Ind. Kids School Scissors

Wisco Ind. Pruning Shear Blades

Wisco Ind. Medical Wrist Tag

Wisco Ind. Purina Checkerboard Pet Tag

Wisco Ind. Mini Churro Warmer

Vollrath Stainless Steel Pots

Vollrath Pans

Vollrath Bowls

Vollrath Home Cookware

Vollrath Home Bakeware

Vollrath Utensils

Durex Maverick Barbecues

Lawn Care

Ames Co. Rakes

Ames Co. Snow Shovels

AZL Post Hole Diggers

Medical Supplies

EyeDx Eye Glasses

EyeDx Contact Lenses

Hollister Ostemy Supplies

Optiview Vision Centers (Eye Glasses)

Riverfront Optical (Eye Glasses)

TK Optical (Eye Glasses)

Winchester Optical (Eye Glasses)

ValueRx Mail Order Drugs

Music

Yamaha Piccolos

Yamaha Trumpets

Yamaha Trombones

Yamaha Saxophones

Yamaha Clarinets

Office Products

American Seating Office Cubicles

American Seating Filing Drawers

American Seating Biochairs

Ames & Rollinson Calligraphers

Cecilware Cappuccino Dispensers

Cecilware Coffee Urns

First Alert Safes

Fawn Engineering Vending Machines

Modern Fold Accordian Doors

Northland Montisa File Cabinets

Northland Montisa Desk Units

Simco Plaques and Pins

Publications

Mother Jones Magazine

SIERRA Magazine

Progressive Magazine

Viking-Penguin Magazines and Books

Village Voice Magazines and Books

Harper Collins Magazines and Books

Monthly Review Magazine

AMSCO Magazines and Books

Wayne State University Press Books

Sports & Hobby

Charles Rice Boat Covers

Colt Handguns and Rifles

Colt Commemoratives

Dare Products Corp. Boat Ropes

FNT Fish Net and Twine

FNT Tennis Netting

FNT Volleyball Netting

Sports & Hobby (cont.)
FNT Backstop Netting
ITT Jabsco Water Pumps
ITT Jabsco Impellers
ITT Jabsco Bilge Pumps
ITT Jabsco Macerators
ITT Jabsco Pool Electric
   Motors
ITT Jabsco Pool Pumps
LML Corp. Pontoon
   Boats
Anchor Horse Hardware
Wilcox-Crittenden
   Marine Hardware
Remington Arms
   (DuPont) Clay Pigeons

Tools
American Beauty
   Soldering Irons
American Tape Co.
   Masking Tape
American Tape Co.
   Double-Faced Tape
American Tape Co.
   Diaper Tape
American Tape Co.
   Electrical Tape
Apex Screwdrivers
Apex Socket Wrenches
Clauss Cutlery Shears
Clauss Cutlery Scissors
Clauss Cutlery Tweezers
Red Devil Razor Blades,
   Scrapers and Cutters
Hyde Razor Blades,
   Scrapers and Cutters
Stanley Tools Razor
   Blades, Scrapers and
   Cutters
L-Tec Welding Wire and
   Welding Rods

Dual Shield Welding
   Wire and Welding
   Rods
Fabricated Wires
   Welding Wire
   and Welding Rods
Spool Arc Welding Wire
   and Welding Rods
Arc Alloy Welding Wire
   and Welding Rods
Black & Decker Radial
   Wire Brushes and
   Cup Brushes
Compo Industries
   Radial Wire Brushes and
   Cup Brushes
United Abrasives Radial
   Wire Brushes and Cup
   Brushes
KD Tools Radial Wire
   Brushes and Cup
   Brushes
Pherd Radial Wire
   Brushes and Cup
   Brushes
Onan Portable
   Generators
Ray-O-Vac Batteries
Reed Mfg. Pipe
   Wrenches
Reed Mfg. Vises
Reed Mfg. Pipe Cutters
Reed Mfg. Threading
   Tools
Rotor Tools
Seagrave Coatings
Plextone Multicolor
   Paint
Service Supply Clips
Service Supply Screws
Service Supply Nuts
Service Supply Bolts

Toys
Fisher Price Sandboxes
Fisher Price Playhouses
Golden Family
   Entertainment Activity
   Boxes
Golden Family
   Entertainment Cloth
   Blocks for Infants
Golden Family
   Entertainment Games
   and Puzzles
Leister Games and Gag
   Gifts
Testor Hobby Kits and
   Supplies

UFCW (United Food & Commercial Workers) Union-Made Products

Food & Beverage

Alcoholic Beverages

4 Roses Bourbon
4 Roses Fine Old
  Bourbon
4 Roses Super Premium
  Bourbon
99 Bananas
99 Blackberries
After Shock
Amar Di Amore
Amaretto De Sabroso
  Apricot Brandy
Amaretto De Sabroso
  Coffee
Amaretto De Sabroso
  Ginger
Amaretto De Sabroso
  Peach
Amaretto De Sabroso
  Wild Cherry
Ancient Age
Aristocrat
Avalanche Blue
Bakers
Baronof
Barren Vonschoter
Barton 5 Star Brandy
Barton California
  Deluxe
Barton Captain T & T
Barton Gin
Barton Peach Schnapps
Barton T & T
  Concentrate
Barton Triple Sec
Barton Vodka
Basil Hayden

Beam 8 Star
Beam's 7 Year Reserve
Beam's Choice
Bellows
Bellows Blend
Bellows Blended
  Whiskey
Bellows Gin
Bellows Light Rum
Bellows Scotch
Bellows Vodka
Benchmark
Blanton's
Blue Light
Bonded Beam
Bookers
Brigadier
Brigadier Gin
Bud
Bud Light
Buffalo Trace
Burnette
Bush Pilot
Cactus Juice
Calvert
Calvert Extra
Calypso Dark Rum
Calypso Light Rum
Canada House
Canadian Barclay
  Bourbon
Canadian Barclay Gin
Canadian Barclay Vodka
Canadian Hunter
Canadian Ltd.
Canandian Host
  Supreme
Captain Gold Tequila
Captain Morgan

Captain Morgan
  Original Spiced Rum
Captain Morgan Private
  Stock
Captain WhiteTequila
Carribean Gold Rum
Carribean White Rum
Carstairs
Chateaux
Chi Chi Carribean
  Mudslide
Chi Chi Gold Margarita
Chi Chi Margarita
Chi Chi Mexican
  Mudslide
Chi Chi Pina Colada
Chi Chi Strawberry
  Margarita
Chi Chi White Russian
Claymore Scotch
Clear Springs Grain
  Alcohol
Cluny
Cockspur
Colonel Lee
Conquistador
Copa de Oro
Corby's Reserve Blend
Coronet
Crown Russe
Crystal Palace Gin
Crystal Palace Vodka
Crystal Palace Vodka
Dark Eyes
Dark Eyes Vodka
Dekuyper Butterscotch
Dekuyper Flavored
  Brandy
Dekuyper Hot Damn

Alcoholic Beverages (cont.)

Dekuyper Peachtree
Dekuyper Schnapps
Dekuyper Schnapps
   Liqueur
Denaka
Distiller's Pride
Dr. McGillicuddy
Dubonet
Eagle Rare
El Jimador Tequila
El Toro Gold
El Toro White
Elijah Craig
Elmer T. Lee
Evan Williams
Feeney's
Fighting Cock
Fleischmann's Preferred
Fleischmann's Royal
   Brandy
Fleischmann's Royal Gin
Fleischmann's Royal Rye
Fleischmann's Royal
   Vodka
Fleischmann's Royal
   Whiskey
Fuki
Gilbey's
Gilbey's Gin
Ginger Ale Mix
Glenrarclas
Godiva
Golden Grain
Golden Grain Alcohol
Grand Dad Bourbon
Great Jackson Export
Hancock's
Harley & Almaden
   Brandy
Harwood
Henri Brandy
Henry McKenna

Herradura Praline
Herradura Tequila
Holland House
House of Stuart Scotch
Imperial Blend
J.T.S. Brown
J.W. Dant
Jacob's Well
Jacques Bonet Brandy
James Foxe
Jim Beam Black Label
Jim Beam Rye
Jim Beam White
Kamachatka
Kamchata
Kamchatka Vodka
Kamora
Kamora Coffee Liqueur
Keith's
Kentucky Gent Black
Kentucky Gentlemen
Kentucky Tavern
Kessier
Kessler Blended Whiskey
Knob Creek
Labatt's Blue
Lauders Scotch
Lemon Gin
Leroux Flavored
Leroux Schnapps
Lord Calvert
Margaritaville
Masterpiece
Mattingly
McNaughton
Mint Gin
Montezuma Blue Tequila
Montezuma Triple Sec
Montezuma White
   Triple Sec
Moore
Mr. Boston
Mt. Gay

Mt. Vernon Blended
   Whiskey
Nikolai
Northern Light
   Canadian
Oland Export
Oland Schooner
Old Charter
Old Crow
Old Fitzgerald
Old Taylor
Old Thompson
Overholt Rye Whiskey
P-51
Pallo Viejo Gold Rum
Pallo Viejo White Rum
Palo Viejo
Parrot Bay
Passport Scotch
Paul Mason Grande
   Amber Brandy
Pikeman Gin
Pimm's
Pleasant Moments
   Whiskey
PM Blend
Puckers
Pussers
Rain Vodka
Rare Breed
Riva Gim
Rock and Rye
Rock Hill Farms
Ron Merito Rum
Ron Rico
RonRico Gold Puerto
   Rican Rum
RonRico Spiced Rum
RonRico White Puerto
   Rican Rum
Royal Canadian
Royal Club Blend
Royal Gate Vodka

Sabroso
Sambuca DiAmore
Sazerac Bourbon
Sazerac Rye
Schenely Reserve Dry
  Gin
Schenely Reserve Gold
  Rum
Schenely Reserve White
  Rum
Seagram 7 Crown
Seagram's Coolers
Seagram's Gin
Seagram's Grapefruit
  Twisted Gin
Seagram's Lime Twisted
  Gin
Seagrams Gin
Seagrams Gin and Juice
Seven Crown
Single Barrel
Skol Gin
Skol Rum
Skol Vodka
Sloe Gin
Sourz
Taaka
Tangle Ridge
Taylor Straight Bourbon
Tom Collins
Tom Moore
Very Old Barton
VO
Vodka Screwdriver
Weber Premial
Wet Willie's
WI Weller
Wild Turkey
Windsor
Windsor Canadian
  Whiskey
Wolschmidt

Bacon
Black Label
Daisyfield
Domino's Bacon
  Topping
Dunkin' Donuts Bacon
Falls Brand
Farmer John
Farmland 101 Regular
  Hickory Smoked
  Bacon
Farmland Cider House
  Bacon
Farmland Honey/Maple
  Bacon
Farmland Low-Sodium
  Bacon
Farmland Regular
  Hickory Smoked
  Bacon
Farmland SP Low
  Sodium Bacon
Farmland SP Regular
  Hickory Smoked
  Bacon
Farmland SP Vac Bacon
Farmland T/S Peppered
  Bacon
Farmland T/X Sliced
  Bacon
Farmland Thick Sliced
  Bacon
Farmland Tocino
  Ahumado
Farmland Tray-Pack
  Bacon
Farmland Xtra Thick
  Sliced Bacon
Fast 'n' Easy Bacon Bits
HEB
Henry's
Henry's Hickory House
Hofmann

Hormel
Hormel Bacon Bits
Hormel Cooked Bacon
Hormel Fully Cooked
  Jalapeno Bacon
Hormel Fully Cooked
  Regular Bacon
Hormel Microwave
  Bacon
Hormel Old Fashioned
  Canadian Bacon
Hormel Pre-Cooked
  Bacon
HyGrade
HyVee Frontier
Jimmy John's Fine Bacon
John Morell
John Morrell Stack
  Packed Bacon
Krystal Precooked Bacon
Marshallville
Orion Fully Cooked
  Bacon
Oscar Meyer
Our Family
Patrick Cudahy
Plumrose
Private Label (Copack)
Heinz
Valleydale Bacon

Bakery Goods -
Miscellaneous
Blue Ridge
Bunge Foods Dry Mix
Flour-I-Strip
Post
Weetabix

Bottled Water
American Springs
Northern Fall's
Pocono
Poland Spring

Bread, Baked Goods, Dessert
Aunt Millie's
Aunt Millies
Butternut
Carvel
Chicago Flats
Country Hearth
Dawn Foods
Earthgrain
Holsum Soft Twist
Merita
Mission Foods
Old Home
Perfection
Pie Piper
Quaker Oats
Sara Lee
Tops

Baked Beans
Ebro
Vankamps

Canned Foods
Del Monte
Dinty Moore
Green Giant
Hanover
Hormel
Hormel Beef Stew
Hormel Chili
Hormel Chili With
   No Beans
Libby's
Salcihllas Carmelas

Champaign/Wine
Almaden
Anapamu
Andre
Arbor Mist
Barelli Creek
Bartles & James
Boone's Farm
Bronco
Burlwood
Carlo Rossi
CC Vineyards
Champs Elysees
Charles Krug Vintage
Chase - Limogere
Cisco
CK Cellars
CK Mondavi
Coastal Vinters
Cook's
Cooperfield
Corbett Canyon
Cresta Blanca
Cribari
Deer Valley
DeFleu
Dunnewood
E & J Brandy
Eden Roc
Ernest & Julio Gallo
Estate Cellars
Estate Inglenook
Fairbanks
Fortune
Franzia
Gossamer Bay
Great Western
Green Hungarian
Holland House
Hornsby's
Indigo Hills
Inglenook Premium
J. Roget

Jacques Bibet
Jacques Bonet
Jacques Reynard
JFJ
Krug
Lafayette
Laguna
Le Domaine
Lejon Vermouth
Livingston Cellars
Manischewicz
Marcelina
Mogen David
Montpelier
Mystic Cliffs
Napolean
Oakridge Vineyards
Paul Masson
Peter Vella
Rancho Zabaco
Richard's Wild Irish
   Rose
Scheffield
Seagram's Coolers
Select
Sonoma Tier
Stanford
Stefani
Taylor California Cellars
Taylor New York State
Totts
Tribuno Vermouth
Turning Leaf
Via Firenze
Wedding Celebration
Weibel
Wycliff
Zonin

Chili
Dinty Moore
Hormel

Coffee/Tea

American Air Lines
    Coffee
Best Choice
Braniff Air Lines Coffee
Darj Green
Delta Air Lines Coffee
Great Value
Maxwell House
McDonald's Coffee
Mr. & Mrs. Tea
S.S. Pierce Teas
Tetley

Condiments

Aunt Jemima
Cattlemen's
Colonial
Colonial Salt
Diamond Crystal Salt
Durkee
Dutch Mlll
Ebro
Flake
French's
Fry Krisp
Gulden's Mustard
Heinz Catsup
Heinz Ketchup
Hidden Valley Ranch
Hormel
Jefferson Island
JIF Peanut Butter
Ken Salad Dressing
Kernal Fresh
Kitchen Bouquet
Leslie
Lucky Whip
Monarch Salt
Monterey Mushrooms
Morton Salts
Mrs. Butterworth's
Nifda Salt

Open Pit Onion
Open Pit Sweet
Open Pit T & T Smoked
    Grill
Open Pit T & T Sugar
    and Spice
Open Pit Thick and
    Tangy Original
Open Pit Thick Hickory
Open Pit Thick Original
Open Pit Traditional
Pace
Peanut Butter Crunch
Red & White Salt
Red Cross
Red, White and Blue
Saucy Sweet and Sour
    Sauce
Sorrell Ridge
Sterling Salt
Sunflower & Scotts
Susan & Polynesian
Sysco Salt
Van Holtens
Vince & Son's
Vlasic
Watkins Sauces
Watkins Spices

**Cooking
Oils/Shortening**

Albertson's
All Kitchens
Almost Butter
Always Save
America's Choice
Armour
Armour Lard Carton,
    Tub, Pail
Arthur Treechers
Astor
Avanza
Bake Mark

Bake Rite
Baker Boy
Bakers & Chefs
Bakers Choice
Bell-View
Best Brands
Best Choice
Best O'Corn
Best O'Veg
Best Yet
Better Valu
Big Y
Breakthrough
Brechet & Richter
Brookfield
Bunge
Buttercup
Centrella
Chef Mark
Chef's Pride
Churn Spread
Cinnabon
Citation
Clark
Classic Gourmet
Club Store
Coburn Farms
Code
Comsource
Country Delight
Country Fare
Cousins
Crystal Springs
Cub Foods
D & W
Dairy Fresh
Dan's
Darling International
Delmar
Dierbergs
Dress-All
El Mexicano
EMGE

Cooking Oils/Shortening (cont.)

Exceptional Value
Fastco
Fiesta
First Prize
Flavorite
Food Club
Fri-Gold
Frosty Acres
Gem
GFS
Godfathers
Gold 'n Rich
Gold n' Soft
Gold n' Sweet
Golden Chip
Good Day
Goya
Grandioso
Great Value
Haolm
Hidden Valley
High Plains
Holsum
Holsum Precreamed Shortening
Holsum Vegetable Oil
Home Harvest
Hormel
HyVee
IGA
Indian Head
Instant Whip
Jay C
Kaola Gold
La Preferida
Lil' Orbit
Little Caesars
LouAnna
Mar Parv
Market Choice
Meadow Gold

Meijer
Mel-Fry
Melvo
Metz
Migdal
Miller
Miolo
Mother's
Nifda
Nu-Maid
Old Time
Otis Spunkmeyer
Our Family
Parade
Perkins
Phase
Pocahontas
Pop All Canola Popping Oil
Pop-All
Poppin Toppin
Pride of Life
Red & White
Richmade
Roundy's
Royal Bear
Safeway
Sara Lee
Satin Gold
Savers Choice
Savory
Shamrock
Shop & Save
Shurfine
Shurfresh
Smartbeat
Spartan
Special Value
Springfield
Stater Brothers
Stew Leonard
Stouffers
Sun Glow

Sunnyland
Super American Chef
Supreme
Sysco
Tablemaid
Taco John's
Tastee Gold
Thrifty Maid
Tony Romas
Triumph
Ultra Fry
V & V
Valley Bakers
Valu Time
Value Buy
Value Check
Value Choice
Ventura
Ventura Butter Margarine Shortening
Vons
Weis
Western Family
White Rose
Winn Dixie

Dairy Products

A & P
Barber
Beatrice
Breakstone
Breyers Ice Cream
Chianti Cheeses
Country Fresh
Dairy Ease
Dairy Fresh
Dannon
Dean Foods Ultra
Dean's
Delisle Yogurt
Eagle
Flav-O-Rich
Good Humor Ice Cream

Half & Half
Hiland Dairy
IGA
International Delight
Knechtel
Labelle Ice Cream
Laura Secord Ice Cream
Leche Tres Monjitas
Lite & Lively
MacArthur
Meadow Brooks
Orchard Harvest
   Ice Cream
Prairie Farms
President Choice
Quality Chekd
Roberts
Sun-Re Cheese
T.G. Lee
Tres Monjitas
Vitamite 100 Lactose
   Free Non Dairy
   Beverage
Yoplait

Frozen Dinners
Albertson's
America's Choice
Angela Mia
Banquet
Bertucci's
Best Yet
Food Club
Great Value
Healthy Choice
Kroger
LaChoy
Market Day
Rosalini
Rosarita
Schwan's

Fruits
Appletime

Lincoln
Lucky Leaf
Musselman

Ham
Alexander & Hornung
Appleton
Armour
Armour Golden Star
Ashley Farm
Best Choice
Best Yet
Big V
Big Y
Black Forest
Boar's Head
Brookside
Carando
Carando
Cooks
Copperfields
Daisyfield
Eckrich
Extra Tender Fresh Pork
Falls Brand
Farm Fresh
Farmland
Farmland Lean Pit Ham
Farmland NJ Classic
   Cure Ham
Farmland Old Fashioned
   Pit Ham
Farmland Original NJ
   Hickory Smoked Ham
Farmland Original NJ
   Honey Ham
Farmland Original NJ
   Peppered Ham
Farmland Original Pit
   Ham
Farmland Special Select
   Sliced Ham
Farmland Special Select
   Sliced Honey Ham

Farmland Sunday Buffet
   Ham
Farmland Traditional
   WA Ham
Figis
Fricks
Gallery Gourmet
Goodies
Harriet & David
Harry & David
HEB
Horizon Foods
Hormel Bavarian
   Boneless Ham
Hormel Black Forest
   Ham
Hormel Boneless Buff
   Ham
Hormel Diced Ham
Hormel Ground Ham
Hormel Smoked Honey
   Maple Ham
John Morrell EZ Cut
John Morrell Spiral Cut
   Hams
Kings
Kirkland
Kroger
Lancaster
Levonian
Lykes Sunnyland
Margaritta
Marshallville
Master Choice
Mountain Hams
Nicks
Our Family
Patrick Cudahy
Perfect Choice Honey
   Ham
Peter Eckrich
Prestige
Ridge Creek

Ham (cont.)
Rosewood Farms
Safeway
Sahlen's
Schwann's
Seneca
Shaws
Shaws
Sherwood
Shoppers
Smithfield
Stevens
Sugar Tree
Sugardale Foods
Swift
Tops
Up Country
Wellsley
Wilson Continental Deli

Hot Dogs
Al-Pete
Armour - Swift - Eckrich
Ball Park
Boar's Head
Brummel & Brown
Bryan
Conti's Texas Brand
Country Crock
County Fair
Disney Beef Frank
Falls Brand
Farmland
Foster Farms
Hebrew National
Hofmann
Hormel Beef Franks
Hormel Fat Free Beef
    Franks
Hormel Franks
Hormel Pork & Chicken
    Franks
Hormel Red Franks

Hormel Smokie Links
Hormel Smokies
    w/Cheese
Imperial
John Morrell All Beef
    Hot Dogs
Koegel's
Levonian
Luther's Hot Dogs
Lykes and Sunnyland
Lykes Beef Plumper Dogs
Lykes Jumbo Franks
Lykes Jumbo Turkey
    Franks
Nathan's Ball Park Hot
    Dogs
Oscar Meyer
Poultry, Inc.
Sahlen's
Smithfield & Sunnyland
Snappy's
Sugardale Foods
Ted's
Top's Bun Busters
Wardynski
Wenzel's

International Foods
LaChoy
Rosarita

Juices
Appletime
Bright Stock
Clamato
Fruit Blasters
Guana
Guava juice
Hawaiian Punch
Hiland Dairy
International Delight
Lincoln
Lucky Leaf

McCain Foods
Melody Farms
Minute Maid
Musselman
Pineapple Juice
Red Cheek
Roberts
Southern Belle
Speas
Tres Monjitas
V8 - Splash
Welch's

Margarine
Blue Bonnet
Brookfield Spread
Gold - n - Sweet
    Whipped Margarine
I Can't Believe It's Not
    Butter
Mrs. Filbert's
Nu-Maid
Parkay
Promise
Satin Gold Buttermatch
    Spread Tub
Satin Gold Spread Krocks
Satin Gold Vegetable
    Margarine Bowls &
    Quarters
Shedd's
Sun Glow Butter Blend
    Euro
Tastee Gold

Meat - Bulk Products
Banquet
Becker
Beef Products, Inc.
Better Beef
Buffets, Inc. (OCB)
Burger King
Byron's Bar-B-Q

Chiappetti
ConAgra
Daisyfield
Eagle
Elbee Meats
Ember
Excel
Farmland
Ferko
Fischer
Holten Meat Company
Hormel
Hormel Always Tender
Jemm
JJ Derma
Kirshner
Kraft Foods
Levonian
Marcel & Henry
Marie Calendar
McDonald's Restaurant
Omaha Steaks
Ozark Mountain Pork
Packerland
Raleys
Rich's Smoke House
Rose
Sara Lee Premium
Shoney's
Siena Foods
Sterling Silver
Strauss
Swift & Company
Thumann's
Tyson
Waffle House
Wispak

Meats - Deli and Specialty
Alexander & Hornung
Always Tender Honey-
    mustard Pork Loin
Always Tender Lemon
    Garlic Pork Tenderloin
Always Tender Mojo
    Pork Picnic Roast
Always Tender
    Peppercorn Pork Chop
Always Tender
    Peppercorn Pork
    Tenderloin
Always Tender Salsa Pork
    Loin
Always Tender Sliced
    Boneless Rib End
Always Tender Teriyaki
    Beef Kabob
Always Tender Teriyaki
    Beef Kabob
Always Tender Teriyaki
    Pork Chop
Armour
Ball Park
Battistoni
Boar's Head
Butterball
Byron's Bar B Q
Calumet
Cattleman's
Citterio
County Fair
Dearborn Sausage
    Company
Decker
Eckrich
Excel's Tender Choice
Farmer John
Farmland
Healthy Choice
Hebrew National
Hillshire Farm
Hofmann
Hormel Boneless Smoked
    Pork Loins
Hormel Philly Steak

Kahn's Deli Select
Kirshner Brand
Koegel's
Lykes Sunnyland
Marcel & Henry
Margaritta
NYS National Brand
Powerpak Lykes
    Sunnyland
Rich's Smoke House
Sara Lee Refrigerated
Smithfield Deli Meats
Smithfield Sunnyland
Sunnyland
Swift
Wardynski
Winter Sausage
Zweigles

Olives/Pickles
Anchor's
Bicks
Cisco
McDonald's
Moore's
Ore-Ida
Pickles In A Bag
Red Brand
Vlasic Bread and Butter
    Chunks
Vlasic Bread and Butter
    Spears
Vlasic Cherry Peppers
Vlasic Crunch Whole
    Dills
Vlasic Deli Midgets
Vlasic Dill Relish
Vlasic Hamburger Dill
    Chips
Vlasic Hearty Garlic
    Stacker
Vlasic Hot 'n' Spicy
    Garden Mix

Olives/Pickles (cont.)
Vlasic Hot 'n' Spicy
  Garden Mix
Vlasic Hot and Spicy
  Cauliflower
Vlasic Hot Banana
  Pepper Rings
Vlasic Hot Dog Relish
Vlasic Jalapenos
Vlasic Kosher Baby Dills
Vlasic Kosher Crunchy
  Dills
Vlasic Kosher Dill
  Gherkins
Vlasic Kosher Dill Spears
Vlasic Kosher Snack
  'Ems
Vlasic Mexican Hot
  Chili Peppers
Vlasic Mexican Jalapeno
  Peppers
Vlasic Mild Cherry
  Peppers
Vlasic Mild Pepper
  Rings
Vlasic Mild Pepperronici
Vlasic No Garlic Spears
Vlasic Polish Dill Spears
Vlasic Refrigerated Dill
Vlasic Roasted Red
  Peppers
Vlasic Sour Whole
  Pickles
Vlasic Sweet Bread and
  Butter Chips
Vlasic Sweet Gherkins
Vlasic Sweet Pickles
Vlasic Sweet Relish
Vlasic Sweet Salad Cubes
Vlasic Tiny Sweet
  Midgets
Vlasic Zesty Baby Sweets

Vlasic Zesty Bread and
  Butter Snack 'Ems
Vlasic Zesty Dill Spears
Vlasic Zesty Garlic Dills
Vlasic Zesty Polish
  Crunchy Dills

Pasta
American Beauty
Chef Boy Ar Dee
  Products
Light N' Fluffy
Ronzoni
Royal Brand
San Giorgio
Skinner
Turris Italian Foods
Vince & Son's

Pasta Sauces
Heinz
Prego
Prego – Pace

Poultry Products
All States Quality Foods
Applebee's
Arby's
Banquet
Banquet Kid Cuisine
Bon-EE-Best
Burger King
Butterball
Byron's Bar-B-Q
Chic-Filet
Church's
ConAgra
Crider
Draper Valley
Easy Entire
Empire
Farmland Special Select
  Sliced Turkey Breast

Fresh Pack
Gold Kist
Healthy Choice
Holly Farms
Hooter's
Hormel White Chicken
  Chunk
House of Raeford Farms
Jane Family Foods
KFC
Koch Foods
Legs QT.
Maple Leaf Farms
Maple Leaf Prime
McDonald's
Nature's Best (Copack)
Earth's Best
Outback Steakhouse
Park Farms
Pennfield
Pierce Foods
Pizza Hut
Private Label (Copack)
Heinz
Rich's Smoke House
Ruby Tuesday's
Sanderson Farms
Smithfield
Taco Bell
Tyson
Valley Fresh Chicken
Vita Fish
Wayne Farms
Wendy's

Salads
Blue Ridge
Country Maid
Fresh Express 3-Color
  Deli Cole Slaw
Fresh Express Angel Hair
  Cole Slaw

Fresh Express Baby
Spinach Salad Blend
Fresh Express Caesar
Salad Kit
Fresh Express Caesar
Supreme Salad Kit
Fresh Express Caesar
with Light Dressing
Salad Kit
Fresh Express Cole Slaw
kit w/Sweet & Creamy
Dressing
Fresh Express Fancy Field
Greens Salad Blend
Fresh Express Green
Crisp with Double
Carrots
Fresh Express Green
Crisp with Iceberg &
Romaine
Fresh Express Greener
European Salad Blend
Fresh Express Hearts of
Romaine Salad Blend
Fresh Express Italian
Salad Blend
Fresh Express More
Carrots American
Salad Blend
Fresh Express Old
Fashioned Cole Slaw
Fresh Express Oriental
Salad Kit
Fresh Express Original
Iceberg Garden Salad
Fresh Express Original
Iceberg Garden Salad
with Zip
Fresh Express Ranch
Salad Kit
Fresh Express Riviera
Salad Blend

Fresh Express Royal Salad
Blend
Fresh Express Shredded
Carrots
Fresh Express Shredded
Red Cabbage
Fresh Express Spring Mix
Salad Blend
Fresh Express Taco Fiesta
Salad Kit
Fresh Express Veggie
Lover's Salad Blend
Grandma's Original
Recipe
Grandma's Original
Recipe Macaroni Salad
Grandma's Original
Recipe Potato Salad
with Egg
Green Hills
Kitchen Fresh
Melch'o Country Reciper
Potato Salad
Sandridge Gourmet
Salads

Sausage Products
Alexander & Hornung
Battistoni
Carmela
Dearborn Sausage
Company
Eckrich
Farmer John
Farmland
Gianelli
Griddlemaster Sausage
Patty
Hofmann
Hormel Smoked Sausage
for Pickling
Johnsonville
Klements

Koegel's
Kroger
Lykes
McDonalds
Oldhams
Premio
Salchillas Carmelas
Siena Foods
Smithfield
Sunnyland
Usinger
Wardynski
Wenzel's
Winter Sausage
Zweigles

Seafood Products
Country Select
Country Select Catfish
Delta Pride
Fresh Water Catfish
Haring's Pride Catfish
Jane Family Foods
Koch Foods
Long Beach Seafood
(Long Beach, CA)
Ocean Beauty a/k/a
Three Starfish a/k/a
Los Angeles Smoking
Curing Company
(LASCO)
Pride of the Pond
Sea Cat
Simmons
Singleton Seafood
State Fish
(San Pedro, CA)
U.S. Farm Raised Catfish
Vita Fish
Wayne Farms

Smoked Meat Products
Armour
Conti's Pride
Cure 81
Eckrich
Galileo
Hillshire Farm
Hormel Black Forest
    Ham
Hormel Diced Pork
Hormel Honey Roasted
    Ham
Hormel Luncheon Meat
Hormel Marianated
    Meats
Hormel Premium
    Ground Pork
Jamonada
Kahns
Margaritta
Patrick Cudahy
Spam
Spam BBQ Flavored
Spam Hot & Spicy
Spam Lite
Spam Oven Roasted
    Turkey
Spam With Cheese
Spam With Less Salt
Swift

Snacks
Anchor
Bob's Candies
Candy Lipstick
Cangel
Carvel
Chi-Chi's
Crunch N' Munch
Evans & Macs
Farmer Jack
Gulden's Mustard
Hershey
K-Mart
Kroger
Leche Tres Monjitas
Mission Foods
Moore's
Mott's
Ore-Ida
Pace Frito Lay
Pepe's
Peter Pan
Pie Piper
Slim Jim
Smarties
Snyder of Berlin
Tres Monjitas
Wise
World Candies

Sodas
American Beverage
    Company
Bart's
Coke
Diet Coke
Diet Sprite
Pepsi
Sprite

Soups
Campbell
College Inn
Ebro - Galican
Healthy Choice Soups
Homestyle Bakes
MC Soups
Snider Soups

Sugar, Sweeteners, Jellies
Domino's
Imperial Sugar
Nutrataste
Sugar in the Raw
Sweet & Low
Welch's

Vegetables
Andy Boy
Bicks
Cortland Valley
EBRO
Eurofresh
Flanagan
Krrrrisp Kraut
Mann's Broccoli &
    Carrots
Mann's Broccoli &
    Cauliflower
Mann's Broccoli Cole
    Slaw
Mann's Broccoly Wokly
    Stir Fry
Mann's Cauliettes
Mann's Party Platter
Mann's Peas & Carrots
Mann's Rainbow Salad
Mann's Stringless Sugar
    Snap Peas
Mann's Vegetable Medley
Purely Idaho
Rose Brand
Silver Floss
Spartan
Sunny Shores
Sunripe Jackie Tomatoes
Sunripe Roma Tomatoes
Topless Cabbage
Topless Leaf Lettuce
Topless Spinach
Vlasic Old Fashioned
    Sauerkraut

Personal Products

Baby, Child-Related Products
Chubs
Cream of Rice
Cushies

Diaperene
Gerber
Heinz
Nestle
Wet Ones

Clothing
Avon
Ben Davis
Carhartt
Graybear
King Louie
Kodiak
Nemesis
Oshkosh B'Gosh
Outdoor Outfit
Platinum Sportswear
Powers
Pro-Fit
Rubin Brothers
Stone Cutter
Stone Cutter, Sure-fit
Sure-Fit
Team Safety Apparel
Thinc Actionwear
Time Out For Her
Union Jeans
Union Line
Wagoner
Wigwam

Carry Bags
Platt
Winston

Home Hardware
Aqua Chem
Dow Corning Sealants
Hunter Douglas Venetian
  Blinds
Keroseal Upholstery
Keroseal Wallcoverings
Pool King

PPG Paints & Coatings
Red Spot Paints
Red Spot Varnishes
U-Vac
United
United Brand
United Windows and
  Doors

Home Health Care
Advil
Aftate
Alka-Seltzer
Aspergum
Bactine
Bayer Aspirin
Broxodent
Bugs Bunny Vitamins
Calcitrel
Campho-Phenique
Centrum Vitamins
Chloraseptic
Chooz
Correctal
Demoplast
Di-Gel
Duration
Feen-a-mint
Flintstone Vitamins
Haley's M-O
Head & Chest
Laxcaps
Milk of Magnesia
Mydol
Neo-Synephrin
One-A-Day
Panadol
Pepto-Bismol
Premarin
Regitol
Riopan
Solarcaine
Specrrocin

Spect-T Lozenges
Squibb Angle
St. Joseph's
Theragran
Trigesic
Valadol
Vanquish
Vigran
Watkins Salves &
  Ointments
Watkins Vitamins

Household Products
Ajax
All
Axion
B 'n' B
Beacon
Bleach Tab
Blu-Flush
Blue Automatic
Blue Tab
BluWater
Borateem
Boraxo
Bowl Fresh Lemon
  Scented
Bowl Fresh Perfumed
Bowl Fresh Potpourri
  Scented
Bowl Fresh Strawberry
  Scented in shelf tray
Bowl Fresh Tissue Roll
  Holder
Bowl Fresh Tissue Roll
  Holder Refill
Cedar Pine Moth Balls
Cedar Scented Mildew
  Cake
Cedar Tree
Cedar-Ize Moth Bar
Citrus Spice in shelf tray
Clorox

Household Products (cont.)
Combat Pest Controllers
Crystal Clear
D-Con
Dan River Bedding (Martha Stewart)
Dermassage
Dynamo
Ecolab Products
Enoz
Exact
EZ-Drain
Fab
Fiber Guard
Final Touch
Fizz Tab Carton in shelf tray
Floral Bouquet in shelf tray
Fly Swatter Wire Mesh
Fly Swatter, Plastic with Wire Handle
Fly Traps - 4 pack fly traps in shelf tray
Four/Gone
Franklin Poly
Fresh Start
Gonesh
Hi-Lex (Ultra)
Keep
Keep it Dry
Lavender Closet Freshener
Lemon Closet Freshener
LePages Adhesives Tapes
Liquid Plumber
Love My Carpet
Lysol
Mini Safe Scour
Minwax
Mop & Glo

Moth Sachettes Lavendar Scent
Moth-Tek Packets Cedar Fresh Scent
Moth-Tek Packets Lavendar Scent
Mountain Pine Vacuum Freshener
Nel-Naphtha
Octagon
Old Dutch
Old Fashioned Moth Balls
Old Fashioned Moth Flakes
Palmolive
Perk
Pine Drop
Plastic Moth Killer With Case
Pleasantly Scented in Shelf Tray
Prime Choice
Punch
Purex
Reed & Barton
Rinso
Roach Away Powder
SKAT! Animal Repellent
Snap Trap - 2 pack mouse traps in shelf tray
Snap Trap - 4 pack mouse traps in shelf tray
Snuggles
Soft Scrub
Sunbeam Teflon
Sunlight
Surf
Tide Soap
Twice As Fresh
Uniflex

Watkins Household Products
Watkins Insecticides
Willert Products
Wisk

Leather Products
Art Craft Leather
Bosca
Elco Manufacturing Company, Inc.
Gutmann
Horween
Leathermark Accessories
Paul May Company, Inc.
Seidel
Winston Manufacturing Corporation

Personal Care Products
Alberto VO5
Caress
Cashmere Bouquet
Chapstick
Colgate
Coppertone
Cosmepak
Dove
FDS
Garden Bouquet
Grey Flannel
Halo
Irish Spring
Jasmin
Lady's Choice
Lander Personal Care Products
Lifebouy
Lux
Mexsana
Ogilvie
Old Spice

Phiso-Derm
Pierre Cardin
Pure & Natural
Rapid Shave
Sardo
Shield
Stri-Dex
Sweetheart
Tussy
Ultra-Brite
Vel
VO5
Watkins Personal Care
  Products

Pet Products
9 Lives
Anchor
Boehringer Ingelheim
  Vetmedica, Inc.
Fresh Step
Friskies
Litter Green
Sanderson Farms
Science Diet
Skippy
Wayne Farms

Plastic Products
Uniflex
Western Plastics

Shoes
Air Step
Belleville Shoe Company
Carolina
Danner
Matterhorn
Natural Sport
Naturalizer
Nunn-Bush
Red Wing Shoes

Stacy Adams
Totes Boots
Wolverine

Yard and Garden
Bonanza Fertilizer
Champions Choice
M & M Moulding
Vim Fertilizer

Miscellaneous
ADM Milling
Aflex
Airco Industrial Gases
Algoma Net
Anaconda
Archer Daniels Midland
B-Line
Baldwin Pianos &
  Organs
Bell Sports
Captain Crunch
Caro-Net
Conseal
Cop
Costco
CR Daniels
Delft Blue
Diamond Crystal Halite
  Winter Melt
Dupont Automotive
  Paints
Eveready
Firestone
Ford Harley-Davidson
Fuji Film
General Motors
General Motors -
  Hummer
Gonesh
Hershey-South Bend
  Chocolate

Inland
International Paper
King Edward
Kroger
Kroger Plus
Lenzing
Life
Marshal Fields
Monopoly
New Clo
OfficeMax
Optimo
Peak
Pierce
Platt
Play-Doh
Register Rolls
Rubber Association
Safe Step
Santa Fe
Scrabble
Sealy Mattress
Shelby Williams -
  EPIC/Charlotte
Skoal
Sparkle Conquest
Sunflour & Scotts
Surefit
Swisher
Tee-Pak, LLC
TRW Electronics
Union Getaway
United Memorial Bible
UNR - Rohn
Walden Books
Wearever Teflon
Yale

Chapter 17

American Hero Companies

ZebulonUSA

What would you do if you worked in manufacturing and watched your co-workers lose their jobs as a result of corporate downsizing? Would it frustrate you to notice that there was no corresponding downsizing in consumer purchasing? More and more Americans today recognize that their country seems to be getting the short end of the stick when they visit their local retail outlets and find all too often that American-made products just aren't available.

Paul Stanuch, owner of the website www.ZebulonUSA.com, decided to turn his frustration of these realities into a passion for offering a wide range of American products in one place. He rightly realized that more patriotic consumers would purchase Made in USA products if they could find them more easily. And with today's Internet giving us greater access to American-made products that oftentimes can't be found in retail stores, anyway, it's actually easier to Buy American than most might think.

At ZebulonUSA.com, they understand that oftentimes there is little difference in price between the products they offer and imported products offered by foreign producers. Next time you hear about a U.S. factory about to close and move overseas, check the price tag of that product currently made by the domestic factory, and then check it again once that product begins to be sourced offshore. You might be surprised that there is little, if any, price difference; and ZebulonUSA.com challenges anyone to compare its prices to other well-known brands of similar quality.

ZebulonUSA.com also understands that when a price difference does exist, many times it is because of the difference in production volume. The more one produces, the lower the cost of producing. Since most of the companies bucking the trend of the ever-increasing import flood from overseas are small or medium-sized businesses, these patriotic businesses compete against larger manufacturers overseas that can produce more at a lower cost.

What does all this mean? It means that buying American-made products from places like www.ZebulonUSA.com can make it easier to buy American in the future by making domestic manufacturers more price-competitive against larger offshore rivals. It also means that the reason we have trouble buying American now is that we haven't been buying American as much as we should have in the past. And we often don't because we aren't aware, and awareness is the key.

So now that you've been made aware of a place to go where everything is made in USA, help American manufacturing expand and make it possible to buy American so that there will always be American left to buy. Visit www.ZebulonUSA.com and support our workers and manufacturers to keep America working.

USA Coffee Company

If you're like most people, you probably figured that buying American-grown coffee was just about as possible as buying American-grown bananas. I use to think the same thing, but I found out I was wrong when I discovered the USA Coffee Company.

Only American workers and American jobs are involved when you buy any of the many types of coffee and other related products from the USA Coffee Company, which grows all of their coffee in the great state of Hawaii. Whether you try the All American Union Roast, Island Paradise, or 100% American Kona coffee, the USA Coffee Company is true red, white, and blue from tree to cup.

They also offer chocolate-covered espresso beans, macadamia nuts, maple syrups, or Maui sugar and even have American-made coffee mugs to make the best of your Buy American experience. You won't find these great American products in stores, so be sure to visit their website at www.usacoffeecompany.com.

Union Built PC

One of the hardest areas to buy American is in electronics. This is an especially difficult realization to patriotic Americans since it's nearly impossible to get by without a computer of some sort these days. Fortunately there's a company that builds all of its computers in the U.S. and gets as many parts from domestic sources as possible. If you own a computer from www.unionbuiltpc.com, you'll take comfort in knowing there isn't another one on the planet with more American parts than yours.

All company technical support, sales and accounting is U.S.-based, so you won't ever have to worry about dealing with someone you can't understand on the phone should you ever have a problem with your computer.

With a UnionBuiltPC computer, your computer case, power supply and RAM can be sourced domestically (only the RAM is domestically-available for laptops) and you can also upgrade to an American-made video card as well. UnionBuiltPC is already doing what we should all be doing: Ordering American-made products whenever possible.

White Creek Tile

At www.whitecreektile.com, you'll see American-made, hand-crafted, kiln-fired ceramic tiles that are perfect for leaving notes or messages for anyone in the family. No more worrying about what happened to that piece of paper with your notes on it. These write-on tiles won't scratch your table or kitchen counter, and wipe off effortlessly with any towel or napkin. You can choose from all kinds of designs for your tile like, birds, sports, animals, farm, floral and nature just to name a few. So if you're looking for that unique gift for someone who has everything, this is it.

BUY AMERICAN LINKS

Listed below are links to some of my favorite websites. Many of these companies don't have the "corporate horsepower" to get their products into a big-box store, and are online-based small companies that prefer to make things USA out of their patriotic beliefs. Not all products on all websites are U.S. made (check the product descriptions), but many of them produce a high majority of their products in America. Links will continue to be added to the webpage www.howto-buyamerican.com/links, so please check for additional updates often.

www.shopforamerica.com

www.zebulonusa.com

www.sets-systems.com

www.unionbuiltpc.com

www.usacoffeecompany.com

www.unionjeancompany.com

www.theunionshop.org

www.buyamerican.com

www.radamfg.com

www.toughtraveler.com

www.whitecreektile.com

www.usaamericanshrimp.com

www.unionmi.com

www.unionhouse.com

www.padlocks.com

www.buzzardtowne.com

www.firemanschore.com

www.americantuna.com

www.mageyes.com

www.makeamerica.com

www.localharvest.org

www.bentwoodfurn.com

www.tigercandyarts.com

www.staber.com

www.scalemodeltoys.com

www.needaprons.com

www.bulkaprons.com

www.americansworking.com

www.wickers.com

www.okabashi.com

www.athleticappeal.com

www.sheetmetalworkerjacket.com

www.igourmet.com

www.plowhearth.com

www.nosweatapparel.com

www.texasjean.com

www.conklinsteel.com

www.weavermodels.com

www.sosfromtexas.com

www.footwearbyfootskins.com

www.nstarleather.com

www.kentuckybarrels.com

www.specialtyemporium.com

www.counciltool.com

www.pinnaclecandle.com

www.usmilitarystuff.com

www.waveshoppe.com

www.traintablesonline.com

www.butlerbags.com

www.getagauge.com

www.solidoak4u.com

www.amishoutletstore.com

www.bellevilleshoe.com

www.juicycouture.com

www.buddysjeans.com

www.kodiakcuttingtools.com

www.bamboosa.com

www.americanleather.com

www.americantechsupport.net

www.americansafestore.com

www.cdsportswear.com

www.gotfruit.com

www.caregiversworld.com

www.carringtoncourtdirect.com

www.overthehillcarpeople.com

www.usamadeboutique.com

www.carllectibles.com

www.driversarmshade.com

www.pottytrainingstuff.com

www.ironwoodbats.com

www.shopunionmade.org

www.alore.net

www.cubbyholetoys.com

www.huntwithgrandpajoe.com

www.stryder-store.com

www.camapp.com

www.lainaline.com

www.qualityusaproducts.com

www.customglove.com

www.usmadetoys.com

www.americancarsfirst.com

www.madeinusa.com

www.intextile.com

www.buydirectusa.com

www.thepatriotscorner.homestead.com

www.support-usa.com

www.louisvillestoneware.com

www.ichordcart.com

www.mo8designs.com

http://stores.ebay.com/Pieces-of-Places

www.unionstuff.com

www.americanjoblog.com

www.usa-mfg.com

www.leatherartisan.com

www.schottnyc.com

www.bragelets.com

www.christmasdepot.com

www.allamericanclothing.com

www.amtacdc.org

www.candle-licious.com

www.todaysamericandream.com

www.woodboxesetc.com

www.craftedwithpride.org

www.bac-america.org

www.americaneconomicalert.org

www.mypersonalstyle.com

www.nbwebexpress.com/madeinusa_nb.htm

www.madeinusa.org

www.filson.com

www.peoplefriendlyplaces.com

www.onesole.com

www.byerschoice.com

www.allamericanclothing.com

Index by Chapter

Index by Category

Bibliography

Business Week, The McGraw-Hill Companies, New York, NY, Various issues.

Consumer Reports, Consumers Union of U.S., Inc., Yonkers, NY, Various issues.

Corporate Affiliations, LexisNexis Group, 2005, 2006 New Providence, NJ

The Wall Street Journal, Dow Jones & Company, Inc., New York, Various issues

Bernstein, Richard and Munro, Ross H., *The Coming Conflict with China*, Alfred A. Knopf, New York, 1997

Brown, Sherrod, *Myths of Free Trade*, The New Press, New York, 2004

Buchanan, Patrick J., *A Republic, Not an Empire*, Regnery Publishing, Inc., Washington, DC, 1999

Buchanan, Patrick J., *Death of the West*, St. Martin's Press, New York, 2002

Buchanan, Patrick J., *Where the Right Went Wrong*, St. Martin's Press, New York, 2004

Burkett, Larry, *The Coming Economic Earthquake*, Moody Press, Chicago, 1994.

Dobbs, Lou, *Exporting America*, Warner Books, New York, 2004

Donoho, Annette, *Buy American*, Waikoloa, HI, 1991

Gephardt, Richard, *An Even Better Place*, Public Affairs, New York, 1999.

Greider, William, *The Soul of Capitalism*, Simon & Schuster, New York, 2004

Greider, William, *Who Will Tell the People*, Simon & Schuster, New York, 1992

Sanders, Bernie, *Outsider in the House*, Verso, New York, 1997

Stelzer, Gus R., *Free Trade and the Constitution*, Liberty Lobby, Inc., Washington, DC, 1993

Stelzer, Gus R., *The Nightmare of Camelot*, Peanut Butter Publishing, Seattle, 1994

Stiglitz, Joseph E., *Globalization and Its Discontents*, W. W. Norton Company, New York, 2002

Stiglitz, Joseph E., *The Roaring Nineties*, W. W. Norton Company, New York, 2003

Soros, George, *George Soros on Globalization*, Public Affairs, New York, 2002

Soros, George, *The Crisis of Global Capitalism*, Public Affairs, New York, 1998

Tonelson, Alan, *The Race to the Bottom*, Westview Press, Boulder, Colorado, 2000

More Praise for *How Americans Can Buy American*

Pat Choate
Economist and 1996 Vice Presidential Candidate:
    "*How Americans Can Buy American* is an invaluable guide to consumers who want to buy products made in American factories by American workers."

Charley Reese
Syndicated Columnist:
    "...It's easy to say we should buy American but it's not easy to actually do it. *How Americans Can Buy American* goes a long way toward turning a good idea into reality. It is essential for America to once again be as nearly a self-sufficient nation as possible. Mr. Simmermaker has performed a public service."

Gus R. Stelzer
Retired Senior Executive, General Motors:
    "No American should leave home without a copy of *How Americans Can Buy American* It is a must guide for every consumer."
Gus Stelzer is the author of *The Nightmare of Camelot*

James A. Traficant, Jr.
Former Congressman, U. S. House of Representatives:
    "For years I have been working to promote the virtues of buying American-made products. *How Americans Can Buy American* provides consumers with the information they need to make intelligent, and patriotic, choices when purchasing anything from candy bars to refrigerators to cars. Any American concerned about our economic future should have this book."